The Military West
in 1860

DEPARTMENT HEADQUARTERS ■ MAJOR POSTS ⠿ MAJOR TRANSCONTINENTAL TRAILS

DEPARTMENT OF OREGON

DEPARTMENT

DEPARTMENT OF UTAH

DEPARTMENT OF CALIFORNIA

DEPARTMENT OF NEW MEXICO

Salt Lake City

Denver

San Francisco

Los Angeles

Santa Fe

Albuquerque

San Diego

Tucson

El Paso

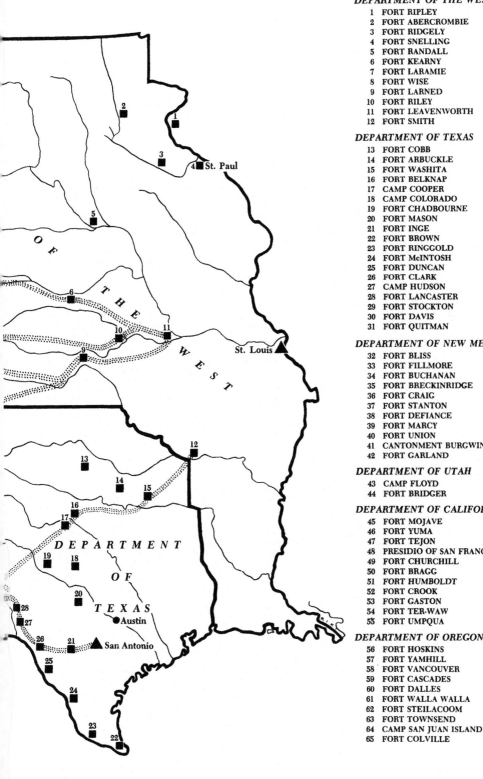

DEPARTMENT OF THE WEST

1 FORT RIPLEY
2 FORT ABERCROMBIE
3 FORT RIDGELY
4 FORT SNELLING
5 FORT RANDALL
6 FORT KEARNY
7 FORT LARAMIE
8 FORT WISE
9 FORT LARNED
10 FORT RILEY
11 FORT LEAVENWORTH
12 FORT SMITH

DEPARTMENT OF TEXAS

13 FORT COBB
14 FORT ARBUCKLE
15 FORT WASHITA
16 FORT BELKNAP
17 CAMP COOPER
18 CAMP COLORADO
19 FORT CHADBOURNE
20 FORT MASON
21 FORT INGE
22 FORT BROWN
23 FORT RINGGOLD
24 FORT McINTOSH
25 FORT DUNCAN
26 FORT CLARK
27 CAMP HUDSON
28 FORT LANCASTER
29 FORT STOCKTON
30 FORT DAVIS
31 FORT QUITMAN

DEPARTMENT OF NEW MEXICO

32 FORT BLISS
33 FORT FILLMORE
34 FORT BUCHANAN
35 FORT BRECKINRIDGE
36 FORT CRAIG
37 FORT STANTON
38 FORT DEFIANCE
39 FORT MARCY
40 FORT UNION
41 CANTONMENT BURGWIN
42 FORT GARLAND

DEPARTMENT OF UTAH

43 CAMP FLOYD
44 FORT BRIDGER

DEPARTMENT OF CALIFORNIA

45 FORT MOJAVE
46 FORT YUMA
47 FORT TEJON
48 PRESIDIO OF SAN FRANCISCO
49 FORT CHURCHILL
50 FORT BRAGG
51 FORT HUMBOLDT
52 FORT CROOK
53 FORT GASTON
54 FORT TER-WAW
55 FORT UMPQUA

DEPARTMENT OF OREGON

56 FORT HOSKINS
57 FORT YAMHILL
58 FORT VANCOUVER
59 FORT CASCADES
60 FORT DALLES
61 FORT WALLA WALLA
62 FORT STEILACOOM
63 FORT TOWNSEND
64 CAMP SAN JUAN ISLAND
65 FORT COLVILLE

Frontiersmen in Blue

THE UNITED STATES ARMY

AND THE INDIAN

☆ 1848-1865 ☆

by *ROBERT M. UTLEY*

University of Nebraska Press
Lincoln and London

First Nebraska paperback printing: 1981

Library of Congress Cataloging in Publication Data

Utley, Robert Marshall, 1929–
  Frontiersmen in blue.

  Reprint of the ed. published by Macmillan, New York.
  Bibliography: p. 350
  Includes index.
  1. Indians of North America—Wars—1815–75. 2. United States.
Army—History—19th century. 3. The West—History—1840–
1950. I. Title.
[E81.U745 1981]   355.3′51′0973   80–27796
ISBN 0–8032–4550–5
ISBN 0–8032–9550–2 (pbk.)

Published by arrangement with Robert M. Utley

☆ CONTENTS ☆

☆ LIST OF MAPS ☆

Abbreviations Used in Footnotes

AG	*Adjutant General*
AAG	*Assistant Adjutant General*
AAAG	*Acting Assistant Adjutant General*
AGO	*Adjutant General's Office*
CIA	*Commissioner of Indian Affairs*
GO	*General Order*
Hq.	*Headquarters*
LB	*Letter Book*
LR	*Letters Received*
LS	*Letters Sent*
NARS	*National Archives and Record Service*
NM	*New Mexico*
OIA	*Office of Indian Affairs*
O.R.	*Official Records of the Union and Confederate Armies*
RG	*Record Group (in National Archives)*
SO	*Special Order*
SI	*Secretary of the Interior*
SW	*Secretary of War*

Errata

p. 67, line 21:   a year later should be 1851

        line 26:   1845 should be 1854

p. 162, line 9:   Feb. 4 should be Feb. 3

p. 165, line 26:   1853 should be 1852

p. 167, line 32:   1857 should be 1856

p. 238, fn. 18:   J. Francisco Chavez should be Manuel Chavez

p. 239, line 17:   400 should be 300

p. 240, line 27:   Chief Barboncito was not killed in this fight; General Sherman made him Navajo Head Chief in 1868, when the Navajos returned to their homeland from exile.

p. 267, fn. 11:   The two Sibleys were distantly related.

p. 378,

    2d column: 5th Minnesota through 30th Wisconsin misplaced; should follow 3d Minnesota, below.

The portrait identified as General Twiggs is General William J. Worth.

Introduction

IN THE SUMMER of 1866, the plains, mountains, and deserts of the Trans-Mississippi West played host to a group of high-ranking army officers whose only mission was to travel and report their observations. The Civil War had ended, and the dissolution of the great volunteer armies of the Union had been all but completed. Yet the exact form and dimensions of the peacetime Army had not been fixed, and the high command was encumbered by an embarrassing surplus of colonels and generals for whom positions remained to be found. Assigned as inspector-generals, some were sent west to inquire into the state of military affairs. The most distinguished traveler was hardly surplus, but the observations of Major General William Tecumseh Sherman, touring his new command, added richly to the detailed picture of the West that emerged from the reports of the inspectors.[1]

Perhaps what struck the touring officers most forcibly about the West of 1866 was a sense of tremendous energy and activity. Miners panned streams and hacked at mineral veins the length and breadth of mountain chains great and small. Dirt farmers advanced up the rivers draining the High Plains, marked off fields at the base of the Rockies, spread over the great interior valleys of the Pacific Slope, and planted themselves wherever else they could detect the faintest promise of adequate water and

---

[1] Besides Sherman, the most prominent of the inspectors were Generals Orville E. Babcock, James Rusling, William B. Hazen, Rufus Ingalls, and Colonel Delos B. Sackett. See House Ex. Docs., 39th Cong., 2d sess., Nos. 20, 23, 45, 111.

local markets. Linking the settlements was a spiderweb of roads filled with freight and emigrant wagons and stagecoaches. Way-stations, called ranches, dotted the principal roads every dozen or so miles. Of enormous portent, the ties and rails of the first transcontinental railway advanced west from the Missouri and east from the Pacific. Population centers old and new—Sacramento, San Diego, Portland, Denver, Santa Fe, San Antonio, Austin, Salt Lake City, Helena—were evolving into established cities or—San Francisco, for one—had already attained the distinction. Everywhere the military inspectors recorded scenes of people on the move.

Of particular interest to the inquiring officers was the state of military and Indian affairs. A postwar military system had yet to take shape in Texas, so recently under the Confederate flag, but spread over the rest of the West was a network of nearly sixty military posts, some of fine stone or frame construction, but most collections of vermin-infested sod or adobe shacks. "Surely," noted General Sherman, "had the southern planters put their negroes in such hovels, a sample would, ere this, have been carried to Boston and exhibited as illustrative of the cruelty and inhumanity of the man-masters." The Regular Army, reduced to a skeleton by the Civil War and not yet reconstructed, was just regarrisoning the forts and resuming police responsibilities borne for the past five years by units of U.S. Volunteers.

The Indian situation gave faint cause for optimism. Open warfare raged in the Southwest and along the northern edges of the Great Basin. The tribes of the upper Missouri were "very bold, defiant, and somewhat troublesome." On the Great Plains, Sherman observed, "the poor Indian finds himself hemmed in" between the farmer's frontier on the east and the Rocky Mountain miner's frontier on the west—"and so the poor devil naturally wriggles against his doom." "There is a universal feeling of mistrust on both sides," he added, and "all the people are clamorous for military protection."

What the inspectors-general saw and reported about the West in the summer of 1866 foreshadowed a new phase of the westward movement, one in which national energies released by the close of the Civil War would carry the conquest of the West to completion within little more than two decades. The postwar Regular Army and the increasingly hemmed-in Indian, "wriggling against his doom," played a large role in this final stage of the frontier movement. They, too, began a new phase of their historic confrontation at the close of the Civil War.

That the inspectors of 1866 could find in the West such a bustle of political, economic, and social activity; that they could find an elaborate and well-established military system; and that they could find Indians and whites filled with such mutual animosity, not only foreshadowed the significant developments to come but also gave the measure of how much had gone before. Only seventeen years had elapsed since the territorial acquisitions of the Mexican War and the discovery of gold in California had set off a migration that scattered miners, farmers, businessmen, artisans, and soldiers over vast areas of the West. In this earlier phase of the westward movement, so vital as a platform for the thrust of the later phase, the Army and the Indian had also played a key role.

This role is commonly ignored or only briefly and superficially treated in most histories of the conflict between Indian and white in the Trans-Mississippi West. The dramatic stories of the Minnesota outbreak of 1862 and the Battle of Sand Creek in 1864 are often thrown in by way of introduction to the big story that began in 1866 and ended with the passing of the frontier in 1890. Only rarely is a fleeting glance cast at the events of the pre-Civil War West.

Yet for the Army and the Indian the two decades that began with the Mexican War and closed with the Civil War held much greater significance than implied by the attention devoted to it by historians. During this period the United States filled out its continental dimensions, and its emigrating citizens first came into meaningful contact with the Indians of its vastly enlarged western domain. The Nation's military and civil policies toward these Indians, together with the channels for their application, were evolved. The tiny Regular Army, and the larger Volunteer Army that replaced it during the Civil War years, planted the U.S. flag on the Great Plains, in Texas, the Rockies, the Southwest, and the Great Basin, and on the Pacific Slope. The Army laid out and manned a group of regional defense systems whose basic outlines endured without fundamental change until the Indian problem ceased to require military involvement. It established relations sometimes amicable, sometimes hostile, but most of the time ambiguous with a native population that resisted convenient classification as friend or foe. It met and struggled with new, more hostile conditions of climate and geography that were never to be wholly mastered, and it met and struggled with a new kind of enemy that had mastered the conditions of climate and geography.

With nearly all the tribes during this period the blueclad frontiersmen of the Regular and Volunteer Armies skirmished inconclusively, and with a few they fought conclusively. In protecting the settlements, in policing the travel routes, and in warring with the Indians, their achievements and failures between 1848 and 1865 contributed importantly to a major chapter in the history of westward expansion and are fundamental to understanding the better known military contributions to the final chapter that General Sherman and his associates saw beginning to unfold while touring the West in 1866.

The story of these achievements and failures is the subject of this volume. The story of the achievements and failures of the postwar Regular Army shaped by Sherman and his fellow commanders is reserved for a later volume in this series.

An expression of appreciation is due a number of people who contributed to the pages that follow. For reading the entire manuscript and offering constructive suggestions for revision, I am deeply indebted to my colleague in the National Park Service Franklin G. Smith, superintendent of Fort Davis National Historic Site, Texas; to Louis Morton of Dartmouth College, editor of the series in which this volume appears; and to Peter Ritner, executive editor of the Macmillan Company. Other associates in the National Park Service who kindly reviewed portions of the manuscript were Roy E. Appleman and John D. McDermott of the Washington office and Albert H. Schroeder and William E. Brown of the Santa Fe office. Also offering helpful suggestions for improving certain chapters were Harry H. Anderson, executive director of the Milwaukee County Historical Society; James S. Hutchins and Donald E. Kloster of the Smithsonian Institution; Andrew Wallace, Odie E. Faulk, and Sidney B. Brinckerhoff of the Arizona Pioneers Historical Society in Tucson; John Alexander Carroll and Harwood P. Hinton of the University of Arizona; Oscar O. Winther, Indiana University; and Keith A. Murray, Western Washington State College. Helpful in other ways were Kenneth F. Neighbours of Midwestern University, Wichita Falls, Texas, and Homer Hastings, Edwin C. Bearss, and Lee Wallace of the National Park Service. Special thanks go to Walter T. Vitous of Olympia, Washington, for the maps.

Permission to include passages from the following copyrighted works is gratefully acknowledged: *The Navaho*, by Clyde Kluckhohn and Dorothea Leighton, Harvard University Press; *General George Crook, His Autobiography*, and *The Southern Cheyennes*, by Donald J. Berthrong, University of Oklahoma Press; *Campaigns in the West*, by John V. D. DuBois, Arizona Pioneers Historical Society; *The Texas Rangers*, by Walter Prescott Webb, University of Texas Press and Terrell Maverick Webb; *The West of Philip St. George Cooke*, by Otis E. Young, Arthur H. Clark Co.; and *Forts and Forays*, by Clinton E. Brooks and Frank D. Reeve, University of New Mexico Press.

Washington, D.C.
January 1967

ONE

Manifest Destiny and the Army

THE United States Army counted September 14, 1847, one of the most glorious days in its half-century of history. It opened as General John A. Quitman led the Fourth Division of Winfield Scott's army through the narrow streets of Mexico City. In the spacious Plaza de Armas, bordered by the twin-spired cathedral and the looming National Palace recently vacated by Santa Anna, a conquered populace watched silently as the begrimed citizen-soldiers from the north formed in line facing the seat of government. Captain Benjamin S. Roberts of the Mounted Rifles climbed to the roof and as the division presented arms hoisted the American flag on the staff surmounting the dome.

The political general's premature entrance on the scene detracted only slightly from the next act of the pageant. "Old Fuss and Feathers" was hard to upstage. Preceded by Harney's dragoons and a mounted band blaring "Yankee Doodle," General Winfield Scott swept into the plaza, followed by the well-dressed ranks of Worth's division of Regulars. Astride a big bay, his imposing frame resplendent in blue and gold, he produced every bit the effect he doubtless intended. The victorious army cheered as their chief, doffing his plumed chapeau, trooped the line of the two divisions. The ceremony even drew scattered applause from the unhappy capital residents crowding the plaza. Dismounting, Scott and his generals strode into the National Palace, where the general-in-chief seated himself at an ornate desk and wrote out the order announcing the triumph of American arms.[1]

---

[1] Charles W. Elliott, *Winfield Scott, the Soldier and the Man* (New York, 937), pp. 551–52.

Although divided on the issues of the conflict, Americans ex-
ulted in the brilliant performance of their Army in the Mexican
War. With a combined force of slightly more than a hundred
thousand officers and men, Taylor, Scott, Kearny, and Wool had
separately invaded a foreign country and put to rout an army
five times the size of their own, Scott seizing Mexico City with
less than six thousand. Blunders there had been—notably in
recruiting, supply, and civilian management—but the succession
of hard-won victories beginning with Palo Alto and Resaca de la
Palma and ending with Buena Vista and Chapultepec dramatically exhibited the fighting qualities of the American soldier and
the professional competence of his career officer. The U.S. Army
had won its first unqualified success in a major war with a
foreign enemy. It had inspired new respect at home and abroad
and, equally important, among its own ranks.

Now the volunteer regiments disbanded and the shrunken
Regular Army prepared to return to its peacetime pursuits.
Among these were manning the coastal defenses, arsenals, and
supply installations, policing the international boundaries, and
preparing for the next war. The principal mission, however,
derived from the imperatives of national expansion. Although
American soldiers had fought three major wars with a foreign
enemy since the Nation's birth seventy-two years earlier, the
chief employment of the U.S. Army for all but a dozen of
these years had been fixed by the requirements of the westward
movement rather than the menace of a foreign power. Exploration, mapping, and construction of internal improvements formed
some of the duties, but protection of the frontier population and
travel routes from hostile Indians placed the largest demand on
the Army. From the Appalachians to the Mississippi, few native
groups had shown a willingness to submit to dispossession or
subjugation. The standing army so distasteful to the architects
of the new nation had thus proved indispensable to the advance
of the frontier. Indian hostility had prompted the creation of the
Regular Army and had sustained it through the formative decades of the Republic.

East of the Mississippi, except in Florida,[2] Indian resistance
had all but collapsed by the 1840s. But the martial ceremony

[2] Although falling within the chronological span of this volume, the Florida conflicts of the 1850s formed a final chapter in a story that began four
decades earlier and are treated in a companion volume of this series.

enacted by Scott and Quitman in the Plaza de Armas of Mexico City symbolized the dawn of a new era in the drama of national expansion, one whose setting would be the plains, mountains, and deserts of the Trans-Mississippi West. The United States had owned an empire west of the Mississippi since Thomas Jefferson's Louisiana Purchase of 1803, but it had intruded on the national consciousness only dimly and under the unalluring label of "Great American Desert." Then in the decade of the 1840s the cry of Manifest Destiny lifted the Nation's vision beyond the Mississippi. In quick succession came the annexation of Texas in 1845, the resolution of the Oregon boundary dispute in 1846, and finally, in February 1848, the peace settlement of Guadalupe Hidalgo, which forced Mexico to cede California, the Great Basin, and the Rio Grande Southwest. In three years the United States had enlarged its domain by more than a million square miles and had transformed itself into a continental nation. For another half century, with time out for the Civil War, the U.S. Army would find its primary mission and its main reason for existence in the requirements of the westward movement beyond the Mississippi.

The new territories beckoned. Although Americans were persuaded by expansionist orators that it was their manifest destiny to overspread the continent, more practical motives impelled them westward. The agricultural potential of Texas, Oregon, and California had lured many before the cry of Manifest Destiny rang through the land. A few merchants had made their homes in New Mexico, and Mormons had been drawn to the Salt Lake Valley by hopes of finding a remote corner of the continent in which to pursue the tenets of their faith free of persecution. By the close of the Mexican War, residents of the territory between the first tier of states west of the Mississippi and the Pacific Ocean numbered slightly more than four hundred thousand, including former Mexican nationals in New Mexico and California. Texas claimed about half of this population.

Then on January 24, 1848, less than two weeks before the diplomats put their signatures to the Treaty of Guadalupe Hidalgo, James Marshall saw flecks of gold in California's American River. Word reached Washington the following August; authenticated by President Polk in December, it electrified the Nation and set off a mass migration unprecedented in its history. By land and sea the Argonauts raced for the Pacific slope. Throughout the decade of the 1850s the principal transcontinental routes—the Oregon-California Trail, the Santa Fe Trail, the Gila Trail, and a host of alternate and feeder trails—bore a stream of travelers westward. Other mineral strikes brought miners to mountainous districts all over the West. Few got rich, but gold dramatized the new territories, invited immigration, and stimulated agriculture, commerce, transportation, and ultimately industry. By 1860 settlement had multiplied more than threefold, with Texas alone claiming 604,215 and California 379,994.[3] California and Oregon had joined Texas in statehood, and nearly all the rest of the land west of the Missouri River had been organized into the Territories of New Mexico, Utah, Washington, Kansas, and Nebraska. The expansionism of the 1850s seemed to confirm the continental destiny so clearly manifest to the orators of the 1840s.

To the Indian inhabitants of the West, the white man's advance foreshadowed a destiny not altogether manifest but still deeply disturbing. At mid-century, in addition to 84,000 people in the sedentary "Five Civilized Tribes," perhaps 75,000 nomads occupied the unorganized portion of the Louisiana Purchase. For three decades U.S. policy makers had regarded this "Great American Desert" as unfit for civilized habitation. Acting on this theory, they had uprooted many woodland groups from homes east of the Mississippi and herded them to the "Indian Country" west of the borders of Arkansas and Missouri. A line of military forts defined the "Permanent Indian Frontier," beyond which emigrant and resident Indians alike would forever enjoy security from white encroachment. The territorial acquisitions of the 1840s, adding new lands west of the Indian Country, doomed the concept of a Permanent Indian Frontier and placed an additional 200,000 or so natives in the paths of expansion—an estimated 25,-000 in Texas, 150,000 in the Mexican Cession, and 25,000 in the Oregon Country.

The Permanent Indian Frontier, if it existed anywhere but in men's minds, began to give way even before the new territories came under the U.S. flag. The modest emigration of the

---

[3] The Census of 1860 exhibited the following breakdown of the non-Indian population: Kansas 107,206; Nebraska 28,841; Dakota 4,837; Texas 604,215; New Mexico 93,516; Nevada, 6,857; Utah 40,273; Colorado 34,277; Washington 11,594; Oregon 52,465; and California 379,994.

early 1840s to disputed Oregon and Mexican California pierced it. The swelling tide loosed by the gold discovery of 1848 widened the breech. And the settlers spilling onto the prairies of eastern Kansas and Nebraska in the middle 1850s destroyed it altogether. The flow of travelers across the continent and the expanding and multiplying pockets of settlement in Texas, New Mexico, California, and Oregon created severe pressures on the fragile balance between the Indian and his environment. Game animals, even the seemingly limitless bison of the Great Plains, grew suddenly less abundant and in places disappeared from their customary haunts. Diseases such as cholera and smallpox swept whole tribes with terrible fatality. Alcohol drained the vitality from those attracted to the settlements and travel routes and locked them in a fatal dependence on the hordes of whisky peddlers that sought them out. Tribal ranges, at best never very stable, shifted constantly as groups dispossessed or shouldered aside encroached on others not yet affected. Lasting divisions opened within and between tribes as quarrels erupted over whether to resist, surrender, or accommodate to the white threat. Torn between hatred and fear of the invading aliens and a growing dependence on their manufactures, the various tribes attempted at various times all three responses and every possible shading of each.

The sudden enlargement of the national domain coupled with the precipitate population movement that followed confronted the federal government with new responsibilities clearly perceived by only a few political leaders. Among these were obligations to explore and map the western territories, to improve existing travel routes and open new ones, to aid the emigration, and to foster means of transcontinental transportation and communication. But most important was the obligation to police the West —to protect travelers and settlers from hostile Indians, to protect peaceful Indians from hostile or ignorant whites, and to perfect a scheme for managing the Indians that balanced the requirements of national expansion against those of humanity to an alien minority destined for subjugation. It was a large order, impossible of complete fulfillment given national attitudes that shaped policy. In the quest, the U.S. Army played a key, often decisive, role.

Not simply by more of the same had the Army's responsibilities been enlarged. Officers who had ridden with the occasional expedition that probed beyond the Permanent Indian Frontier in the prewar decades knew that the new scene of operations presented conditions of weather and terrain unlike any encountered east of the Mississippi River. They knew, too, though perhaps less explicitly, that the Indians now to be met differed in many ways from those of the eastern woodlands. A new geography and a new enemy decreed that the Army evolve new attitudes and new capabilities.

West of the Mississippi River the prairies and High Plains stretched from Canada nearly to Mexico. Beyond rose the peaks of the Rockies. Describing an arc around their southern flank and reaching northward into the Great Basin, the southwestern deserts, relieved by craggy, barren mountain ranges, pushed across the Colorado River against the looming face of the Sierra Nevada. Rugged, pine-clad mountains and upland plateaus circled the Great Basin on the north, connecting the Sierra with the Rockies. Vast distances, climatic extremes, and scarcity of such life-sustaining resources as water, food, and fuel characterized this land and severely limited the militarily possible. War with the hostile environment consumed a proportion of the total military effort that left little margin for war with the human enemy.

To aggravate this condition, the human enemy had achieved a near perfect adaptation to the environment.[4] The tribes of the plains, mountains, and deserts had learned how to make the land sustain life and, of graver import for the challenger, how to turn the hostile features of their particular environment to military advantage. Unlike their brethren of the East, most of these Indians were mounted on wiry ponies as finely attuned to the environment as their riders. Also unlike the easterners, most of the western groups were partially or wholly nomadic, living off

---

[4] The ethnological generalizations in this section apply particularly to the Plains Indians but also, with perhaps less exactitude, to most of the other horse Indians with whom the Army came into conflict. The literature is vast, but see especially Clark Wissler, *North American Indians of the Plains* (2d ed.; New York, 1938); Marian W. Smith, "The War Complex of the Plains Indians," *Proceedings of the American Philosophical Society*, 78 (1938), 425–64; and Bernard Mishkin, *Rank and Warfare among the Plains Indians*, Monographs of the American Ethnological Society, 3 (New York, 1940). E. S. Curtis, *The North American Indian* (20 vols.; Norwood, Mass., 1907–30), is a rich compendium of data on the subject. A useful brief generalization will be found in Frederick Webb Hodge, ed., *Handbook of American Indians North of Mexico* (2 vols.; Washington, D.C., 1912), 2, 914–15.

the country and practicing no more than a rudimentary agriculture that did not fix them for long periods at predictable locations.

Frontier army officers often called the horse warriors the finest light cavalry in the world, and historians have repeated the judgment ever since. The individual warrior came close to deserving the distinction. From childhood, indeed almost from infancy, he had devoted himself wholeheartedly to the task. He excelled in horsemanship—in maneuvering his mount in combat and in calling forth its full effort in the chase. Mounted or dismounted, he used his bow and arrows, lance, tomahawk, and knife with skill born of long practice. He had developed in himself qualities that every commander strives to inculcate in his men—an aggressive, warlike spirit, courage, physical strength and endurance, mental alertness, stealth, cunning, and a thorough knowledge of the land and how to make full military use of it. Beyond this, he was of a people whose highest values centered on war and whose highest rewards—material, social, political, and religious—were earned by success in war. In training and in combat, the warrior rarely lacked motivation.

The analogy cannot be carried much farther. If the western Indian was a first-rate light cavalryman, he did not often function as a member of a first-rate combat unit of light cavalry. If individual abilities attained the highest expression, group abilities suffered severe limitations.

The explanation lay in a loose social and political organization that exalted the individual at the expense of the group. Never was a tribe or even a band a monolithic entity with a leadership hierarchy that controlled the actions of the people. Indians practiced a democracy so extreme as to be incomprehensible to white Americans. This led to endless friction with the whites. Their assumption that a chief "commanded" in battle was harmless enough, but their assumption that a chief who signed a treaty or professed peace could bind his people by the pledge caused constant misunderstanding and underlay more than one war. Many an innocent chief suffered charges of bad faith from government officials who viewed Indian institutions from the frame of reference of their own.

The emphasis on individual freedom expressed itself both in the objectives and methods of war. The objective was rarely, as in "civilized" warfare, to smash the enemy and compel his

submission. Rather it was principally for the individual to enrich himself by seizing booty and to gain war honors by performing feats culturally ordained as the means of personal aggrandize-
ment. This held true whether the immediate cause of hostilities
was defense against invasion or raiding, revenge for casualties
sustained in previous encounters, retaliation for real or imagined
injuries, simple aggression aimed at reaping honors, or even,
as it became with the passage of time, racial preservation.

War expeditions customarily numbered five to thirty men,
sometimes more, and on rare occasions the whole strength of a
band or tribe. A war party set forth under the loose leadership
of any warrior with the prestige to enlist and organize one. In
the field he "commanded" only to the extent that his followers
chose to obey. From the moment such an expedition departed
until it returned, the group and each member of the group had
to perform certain religious rituals and respect certain religious
taboos, any or all of which, possible divine benefits aside, might
in fact interfere with the accomplishment of the mission. Close
combat, unless the odds overwhelmingly favored success, was to
be avoided, for casualties, no matter how complete the victory,
mitigated the triumph.

For the white soldier who moved west to grapple with the
nomadic tribesmen after the Mexican War, this mode of warfare had advantages as well as disadvantages. The most serious of the latter was the Indian's reluctance to stand and fight
unless his family was endangered, coupled with his consummate
skill at guerrilla tactics. "In a campaign against Indians," observed a veteran company commander, "the front is all around,
and the rear is nowhere."[5] One fruitless, disheartening pursuit
after another made up by far the largest share of the soldier's
field service. Sometimes there were skirmishes, but they rarely
lasted any longer than it took the Indians to break contact and
escape. "An Indian war is a chapter of accidents," remarked
Lieutenant Lawrence Kip in 1859.[6] Most of the big battles of
frontier history were just such accidents—the result of a rare
stroke of luck for the Army or a grave miscalculation by the Indians. Far more common was the experience lamented by Captain E. Kirby Smith: "We travelled through the country, broke

[5] Erasmus D. Keyes, *Fifty Years Observation of Men and Events* (New
York, 1884), p. 254.
[6] Lawrence Kip, *Army Life on the Pacific* (New York, 1859), p. 51.

down our men, killed our horses, and returned as ignorant of the whereabouts of Mr. Sanico [a Comanche chief] as when we started."[7]

The Indian style of warfare presented the Army with certain advantages, too. A team of mediocre fighters may well best a mob of superb ones if really acting as a team. The Army had the capability, and when its teams stuck together as disciplined combat units instead of fragmenting for the Indian method of personal encounter, it won some striking victories. Another big advantage lay in the inability of a tribe or group of tribes to unite for a vigorous and sustained offense or defense employing its full military potential. With their very existence as a people endangered by the white advance, the western tribes could never, collectively or even individually, present a solid front of opposition for very long or respond with anything more original than sporadic raids in the traditional pattern. When the bluecoats invaded the Indian homeland in force, it was every band for itself, with all the effort directed at eluding the aggressor and little or none at resisting him. If the troops could manage the logistics and find the quarry, victory was probable.

And herein lay the two looming military requirements dictated by the nature of the terrain and the nature of the enemy. A vast and inhospitable terrain demanded an army that could live off the country in the Indian manner or a logistical system so supremely developed as to permit operations not dependent on the resources of the country. A highly mobile enemy skilled in guerrilla tactics demanded either a highly mobile counterguerrilla force or a heavy defensive army large enough to erect an impenetrable shield around every settlement and travel route in the West. That the Army, for reasons not wholly or even largely within its control, never met these requirements explains its not too creditable record in the half century of Indian operations beginning in 1848.

[7] Joseph H. Parks, *General Edmund Kirby Smith* (Baton Rouge, La., 1954), pp. 89–90.

The Mandate of Congress

THAT the country's military leaders would have put together a truly effective Indian-fighting army if provided adequate resources is doubtful. The fact is, they never had a real chance to demonstrate the possibilities. Congress fixed the framework within which the Executive shaped the Army, and a restrictive framework it was.

Part of the problem lay in the difficulty of defining exactly what the problem was. How to deal with a people friendly at times, hostile at other times, but of uncertain disposition most of the time posed a hard dilemma. Obviously it was not exclusively a military task, and to many at mid-century the dawning hope of "civilizing" the Indian made it seem not even primarily so. Given "the interesting progress of so many tribes in Christianity, knowledge, and civilization," Treasury Secretary Robert Walker argued in 1848, the duties of Indian administration "do not necessarily appertain to war, but to peace." The Indian Bureau, he urged, together with certain other agencies not strictly military, should be detached from the War Department and lodged in a new executive department. Walker's proposals bore fruit in the creation of the Department of the Interior in 1849, and the Army, ascendant in Indian affairs since the adoption of the Constitution, protestingly yielded part of its responsibility.[1] How much no one could say with certainty, for the line dividing civil and military requirements, especially in dealing with the nomadic tribes of the West, was often badly

[1] George D. Harmon, *Sixty Years of Indian Affairs, 1789–1850* (Chapel Hill, N. C., 1941), pp. 172–73.

blurred. As controversy raged over whether soldiers or civilians were best fitted for the clearly nonmilitary phases of Indian management, competition and conflict between the two departments and their field officials complicated relations not only with the tribes but also with Congress on which both depended for appropriations.

Vastly more consequential for both agencies was the persistent inability of most congressmen to face up to the fiscal realities of territorial growth. Expansionist legislators gloried in the Nation's new stature as a continental power, but the few who perceived its monetary implications failed to persuade a majority of their colleagues that the federal budget could never return to the scale of 1845. For the Army, congressional parsimony focused most sharply on the two elements of military strength crucial to meeting the requirements peculiar to the frontier enemy and terrain—size of the Army and its logistical support.

To military leaders it was a truism too patent to need elaboration that enlargement of the national domain demanded enlargement of the military force expected to police it. On two occasions during the 1850s Congress grudgingly agreed, but the legislators never responded with a liberality permitting anything approaching a strength equal to the task. So far from appreciating the military implications of the orgy of expansion in which he had led the Nation, President Polk informed Congress on July 6, 1848, that "the old army, as it existed before the war with Mexico," would serve peacetime necessities.[2] Six months later, in the very message in which he confirmed the news of gold in California, the President explained that a "suitable number" of Indian agents would preserve peace with the Indians and make unnecessary the employment of more than a small military force.[3] Congress cheerfully agreed, and the Regular Army undertook its new duties with an authorized strength of little more than ten thousand officers and men.[4]

Succeeding Presidents, however, confronted with an actuality instead of a prospect, saw the need more clearly. One after another, Presidents Taylor, Fillmore, Pierce, and Buchanan

---

[2] House Ex. Docs., 30th Cong., 1st sess., No. 69, p. 4.
[3] James D. Richardson, comp., *Messages and Papers of the Presidents* (20 vols., New York, 1897), *4*, 645–46.
[4] 9 Stat. 305 (Aug. 14, 1848).

urged on Congress the necessity of expanding the Army,[5] and in nearly every annual report the Secretary of War and the general-in-chief spelled out the reasons in detail. Pierce's able Secretary, Jefferson Davis, analyzed the situation with compelling logic. In 1853 he pointed out that in less than half a century the national domain had doubled, the Indian population had doubled, white population had soared by eighteen million, and yet the peacetime strength of the Army had rarely exceeded ten thousand. The following year he demonstrated with statistics gathered from each geographical command the military implications of expansion that had escaped President Polk. "We have a sea-board and foreign frontier of more than 10,000 miles," he summarized, "an Indian frontier, and routes through an Indian country, requiring constant protection, of more than 8,000 miles, and an Indian population of more than 400,000, of whom, probably, one-half, or 40,000 warriors, are inimical, and only wait the opportunity to become active enemies."[6]

Swayed by such arguments, Congress twice allowed modest increases. Both could be credited largely to the persuasive logic and high stature of Jefferson Davis, first as a senator from Mississippi, later as War Secretary in Pierce's cabinet. The first, in 1850, authorized the President to raise to 74 the number of privates in each company serving on the frontier, which had the effect of elevating the legal strength of the Army to nearly fourteen thousand.[7] Again in 1855, responding to forceful appeals of President Pierce and Secretary Davis, Congress sanctioned the creation of four new regiments and a consequent lifting of the ceiling to around eighteen thousand.[8] The gain was more than offset by the assignment of regular troops to Kansas in 1855–56 to keep the peace between slavery and free-soil forces and by the dispatch of an army to Utah in 1857–59 to coerce the Mormons into submitting to U.S. authority. But

[5] Richardson, *Messages and Papers* . . . , 5, 21, 87, 132, 215, 286, 456.

[6] SW, *Annual Report* (1853), pp. 11–12; (1854), pp. 5–6.

[7] 9 Stat. 438–39 (June 17, 1850). The postwar army reduction in 1848 fixed dragoon companies at 50 privates, Mounted Rifle companies at 64, and infantry and artillery companies at 42.

[8] 10 Stat. 639–40 (March 3, 1855). In addition to urging an increase in his annual message to Congress, President Pierce transmitted a special message in January 1855 stressing the critical situation on the frontier that demanded more troops at once. Richardson, *Messages and Papers* . . . , 5, 286. Senate Ex. Docs., 33d Cong., 2d sess., No. 22.

Congress refused to yield to a strenuous Executive attempt in 1858 to win still another augmentation of the Army.

That the Regular Army was so small and so unprepared for the enormous demands suddenly thrust on it by the firing on Fort Sumter in 1861 has been a matter of reproachful remark by analysts of U.S. military policy from Emory Upton to the present. Upton contended that twenty thousand trained Regulars at Bull Run would have crushed the southern rebellion and ended the Civil War at the outset.[9] In response, it has been argued that a Regular Army large enough to have permitted such a concentration could not have won approval in the 1850s: its only purpose would have been coercion of the South, and the southern legislators who dominated Congress in the prewar years would not have acquiesced in it.[10] Yet another purpose was repeatedly demonstrated by every administration from Taylor to Buchanan, and it was perceived by enough prominent southerners to suggest that fear of sectional coercion motivated little of the opposition to a larger Regular Army. Such southern stalwarts as Jefferson Davis, John B. Floyd, James M. Mason, John J. Crittenden, and Stephen Mallory championed enlargement of the military establishment as necessary for frontier defense, while among the opponents stood such northern leaders as John P. Hale, Zachariah Chandler, Charles Sumner, Benjamin Wade, and William P. Fessenden. In truth, the debates and votes on military legislation in the 1850s reveal no discernible sectional pattern.[11]

Not that the sectional struggle played no part in the failure of Congress to heed the repeated cries of alarm from the Executive branch. By monopolizing the time and energies of the leg-

[9] Emory Upton, *The Military Policy of the United States* (Washington, D.C., 1917), p. xv. Uncompleted at his death in 1881, Upton's manuscript was not published until 1904.

[10] Walter Millis, *Arms and Men: A Study of American Military History* (Mentor ed.; New York, 1956), pp. 104–5.

[11] The House approval of the 1855 legislation, which was an amendment to the Army appropriation bill, was registered by voice vote and thus cannot be analyzed. The Senate vote, however, shows that thirteen senators from states later part of the Confederacy favored the measure while seven voted against it. Two of the seven Southerners opposing the amendment were the Texans Houston and Rusk, both of whom advocated rangers for frontier defense instead of Regulars. Of senators from states that remained in the Union, eighteen voted for the increase, thirteen against. *Cong. Globe*, 33d Cong., 2d sess., p. 515 (Feb. 1, 1855).

islators, it barred effective consideration of western needs, of which defense against Indians was but one. The western territories engaged the sustained attention of Congress in the debates over the extension of slavery, but the handful of state senators and congressmen and voteless territorial delegates could rarely win very thorough ventilation of other questions of concern to the West. When such questions arose in the regular course of business, the debates demonstrated mainly that the majority of the Nation's lawmakers, while happy to exult in the continental destiny of the Republic, could not bring themselves to pay its price.

The opposition to an enlarged army played on several themes. All the traditional clichés about the threat to democratic institutions posed by a regular army were repeated and embellished. Thus did Senator Hale of New Hampshire in 1858 recall "a lesson of wisdom which the fathers of my native state inscribed on the first constitution they ever wrote, and which, I hope in God, will remain as long as we have a Constitution—that standing armies are dangerous to liberty."[12]

Enlarging on this warning, such frontier spokesmen as Houston and Rusk of Texas and Benton of Missouri urged the enrollment of volunteer units to fight Indians. They cost less, they fought Indians more effectively, and they could be demobilized after the threat subsided. Unsaid in the halls of Congress but not unappreciated at home, they also furnished a mechanism for funneling federal money into the pockets of a community's citizens. "School-house officers and pot-house soldiers" could never conquer the Indians, exclaimed Representative Thomas Hart Benton in 1855, "and at last the Indian wars will have to be ended as others have been, by citizen rangers and volunteers."[13] And combining the arguments of Hale and Benton, Senator Robert Toombs of Georgia declared: "A republican Government should rest upon and be defended by the people; and when they are unwilling or unfit to defend it, the sooner they get a master the better."[14]

But the great objection to a larger army was the cost. Even those who orated on the lofty plane of constitutional theory usually at length got down to the fundamentals of cost and

[12] *Ibid.*, 35th Cong., 1st sess., p. 409 (Jan. 26, 1858).
[13] *Ibid.*, 33d Cong., 2d sess. (Appendix), pp. 334–41 (Feb. 27, 1855).
[14] *Ibid.*, 35th Cong., 1st sess., p. 407 (Jan. 26, 1858).

ended by voicing more concern for the Treasury than for the free institutions that the Regulars would supposedly menace. "I represent a people who are in the habit of working hard for what little money they get," asserted Senator Hale, one of the most vocal of those who deplored a standing army, "and they are not willing to vote away money unless there is an absolute necessity for it."[15] And after listening to Senator Davis set forth the most pressing exigencies, Senator Fessenden echoed Toombs, Hale, Hunter, and others: "I say, then, sir, seeing no reason, illustrated and enforced, calling upon me to vote an increase to our expenditure of $10,000,000 in time of peace and a time of bankruptcy . . . I must necessarily vote against the bill in any shape in which it may be presented."[16]

Advocates could expose the fallacy of apprehending dangers to liberty in a regular army: "This country will never be conquered by its own military force till it is fit for nothing else but to be conquered," trumpeted Senator Lewis Cass. "So long as the American people are qualified for the blessings of liberty, so long they will enjoy them."[17] Advocates could show that volunteers were more costly and less amenable to control: "It is argued that if we raise volunteers they can be got rid of," said Jefferson Davis. "Yes, sir, and we can get rid of the Treasury of the United States in the same way: we can keep its organization, but empty its coffers." Furthermore, authorization of border volunteers was a mandate "to exterminate the Indians."[18] Advocates could show the necessity for more troops on the frontiers: "Sir, if we will have a nation embracing half a continent," pointed out Senator George Badger of North Carolina; "if we will have internal and external frontiers to defend; if we will stretch from ocean to ocean, and from sea to sea, we must necessarily multiply our military means to meet the emergency which we have thus assumed."[19] But advocates could not deny that a larger army would cost more money, and on this rock any effort to win an increase truly responsive to the need was sure to shatter.

The country needed a larger army in the 1850s, not to prepare for a civil war that only a few alarmists foresaw but to

[15] *Ibid.*, p. 409.
[16] *Ibid.*, p. 412.
[17] *Ibid.*, 33d Cong., 2d sess., p. 515 (Feb. 1, 1855).
[18] *Ibid.*, 35th Cong., 1st sess., p. 515 (Jan. 27, 1858).
[19] *Ibid.*, 33d Cong., 2d sess., p. 517 (Feb. 1, 1855).

perform the mission that, with two exceptions, had been its principal reason for existence since 1792—to protect frontier citizens from the Indians. An army three times the sixteen thousand of 1860, with the same proportion stationed in the West, would still have afforded less than fifty officers and men for each post and no more than one soldier for every forty square miles of territory, every four hundred settlers, and every eight hostile or potentially hostile Indians. The U.S. Army was unprepared for the Civil War as it was inadequate for the Indian Wars very largely because the Nation, through its elected representatives, declined to pay the price of Manifest Destiny.

If Congress balked at allowing meaningful increases in the Army, so also it repeatedly expressed outrage at the cost of maintaining what it had already authorized. Quartermaster expenditures leaped from less than a million dollars in 1845 to around five million in 1851, and throughout the decade of the 1850s the estimates mounted steadily. The reasons were abundantly clear and repeatedly explained to the appropriations committees: the Army of 1845 was largely in garrison; that of 1850s was largely engaged in field operations. The military posts of 1845 were all on or very near navigable streams by which they could be supplied; those of the 1850s were for the most part accessible only by land routes hundreds of miles in length. The forts of 1845, located in a fertile and increasingly settled country, drew much of their supplies from the neighborhood; those of the 1850s, situated in a sterile and sparsely inhabited country, had to depend on overland shipments from the States for nearly every necessity. And the enlargement of territorial responsibilities, unaccompanied by a proportionate enlargement of the Army, meant more frequent movement of troops over vaster distances.[20]

Patiently the capable quartermaster general, Thomas Jesup, demonstrated with statistics that the increased cost stemmed wholly from the character and extent of the new lands—transportation registering the most notable rise, from $130,000 in 1845 to more than $2 million in 1851. But only slowly did the appropriations committees yield to his logic. The usual reaction was to slash his estimates arbitrarily, forcing an accumulation of arrearages and ultimately the unpleasant necessity of

[20] Cf. statement of Secretary of War Charles M. Conrad in SW, *Annual Report* (1851), pp. 109–13.

a deficiency appropriation. In vain did Jesup plead that "Money cannot be saved by cutting *estimates* down . . . ; to save money, *objects* of expenditure must be dispensed with." And the objects were fixed by authority higher than the quartermaster general.[21]

Congressional parsimony in quartermaster appropriations placed serious limitations on the Army's capabilities in the West. Often it meant that manpower had to be diverted from military tasks to such ordinarily civilian tasks as constructing buildings, cultivating crops, tending herds of beef and draft animals, and gathering forage. Often, too, it meant that necessary field operations were handicapped, postponed, or not even prosecuted because available supplies or the means of moving them were not at hand.

Far more than military requirements or military leadership, the congressional passion for economy shaped the frontier Army. The trauma of the annual confrontation with the appropriations moguls of Congress lay heavy on every decision and program of the War Department and permeated down the chain of command to the newest subaltern. Within the narrowly constricting boundaries thus drawn by the national legislators, the Army forged the instrument expected to overcome the hostile western landscape and its primitive inhabitants.

---

[21] Jesup's report in *ibid.*, pp. 217–25. Senator Davis argued this thesis with clarity on the Senate floor. *Cong. Globe*, 31st Cong., 2d sess., p. 826 (March 3, 1851). In the House a congressman charged that the War Department had become a tool of speculators. "That in time of profound peace," he thundered, "with no armies for aggressive war—when the whole world were extending their hands to shake the hand of peace with us . . . ; at this time of profound security and unbroken peace, the resources of the Quartermaster Department should run up to $5,000,000, is a thing unheard of in the history of expenditure." *Ibid.*, 32d Cong., 1st sess., p. 515 (Feb. 9, 1852).

THREE

The Frontier Army, 1848-61

ALTHOUGH top military leaders based their pleas for a larger Army on the needs of the frontier, they did not consciously design the frontier army to meet the special requirements of its frontier mission. Preoccupied with the next foreign war rather than the current domestic conflict, they rarely stepped from the pathways marked out by the military intellects of Europe to explore more than superficially the doctrinal implications of continuing warfare with a primitive people. Hard frontier experience, however, freed many of the junior officers from traditional dogma. Under their leadership an army organized for formal warfare adapted itself to circumstances and provided a frontier constabulary often surprisingly efficient at irregular warfare. Within the limits of strength and composition drawn by law, it did as well as could be expected.

Strength and composition imposed severe handicaps. Scattered in driblets at scores of tiny outposts all over the West, the Army rarely at any place had enough men to do its job. The low ceilings set by Congress hardly revealed the magnitude of the manpower problem. Desertion, discharge, and death produced an annual turnover of about 28 per cent, and this, coupled with the time required by the adjutant general to receive and consolidate regimental returns and sign up fresh recruits, decreed that actual strength always fall below authorized strength by as much as 18 per cent.[1] Furthermore, much of the Army's housekeeping was performed by personnel on

[1] SW, *Annual Report* (1853), pp. 7-8.

detached service from their units, either at the assigned post or some distant headquarters, and at any given time many officers and men were absent on furlough. Thus in June 1853, as a typical example, the authorized size of the Army was 13,821, the actual size 10,417; and of the 8,342 officers and men in units stationed on the western frontier, 6,918 were actually at their posts, or an average of 124 for each of the 54 stations in the western commands.[2] Allowing for men in confinement, on guard, sick, and detailed to fatigue duties, a post commander could not often count enough men to man the fort, much less to take the field. And this condition persisted throughout the 1850s, for civil disturbances in Kansas, Utah, and along the Mexican border nullified the gains allowed in 1855.

All too typical was the situation that Inspector General Joseph K. F. Mansfield discovered in August 1853 at Fort Jones, a strategic post in northern California garrisoned by Company E, 4th Infantry. Serving on the frontier, this company was authorized 3 officers, 8 noncommissioned officers, and 74 privates. Instead, its rolls bore 34 names. The captain, U. S. Grant, had just resigned his commission, one sergeant was on detached service at department headquarters and another on furlough, and a private was in the hospital at Fort Vancouver. Actually present were the commanding officer, Lieutenant J. C. Bonneycastle; Lieutenant George Crook, acting as both quartermaster and commissary of subsistence in addition to his troop duties; Lieutenant John B. Hood, newly graduated from West Point and awaiting a regimental vacancy; Surgeon Francis Sorrel; and 26 enlisted men. With 2 privates in the guardhouse, 2 sick, and a sergeant, corporal, and 7 privates on daily extra duty, Fort Jones boasted a disposable force of 4 officers, 1 sergeant, 2 corporals, and 11 privates—hardly sufficient to produce much effect on the neighboring Indians.[3]

Congress fixed not only the size of the Army but its composition as well, and here, too, economy was the guiding consideration. Part of what it lacked in strength of numbers the Army might have made up in mobility. Indeed, since weakness in numbers precluded reliance on static defense, the mobility of the enemy clearly demanded it. "The great extent of our frontiers, and the peculiar character of the service devolving on

[2] *Ibid.*, pp. 116–23.
[3] Frazer, *Mansfield on Western Forts*, pp. 165–66.

our troops, render it indispensable that the *cavalry* element should enter largely into the composition of the army," General Scott pointed out in 1850. "No other description of troops will answer for the protection of our immense lines of emigration and frontier settlements."[4] Texas Congressman Volney Howard agreed. The Indians were "well mounted and the most expert riders in the world, not excepting even the Arabs. You can neither fight nor pursue them with infantry or artillery. Out of reach of the guns of the fort and these corps might as well be a thousand miles distant. They never can come up with the enemy."[5]

But to Howard's colleagues a more compelling truth was that mounted troops cost much more than foot troops. Like their masters, Indian ponies could live off the country. The big grain-fed "American" horses could not, and most of their forage had to be hauled from the States. Major Herbert M. Enos, a quartermaster of long experience in the West, estimated in 1865 that annual supply expenses for an infantry regiment ran between $250,000 and $300,000, for a cavalry regiment, $500,-000 to $600,000. "This would not include the purchase of horses, nor the payment of troops, but simply the expense of the quartermaster's department to keep the regiment in serviceable condition and transportation." And this was only for routine service. "To keep a regiment of mounted men in the field, besides their pay and original cost of horses and arms, it would cost $1,500,000 per annum."[6] Such statistics hardly encouraged congressional economizers to grant more cavalry. And limiting the employment of what had been granted was the annual custom of cutting quartermaster estimates, which on occasion, to meet the necessity of reducing forage transportation expenditures, led to the replacement of cavalry with infantry at distant stations.[7]

Because of its expense, therefore, the mounted arm of the service never attained dimensions commensurate with its mission. As constituted at the close of the Mexican War, the line of the Army consisted of four artillery regiments, eight infantry regiments, and three mounted regiments. The legislation of 1855 added two foot and two mounted regiments. Except

---

[4] SW, *Annual Report* (1850), pp. 114–15.
[5] *Cong. Globe*, 31st Cong., 2d sess., p. 722 (Feb. 27, 1851).
[6] "Condition of the Indian Tribes," Senate Reps., 39th Cong., 2d sess., No. 156, pp. 340–41.
[7] See for example p. 112.

for the garrisons of seacoast fortifications, the peacetime artillery for the most part served as infantry. Thus at a time when about three-fourths of the Army was stationied on the frontier, only about one-third could be counted as effective for any but a passive mission of guard and escort.

Although the field employment of cavalry raised staggering logistical problems that once impelled a department commander to ask to be relieved of all his cavalry,[8] experts generally united in the judgment that only mounted troops could fight Indians with any hope of success. Two alternatives to additional regular regiments were now and then tried. One, the mounting of infantry on mules, won congressional sanction in 1850.[9] Such tampering with foot soldiers, warned General Scott, "can only result in disorganizing the infantry, and converting them into extremely indifferent horsemen."[10] Reports from the field confirmed this judgment,[11] but for half a century, when cavalry was simply not to be had, mule-mounted infantry often served as an inferior substitute. The other alternative, immensely appealing to frontier settlers and their congressional spokesmen, was the enrollment of frontiersmen as volunteer rangers for short enlistments. Such troops, although vastly more expensive and given to undisciplined excesses, were frequently mustered —usually by a state or territorial governor over the protest of the local regular army commander.

None of the various types of frontier troops attained the ideal set by Captain Randolph B. Marcy of "a union of discipline with the individuality, self-reliance, and rapidity of locomotion of the savage."[12] Infantry, even mule-mounted infantry, lacked rapidity of locomotion. Volunteers, although noted for individuality and self-reliance, were lamentably deficient in discipline. For all its weaknesses, then, the regular cavalry came closest to the ideal. For all its failures, it could also point to some

[8] Colonel Edwin V. Sumner, who remarked that cavalry could not act offensively because the horses invariably broke down. He requested that all his cavalry be replaced with infantry. The proposal was doubtless made in a fit of exasperation; none knew better than the veteran Sumner that infantry had even less capability of acting offensively against Indians. Sumner to Jones, Fort Union, N. M., Oct. 24, 1851, in Annie H. Abel, ed., *The Correspondence of James S. Calhoun* (Washington, D.C., 1915), pp. 416–19.

[9] 9 Stat. 438–39 (June 17, 1850).

[10] SW, *Annual Report* (1850), p. 114.

[11] Cf. General George M. Brooke, March 7, 1850, *ibid.*, pp. 26–27. They were "miserable riders," broke down their horses through improper care, and could not use their arms when in the saddle.

[12] Marcy, *Thirty Years of Army Life on the Border* (New York, 1866; Lippincott ed. Philadelphia, Pa., 1962), p. 252.

remarkable accomplishments. Concluded a well-traveled soldier-of-fortune: "For the work I have seen a squadron of United States Cavalry performing on the plains, Germany would send two regiments, and deem it hard service."[13]

The mounted arm consisted of the 1st and 2d Dragoons, dating from 1833 and 1836, respectively, and the Regiment of Mounted Riflemen, organized in 1846. The 1st and 2d Cavalry joined the establishment in 1855. Minor distinctions of uniform, arms, and equipment differentiated the three varieties of horsemen, most notably the Mounted Riflemen, who carried rifles and in theory traveled on horseback and fought on foot. But in reality none conformed to the generally accepted European meaning of the terms; all were in fact light cavalry. The efforts of Secretary Davis and General Scott to eliminate distinctions and designate all the mounted regiments as cavalry failed to overcome congressional inertia and the pride of the regiments in their history and traditions.[14]

Cavalry and infantry were organized into ten companies each, artillery twelve, ten of which were infantry in all but name. The tables of organization allotted each cavalry and dragoon company 50 privates, each company of Mounted Rifles 64 privates, each infantry company 42 privates, and each artillery company 42 if heavy, 64 if light. The law of 1850, authorizing 74 privates to frontier companies regardless of arm, set a maximum that was rarely reached. A captain, assisted by a first and second lieutenant and an orderly sergeant, commanded the company, and a sergeant and corporal headed each of the four squads. Regimental field and staff consisted of the colonel, lieutenant colonel, two majors, and an adjutant and quartermaster detailed from the line subalterns. A sergeant major, quartermaster sergeant, and musicians—buglers for cavalry, fifers, drummers, and bandsmen for infantry and artillery—composed the noncommissioned staff. Thus the authorized aggregate of an infantry regiment was 559, an artillery regiment 748, a cavalry or dragoon regiment 652, and the Mounted Rifle regiment 802.[15] On the frontier any regiment could theoretically number nearly 900. In fact, 1 or 2 officers and 30 to 40 men per company, or 300 to 400 per regiment, was the usual average.

[13] General Charles P. Stone in *Journal of the Military Service Institution of the United States*, 4 (1883), 394.
[14] SW, *Annual Report* (1854), pp. 16-17; (1858), p. 763.
[15] See for example table of organization in *ibid.* (1856), pp. 230-31.

Spread thinly over the West, the regiments rarely found occasion to assemble as such. The company tended to become the basic tactical unit and the organization on which individual pride and loyalty focused. In five years of active plains service, for example, Sergeant Percival Lowe's company of the 1st Dragoons had never taken the field with another company.[16] "During my entire ten years' service," recalled Augustus Meyers, who signed up as a drummer boy in the 2d Infantry in 1854, "I never saw more than six companies of the regiment together at one time"—and that was in the Civil War.[17]

Even so, the regiment did not fade from the consciousness of its rank and file. Common traditions bound the companies and clothed each regiment with a distinctive personality and "tone" for which it became known throughout the Army. Twiggs, Harney, Cooke, and "Old Ben" Beall, for example, shaped the 2d Dragoons to fit Professor Mahan's definition of the hussar as "that epitome of military impudence"—an image quite in contrast to that of the more dignified and methodical 1st Dragoons of Kearny and Mason. Similarly, the 2d Cavalry, heavy with future generals and basking in the favor of the War Department hierarchy, developed an *élan* that set it apart from its less colorful twin, the 1st Cavalry. The Mounted Riflemen, riding behind a "cantankerous lot" of officers appointed largely from civil life but fully as experienced as the West Pointers, regarded themselves as irresistible because in the Mexican War the awkwardness of the rifle encouraged them to ride down the enemy with the saber. No less did the foot regiments cultivate their individuality. Bonneville's 3d, Clarke's 6th, Garland's 8th, Wright's 9th, and even the "Marching 3d" Artillery boasted feats of endurance and perseverance that, though only occasionally ending in action, nonetheless consistently outshone the cavalrymen and their fragile horses.[18]

Distinctive facings on the navy-blue uniform differentiated the various arms of the service—orange for dragoons, yellow

---

[16] Percival Lowe, *Five Years a Dragoon* (Kansas City, Mo., 1906), p. 158.

[17] Augustus Meyers, *Ten Years in the Ranks, U.S. Army* (New York, 1914), p. 179.

[18] For histories of all the regiments see Theo. F. Rodenbough and William L. Haskin, eds., *The Army of the United States* (New York, 1896). Good histories of the 2d Dragoons and 2d Cavalry are Theo. F. Rodenbough, *From Everglade to Cañon with the Second Dragoons* (New York, 1875); and George F. Price, *Across the Continent with the Fifth Cavalry* (New York, 1883; facsimile reprint, New York, 1959).

for cavalry, green for Mounted Rifles, sky blue for infantry, and scarlet for artillery. Mounted troops sported a waist-length shell jacket, foot troops a long-skirted blouse. Worsted epaulettes and a pompom-topped shako gave way late in the decade to brass scales and the wide-brimmed "Jeff Davis" hat with ostrich feathers. The latter, reputedly designed by the Secretary of War himself for the new cavalry regiments, was ultimately adopted by the whole Army and inspired much ridicule—one veteran quipped that "If the whole earth had been ransacked, it is difficult to tell where a more ungainly piece of furniture could have been found."[19]

For the hard field service of the western frontier, however, the ornate uniforms prescribed by the regulations yielded to less military, more functional attire. Few officers insisted on uniformity. Picturing himself on the Texas frontier in 1855, Captain E. Kirby Smith of the 2d Cavalry wrote that "corduroy pants; a hickory or blue flannel shirt, cut down in front, studded with pockets and worn outside; a slouched hat and long beard, cavalry boots worn over the pants, knife and revolver belted to the side and a double barrel gun across the pommel, complete the costume as truly serviceable as it is unmilitary."[20] Returning from the Spokane campaign in 1858, a lieutenant described the soldiers as "begrimed with mud and rain and dust. The artillery and infantry wore blue flannel shirts drawn over their uniforms and belted at the waist; the dragoons had a similar dress of grey flannel. The officers had adopted the same, with slouched hats. The only marks of their rank were the shoulder-straps sewed on to the flannel."[21] At a Texas fort in 1856 the Mounted Rifles "drill with blue flannel hunting shirts and felt hats."[22] And a 6th Infantryman in Kansas in 1857 told his parents not to imagine him in uniform: "Every man is wearing a broad-brimmed hat, each of a different color;

[19] Albert G. Brackett, *History of the U.S. Cavalry* (New York, 1865), pp. 160–61. Uniforms are illustrated and described in the Quartermaster General's *The Army of the United States: Illustrated by Forty-four Facsimile Plates from Water Color Drawings by H. A. Ogden* (Washington, D.C. 1890). A new edition was published by Thomas Yoseloff in 1959. More accurate data are scattered through the files of the *Military Collector and Historian*, journal of the Company of Military Historians.

[20] Parks, *Edmund Kirby Smith*, p. 90.

[21] Kip, *Army Life on the Pacific*, pp. 122–23.

[22] John Van Deusen DuBois, *Campaigns in the West, 1856–1861*, George P. Hammond, ed. (Tucson, Arizona Pioneers Historical Society, 1949), p. 114.

white trousers of rough material; a woolen shirt of red, green, blue, or brown . . . usually open in front and worn like a coat."[23]

Of more vital concern than attire were weapons, for fire-power united with discipline to offset somewhat the enemy's advantage in mobility and individual fighting qualities. The Indians "had learned enough to convince them that the superiority of the soldier was in his arms," commented a dragoon sergeant, "not in his horsemanship . . . nor in his strength and prowess as a warrior."[24] It was a time of far-reaching advances in weapons technology—percussion-cap ignition systems, efficient revolving pistols, elongated expanding rifle balls, and breech-loading shoulder arms—and despite the Ordnance Department's ingrained conservatism, the troops profited from the improved accuracy, range, and firepower before their enemies did. Although the Indians were not without firearms even as early as the 1850s, not until much later could any significant number of them boast equal or better weapons than the Army.

Principal dragoon arms were the musketoon and pistol. No one had much good to say about the musketoon. It was, recalled a veteran of the period,

a sort of brevet musket. It was nothing but an old musket sawed off to about two-thirds of its original length, and the rammer fastened to the barrel by a swivel to prevent its being lost or dropped when loading on horseback; it used the same cartridge as the musket, kicked like blazes, and had neither range nor accuracy, and was not near as good as the musket, and was only used because it could be more conveniently carried on horseback.[25]

Inspector General Mansfield, adding that the ball was likely to roll out when the weapon was slung, called the musketoon

[23] Eugene Bandel, *Frontier Life in the Army, 1854–1861*, Ralph P. Bieber, ed. (Glendale, Calif., 1932), p. 124. See also Lowe, *Five Years a Dragoon*, p. 105.

[24] Lowe, *Five Years a Dragoon*, p. 112.

[25] "Extracts from the Unpublished Memoirs of Major General Z. R. Bliss," *Journal of the Military Service Institution of the United States, 38* (1906), 128. This was the U.S. Musketoon, model 1847. As Bliss stated, it was the standard infantry musket shortened and adapted in minor details for mounted use. It was a smoothbore, caliber .69, 41 inches long, and weighed 6 lbs. 6 ou. None was made after 1856. James E. Hicks, *Notes on United States Ordnance* (Mt. Vernon, N. Y., 1946), pp. 72–75. Arcardi Gluckman, *United States Muskets, Rifles and Carbines* (Buffalo, N. Y., 1948), p. 353.

"a worthless arm" that had "no advocates that I am aware of." He urged its replacement with the breech-loading Sharp's carbine such as had been experimentally issued to a few dragoon companies.[26] In fact, the Ordnance Department experimented throughout the decade with rifled weapons, and the musketoon gradually gave way in the late 1850s to a variety of experimental rifled carbines: Merrill, Perry, Burnside's Sharp's, and the new U.S. Carbine and U.S. Pistol-Carbine —the latter a single-shot weapon with detachable stock that could be used as a hand or shoulder weapon.[27] By 1858 the Sharp's carbine led the field. The 1st and 2d Dragoons both carried it, as did eight companies of the 1st Cavalry and two of the 2d. Two companies of the 1st Cavalry retained Burnside's carbines, and eight of the 2d the U.S. Carbine.[28]

Mainstay of all the mounted regiments was Colt's cap-and-ball six-shooter, popularized in the Mexican War by the Texas Rangers. First issued to the dragoons in 1849, by the early 1850s the revolver had largely replaced the old single-shot muzzle-loading horse pistol. Although military men debated the relative merits of the Navy and heavier Army models, on the utility of Samuel Colt's product all agreed: a weapon that enabled a horseman to fire six shots without reloading had revolutionary implications.[29] Against mounted Indians, declared General Persifor Smith, mounted troops had to have a repeater. "They charge them suddenly, are in contact with them but a few minutes, and in that time must do all the execution they

[26] Frazer, *Mansfield on Western Forts*, p. 168. In 1849 the musketoon replaced the Hall carbine in use since the organization of the dragoons. Craig to McDowell, July 19, 1856, Office Chief of Ordnance LS, vol. 49, p. 284, RG 156, NARS.

[27] Price, *Across the Continent*, pp. 29-30. Both the official weapons, model 1855, were fabricated at Springfield Armory. Both were caliber .58 and muzzle-loading. The pistol-carbine was never popular because its characteristics when fired without the stock differed so markedly from those when fired with the stock. Hicks, *Notes on United States Ordnance*, pp. 81-82. Gluckman, *Muskets, Rifles, and Carbines*, pp. 354-58.

[28] Charles E. Fuller, *The Breech-Loader in the Service* (New York, 1933), pp. 76-77.

[29] The Navy Colt was .36 caliber, weighed 2 lbs. 10 ou., and was 13 in. long. Arcardi Gluckman, *United States Martial Pistols and Revolvers* (Buffalo, N. Y., 1944), pp. 173-85. Commented Captain Randolph B. Marcy: "Notwithstanding Colt's army and navy sized revolvers have been in use for a long time in our army, officers are by no means of one mind as to their relative merits for frontier service. The navy pistol, being more light and portable, is more convenient for the belt, but it is very questionable in my mind whether these qualities counterbalance the advantages derived from the greater weight of powder and lead that can be fired from the larger pistol, and the consequent increased projectile force." *Thirty Years of Army Life*, p. 244.

expect to do, and for that purpose the revolving pistol is absolutely necessary."[30] "To a few men," added Captain William J. Hardee of the 2d Dragoons, Colt's pistol "gives the strength and confidence of numbers and inspires the savage with dread."[31]

As for the saber, Hardee continued, it was unnecessary: "in marching it makes a noise which may be heard at some distance, perhaps preventing a surprise, and in a charge, when not drawn, is positively an encumbrance."[32] A great many officers agreed with Hardee, but the weapon was issued to all the mounted regiments. Even the Mounted Riflemen, who were supposed to have hunting knives instead, received sabers, although one of their officers recalled that they rarely were used.[33] Officers often permitted their men to leave the saber in the barracks, but it figured importantly in too many engagements of the 1850s to be discounted altogether.

Foot troops in the early 1850s continued to carry the .69 caliber percussion smoothbore musket adopted in 1842. Mounted Riflemen used the famed Mississippi or "Yager" rifle popularized by Colonel Jefferson Davis' Mississippi Rifles in the Mexican War. This was the .54 caliber U.S. Percussion Rifle, model 1841. Rifles offered superior range, accuracy, and velocity, but the difficulty of seating the ball made them slow to load. In 1850 a French captain mastered the problem by a device satisfactory to U.S. ordnance officers: the elongated Minie ball contained an iron plug that the explosion drove into the lead, forcing it to fill the grooves of the bore. Adopting the Minie principle in 1855, U.S. armories began to turn out the U.S. Rifle and U.S. Rifled Musket, model 1855, both calibered at .58 and provided with long-range sights as well as attachments for the 22½-inch saber-bayonet. The 1841 rifles and the 1842 muskets were turned in for alteration to the new caliber and then reissued. The first eight infantry regiments received the rifled muskets, the new 9th and 10th Infantry together with the Mounted Riflemen the rifles.[34]

[30] July 18, 1852, SW, *Annual Report* (1852), p. 18.
[31] Hardee to AAG San Antonio, Nov. 20, 1850, encl. to Hardee to AG, Nov. 23, 1850, H458/1850, RG 94, NARS.
[32] *Ibid.*
[33] Dabney H. Maury, *Recollections of a Virginian in the Mexican, Indian, and Civil Wars* (New York, 1894), p. 105.
[34] Gluckman, *United States Muskets, Rifles and Carbines*, pp. 167–69, 181–82, 213–16, 221–23, 227–29. Hicks, *Notes on United States Ordnance*, 70–71, 82–84. The 1842 musket weighed 9 lbs. 3 ou. and was 57¾ in. long, the 1841 rifle 9 lbs. 12 ou., 48¾ in. The 1855 rifle-musket weighed 9 lbs. 2 ou., measured 59⅞ in.; the 1855 rifle 10 lbs. 49⅜ in. All were muzzle-loaders.

Although rarely included in the popular image of Indian warfare, artillery served more purposes than the ornamental and ceremonial. Nearly every post boasted its cannon, and howitzers or field guns rattled in the wake of nearly every formidable offensive column. In many engagements artillery figured importantly, in a few decisively.

The most popular and widely employed piece was the 12-pounder mountain howitzer, series 1840–41, which was used throughout the 1850s and 1860s and even later. Originally designed for pack use and later provided with several variants of field carriage, it threw an 8.9-pound shell for 900 yards at a 5-degree elevation, and it could carry for more than a mile at greater elevations. With the "prairie carriage," which became standard, the 12-pounder howitzer was as easily portable as it was effective in scattering and demoralizing concentrations of Indians. Gun crews were normally drawn from the infantry or cavalry and trained as "instant artillerymen."[35]

With its arsenal of modern rifles, carbines, revolving pistols, and "guns that shoot twice," the frontier army easily outmatched the Indians in weaponry. It was without doubt the most important single advantage the soldiers enjoyed over their adversary, and time and again, when a test of arms could be engineered, it carried the day.

The Regulars came home from the Mexican War in high spirits, with soaring morale born of solid achievement. Officers and men alike, they had consistently outshone the Volunteers in every test of military ability and had been largely responsible for the succession of triumphs that culminated in Mexico City's Plaza de Armas. The youthful West Pointers had fully vindicated the national military school that had so recently been assailed—and almost abolished—as an aristocratic parasite on a democratic society. Proud and confident, infused with the chivalrous traditions of the Plantation South from which so many of the officers sprang, the Regular Army embarked on its postwar duties with zest. But a variety of influences soon smothered this spirit and turned the talented and ambitious

[35] See William E. Birkheimer, *Historical Sketch of the Organization, Administration, Materièl and Tactics of the Artillery, United States Army* (Washington, D.C., 1881); Alfred Mordecai, *Artillery for the Land Service of the United States* (Washington, D.C., 1848); and Harold L. Peterson, *Notes on the Ordnance of the American Civil War* (Washington, D.C., 1959).

to other pursuits. Able officers and men there were, but the mediocre and incompetent formed too large a proportion for the Regular Army to retain more than a shadow of its wartime energy and ability.

Frontier service meant abominable food and living conditions, grinding monotony punctuated at infrequent intervals by the hardest and least rewarding kind of field duty, long separation from friends and family and the comforts of civilization, and the prospect of death or disability from disease, enemy action, or a constitution broken by exposure and improper diet. It meant low pay, little chance of advancement or personal recognition, and for enlisted personnel harsh, often brutal discipline. Except during the Panic of 1857, it meant foregoing opportunities in civil life that offered nearly every advantage that the Army did not. It meant persisting in a profession commonly held in contempt: "A soldier at that period was but little respected by civilians in the east," recalled an infantryman; he "was looked upon as an individual too lazy to work for a living."[36] And it meant enduring abuse when proper recognition of his services was proposed: "We see our officers now in almost every city strutting about the streets in indolence," complained an Ohio congressman on the House floor, "sustained by the laboring people, fed from the public crib, but doing nothing whatever to support themselves or to increase the wealth of the nation."[37] Although unfair to many able officers and soldiers to whom love of military life outweighed all other considerations, there was still a kernel of truth to the common charge that the Army formed a haven for men who could not succeed in any other pursuit.

The officer corps exhibited contrasts of competence and incompetence, youth and age, energy and lethargy. On the one hand there were the vigorous and ambitious young line officers glorying in the traditions of professionalism so dramatically established on the battlefields of Mexico and striving to perpetuate them in the dismal little forts of the West. From their ranks both Union and Confederate armies would soon draw their generals—Pleasanton, Reynolds, Sturgis, Ord, Maury, Buford, Garnett, Ewell, Phil Kearny, Van Dorn, Hood, A. J. Smith, Kirby Smith, Fitzhugh Lee, Sheridan, Crook. There were also the older officers who had laid the groundwork for

36 Meyers, *Ten Years in the Ranks*, p. 22.
37 *Cong. Globe*, 31st Cong., 2d sess., p. 379 (Jan. 30, 1851).

the new professionalism back in the 1830s and 1840s and who still had years of valuable service ahead of them—Cooke, Sumner, Harney, Wright, Casey, Marcy, R. E. Lee, Longstreet. Hardee, Keyes, C. F. Smith, Abercrombie, Thomas, Heintzelman. To such officers goes most of the credit for the Army's frontier achievements in the 1850s. They merited accolades like Sergeant Lowe accorded his company commander, Captain Robert H. Chilton—"bold, unyielding, self-reliant, quick to comprehend an emergency, and so vigilant that he could not be surprised";[38] or such as Private Peck applied to Lieutenant J. E. B. Stuart—"worth a dozen ordinary men . . . always prolific of expedients for working his way out of difficult or embarrassing situations."[39]

On the other hand, there were the deadbeats, timeservers, and narrow martinets whose abilities had been dulled by age, boredom, and alcohol. Lieutenant George Crook thought most post commanders "petty tyrants." "They lost no opportunity to snub those under them, and prided themselves in saying disagreeable things. Most of them had been in command of small posts so long that their habits and minds had narrowed down to their surroundings. . . . Generally they were the quintessence of selfishness."[40] In Major John S. Simonson, veteran of the War of 1812, a new lieutenant in 1857 saw "a simple, but kind old fellow . . . deficient in reason, cramped in his understanding, and warped in his judgment."[41] Private Augustus Meyers served under a company commander whom twenty-three years in the 2d Infantry had converted into "an elderly man, very corpulent and unable to stand the hardships of a campaign," a lover of "his ease and comfort."[42] Most frontier officers were hard drinkers, and all too many slipped into the grip of alcoholism. At Fort Vancouver in 1849 Major John S. Hatheway suffered a series of seizures of delirium tremens, during which he tried to kill himself; four years later, in New York, he succeeded.[43] And delirium tremens kept Captain Henry Judah with

[38] Lowe, *Five Years a Dragoon*, p. 85.
[39] Robert M. Peck, "Recollections of Early Times in Kansas Territory from the Standpoint of a Regular Cavalryman," *Transactions of the Kansas State Historical Society, 8* (1904), 505.
[40] *General George Crook, His Autobiography*, Martin F. Schmitt, ed. (Norman, Okla., 1946), p. 10.
[41] Frank D. Reeve, ed., "Puritan and Apache: A Diary [of Lt. H. M. Lazelle]," *New Mexico Historical Review, 23* (1948), 276.
[42] Meyers, *Ten Years in the Ranks*, pp. 163, 175.
[43] Robert C. Clark, "Military History of Oregon, 1849-1859," *Oregon Historical Quarterly, 36* (1935), 21.

the packs while his company of the 4th Infantry assaulted a party of Indians barricaded in a California cave.[44] In truth the frontier army not only attracted mediocrity but impaired the usefulness of all but a select few of the promising.

Low pay and slow promotion coupled with a dearth of other forms of reward and recognition exacted a heavy toll on the officer corps, prompting the resignation of such promising men as Grant, McClellan, Halleck, Buckner, Sherman, Burnside, Bragg, and T. J. Jackson. When his daughter announced her intention to marry Lieutenant Ambrose P. Hill, Captain Randolph B. Marcy exploded: "You would have to go to a company where his pay could hardly give you a miserable living, with a house that a man in civilized society would actually be ashamed to keep a horse in."[45] He could point to pay scales basically unaltered for half a century, ranging from $25 a month for a second lieutenant to $75 for a colonel.[46] Allowances for rations, fuel, forage, servants, quarters, and other necessities as much as trebled the base pay, but the total still fell far below salaries in comparable civilian occupations. Even the general-in-chief, with a base pay of $2,400 a year, drew less than $7,000 after counting all allowances.[47] In 1850 Congress granted an additional $2 a day to officers serving in California and Oregon and subsequently extended the provision to those elsewhere on the frontier.[48] In 1857 it went a step further and raised the base pay of officers in all grades by $20 a month.[49]

Slow promotion added to the discontent. Officers advanced strictly by seniority—in their regiments through captain, in their corps (infantry, cavalry, engineers, and so forth) through colonel, and in the army at large beyond. Absence of a retired list made progress agonizingly slow. Repeatedly succeeding administrations urged Congress to allow compensated retirement for age,[50] only to be met with such replies as that of Representative Joshua Giddings: "Sir, when this retired military list shall once be established, it will remain an incubus upon the people while the Government shall exist. Like that of Great Britain and of other despotic nations, it will bear down the

[44] Crook, *General George Crook*, p. 19.
[45] Quoted in W. Eugene Hollon, *Beyond the Cross Timbers: The Travels of Randolph B. Marcy, 1812–1887* (Norman, Okla., 1955), p. 194.
[46] 2 Stat. 132 (March 16, 1802).
[47] "Army Register, 1853," House Ex. Docs., 33d Cong., 1st sess., No. 59.
[48] 9 Stat. 508 (Sept. 28, 1850). 10 Stat. 108 (Aug. 31, 1852).
[49] 11 Stat. 163 (Feb. 21, 1857).
[50] Richardson, 5, 21, 88, 287–88, 338.

energies of the people, and oppress those who toil for a living."[51] To establish a retirement system, contended the majority of congressmen, would set a dangerous precedent and ultimately lead even to retirement for the civil service.[52]

The consequence was twofold. First, it burdened the top ranks of the Army with ancient and wornout officers unable to perform their duties. The adjutant general estimated in 1850 that twenty-five officers fell in this category and ought to be retired.[53] Of the nineteen regimental colonels in 1860, eleven were veterans of the War of 1812, and two had entered the Army in 1801; and of the remaining eight, only four counted less than forty years of service.[54] Second, the absence of a retired list blocked the channels of promotion and barred juniors, good and bad alike, from the field grades until past their prime. An officer commonly spent twenty to thirty years reaching the rank of major, and by then his horizons were apt to be so limited by company concerns as to make his usefulness in broader responsibilities dubious. As a random example, Nathaniel C. Macrae was graduated from West Point in 1826 and posted to the 3d Infantry. He was promoted to first lieutenant in 1835, to captain in 1839, and to major in 1857, retiring in 1861 after 35 years in the same regiment.[55] Such prospects hardly infused a new leutenant with ambition or roused his hopes for reward based on achievement. Although President Pierce and Secretary Davis mounted a strong drive for reform, proposing a retirement system coupled with limited promotions for merit,[56] not until 1861 was the retirement issue won and not until near the close of the century did the first cracks appear in the seniority system.

Chief means of recognizing battlefield achievement was the award of brevet ranks, although Indian engagements did not qualify as battles for this purpose. Most of the Mexican War veterans had received one or more brevets for gallantry in action. Many a lieutenant and captain claimed brevet grades of major or lieutenant colonel, while more than half the colonels enjoyed

[51] *Cong. Globe*, 31st Cong., 2d sess., p. 379 (Jan. 30, 1851).
[52] Cf. *ibid.*, 30th Cong., 2d sess., pp. 570-71 (Feb. 20, 1849).
[53] Jones to Davis, Jan. 14, 1850, AGO LB No. 27, pp. 17-19, RG 94, NARS.
[54] Compiled from F. B. Heitman, *Historical Register and Dictionary of the U.S. Army* (2 vols.; Washington, D.C., 1903), *1*.
[55] *Ibid.*, p. 682.
[56] Richardson, *Messages and Papers . . .*, *5*, 287, 338.

brevets of brigadier or major general. Had the brevet system been purely honorary, it would have been harmless. But brevet rank took effect, in both authority and pay, by special assignment of the President, in commands composed of different corps, on courts-martial, and in detachments composed of different corps. Thus under certain conditions a captain with no brevet might find himself serving under a lieutenant who had picked up a brevet of major in Mexico. The system had so many ramifications and nuances that it produced endless dispute and uncertainty, to say nothing of chaos in the computation of pay. Senator Davis declared in 1851 that it had "grown upon our service until it has produced such confusion in the Army that many of its best soldiers wish it could be obliterated." But compensating for slow promotion and offering the only means of winning recognition for gallantry, the brevet system was not to be relinquished lightly.[57]

By the middle 1850s, 73 per cent of the officer corps boasted a West Point education.[58] Although mainly an engineering college, the Academy instilled a sense of professionalism that flowered in Mexico and persisted on the frontier. It did not teach a prospective officer how to fight Indians. The incisive lectures of old Professor Dennis Hart Mahan probed the nature and art of war and laid down the principles by which his students would conduct the coming Civil War, but his teachings remained barren of guidance on how to employ a company of dragoons against the only enemy any of them could see in their future. West Point provided a superior selection apparatus for the officer corps and gave its graduates a slight edge in the military fundamentals, but it sent them forth to learn Indian fighting by hard experience.[59]

[57] The Davis statement is in *Jefferson Davis, Constitutionalist: His Letters, Papers, and Speeches*, Roland Dunbar, ed. (10 vols.; Jackson, Miss., 1923), 2, 23. For a thorough discussion of the subject consult James B. Fry, *The History and Legal Effect of Brevets in the Armies of Great Britain and the United States* (New York, 1877). Brevets have created perhaps as much confusion among historians of the Indian Wars as they did among their bearers, leading in much historical writing to such spectacles as colonels commanding companies and generals commanding regiments. There is no wholly satisfactory usage that does not tend toward the pedantic. In this volume I have tried to draw the distinction where it seemed desirable without unduly laboring the point. As a general rule, I have used an officer's brevet rank only if he was actually serving in it.

[58] See below, p. 34, n. 60.

[59] A standard history of the Academy for this period is Sidney Forman, *West Point: A History of the United States Military Academy* (New York,

Not until after the Civil War did the West Point influence dominate the top ranks of the Army. In the 1850s the example of Scott, Taylor, Wool, Worth, Twiggs, and others in the military hierarchy seemed to buttress the Minute Man tradition against the growing notion that a man needed a formal military education to lead troops in battle. Nearly one-fourth of the officer corps had been drawn from civil life, and the Pierce administration in 1855–56 filled 116 commissioned vacancies, chiefly in the four new regiments, with civil appointees—a source of resentment to officers ranked by the newcomers and to graduates brevetted to their regiments as supernumeraries until a vacancy opened. Many unfortunate appointments there were, but many, too, rested on prior service as well as political preferment. And since the appointee learned his frontiersmanship in the same school as the West Pointer, distinctions of academic background tended to fade.[60]

1950), pp. 36–133. American military thought as expressed at West Point in Mahan's day is discussed in Russell Weigley, *Towards an American Army: Military Thought from Washington to Marshall* (New York, 1962), chap. 5. See also Leonard D. White, *The Jacksonians: A Study in Administrative History, 1829–1861* (New York, 1963), pp. 205–12; and the annual reports of the Board of Visitors to the Academy in the annual reports of the Secretary of War. It is true that appointments to the Academy were political, but the entrance examination and four—for a time five—years of rigorous academic work and strict discipline eliminated most of the unfit.

[60] A comparison of the 1856 Army Register (House Ex. Docs., 34th Cong., 3d sess., No. 24) with Heitman's *Historical Register and Dictionary* reveals some interesting statistics:

| | Source of commission | | | | Civil Appointments |
	USMA	Civil	Ranks	Total	1855–56
Staff (Excluding 101 officers of Med. Dept.)	188	35	1	224	
Cavalry (5 regiments)	117	62	8	187	37
Artillery (4 regiments)	173	43	4	220	18
Infantry (10 regiments)	236	102	13	351	61
Total	714	242	26	982	116

Civil appointments cluster in four distinct periods—1812–14, 1836–38, 1846–48, and 1855–56. In the four new regiments organized in 1855, about one-half the commissioned grades were filled by political appointment, together with a scattering of second lieutenant vacancies in the older regiments. This led to bitter recriminations against Jefferson Davis and his "creatures"—mainly, it should be noted, after Davis became Confederate President. I have not found evidence to explain the rash of civil appointments at this time, but it may be speculated that they represent the price Davis paid for the congressional votes that won authorization of the new regiments. Of the 116 civil appointees in 1855–56, 37 came from states that later formed the Confederacy, which is not the undue proportion often charged. Of the 116, 66 claimed prior service either as West Pointers who failed to graduate (12) or as veterans of the

Other distinctions did not. The officer corps was anything but a tight little band of like-minded professionals bound by common traditions and loyalties. Harmony never settled on the quarreling factions—infantry against cavalry, staff against line, North against South. Especially North against South; as the sectional controversy flamed, northern and southern officers, particularly the extremists, waged a bureaucratic war between the States that ended only with the firing on Fort Sumter.[61] Jealous of prerogatives, quick to prefer charges for the most trivial offenses real or imagined, eternally quarreling over precedence, from general-in-chief down the officers engaged in prodigies of disputation and decreed that a large share of one's service be spent on court-martial duty.[62]

Most of the adverse influences operating on the officer corps weighed even more heavily on the enlisted complement, with predictable results. "The tone of the rank and file needs elevation extremely," remarked Secretary of War Floyd in 1857,[63] and the few literate soldiers who set down their observations confirmed the judgment. Eugene Bandel informed his parents in Germany that his associates were "not such as I have been accustomed to live with." "The greater part of the army," he concluded, "consists of men who either do not care to work, or who, because of being addicted to drink, cannot find employment."[64] Augustus Meyers was more charitable. A company soon separated into two parties, he said, the larger including the men who kept themselves clean and took some pride in soldiering, the smaller consisting of the slovenly, disorderly, quarrelsome, and sometimes vicious.[65] In the former class, in Percival Lowe's opinion, were many faithful and reliable men whose main shortcoming was lack of "the strong will and sound

---

Mexican War. Of these 66, 9 won general officer rank and 17 field rank in the Union or Confederate armies. Of the 50 civil appointees without military experience, 6 won stars, 15 field rank. Among the balance of the civil appointees, 16 resigned before 1860, 4 were dismissed, 2 were cashiered, and 1 was dropped.

[61] This theme runs through most of the writings of officers who served in the 1850s but with special clarity in the recollections of abolitionist E. D. Keyes, *Fifty Years Recollections of Men and Events.* See also Brackett, *History of the U.S. Cavalry,* for expressions of sectional animus. As Southerners dominated the officer corps, Northerners had the worst of it.

[62] For a brief discussion of this problem, see White, *Jacksonians,* pp. 194–96.

[63] SW, *Annual Report* (1857), p. 12.

[64] Bandel, *Frontier Life in the Army,* pp. 110, 114.

[65] Meyers, *Ten Years in the Ranks,* p. 43.

judgment to act independently—to blaze the way and decide their own destiny."[66] Samuel Chamberlain probably drew the best characterization of the enlisted force of this or any other regular army. There were the "deadbeats"—dirty, malingering, and untrustworthy; the "old soldiers"—quiet, dutiful, subordinate, of limited intellect and initiative, often corporals but never sergeants; and the "daredevils"—"first in a fight, frolic or to volunteer for duty," faultlessly uniformed, often in the guardhouse but never the hospital, "the pride of the officers and the admiration of their companions."[67]

The Army offered little to attract enterprising men or to elevate them once enlisted. A recruit signed up for a five-year hitch. He received $7 a month in the infantry and artillery, $8 in the cavalry, and he could anticipate $13 a month if he ever made sergeant. The Pierce administration, with the aggressive Davis heading the War Department, managed to get a pay bill through Congress in 1854 that added $4 a month to enlisted pay in all grades and for the first time provided longevity pay—$2 a month extra for the second enlistment and $1 for each thereafter.[68] Although regulations required a visit by the paymaster at least every two months, this provision was rarely complied with on the frontier, where remote garrisons and commands on extended field service often went six months or more without pay.

In addition, of course, the enlisted man received his uniform, rations, and quarters. The daily ration, repeated with deadly monotony day after day, consisted of fresh or salt beef or pork, bread, coffee, and beans, peas, or rice.[69] In the West the soldiers sought to vary the fare whenever opportunity offered for hunting or fishing, and buffalo, elk, deer, wild turkey, grouse, and other game often appeared on the mess tables. Fresh vegetables were priceless rarities. In 1851, as an economy measure, Secretary of War Conrad launched an experiment in self-support by directing all frontier post commanders to plant a vege-

---

[66] Lowe, *Five Years a Dragoon*, p. 49 and passim.

[67] Samuel Chamberlain, *My Confession* (New York, 1956), pp. 186–87.

[68] 10 Stat. 575–76 (Aug. 4, 1854). Pay scales from 1873 to 1875 are printed in Thos. H. S. Hamersly, comp., *Complete Regular Army Register of the United States* (Washington, D.C., 1881), pp. 190–92.

[69] One ration consisted of ¾ lb. pork or bacon or 1¼ lbs. fresh or salt beef; 18 ou. bread or flour, or 12 ou. hard bread, or 1¼ lbs. corn meal; and for every 100 rations 8 qts. peas or beans or 10 lbs. rice, 6 lbs. coffee, 12 lbs. sugar, 4 qts. vinegar, 1½ lbs. tallow, 4 lbs. soap, and 2 qts. salt. *Army Regulations*, 1857.

table garden, but it proved a costly failure at nearly every post.[70] Officers or their wives frequently tended small garden plots, but for the enlisted man it was beans and more beans, sometimes relieved by the desiccated vegetables with which the Subsistence Department experimented throughout the decade.[71]

The usual quarters afforded few comforts. Because of the constantly shifting frontiers, remarked General Scott in 1857, "the troops are . . . either in tents (winter as well as summer) or such miserable bush and mud huts as they have hastily constructed for the moment."[72] Although work on permanent barracks got under way at many western forts in the 1850s, the general did not seriously overstate the case. The surgeon at Fort Union, New Mexico, reported in 1856 that one set of barracks, though only four years old, had been demolished to prevent its falling on its tenants. The other barracks, built of unbarked pine logs, harbored "that annoying and disgusting insect the *Cimex lectularius*," and most of the men slept in the open when weather permitted.[73] Similar conditions prevailed at Fort Davis, Texas, where the 8th Infantry occupied rude shelters built of oak and cottonwood pickets thatched with grass (jacales).[74] At Fort Yuma in 1854 Colonel Mansfield found the men living in willow huts that he judged "worthless."[75] And Harney's troops on the upper Missouri wintered in 1855–56 in dark log structures crowded with bulky wooden bunks and barely heated by fireplaces that regularly ignited the chimneys, kept the surrounding dirt floors a muddy quagmire, and left more distant areas frozen solid in temperatures that sank to forty below zero.[76]

The prospect of serious illness and perhaps death also greeted the recruit. Primitive medical facilities combined with primitive medicine practiced by a corps of physicians always too small to meet its responsibilities produced a high rate of sickness and mortality in the frontier army. For the first five years after the

---

[70] SW, *Annual Report* (1851), p. 111; (1852), p. 4. See below, p. 86.

[71] Cf. *ibid.* (1858), p. 801.

[72] *Ibid.* (1857), p. 49.

[73] Quoted in Chris Emmett, *Fort Union and the Winning of the Southwest* (Norman, Okla., 1965), p. 202.

[74] M. L. Crimmins, ed., "Colonel J. K. F. Mansfield's Report of the Inspection of the Department of Texas in 1856," *Southwestern Historical Quarterly, 42* (1938–39), 351–57.

[75] Frazer, *Mansfield on Western Forts*, p. 147.

[76] Meyers, *Ten Years in the Ranks*, p. 93.

Mexican War, when the mean strength of the Army hovered around 10,000, the Medical Department treated 134,708 cases and lost 1,835 to death. In 1849 alone cholera attacked some 700 soldiers, of whom nearly half died. In this same year more than 7,000 cases of acute dysentery prostrated the Army and killed 151 men. Various fevers, especially among troops crossing the Isthmus en route to the Pacific, ran to several thousand cases each year. Respiratory ailments and venereal diseases took heavy toll in lost time. Scurvy debilitated men deprived of fresh vegetables. On the average each soldier had to be hospitalized three times a year, and each year one in 33 men died of disease.[77]

Also stripping military life of its appeal was the fact that much of it was so very unmilitary. The soldier found himself more often employed with shovel or ax than with musket or saber. With economy the watchword, the civilian payroll had to be kept down, and nearly every task in the construction and operation of a fort had to be performed by the troops in addition to their military duties. This, observed Secretary Floyd in 1857, made them "feel degraded because they are deprived of both the emoluments and the sturdy independence of the laboring man." The recruit who signed up to be a soldier "can but resent as a wrong the order which changes him from his legitimate vocation to that of a mere operative deprived of his wages."[78] Yet the work had to be done, and the soldier was usually the only one on hand to do it.

And finally, discipline was harsh and unremitting. As Drummer Meyers observed when he signed up in 1854, the Articles of War catalogued every offense imaginable, and the ninety-ninth, conduct "to the prejudice of good order and military discipline," covered everything that had been missed in the first ninety-eight. "It seemed," he thought, "to fit nearly every case." Solitary confinement on bread and water or forfeiture of pay and allowances were normal sentences of a garrison court-martial for minor transgressions, but for major offenses, except desertion, the Articles of War left the punishment pretty much

[77] Richard H. Coolidge, *Statistical Report on the Sickness and Mortality in the Army of the United States*. . . . [1839-55], Senate Ex. Docs., 34th Cong., 1st sess., No. 96. See especially tables on pp. 488-93. See also annual reports of the Surgeon General in the annual reports of the Secretary of War; and P. M. Ashburn, *A History of the Medical Department of the United States Army* (Boston, Mass., 1929), chap. 2.

[78] SW, *Annual Report* (1857), p. 12.

to the discretion of the officers composing the court. Thus a man might be whipped, confined with ball and chain and perhaps even an iron collar with spikes projecting in such manner as to prevent reclining in comfort, bucked, hung by the wrists or thumbs, marched around the parade ground for days with a pack full of bricks, or subjected to almost any other torture that an officer's ingenuity might conceive. And these punishments were often administered by company officers without the formality of a court-martial.[79]

The Articles permitted a sentence of death for desertion, but in practice the punishment stopped short of this finality. Stripped to the waist, the deserter was tied to a pole and in a formal ceremony his back flogged with up to fifty lashes, "well laid on" with a rawhide whip. Later, his head shaved and his hip indelibly branded with a large D, he was drummed out of the post to the strains of the "Rogue's March." After witnessing such a spectacle, Eliza Johnston, wife of the colonel of the 2d Cavalry, wrote in her diary that "surely, surely, some less degrading mode of punishment can be substituted."[80] Most contemporaries who set their thoughts to paper agreed.

General Scott recognized the weaknesses in a code that left so much discretion to the administering officers and that, because of the perennial shortage of officers to compose courts-martial, produced so much punishment that had not been judicially decreed. He urged the formation of a board of officers charged with revising the Articles of War, and he hoped that they would come up with a system that combined specific punishments with specific rewards and also provided for garrison courts composed of sergeants where sufficient officers were not available.[81] Not until long after Scott's time, however, was the system of military justice overhauled.

The contrast between conditions in the Army and out manifested itself at the recruiting "rendezvous." "The material offered

[79] For the Articles of War see *Army Regulations, 1857*. Especially good descriptions of the punishments administered are in Meyers, *Ten Years in the Ranks;* M. R. Morgan, "Memories of the Fifties," *Journal of the Military Service Institution of the United States*, 37 (1905), 147–67; Bliss, "Extracts from the Unpublished Memoirs of Maj. Gen. Z. R. Bliss," pp. 120–34; and Clinton E. Brooks and Frank D. Reeve, eds., *Forts and Forays; James A. Bennett: A Dragoon in New Mexico, 1850–1856* (Albuquerque, 1948), passim.
[80] Charles P. Roland and Richard C. Robbins, eds., "The Diary of Eliza (Mrs. Albert Sidney) Johnston [1855]," *Southwestern Historical Quarterly*, 60 (1956–57), 467.
[81] SW, *Annual Report* (1853), p. 96; (1857), p. 48.

in time of peace," concluded an official survey of recruiting statistics, "is not of the most desirable character, consisting principally of newly arrived immigrants, of those broken down by bad habits and dissipation, the idle, and the improvident." Officers preferred native-born American farm boys, but this study showed that most were newly arrived immigrants and city dwellers. Less than four in thirty listed their vocation as farming, and immigrants outnumbered native Americans more than two to one. Ireland supplied more than half the foreign element, Germany about a fifth. Complaints against foreigners were their inability to speak English and their generally debilitated physical condition, stemming from the economic forces that moved them to leave the old country. Although reluctantly, the Army played a large role in the absorption of immigrants into American life: it indoctrinated them in the language and ways of the new country and distributed them at the close of their enlistment along the sparsely peopled frontier.[82]

Springing from the dominant character of the recruits were two scourges of the Regular Army—drunkenness and desertion. The monotony of life at a frontier station, the absence of much else to do with one's leisure time, and the like frailty of large numbers of officers aggravated tendencies that many recruits brought with them to the Army, and the literature of the period testifies overwhelmingly to a chronic turbulence produced by excessive drinking. Officers went to extravagant lengths to keep whisky from their men, but rarely with any success. Although temperance societies occasionally flourished in a garrison,[83] more characteristic was Sergeant Lowe's observation that 10 per cent of his company could be found in the guardhouse for offenses committed while drunk.[84]

Desertion took heavy toll on the undermanned frontier army, especially on the Pacific Coast in the few years after the discovery of gold. Experience demonstrated, declared the Secretary of War in 1853, that in an army of 10,000 nearly 1,300 would receive their discharge each year, while nearly 1,500 would desert.[85] In 1856, with the Army expanded to more than

[82] Coolidge, pp. 625–32. It is interesting to note that more American recruits ended their service by desertion or court-martial than did immigrant recruits.
[83] Cf. Frazer, *Mansfield on Western Forts*, p. 52.
[84] Lowe, *Five Years a Dragoon*, p. 122.
[85] SW, *Annual Report* (1853), p. 8.

15,000, 3,223 men deserted.[86] Of the first 500 men enlisted in the new 10th Infantry in 1855, 275 deserted before completing their five-year term.[87] They simply got their fill of low pay, bad living conditions, and oppressive discipline that stood in such bold contrast to the seeming allurements of the civilian world, especially in the mineral regions. The pay raise of 1854, with its additional reward for longevity, was designed in part as an attack on the desertion problem, but the Panic of 1857, reducing civilian opportunities, had more effect. Even so, about one-eighth of the troops went over the hill in 1860.[88]

No very thorough system of basic training prepared the recruit for his new vocation. Three "schools of instruction" received inductees signed up by recruiting officers in the big eastern cities. Prospective infantrymen went to Governors Island in New York Harbor, cavalrymen to Carlisle Barracks, Pennsylvania, and artillerymen to Newport Barracks, Kentucky.[89] Here the new soldier was supposedly exposed to the rudiments of dismounted drill, care and use of weapons, and at Carlisle horsemanship. But in practice, as General Scott complained in 1857, "Incessant calls for reinforcements received from the frontiers compel us, habitually, to forward recruits without the instruction that should precede service in the field, and on joining their regiments, perhaps in the act of pursuing an enemy, it is long before the deficiency can be supplied."[90] The result was that the replacements received by the regiments, unless they claimed prior service, often could not handle a weapon or, if cavalry, stay in the saddle. When a prairie fire swept the camp of a detachment of recruits bound for New Mexico, for example, the number of unexploded muskets led to an investigation that revealed 140 out of 325 loaded with the ball before the charge.[91]

It remained to the regimental commissioned and noncommissioned officers, therefore, to train their own recruits. But the

---

[86] *Ibid.* (1856), p. 3.

[87] S. Y. Seyburn, "The Tenth Regiment of Infantry," in Rodenbough and Haskin, *Army of the United States*, p. 531.

[88] SW, *Annual Report* (1860), p. 189.

[89] *Ibid.* (1849), p. 186. About three-fourths of the recruits were signed up by the General and the Mounted Recruiting Services at recruiting rendezvous in the eastern cities, the rest directly by the various regiments through what was called the Regimental Service.

[90] *Ibid.* (1858), p. 762.

[91] M. C. Meyer, "Letters of a Sante Fe Army Clerk," *New Mexico Historical Review*, 40 (1965), 143.

chronic shortage of officers on line duty,[92] the dispersed condition of the regiments, and the constant employment of men on fatigue labor made this an unsatisfactory substitute. Sporadic target practice and daily dismounted drill helped a little, but for the most part time and experience had to make up for the absence of formal training.

For officer corps and enlisted complement alike, garrison duty was the principal pastime of frontier service. Although the War Department recorded more than two hundred armed clashes of Regulars with Indians between 1848 and 1861, it has been authoritatively estimated that a frontier soldier might participate in one combat during a five-year enlistment.[93] Field service now and then relieved the tedium, but it is a paradox that an army so grievously undermanned for its mission spent so much time in garrison. The paradox contains its own explanation: garrisoning the forts consumed most of the manpower. And paradoxically, too, garrison routine usually permitted an abundance of leisure in an environment affording few outlets for its enjoyment.

The fort was the central institution of the frontier army. Some were convenient to a settlement, others isolated in the wilderness. A few were stockaded or otherwise fortified in whole or part, most laid out without any concession to the remote possibility of attack. A few were of lasting stone or frame construction and skilled craftsmanship, most hasty patchworks of locally available materials. But all conformed to a basic pattern. "Some, I suppose, have a very vague idea of what a fort is like in this country," wrote a dragoon in his diary at Cantonment Burgwin, New Mexico, in 1852. "The buildings are built of mud brick in a hollow square, leaving in the center what is called a 'parade ground' where the military parades are held every morning. One side of the square is used as officer's quarters; the opposite side as a guard house, commissary department, offices, etc. The other two sides are soldiers' barracks. There is a flag staff in the center from which the stars and stripes flash and wave in the breeze.

[92] Lamenting the lack of officers to conduct training, Colonel Mansfield noted that in 1853 11 of the 21 companies in the Department of New Mexico had only one officer on duty and that in 4 of the 11 the officer also commanded the post and served as quartermaster and commissary officer. Frazer, *Mansfield on Western Forts*, p. 67.

[93] Don Russell in introduction to 2d ed. of Lowe, *Five Years a Dragoon*, p. viii.

Out of this square are to be found a hospital, dragoon stables, yards, etc."[94] With minor variations, the description fitted almost any fort in the West.

The fort was a largely self-contained community, with official and social life following a pattern as unvarying as the physical layout. Military rank ordered the official and social hierarchy and determined the authority, privileges, and social standing of all members of the community. It encompassed the families of officers and enlisted men, whose existence army regulations did not recognize, as well as such civilian residents as sutler, quartermaster employees, and laundresses, whose existence was officially recognized. At the bottom of the pyramid was the private soldier (and laundress, whether married or unmarried), at the top the commanding officer (and his wife). Between commissioned and noncommissioned groups was a gulf that allowed little mobility, either official or social.

Under the post commander, each officer and man had his official role to play. The post adjutant and sergeant major were the administrative voices of the commander, with whom they shared offices at post headquarters. Most of his orders were transmitted through these men. The post quartermaster officer was responsible for clothing, housing, and supplying the garrison, the post commissary officer for feeding it. The post surgeon presided over the hospital and also looked after the sanitary condition of the fort. Company officers could be found supervising their units in the field or occupied with paper work in the company orderly room. Sergeants and corporals of the line usually stayed with the troops. Numerous enlisted specialists— blacksmith, farrier, saddler, wagoner, wheelwright—worked in shops that formed part of the quartermaster and cavalry corrals. At specified times of the day drum or bugle broadcast the appropriate calls that regulated the routine of the military community.

The wives of some officers wrote books in which they described this routine in rich detail and with evident nostalgia. One recalled life at Fort Ringgold, Texas, in 1850–51 in these words:

Garrison life, in the phase that I saw it, was very pleasant. Each hour was marked by some peculiar military signal. At daybreak "reveille" sounded musically on the drowsy ear; then came the "sick

---

[94] Brooks and Reeve, *Forts and Forays*, p. 40.

call," especially agreeable to "Old Soldiers!" Then the dulcet airs
of "peas upon a trencher," or "roast beef," summoned the soldier
with fife and drum, to his frugal repast of "junk" and hard bread.
Guard-mounting, morning and evening drill, parade, and finally
tattoo, systematically divided the day, without rendering it monot-
onous.[95]

Sergeant Eugene Bandel, a participant in the routine rather
than an observer, described it with more authority if less roman-
ticism. For his parents to "see how little there is to vary the
monotony as the weeks go by," he set forth a typical day's program at Camp Prentiss, California, in 1859:

At daybreak I am awakened by the drums and fifes. I get up, read
the roll call of the company . . . and then go back to bed again.
Towards six o'clock I arise once more, dress, etc. In the meantime
the company clerk . . . has completed the sick list and the morning
report. At seven the drum beats the sick call. The sergeant, or corporal who has been assigned the duty for that particular day, takes
the sick list and marches the sick who are in quarters (not in the
hospital) to the tent of the doctor. At half past seven comes the call
to breakfast, though, to be sure, the soldiers have usually eaten by
that time. After signing the morning report, I then take it to the
captain of the company, who also signs. After this it is delivered
to the office of the adjutant. . . . The call to guard muster beats
at eight. I inspect the detail for the company and march them to
parade. At nine the drum beats for drill. The company is then
formed and for one hour is drilled in marching and in the manual
of arms. After this, as a rule, my labors for the day are over until
towards evening, with the exception of the summons for orders
which beats at eleven o'clock. Then I go to the adjutant's office
to receive any possible orders there may be and the details for the
next day. After that I am my own master until five-thirty o'clock,
since the different calls during the day, such as the signal for noon
meal, and the like, do not necessitate my presence. Then, to be
sure, one hour is devoted to exercise. At sundown the drum beats
the signal for retreat. I read the roll call once more, announce the
various details for the following day, and leave the company. Tattoo beats at half past eight. Once more I call the roll and then
am glad that I am one day nearer my discharge.[96]

[95] Mrs. E. L. Viele, *Following the Drum: A Glimpse of Frontier Life*
(New York, 1858), p. 221.
[96] Bandel, *Frontier Life in the Army*, pp. 287-88.

Daily guard mount and weekly dress parade, especially at posts with a regimental band in residence, sparked a small and fleeting flame of martial ardor. But mostly garrison life consisted of drill, guard duty, care and feeding of horses and mules, repair and maintenance of facilities (and often their actual construction), police of the post and other fatigue labor, target practice (when ammunition could be spared), such escort or scouting assignments as became necessary—and the constant quest for diversions to speed passage of the spare time so evident in Sergeant Bandel's typical daily program.

For the entire community reading was a pastime in which supply never caught up with demand. Everyone thirsted for news of the outside world, and newspapers and magazines, usually a month or more old, were passed from hand to hand until read to shreds. Some posts had a small library, paid for by the garrison, that stocked popular paperbound novels and a little heavier reading for the intellectually inclined. Sergeant Lowe recalled how his company commander organized a subscription campaign to establish a company library whose nucleus was a pair of bookcases and "Harper's Classical and Family Libraries."[97]

The community also staged frequent dances, or "hops," and dramatic productions. At Fort Leavenworth in 1852 the dragoon enlisted complement organized a "Thespian Society" whose performances returned enough profit to finance a hop that "was a great success from the soldier's standpoint."[98] Formal dinners, with fine silver, china, and linen assembled from several households and with champagne and tinned delicacies purchased at the sutler's store, were frequent occurrences, often preceding the dances that the officers' wives got up on any pretext. "The hops are more like a family reunion than a gathering of strangers," observed the wife of an officer of Mounted Rifles.[99]

Hunting and fishing afforded a diversion to which many were passionately addicted. Game animals and birds were to be found in the vicinity of most posts, and the rivers, lakes, and streams teemed with fish. Buffalo, deer, elk, antelope, and even bear; geese, wild turkeys, grouse, pheasants, or quail; bass, trout, catfish, or salmon not only provided engrossing sport but supple-

[97] Lowe, *Five Years a Dragoon*, pp. 124–25.
[98] *Ibid.*, p. 97.
[99] Lydia Spencer Lane, *I Married a Soldier, or Old Days in the Army*, p. 86.

mented the dreary fare little less common to the kitchens on officers row than to the barracks mess halls. Many officers kept hunting horses and dogs and elaborate hunting rifles and fishing tackle. Enlisted men, downing game with an army musket and snaring fish with an improvised hook on a piece of string, showed no less enthusiasm for the sport.

These amusements, together with such others as swimming, athletic competition, musical expression, and studying the natural and human phenomena of the West took second place to the commonest forms of diversion—drinking and gambling. Widespread and excessive indulgence in these two pastimes was more symptomatic of isolation and boredom than of the human composition of the frontier army.

The sutler's store stocked package wines and liquors and sold beer and ale by the glass, but for the enlisted men the really wild scenes were in the nearby settlements or, where none existed, the local "hog ranch." Every isolated post boasted its hog ranch —Loma Parda for Fort Union, Chihuahua for Fort Davis—dispensing vile liquor and even viler social diseases to troops who spent much of their pay and spare time there. "Every company," noted Drummer Meyers, "had some men who were slaves to the liquor habit." One in his company, whenever he observed an intoxicated man, would exclaim: "I wish I had half your sickness."[100] Officers were equally addicted but usually slightly more discreet, confining their indulgences to officers' quarters.

Gambling was closely associated with drinking. It centered on horse races, athletic competitions, poker, and even checkers. "Paymaster arrived yesterday," noted Private Bennett in his diary in March 1851. "Paid off the troops. Night came. The long rows of beds in our quarters were occupied. Benches were all full. All were interested in playing cards. Money exchanged hands as fast as possible. Up jumped one cursing himself, his parents, his God, his evil fortune. Another that fiendish smile exhibited because he had won his fellows' money. All much engaged. Morning found many still gambling. Lost their sleep and their money. This is a practice followed very much by soldiers."[101]

Several characteristic forms of diversion were combined in a memorable if not completely characteristic social event recalled

[100] Meyers, *Ten Years in the Ranks*, p. 129.
[101] Brooks and Reeve, *Forts and Forays*, pp. 22-23.

by Private Meyers, stationed with his company of the 2d Infantry at Fort Abercrombie, Dakota, in the winter of 1860–61:

There was a Scotchman in my company, whom we called Sandy, who was an excellent cook and a born caterer. During the winter he proposed to get up a dinner to be followed by dancing in the company's mess-room. Permission was obtained for "Sandy's ball," as we called it; most of the company subscribed, as well as some soldiers from the other companies. Sandy shrewdly collected the cash and gave no credit, then he sent to St. Paul for stone china dishes, for we had only tin cups and plates in our mess-room. He ordered hams, tongues, sardines, pickles, preserves, lemons, etc., not forgetting a few dozen bottles of American champagne, which had been carefully packed with sawdust into barrels both for safety and concealment. These goods arrived in due time and Sandy was a busy man, cooking hams and venison and baking pies and cakes. We helped him put up a few decorations and a lot of candles around the walls.

All was ready when the eventful evening arrived. The dinner was to be at eight o'clock, followed by dancing until midnight, with two fiddlers and a flute player to furnish the music. A half dozen soldiers' wives were the only ladies present; but we had as many more of the younger men dressed up in borrowed female clothes. The dinner was voted a great success and we lauded Sandy. We had bottled ale from the sutler's and topped off with whiskey punch, which continued to be served throughout the evening. Then the tables and benches were moved into a corner, the dishes piled on them, and the dancing commenced.

Everything went well for a while and we had lots of fun, until trouble started between the fiddlers. One of them, Mike Burns, had partaken too much punch and wanted to play an Irish jig, while his German partner held out for a waltz. This enraged Mike so that he exclaimed, "Oi despises no nation, but damn the Dutch!" and smashed his fiddle over his partner's head. The combatants were separated, Mike was put out, order restored and the dancing resumed. While the dance went on Sandy had been busy in the kitchen selling Ohio champagne to the soldiers at steep prices. This, together with liberal quantities of whiskey punch, began to show its effects and the fun became fast and furious, until near midnight a fight started in one end of the room and in a moment a dozen or more of the soldiers were in the midst of it. Bottles and dishes were thrown about the room; the women screamed and rushed for the door; Sandy was up on a table waving his arms and shouting, "Quit yer fetching! dinna be breaking me dishes, I'm a puir mon," when the table upset and he went down to the floor among his broken dishes. The officer of the day and a few files of the guard, together with the corporal, now made their appearance and quelled the disturbance. All those who showed marks of having been fighting or were drunk were marched off to the guardhouse and all others ordered to their quarters.[102]

Such was life, military and social, of the officers and soldiers at the frontier garrisons. Such, rather than stirring scenes of combat with hostile Indians, was what they remembered and put to paper for the benefit of future historians.

The frontier soldiers of the 1850s pursued their mission and met recurring crises largely with policies and courses of action improvised by immediate commanders on the scene. Now and then the Secretary of War, the general-in-chief, or even the President intervened directly to influence the outcome of an operation. More often, the Army's top command confined itself to ratifying the decisions of subordinates in the field and trying to get the available men and supplies to the points of greatest need. No framework of strategy and few policy guidelines emanated from the War Department or army headquarters to give direction and coherence to frontier defense measures. The failure sprang from remoteness, slowness of communication, lack of accurate information about local conditions, and the fact that military responsibilities partook less of warfare than of police operations against an enemy only occasionally identifiable as such. The confusion and uncertainty that characterized U.S. Indian policy, particularly the respective roles of civilian and military agencies, also inhibited leadership. And of large importance, too, command and staff suffered from an organization that blurred lines of authority and made firm central direction impossible.

Under the President as Commander-in-Chief, the civilian Secretary of War and the military general-in-chief, senior of the Army's generals, struggled for supremacy, with most of the advantages favoring the former. Theoretically, the Secretary of War controlled administration, the general-in-chief personnel. In practice the Secretary and the chiefs of the independent staff agencies of the War Department controlled nearly everything,

102 Meyers, *Ten Years in the Ranks*, pp. 167–69.

leaving the general-in-chief largely a figurehead. This situation prevailed mainly because the heads of the staff departments— adjutant general, quartermaster general, commissary general, inspector general, paymaster general, surgeon general, chief engineer, colonel of topographical engineers, and colonel of ord- nance—reported to the Secretary of War rather than the general- in-chief. With no authority over the staff, the general-in-chief could exert very little authority over the line. Staff officers, hold- ing staff commission for life, jealously guarding a deeply en- trenched bureaucracy, and thoroughly knowledgeable in the functions and procedures of their departments, were more often than not the true repositories of administrative power. Only the strongest and most independent Secretary mastered the sys- tem before giving way to another appointee. Most had no choice but to serve as instruments of the staff chiefs, particularly the adjutant general, keeper of records and dispenser of regulations and orders. He was the functionary through whom the Secretary spoke, but more significant he had become the functionary who spoke for the Secretary—to line as well as staff.[103]

Had the general-in-chief been content with no more than the trappings of high office, the Army would have rocked along in quiet inefficiency. Major General Winfield Scott gloried in the trappings—crowned in 1855 by a brevet of lieutenant general— but he also cherished a passionate conviction that the command- ing general ought truly to command. From his headquarters in New York, to which he repaired in 1849 when his arch-rival Zachary Taylor won the presidency, Scott noisily challenged the system and assailed its beneficiaries. The contention reached a peak during Jefferson Davis' administration of the department. For four years the ambiguities of military organization combined with a long-standing mutual antipathy to keep these two strong- willed, hot-tempered egotists locked in a publicly displayed quar- rel that for invective has rarely been equalled in the history of

[103] The problem is analyzed in Weigley, *Towards an American Army*, pp. 164–65; White, pp. 190–94; C. S. Bernardo and E. H. Bacon, *American Mili- tary Policy: Its Development since 1775* (Harrisburg, Pa., 1955), pp. 150–52; Upton, *Military Policy*, pp. 155–59 and passim. An excellent administrative study is A. Howard Meneely, *The War Department, 1861* (New York, 1928). Uncritical is L. D. Ingersoll, *A History of the War Department of the United States* (Washington, D.C., 1879). The fact that the War Department consisted of a group of departments is another evidence of loose administra- tive thinking. Although bureau would be a more precise nomenclature for the departmental subdivisions, the contemporary usage is adhered to in this volume.

U.S. government. On most issues Davis won, but his reputation suffered as much as Scott's, and the polemics further confused and aggravated the underlying problem.[104]

In default of meaningful central direction, commanders of geographical departments emerged as the principal molders of the Army's frontier defense system. From 1848 to 1853 these departments were numbered and brigaded under several division headquarters. Thereafter regionally descriptive designations replaced the numbers, and the divisional echelon was dropped.[105] The two full brigadier generals of the line (three after 1855) took over the most important departmental commands, leaving the rest to be filled with colonels assigned by brevet. The department commanders erected their defenses and employed their troops pretty much as they saw fit. Often, as a matter of form or to arm themselves against later criticism, they obtained higher authority for what they planned to do or had already done. That they applied at times to the Secretary of War (by way of the adjutant general), at other times to the general-in-chief (through his military secretary), illustrates the confusion created by the lack of definition in the relationships of military to civilian head of the Army. Although constantly faced with the dilemma of which source of authority to honor, the department commanders found themselves wielding more authority of their own than would have been likely had true unity of command prevailed at higher headquarters. The system proved reasonably workable when enemy activity did not play across departmental boundaries. Too often, however, the source of a threat to one department lay

---

[104] Scott's viewpoint is championed in Elliott, *Winfield Scott*, chap. 46; Davis' in Hudson Strode, *Jefferson Davis, American Patriot, 1808–1861* (New York, 1955), pp. 287–90. Some of the correspondence between the two is set forth in 254 pages of print in Senate Ex. Docs., 34th Cong., 3d sess., No. 34. Samples: Davis said Scott's fame "has been clouded by grovelling vices" and hoped young officers would imitate "some other model than one whose military career has been marked by querulousness, insubordination, greed of lucre, and want of truth" (Feb. 29, 1856, pp. 239–40). Scott replied that this letter was "a heavy folio . . . of new examples in chicanery and tergiversation; of prodigality in assertion, and utter penury in proofs and probabilities" (March 20, 1856, p. 246).

[105] In the 1850s the western commands were the Departments of Texas, New Mexico, the West, and the Pacific. In 1858 the Department of Utah was carved out of the Department of the West and the Departments of Oregon and California substituted for that of the Pacific. For details see Raphael P. Thian, comp., *Notes Illustrating the Military Geography of the United States* (Washington, D.C., 1881).

within another, and only rarely could the high command bring about the required coordination.

What the architects of army organization had been groping for, of course, was a means of giving effect to the cherished constitutional principle of civilian mastery of the military. Not for half a century would anyone come up with a system that reconciled this principle with the demands of unity of command. Not for half a century, either, would the staff system be overhauled. Increasingly divorced from the realities of line operations, inflexibly resistant to change, burdened with feeble old men, the staff departments could barely service the line in Indian operations.[106] But they represented a powerful vested interest that stood rocklike against all attempts at reform. Jefferson Davis, supported by President Pierce, proposed to dispense with permanent staff commissions and man the staff departments through rotation from the line, thus bringing staff and line into closer association and giving officers essential experience in both.[107] Secretary John B. Floyd championed the same measure, and legislation to accomplish it received favorable committee action in Congress.[108] Each time the staff chiefs headed off the threat. The Civil War was to force some long-overdue personnel changes, but not until after its Indian-fighting years did the Army get an efficient staff organization.

Washington offices of the staff departments consisted of only one or two officers and a few civilian clerks. Most of the personnel took station at the field installations, where their services could be directly rendered. Assistant adjutants general handled the paperwork for the department commanders. Quartermaster and commissary officers in department headquarters and the supply depots looked to supplies, rations, and transportation. Ordnance officers in charge of the arsenals issued new and serviced old arms. Paymasters made the rounds of the garrisons. An assistant surgeon or acting assistant surgeon (the latter a civilian under contract to the surgeon general) provided medical services at

[106] A good picture of staff conditions in this period is in Meneely.

[107] SW, *Annual Report* (1854), pp. 11–16; (1855), p. 6. Richardson, *Messages and Papers*, 5, 287–88, 339. Captain Henry W. Halleck, a leading theoretician, advocated much the same thing in his *Elements of Military Art and Science*. See Weigley, *Towards an American Army*, p. 62, for a discussion.

[108] SW, *Annual Report* (1859), pp. 4–5.

nearly every post. Engineer officers supervised the construction of forts and roads. Topographical engineers conducted explorations and prepared maps of vital importance to tactical commanders.

Of all the staff services, none more directly influenced the scope and success of line operations than those of the Quartermaster Department. Presided over by the able but aging Brigadier General Thomas S. Jesup, the department entered the 1850s with massive new frontier responsibilities. In 1845 it supplied less than a dozen posts along a compact frontier accessible by steamboat and drawing many provisions from fertile surroundings. In 1855 it supplied more than fifty posts scattered over two million square miles of territory almost wholly beyond the reach of navigable streams and dependent on the States for nearly all necessities. This abrupt change in the logistical requirements of the frontier army revolutionized quartermaster operations—at a monetary cost, as already shown, that scandalized Congress.

For the Departments of the Pacific and Texas, the Quartermaster Department could still rely principally on water-borne transportation. Troops and supplies destined for the West Coast went in vessels by way of Cape Horn or the Isthmus to San Francisco. At times the department chartered entire ships, at others contracted with sailing masters for specified services. Costs ran to about $150 per soldier, $225 per officer, and 60 to 90 cents per cubic foot for supplies. From San Francisco coastal steamers or river boats plying the Sacramento took over for such of the remaining distance as could be accomplished by water. Troops and supplies bound for Texas landed at Indianola and were forwarded by land either to the department depot at San Antonio or directly to their destination.

The vast wilderness between the Missouri River and the Pacific Slope raised larger and more costly obstacles. Everything had to be hauled from the principal depot at Fort Leavenworth, Kansas, by mule- or ox-drawn wagon. Logistical support of General Kearny in Santa Fe during the Mexican War had exposed the weaknesses in quartermaster operation of its own trains with hired civilian teamsters, and at the close of the war General Jesup turned in desperation to the contract system. It proved more efficient and economical, and thereafter, with occasional exceptions, he relied on freighting contractors to deliver supplies to the far-flung posts of the Great Plains, Texas, the

Southwest, and the Great Basin. By 1855 the firm that three years later took the name Russell, Majors, and Waddell had achieved a near monopoly of government freighting on the Santa Fe and Oregon Trails, and George T. Howard enjoyed similar supremacy in Texas.[109]

For plains freighting, experts debated the relative merits of mules and oxen—Alexander Majors favored oxen—but for desert transport Jefferson Davis caused the Quartermaster Department to sponsor a notable experiment with a third beast of burden. First as senator, later as War Secretary, Davis contended that camels, as creatures of the desert, would perform more efficiently and at less expense than either mules or oxen, particularly in the arid Southwest. At first treating the proposal lightly, Congress in 1855 sanctioned it, and by early the next year seventy-four of the strange animals had been imported from the Middle East. In extensive tests on the deserts of West Texas, the camels won high praise from their military masters and seemed to confirm the Secretary's faith. But the Civil War intervened, the herds were gradually dispersed, and the contentious army mule retained its customary supremacy in the affections of the U.S. Army.[110]

The enormous transportation bills that burst on Congress as the Army moved to the arid lands beyond the Missouri prompted a searching examination of the fixed-post defense system that had taken shape at the close of the Mexican War. The patchwork of rude villages misnamed "forts," constantly shifting in response to shifting threats, not only sent logistical costs skyrocketing but also gave little evidence of providing effective protection to settlements and travel routes. Hounded by a Congress crying for re-

[109] In addition to Jesup's annual reports in the reports of the Secretary of War, this section is based principally on Erna Risch, *Quartermaster Support of the Army: A History of the Corps, 1775–1939* (Washington, D.C., 1962), chap. 8. Pertinent also are Raymond W. and Mary Lund Settle, *Empire on Wheels* (Stanford, Calif., 1940)—a history of Russell, Majors, and Waddell; Alexander Majors, *Seventy Years on the Old Frontier* (Denver, Colo., 1893); Walker D. Wyman, "The Military Phase of Santa Fe Freighting, 1846–1865," *Kansas Historical Quarterly, I* (1932), 415–28; and Lenora Barrett, "Transportation, Supplies, and Quarters for the West Texas Frontier under the Federal Military System, 1848–1861," *West Texas Historical Association Year Book, 5* (1929), 87–99.

[110] Senate Ex. Docs., 34th Cong., 3d sess., No. 62. Lewis B. Lesley, ed., *Uncle Sam's Camels* (Cambridge, Mass., 1929). Frank B. Lammons, "Operation Camel: An Experiment in Animal Transportation in Texas, 1857–1860," *Southwestern Historical Quarterly, 61* (1957), 40–48.

duced expenditures, military leaders desperately sought some hopeful alternative.

Jefferson Davis, Generals Scott and Jesup, and a host of lesser officers advocated such an alternative, one drawn from recommendations made by Colonel Stephen Watts Kearny after leading a dragoon column up the Platte River to South Pass in the summer of 1845.[111] The proliferation of small posts should be broken up, the argument ran; they were expensive to maintain, they sowed contempt for U.S. authority in the Indian mind, and they protected little beyond their own parade ground. Instead, the troops should be concentrated at a few commodious permanent stations accessible by railway or navigable stream and "within the fertile region." Each spring, when the grass turned green, strong mounted columns would set forth from these posts to patrol the travel routes, show the flag, and hunt up and punish any recalcitrant bands that had given trouble since the last visit. The permanent posts could be cheaply supplied by steamboat or railway, and they would draw provisions for men and animals from surrounding agricultural settlements. The troops would be assembled in tactical units large enough for instruction and discipline rather than scattered in tiny detachments employed mainly in building and maintaining small posts. And the Indians would be more effectively controlled.[112]

The roving patrol concept contained certain flaws. For one, it assumed that settlers would never overspread the arid lands—an assumption already in the 1850s proving false. For another, it ignored the utility of fixed posts as way stations on the travel routes and the consequent political unpopularity of attempts to abandon them. And finally, it could not be put into effect without an army increase of a magnitude unacceptable to Congress, for too much of the existing force was tied to the settlements. Secretary Davis tried to set in motion a concentration in 1854, but he dis-

---

[111] Senate Ex. Docs., 29th Cong., 1st sess., No. 1, p. 212.

[112] The concept is best elaborated by Jefferson Davis in SW, *Annual Report* (1856), pp. 5–8, but see also *ibid.* (1853), p. 6. For Scott, see *ibid.* (1851), p. 161; (1854), p. 51. For Jesup, see *ibid.* (1852), p. 70. Good expositions of the point of view by junior officers are by Captain Rufus Ingalls in *ibid.* (1855), pp. 162–63; by Colonel T. T. Fauntleroy in *ibid.* (1852), p. 127; and by Captain John Pope in a 59-page "Military Memoir" presented to Secretary of War Floyd, for which see A. B. Bender, *The March of Empire: Frontier Defense in the Southwest, 1848–1860* (Lawrence, Kans., 1952), pp. 47–49. Another Pope essay is Robert M. Utley, ed., "Captain John Pope's Plan of 1853 for the Frontier Defense of New Mexico," *Arizona and the West*, 5 (1963), 149–63.

covered "the want of troops in all sections of the country so great, that the concentration would have exposed portions of the frontier to Indian hostilities without any protection whatever."[113]

There were those in the Army, too, who questioned other basic assumptions of the concept. Indians were fully aware of U.S. strength, argued Captain William Hoffman, "and care little about it so long as it is not present." A regiment of dragoons crossing their range in June would not stop them from committing depredations in November. If raiders wished to attack a wagon train, they would simply wait until the roving column had ridden elsewhere, then strike and be gone before help could be summoned.[114] On the other hand, contended Inspector General Mansfield, the Indians respected the soldiers no matter how few in number, "for they seem to understand that there is a power behind, more than sufficient to make up for any present weakness, in case they commit depredations."[115] Scatter the little posts across the Indian homeland, predicted Colonel Edwin V. Sumner, and the warriors would never venture on distant raids because their families and possessions would lie within striking distance of vigilant garrisons.[116]

What Sumner, Mansfield, and Hoffman were groping for, the old mountain man Tom Fitzpatrick, now an Indian agent, expressed with precision. Neither the fixed-post system as it had developed nor the roving patrol concept was the answer. "It must be apparent that a skeleton company of infantry or dragoons can add but little to the security of five hundred miles square of territory; nor can the great highways to Utah and New Mexico be properly protected by a wandering squadron that parades them once a year." These indeed were not even the true alternatives. Instead: "The policy must be either an army or an annuity. Either an inducement must be offered to them greater than the gains of plunder, or a force must be at hand able to restrain and check their depredations. Any compromise between the two systems will only be productive of mischief. . . . It will beget confidence, without providing safety; it will neither create fear, nor satisfy avarice; and, adding nothing to the protection of trade and emigration, will add everything to the responsibilities

113 SW, *Annual Report* (1854), p. 5.
114 Hoffman to McDowell, Dec. 10, 1850, H482/1850, RG 94, NARS.
115 Frazer, *Mansfield on Western Forts*, p. 122.
116 Sumner to Jones, Jan. 27, 1852, Dept. NM LS, vol. 8, pp. 123–24, RG 98, NARS.

of government."[117] If the choice fell to the purely military solution, he made clear, then a system of fixed posts manned by
powerful garrisons had to be established.[118]

Lieutenant Gouverneur K. Warren supported the Fitzpatrick
thesis in an analysis incorporated in his report of explorations in Dakota in 1855. Strong military posts, he said, should be
placed not only near the settlements and along the lines of
travel, but also "well in the country whence the marauders
come" and located so "as effectually to overawe the ambitious
and turbulent, and sustain the counsel of the old and prudent."
The latter posts, designed to restrain through mere presence,
could be manned with infantry. Those near the settlements
should have cavalry, both for rapid pursuit and for economy in
sustaining the horses.[119]

Many military authorities joined with civil officials in sub-
scribing to Fitzpatrick's second alternative, which Secretary of
War Conrad defined succinctly in 1851: "It would be far less
expensive to feed than to fight them."[120] This thought in fact
formed part of the policy that began to emerge in the 1850s
from the wreckage of the Permanent Indian Frontier. The aim
was to shoulder the Indians away from the emigrant roads and
extinguish their title to lands coveted or already preempted by
white settlers. Special commissions and agents of the Indian
Bureau spread over the West to negotiate treaties of peace and
cession with the tribes that held such lands. The treaties promised payment for the cessions and rations and annuities to ease
the transition from the rapidly crumbling nomadic life to the
agricultural life that would have to replace it.[121] But here again,
as Fitzpatrick foresaw, half-measures were worse than none. If
the Army could not win sufficient resources for a military solution, neither could the Indian Bureau win sufficient for a peaceful solution; Congress refused to pay more than a token price
for the land or to sanction more than token issues of food to a
people reluctant to learn new ways of supporting themselves.

The strategy of the Indian wars thus turned out to be the

[117] SI, *Annual Report* (1853), p. 362.
[118] See below, p. 57.
[119] Quoted in Lloyd McFarling, ed., *Exploring the Northern Plains, 1804–
1867* (Caldwell, Ida., 1955), pp. 235–36.
[120] SW, *Annual Report* (1851), p. 113.
[121] For the policy that took shape after collapse of the Permanent Indian
Frontier, see James C. Malin, *Indian Policy and Westward Expansion*, Bulletin of the University of Kansas, vol. 22, no. 17 (Nov. 1, 1921), Pts. 2 and 3.

compromise of military and civil half-measures that Fitzpatrick had warned against. The Indian Bureau took the tribal ranges for a pittance, thus undermining the traditional forms of obtaining a livelihood, then could not offer the inducement that would exceed the prospective gains of plunder. The Army fragmented in an expanding network of little forts whose feeble garrisons intimidated few Indians and protected few whites. Yet every treaty and every agency opened new cracks in tribal unity, diluted old values and customs, and bound the Indian to his overseer with new strands of dependence. And every new army post, weak and ineffectual though it might be individually, formed one more link in a chain that ultimately circled the Indian and helped to strangle him.

While the military strategy of grappling with the Indian received a thorough if often uninformed ventilation in government circles, the tactics by which it might be carried out never found expression in military manuals or other professional publications of the Army. Neither Captain William J. Hardee's *Infantry Tactics*, which appeared in 1855, nor Colonel Philip St. George Cooke's *Cavalry Tactics*, which replaced an obsolete French system in 1861, contained any hint of how to employ troops against Indians.[122] West Point offered no guidance either. True, Cooke and such other frontier veterans as Randolph Marcy dwelt in print on how to operate in the western environment. And Captain George B. McClellan came close to the mark when he advised the development of light cavalry capable of matching Indian mobility and forcing the enemy into combats in which the Army's superior discipline and firepower could be brought to bear.[123] But the tactics manuals and textbooks concerned themselves exclusively with conventional warfare against a civilized foe. Officers and men were left to learn for themselves how to conduct operations against their primitive foe.

Without formal doctrine either strategic or tactical, without firm and purposeful leadership from the high command, with human resources deficient in quantity and quality, and with material resources forever inadequate to the need, the bluecoats of the frontier constabulary set forth to police the Indians of

---

[122] A discussion of this point is in Otis E. Young, *The West of Philip St. George Cooke, 1809–1895* (Glendale, Calif., 1955), pp. 314–19.

[123] McClellan's report of his Crimean tour, Dec. 19, 1856, in Senate Ex. Docs., 35th Cong., sp. sess., No. 1, p. 277.

the newly acquired West. The wonder is not that they so often failed to meet the test but rather, considering what they were and what they had to work with, that they scored as many successes as they did. If they took nearly half a century to do the job, and then had to share the credit with other and more determining historical forces, they still could lay claim to a role of considerable significance in the opening of the West.

FOUR

Garrisoning the Great Plains

THOMAS JEFFERSON bought the Great Plains for the United States in 1803, but for several decades they remained in almost undisturbed possession of the Indian occupants. A handful of trappers, Indian traders, and Missouri entrepreneurs engaging in overland commerce with Mexican Santa Fe came to know the vast emptiness of the Plains, and through them the Indian residents learned something of the white man's curious and sometimes reprehensible behavior. Neither race posed much of a threat to the other, and on the whole they got along fairly well. The Mexican War, adding extensive new territories to the United States beyond the Plains, ended this happy state of affairs.

Bound for Oregon or California, emigrants by the thousands cascaded up the valleys of the Platte and the Sweetwater. Others, seeking more southerly routes to the beckoning goldfields, pushed west on the Santa Fe Trail or struck out on the newly opened routes across Texas. The annual trade caravans that marked out the road to Santa Fe in the two decades before the Mexican War gave way after the war to a nearly continuous stream of freight wagons laden with merchandise for New Mexicans and supplies for the army on the Rio Grande. Later, with the onset of the Pike's Peak gold rush in 1858, still another overland route, the Smoky Hill Trail, took its place with the rest. And finally, the frontier of settlement in Texas spread swiftly up the valleys of the Trinity, the Brazos, and the Colorado toward the Staked Plains escarpment.

All this activity had its effect on the Indians who roamed the Plains. In Texas it actually dispossessed some of them. Elsewhere it merely cut pathways across their domain. For the time being at least, the tribes faced no very serious danger of being deprived of living space. For several centuries the homeland of each had shifted constantly in response to pressures from other tribes and, usually indirectly, from the white man. The Plains still offered a great deal of acreage in which this process might continue. The immediate threat to the Indian lay not in shrinkage of territory available for his use, but rather in the impact of the white invasion on the resources that supported and shaped his way of life—timber, grass, and above all buffalo and other game. These simply did not exist in such abundance as to provide for whites and Indians alike.

Throughout the decade of the 1850s civil agents and military officers repeatedly stressed that, for the Indian, it had become a matter of steal or starve. Stealing was an old and honored pastime, and not unnaturally he turned more often to this alternative than to the other. He was, besides, born and bred a warlike person, and the parade of alien people offered an opportunity that even with a full stomach he saw no reason to ignore. Finally, both races contained their full share of ignorant, inept, perfidious, or belligerent individuals whose actions could be counted on to spark trouble.

To protect their countrymen from the Indian, and sometimes even to protect the Indian from their countrymen, the soldiers of the Regular Army took station on the Great Plains at the close of the Mexican War.

Extending from the Canadian border on the north to the Rio Grande on the south, about a dozen major tribes and a score or more minor ones ranged the Plains country crossed by the overland trails. Along the Missouri River frontier and the western borders of Arkansas—the old "Indian Country" of Monroe and Jackson—and extending southwest into Texas lived a proliferation of weak or docile tribes from which little danger was to be apprehended—Gros Ventre, Mandan, Arikara, Omaha, Ponca, Sac and Fox, Delaware, Waco, Caddo, Tonkawa, Anadarko, Keechi, Tawakoni, Ioni, the "Five Civilized Tribes" earlier moved from their eastern homes (Creek, Choctaw, Cherokee, Chickasaw, and Seminole), and others. Scattered among these or slightly to the west were other groups—Pawnee, Wichita, Kickapoo, Osage, Lipan—that occasionally caused more or less trouble

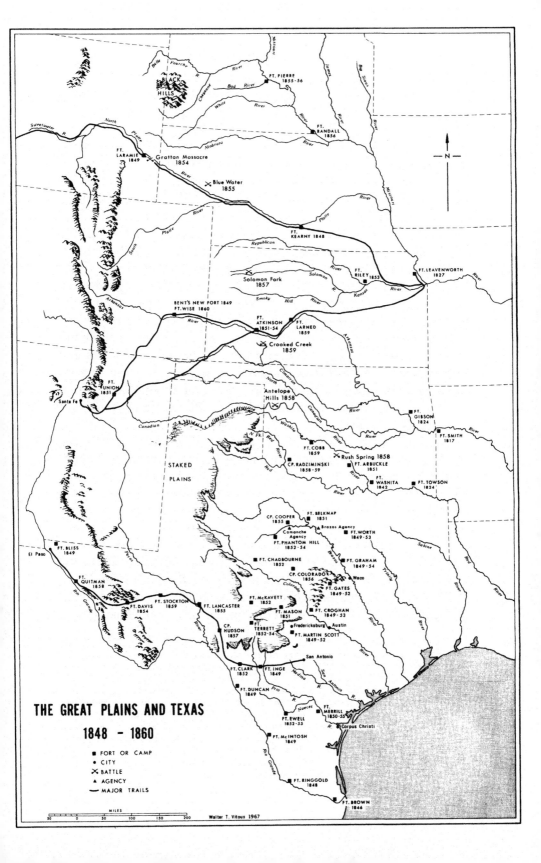

THE GREAT PLAINS AND TEXAS

1848 – 1860

■ FORT OR CAMP
● CITY
✕ BATTLE
▲ AGENCY
— MAJOR TRAILS

MILES
50 0 50 100 150 200

Walter T. Vitous 1967

but that posed no real problem in a military sense. Then, still farther west, were the nomads of the High Plains—notably Blackfoot, Crow, Shoshoni, Sioux, Cheyenne, Arapaho, Comanche, Kiowa, and Kiowa-Apache. In the last six of these, the tribes most directly affected by the overland trails, resided the gravest potential threat to westering Americans of the 1850s.

The Sioux or Dakota blanketed the northern Plains from the sources of the Mississippi to the Powder, Yellowstone, and upper Missouri. Although the Minnesota groups, pressured by Chippewas and white settlers, would react violently later, it was their kinsmen to the west who first collided with the whites. These were the Teton Sioux, a confederation of seven tribes (Oglala, Brule, Hunkpapa, Miniconjou, Sans Arc, Two Kettle, and Blackfoot) that occupied territory bounded roughly by the Missouri, Yellowstone, Powder, and North Platte Rivers. By the 1850s large numbers, chiefly of the Oglala, Brule, and Miniconjou divisions, had descended to the Platte, where traders and government agents at Fort Laramie offered for trade or as gifts manufactured goods that made life easier. Of about 18,000 Teton Sioux, perhaps 7,000 hovered about the Platte Valley emigrant road in this decade.[1]

The Cheyennes and Arapahoes, close friends and allies, claimed as hunting grounds the High Plains between the Platte and the Arkansas. In 1854 the former numbered nearly 4,000, the latter about 2,400. Some 800 Cheyennes preferred more northerly ranges and, with a scattering of Arapahoes, were usually found among the Sioux on the North Platte—the genesis of a tribal division into distinct northern and southern groups. As the Sioux in the prewar years had formed attachments to the whites at the fur post of Fort Laramie, on the North Platte, so their southern neighbors had grown increasingly dependent on the goods to be had at Bent's Fort, on the Arkansas. The Oregon

---

[1] The population figures are 1850 estimates. Evidence bearing on Teton population at various years in the nineteenth century is synthesized in John C. Ewers, *Teton Dakota History and Ethnology* (National Park Service, 1938), pp. 7-8. Able histories of the Sioux are Doane Robinson, *A History of the Dakota or Sioux Indians* (2d ed.; Minneapolis, Minn., 1956); George E. Hyde, *Red Cloud's Folk: A History of the Oglala Sioux Indians* (2d ed.; Norman, Okla., 1957); Hyde, *Spotted Tail's Folk: A History of the Brule Sioux* (Norman, Okla., 1961); and Stanley Vestal, *Sitting Bull, Champion of the Sioux* (2d ed.; Norman, Okla., 1957). Organization, population, and location of the Sioux and all other tribes dealt with in this chapter are set forth in John R. Swanton, *The Indian Tribes of North America*, Bureau of American Ethnology, Bulletin 145 (Washington, D.C., 1952).

and Santa Fe Trails brushed the fringes of the Cheyenne and Arapaho domain, and in 1858 the Smoky Hill Trail pierced the heart of it.[2]

The homeland of the Comanches and their allies the Kiowas and confederated Kiowa-Apaches lay between the Arkansas and Red Rivers and included the Staked Plains of the Texas Panhandle. A number of powerful bands, notably the Yamparika, Kotsoteka, Nakoni, and Kwahadi, composed the Northern Comanches, while the Penateka, residing in Texas on the headwaters of the Brazos and Colorado Rivers, came to be known as the Southern Comanches. The population of the northern bands numbered perhaps as high as 15,000, of the southern little more than 1,000. The Kiowas and Kiowa-Apaches probably totaled less than 2,000 people. The Kiowa-Comanche ranges lay adjacent to the Santa Fe Trail on the north and were penetrated by the little-used emigrant road from Fort Smith to Santa Fe along the Canadian. The advancing settlements of Texas cut into the preserve of the Southern Comanches and gradually pushed them northward.[3]

More than any other tribes, the Kiowas and Comanches ranged far from their homeland. They could sometimes be found north of the Arkansas as far as the Platte, but it was to the south that their great interest lay. For more than a century these tribes had made a custom of regularly raiding the frontier settlements of Texas and Mexico. In Texas, Tamaulipas, Nuevo Leon, Coahuila, Chihuahua, and even remote Durango, they amassed enormous herds of horses and mules, strengthened their numbers through the integration of Mexican captives into the tribe, and accumulated cattle and other plunder to barter for whisky, arms, and ammunition with *Comanchero* traders from New Mexico and

[2] The population figure is from Donald J. Berthrong, *The Southern Cheyennes* (Norman, Okla., 1963), p. 132. This is the most recent and scholarly history of the Cheyennes but should be read in conjunction with George B. Grinnell, *The Fighting Cheyennes* (2d ed.; Norman, Okla., 1956); and Grinnell, *The Cheyenne Indians* (2 vols.; New Haven, Conn., 1923).

[3] Kiowa population figures are discussed in James Mooney, *Calendar History of the Kiowa Indians*, 17th Annual Report of the Bureau of American Ethnology (Washington, D.C., 1898), p. 235. This is the standard source for this tribe, but see also Mildred P. Mayhall, *The Kiowas* (Norman, Okla., 1962). Comanche figures are from Rupert N. Richardson, *The Comanche Barrier to South Plains Settlement* (Glendale, Calif., 1933), p. 216; and Ernest Wallace and E. Adamson Hoebel, *The Comanches, Lords of the South Plains* (Norman, Okla, 1952), pp. 31–32. Agent J. H. Leavenworth in 1865 estimated all the Comanches at eighteen to twenty thousand, in "Condition of the Indian Tribes," Senate Reps., 39th Cong., 2d sess., No. 156, p. 37.

Kickapoo and other Indian traders from the frontiers of Arkansas and Missouri. Of large social and economic significance, the Texan and Mexican raids had become a deeply entrenched feature of Kiowa and Comanche culture and were not to be surrendered lightly.[4]

Like the other Plains tribes, the Kiowas and Comanches had by the end of the Mexican War come to know a little about the white man. They had warred, traded, and negotiated with him in Texas during the period of the Republic, 1836–45; they had traded now and then with William Bent's agents in their own camps or, less frequently, at Bent's Fort itself; and they had occasionally attacked, bullied, or begged from the merchants whose caravans plied the Santa Fe Trail. These experiences had led them to classify white men in two distinct categories—Americans and Texans. That they could never bring themselves to view the two as one people complicated relations with them for a quarter of a century.

In dealing with the Plains tribes after the Mexican War, the federal government faced two distinct problems. On the central Plains the task was to persuade or compel the Sioux, Cheyennes, Arapahoes, Kiowas, and Comanches not to molest travelers on the transcontinental roads up the Platte and the Arkansas. On the southern Plains it was to make the Kiowas and Comanches stop raiding the Texan and Mexican frontier settlements and, in accordance with the Treaty of Guadalupe Hidalgo, to secure the return of Mexican captives from these tribes. In the one area it was to prevent the outbreak of hostilities, in the other to end hostilities that had been going on for more than a century; in the one merely to see people safely through a potential danger zone, in the other to safeguard the lives and property of people who had actually made their homes in the danger zone.

Measures for guarding the overland trails began to take shape before the Mexican War. Although isolated clashes occasionally disturbed the Santa Fe and Oregon Trails, the Plains tribes had not seriously endangered either. That the possibility

[4] Of particular pertinence are C. C. Rister, *Border Captives: The Traffic in Prisoners by Southern Plains Indians, 1835–1875* (Norman, Okla., 1940); Richardson, pp. 193–211; Ralph A. Smith, "The Comanche Bridge between Oklahoma and Mexico, 1843–1844," *Chronicles of Oklahoma*, 39 (1961), 54–69; Smith, "The Comanche Invasion of Mexico in the Fall of 1845," *Southwestern Historical Quarterly*, 38 (1934–35), 157–76.

always existed worried people, however, and it led to demands for military protection. The line of western forts in the two prewar decades crept to the edge of the Plains and faced the fictitious Permanent Indian Frontier. But from the key bastions holding the middle of the line, Forts Gibson and Leavenworth, the soldiers probed beyond. Dragoon expeditions went to the Plains in 1834 and 1835 and to the Rockies in 1845. Sword-and-olive-branch operations, they proved of dubious effect in either frightening or conciliating the Indians. Lieutenant John C. Frémont's three topographical expeditions of 1842–45 stemmed largely from official desire to support the Oregon emigration. And twice, in 1829 and again in 1843, years of apprehended Indian danger, escorts piloted freight caravans on the Santa Fe Trail as far as the Mexican boundary. But the traders, making the journey regularly, soon became experienced plainsmen who protected themselves and their cargoes by observing certain elementary rules of the trail. The Oregon emigrants, on the other hand, knew little about the Plains, and the sentiment for military action focused principally on the road up the Platte Valley.

Both Congress and the Executive expressed this sentiment repeatedly in the first half of the 1840s, and when the Polk administration in the spring of 1846 finally broke the deadlock with Great Britain in the Oregon dispute Congress moved swiftly. An act of May 19, 1846, authorized the addition of the Regiment of Mounted Riflemen to the Regular Army specifically for Oregon Trail duty and appropriated funds for the erection of such forts along the route as the President deemed necessary.[5] The new regiment found itself at once shipped to Mexico rather than to the Plains, but with the close of the war it made ready to perform the mission assigned it by Congress. A year's delay intervened because Congress permitted the discharge of all the unit's veteran personnel who wanted out, and it had to be recruited again. In the spring of 1849, however, Lieutenant Colonel William W. Loring led the regiment out of Fort Leavenworth on the Oregon Trail.

Loring found the first of the new forts already a going concern. It lay on the south bank of the Platte where the trail first struck the river. Missouri Volunteers had been here in 1846–48,

5 9 Stat. 13-14 (May 19, 1846). See J. T. Dorris, "Federal Aid to the Oregon Trail before 1850," *Oregon Historical Quarterly*, *30* (1929), 305-25, for a summary of prewar efforts to protect the migration.

and the previous autumn two companies of the Rifle Regiment under Captain Charles F. Ruff had gone up to relieve them. The new post had been named Fort Kearny in honor of the recently deceased General Stephen Watts Kearny, who, ironically had opposed the fixed-post concept of Plains defense. On up the Platte Loring and his men marched, sharing the trail with waves of California-bound argonauts. On the North Platte, Loring dropped off two more companies, under Major Winslow F. Sanderson. Engineer officers paid the American Fur Company $4,000 for the old trading post of Fort Laramie, and it became the second of the trail stations. Beyond the Plains Loring left another two companies near the former fur post of Fort Hall, on the Snake River, then took position in Oregon at the Hudson's Bay Company post of Fort Vancouver with the rest of the regiment.[6]

The drive for military protection of the Santa Fe Trail, dormant since 1843, revived with the onset of the Mexican War. In the summer of 1846 General Kearny's Army of the West marched over the trail and conquered New Mexico without bloodshed. The occupation force depended on the slender lifeline to the States, and immense supply caravans rolled over the road from Fort Leavenworth to Santa Fe. The new freighters were not the experienced plainsmen of earlier years, and their careless habits invited the Plains warriors to take what they could of the unprecedentedly rich cargoes stowed in the canvas-topped wagons. From the Pawnees on the east to the Kiowas and Comanches on the west, the tribesmen obliged.

In 1847 Missouri Volunteers patrolling the Santa Fe Trail threw up a rude stockade, Fort Mann, below the Cimarron Crossing of the Arkansas, where the shorter "dry route" diverged from the Mountain Branch. The next year Lieutenant Colonel William Gilpin proposed a string of forts on the Arkansas. William Bent offered to sell Bent's Fort, but negotiations collapsed in a dispute over fair price. Disillusioned over the changes wrought on the Plains by the white invasion, Bent in

[6] Documents and journals of the march are in Raymond W. Settle, ed., *The March of the Mounted Riflemen from Fort Leavenworth to Fort Vancouver, May to October 1849* (Glendale, Calif., 1940). For Fort Kearny see Lyle Mantor, "Fort Kearny and the Westward Movement," *Nebraska History Magazine*, 29 (1948), 175–207; and Albert Watkins, "History of Fort Kearny," *Collections of the Nebraska State Historical Society*, 16 (1911), 227–67. For Fort Laramie see LeRoy R. Hafen and Francis M. Young, *Fort Laramie and the Pageant of the West* (Glendale, Calif., 1938), pp. 137–56.

1849 burned the historic old trading station and moved 38 miles down the river to establish a new one at Big Timbers.[7]

Affording plenty of wood, water, and grass, Big Timbers seemed a likely spot for a military station too. But the War Department finally assigned the responsibility for choosing a location to Lieutenant Colonel Edwin V. Sumner. Conceding that Big Timbers had all the practical advantages, Sumner fixed instead on the site of old Fort Mann as the place offering the strategic advantages. Nearly all the overland traffic now followed the cutoff across the Cimarron Desert, and there seemed little purpose in building a fort on the lightly traveled Mountain Route. Although the officer charged with the task dissented, the War Department bowed to Sumner's judgment, and in 1850 Captain William Hoffman replaced the rotting Fort Mann with a shabby sod post named Fort Atkinson.[8] In the end Hoffman's views won out. The absence of building materials and other disadvantages led to the temporary abandonment of Fort Atkinson in 1853 and to its permanent abandonment in 1854. In 1859 Fort Larned was built on Pawnee Fork, Hoffman's choice of location.

At the western junction of the two trail branches a more lasting post rose a year later. Again Sumner was the founder. Sent to assume command of the 9th Military Department in 1851, he founded Fort Union near the Mora River on the eastern edge of New Mexican settlement. Although it had major responsibilities to the west, Sumner also made it a guardian of the Santa Fe Trail on the east. Until 1845 the garrisons of Forts Union and Atkinson cooperated in furnishing patrols and escorts to the intervening segments of the trail, and after 1854 Fort Union continued to look to this duty.[9]

A final link in the defenses of the Oregon and Santa Fe Trails emerged from the thinking of Colonel Thomas T. Fauntleroy, 1st Dragoons, who saw in the confluence of the Kansas and Republican Rivers, 150 miles west of Leavenworth, an ideal

[7] David Lavender, *Bent's Fort* (New York, 1954), chap. 17. Lewis H. Garrard, *Wah-To-Yah and the Taos Trail* (2d ed.; Glendale, Calif., 1938), chaps. 22–25, gives a good firsthand view of Fort Mann in its heyday.

[8] Jones to Scott, June 13, 1850, AGO LB No. 27. Freeman to Clarke, June 19, 1850, S287/1850. Clarke to Freeman (telegram), July 5, 1850; Freeman to Clarke (telegram), July 6, 1850, C360/1850. Sumner to Buell, Sept. 10, 1850, S562/1850. Hoffman to McDowell, Dec. 10, 1850, H482/1850. All in RG 94, NARS.

[9] Robert M. Utley, "Fort Union and the Santa Fe Trail," *New Mexico Historical Review*, 36 (1961), 36–48. A book-length history is Emmett, *Fort Union and the Winning of the Southwest*.

setting for one of the large posts that proponents of roving summer columns hoped to erect. Here every necessity for an economical installation existed—wood, water, grass, and cultivable land upon which farmers, assured a military market, would soon settle. The new station would draw together in a single trace the eastern segments of the two roads. Forts Leavenworth, Scott, Atkinson, Kearny, and Laramie could be abandoned, their garrisons concentrated, and their purpose met by strong mounted columns patrolling the two trails each travel season. Quartermaster General Jesup was delighted, and so was Congress. Fauntleroy's post, Fort Riley, was begun in 1853 and finished in 1855.[10] But none of the other posts was abandoned. Leavenworth continued as the principal base for military activities on the Plains and also as the eastern terminus of the overland trails. In truth the forts had other than military value. They performed vital services as way stations for travelers, and abandonment was not politically expedient.[11]

Military responsibility for the central Plains fell to Brevet Brigadier General Newman S. Clarke, who commanded the 6th Department from Jefferson Barracks, St. Louis, from 1849 to 1856. The 7th Department, Brevet Brigadier General Matthew Arbuckle commanding, lay to the south of the 6th and, headquartered at Fort Smith, Arkansas, embraced Forts Gibson, Towson, and Washita—posts that had been established primarily to guard the interests of the immigrant tribes from the east. The reorganization of 1853 merged the 6th and 7th departments into the Department of the West under General Clarke. His command now extended from the Mississippi to the crest of the Rockies and from Canada to northern Texas. To police this vast domain, Clarke in 1854 had 112 officers and 1,587 enlisted men, for the most part infantry, in twelve posts strung from Fort Ripley, Minnesota, to Fort Washita, on Red River in the Choctaw and Chickasaw country.[12]

---

[10] SW, *Annual Report* (1852), pp. 127–28; (1853), p. 131. W. F. Pride, *The History of Fort Riley* (Fort Riley, Kans. 1926), pp. 60 ff. The post was named for Brevet Major General Bennet Riley, who died on June 9, 1853.

[11] Cf. *Cong. Globe*, 31st Cong., 1st sess., p. 1967 (Sept. 25, 1850); and letter of J. Dougherty to his congressman from Liberty County, Mo., Jan. 29, 1852, quoted in Hafen and Young, *Fort Laramie and the Pageant of the West*, pp. 174–75.

[12] SW, *Annual Report* (1854), pp. 56–57. Clarke's tenure was interrupted at brief but frequent intervals by Colonel Thomas T. Fauntleroy and Brevet Major General David E. Twiggs. Brevet Major General Persifor F. Smith took over from Clarke on July 1, 1856. The sequence is in Thian, *Notes Illustrating the Military Geography of the United States*, p. 105.

The effort to keep the Plains Indians peaceable was expressed through diplomatic as well as military measures. In 1850 Congress authorized the Indian Bureau to bring these aboriginal "nations" into formal relations with the United States. This was accomplished by a treaty concluded with the northern Plains tribes at Fort Laramie in September 1851 and another negotiated with the southern Plains tribes at Fort Atkinson in July 1853. Both treaties aimed at winning security for the overland travel routes by binding the Indians to refrain from warring with one another and with the Americans, to permit the United States to build roads and military posts in their country, and to make restitution for damages inflicted on white travelers.[13] It is doubtful that many of the chiefs fully understood or seriously intended to adhere to these pledges. If so, they failed to see that good intentions could not at once overcome customs solidified by generations of practice. In these treaties, as in practically all others concluded over the next three decades, a powerful force operated to stimulate cooperation. Nearby loomed a pile of presents to be distributed as soon as the chiefs fixed their marks to the paper, and in the paper were words that promised an equally tempting array of presents each year for a certain time in the future. The chiefs signed, and the government officials thought they had bought security for the roads.[14]

For a time it seemed so. The Kiowas occasionally marauded on the Cimarron cutoff of the Santa Fe Trail, but on other segments of the Arkansas route, and along the Oregon Trail, the early 1850s passed in comparative harmony. Each summer the tribes came happily to Fort Laramie and Bent's Fort or an-

[13] The treaties are printed in Charles J. Kappler, comp., *Indian Affairs: Laws and Treaties* (2 vols.; Washington, D.C., 1904), 2, 594–96, 600–602. The Fort Laramie Treaty was negotiated by Agent Thomas Fitzpatrick and Superintendent of Indian Affairs David D. Mitchell with the Teton Sioux, Cheyennes, Arapahoes, Crows, Assiniboins, Mandans, Gros Ventres, and Arikaras. The Fort Atkinson Treaty was negotiated by Fitzpatrick with the Kiowas, Comanches, and Kiowa-Apaches. In addition, the Fort Laramie Treaty specified boundaries for each tribe and committed each to acknowledge a head chief who could speak as the single authority of his people in dealings with the government. The Fort Atkinson Treaty did not contain these stipulations but, in furtherance of the peace treaty with Mexico, bound the signatory tribes to refrain from raiding in Mexico. An excellent discussion of the treaty ramifications is Harry H. Anderson, "The Controversial Sioux Amendment to the Fort Laramie Treaty of 1851," *Nebraska History*, 37 (1956), 201–20.

[14] The influence of presents is evident in nearly all sensitive studies of the various tribes but emerges with special clarity from the Indian viewpoint in Wilbur S. Nye, *Bad Medicine and Good: Tales of the Kiowas* (Norman, Okla., 1962).

other designated spot on the Arkansas to receive their treaty presents and stare in wonder at the procession of white travelers. The treaties thus acted to attract the Indians to the roads, there to be antagonized by the travelers and impressed by the handful of bluecoats with the impotence of the Great Father. Sooner or later a collision was bound to occur.

Entering the American Union in 1845, Texas handed the federal government an Indian situation with several unusual complications. For one, protecting an advancing line of settlement was a more difficult undertaking than protecting passing travelers. For another, the established federal Indian system could not be wholly applied to Texas. Upon joining the Union, the State had retained its vacant lands, which meant that the Indian Intercourse laws could not be extended to Texas and that parcels of land could not be set aside for exclusive Indian occupancy. As the frontier of settlement moved into the Indian country, surveyors laid off the land in sections and counties were created. The process had no place in it for the Indians.[15] Nor did the prevailing sentiment of the settlers, whose views were fixed by two decades of bloody hostility with the warlike tribes of the north. As a distinguished historian has written: "Theoretically they were quite willing to turn the task of protecting the frontier over to the federal government, but practically they were unwilling to accept the federal plan; they soon demanded that the work be done through their institutions and leadership—at federal expense. . . . The Texans demanded that the United States should muster the Rangers into federal service, pay them with federal money, and let them run all the Mexicans into the Rio Grande and all the Indians into Red River."[16] And added to all this was the obligation assumed at the peace table at Guadalupe Hidalgo. Between 1848 and 1854, when released by the Gadsden Treaty, the United States was bound to reverse the tribal customs of generations and keep the Indian marauders out of Mexico.

In 1845, when the Republic became a State, a Texas newspaper acclaimed the happy event with the prophesy that "the giant

[15] For a summary of this problem, see George D. Harmon, "The United States Indian Policy in Texas, 1846–1860," *Mississippi Valley Historical Review*, 17 (1930), 377–403.

[16] Walter Prescott Webb, *The Texas Rangers: A Century of Frontier Defense* (Boston, Mass., 1935), p. 127.

arms of the United States would soon sweep the few bands of hostile Indians from our borders."[17] The arms turned out to be something less than giant. To guard a frontier of nearly 400 miles stretching from Red River to the Rio Grande and another of more than 1,000 extending along the international boundary from El Paso to the Gulf of Mexico, the Army could spare only 93 officers and 1,462 soldiers in 1850. By 1860, chiefly because of the four additional regiments authorized in 1855, the number had risen to 121 officers and 2,727 enlisted men. Mounted troops accounted for only 20 per cent of the total in 1850, 25 per cent in 1860.[18] Throughout most of the period, to deal with some 25,000 Indians in 16 tribes,[19] both resident and transient, the Indian Bureau could win congressional authority for only three agents and four interpreters. The journalistic prophecy of 1845 was not to be fulfilled for forty years.

In 1848 the War Department established the 8th Military Department, renamed the Department of Texas in the reorganization of 1853, to encompass the state. To Brevet Major General George Mercer Brooke, who assumed command in 1849, fell the task of laying the groundwork of the Texas defense system. Along the international boundary he completed a string of border posts whose Indian responsibilities were only secondary— Forts Brown, Ringgold, McIntosh, and Duncan. On the upper Frio, Fort Inge, aided later by Forts Merrill and Ewell, buttressed the borderline in interdicting some of the favorite raiding trails to Mexico and also brought under surveillance the Nueces Plains, which supported immense herds of mustangs that attracted the Indians. The heart of the defenses, however, defined the limit of settlement in 1849. By this year the settlers had worked their way up the river valleys to the curving line of the Balcones Escarpment, where the vast table of the Edwards Plateau breaks away to the lowlands that cradled the first Anglo-American colonies. Slightly in advance of this frontier General Brooke's troops erected a chain of forts in 1849—Fort Worth on the Trinity, Forts Graham and Gates on the Brazos and one of its tributaries, Fort Croghan on the Colorado above Austin, and

[17] Quoted in Bender, *March of Empire*, p. 130.

[18] SW, *Annual Report* (1850), chart following p. 116. *Ibid.* (1860), pp. 218–21.

[19] CIA, *Annual Report* (1849), p. 963. The estimate by Agent Robert S. Neighbors was actually 29,575, but reflects a probable overestimate of Comanches by about 5,000.

Fort Martin Scott on the Guadalupe north of San Antonio. In theory if not always in practice, each of the forts was held by one mounted and one foot company, and their mission was to keep the Indians out of the settlements.[20]

They failed largely because they were so few and because most of them were infantry. The Plains warriors, chiefly Kiowas and Comanches from the north but sometimes Lipans, Kickapoos, and other lesser groups, effortlessly slipped through the cordon of forts, struck at the settlements, and escaped before pursuit could be organized. No citizen was safe, even within sight of such large towns as Austin, San Antonio, and Corpus Christi. Human and property losses rose to alarming levels, and Texas newspapers excoriated the federal government for not living up to its responsibilities. Even with the aid of nearly four hundred federalized Texas Rangers, Brooke could not protect the people from the raiders. "I do not believe," he wrote the adjutant general, "that three thousand men or more stationed at the frontier posts can prevent these deluded people from secretly passing the line of posts in very small parties at different points and afterwards uniting in large bodies in particular neighborhoods where they commit their acts of murder and depredation and instantly return to their own country, neither stopping night or day until they conceive themselves out of danger." The general thought that an offensive into the Indian haunts offered the only hope of easing the menace, but his forces were too weak for effective defense, much less offense.[21]

If the military line failed to turn back Indian raiding parties, it failed equally to discourage the restless push of the settlers. On the contrary, by implying security and affording markets for produce, the forts hastened the advance of the settlements up the valleys to the northwest. Within two years after the completion of Brooke's defense shield, the frontier had left it behind and Texans were demanding a new one. General Brooke

[20] SW, *Annual Report* (1849), pp. 152-53. Martin L. Crimmins, "The First Line of Army Posts Established in West Texas in 1849," West Texas Historical Association *Year Book*, *19* (1943), 121-27.

[21] SW, *Annual Report* (1850), pp. 51-53. See also *ibid.*, pp. 435-36, 45. In early 1850 there were five companies of State Rangers in federal service numbering 15 officers and 356 men. Jones to Jesup, April 30, 1850, AGO LB No. 27, RG 94, NARS. Webb, *The Texas Rangers*, pp. 130-31, 140, indicates that the federal government rarely financed the Rangers before the late 1850s, but in fact Congress usually voted funds for their support. Cf. 9 Stat. 573 ($236,934.34) and 10 Stat. 15 ($80,740).

died in 1851, and his successor, Brevet Major General Persifor F. Smith, came to Texas from California with instructions from Secretary of War Conrad to "revise the whole system both of defense and of administration." Smith's mission was to lay out a new network of forts, protect the people of Texas, defend Mexican territory, carry the war to the Indian homeland, and reduce expenses.[22] An able, conscientious, and beloved officer, General Smith, though of feeble health, attacked this impossible assignment with a will.

In the north troops of the 5th Infantry from the adjoining 7th Department had already begun the job. In 1850 General Arbuckle had concluded that the newly opened trail known as "Marcy's return route" would become the principal transcontinental emigrant road and had prevailed on the War Department to authorize a chain of posts to guard it. This route was explored in 1849 by Captain Randolph B. Marcy on his return from escorting California-bound emigrants as far as New Mexico. It ran southwest from Fort Smith across the Washita, Red, Brazos, Colorado, and Pecos Rivers and struck the Rio Grande at Doña Ana about forty miles north of El Paso. In 1851, pursuant to General Arbuckle's design, Captain Marcy established a fort near the Washita and Brevet Brigadier General William G. Belknap founded another on the upper reaches of the Brazos. The former was named Fort Arbuckle for the department commander, who died in June 1851, the latter Fort Belknap for its founder, who died on his way back to Fort Smith in November 1851.[23]

The line of forts planned by General Arbuckle sliced across the northwestern fringe of General Smith's department, and in fact a secondary purpose of the line was to deflect Kiowa and Comanche raiders from the Texas settlements. Smith toured this portion of his command late in 1851. When he returned to San Antonio, the Arbuckle plan for protecting the Marcy road had

[22] SW, *Annual Report* (1851), pp. 117–18. Colonel E. V. Sumner, assigned to the 9th Department at the same time, received almost identical instructions. See below, p. 86.

[23] Arbuckle to Freeman, March 13, 1850, A46/1850. Arbuckle to Jones, July 24, 1850, A115/1850. Same to same, Sept. 2, 1850, A147/1850. Jones to Arbuckle, April 1, 1851; June 14, 1851, AGO LB No. 27. Jones to Belknap, July 2, 1851, same source. Jones to Smith, Nov. 17, 1851, same source. All in RG 94, NARS. Ben G. Oneal, "The Beginnings of Fort Belknap," *Southwestern Historical Quarterly, 61* (1957–58) 508–21. R. N. Richardson, *The Frontier of Northwest Texas, 1846 to 1876* (Glendale, Calif., 1963), pp. 61–66.

been transformed into the Smith plan for protecting the Texas frontier. On the Marcy road beyond Fort Belknap there appeared to be no sites affording sufficient wood and water for military installations, and in effect Smith bent the Arbuckle line to the south, away from the Marcy road, and carried it in a great arc to the Rio Grande. Enclosing the new frontier of settlement, the Smith line traced the western limit of reliable water flow in the rivers heading on the Staked Plains and the Edwards Plateau. From Fort Belknap on the north, it curved to Fort Phantom Hill on the Clear Fork of the Brazos, Fort Chadbourne on a tributary of the upper Colorado, Fort McKavett at the head of the San Saba, Fort Terrett on the Llano, and Fort Clark, the southern anchor, on Las Moras Creek. Behind this line, between the San Saba and the Llano, Smith also erected Fort Mason to guard the German settlements that had taken a particularly savage beating.

By the end of 1852 Texas had an inner and an outer cordon of defensive works with an intervening zone about 150 miles wide in which the frontier of settlement lay. Smith's defense plan called for manning the outer line with infantry and the inner with cavalry. The infantry would alert the cavalry to the presence of raiding parties between the lines—how was not specified. The cavalry would then pursue and the infantry would shut off the avenues of escape. The plan had the further advantage of economy, for the mounted force, stationed among the settlements, could obtain forage and other supplies locally. Smith also intended to stockpile provisions at the outer posts for use by the cavalry if campaigns beyond the defenses became necessary. The plan looked good on paper, but as it worked out in practice the troops were too few, the Indians too cunning, and Texas too big for it to have much effect. The warriors now had several more places to avoid, but they still raided much as they had in the past.[24]

[24] The concept is set forth in Smith to Lieutenant Colonel W. G. Freeman, July 19, 1853, printed in *Southwestern Historical Quarterly*, *54* (1950–51), 211–16. Regarding the Marcy road, Smith wrote: "The Secretary of War had directed the occupation of the line known as 'Marcy's return route from New Mexico'— but this line although abundant in water and fuel for small parties did not suffice for the establishment of a line of posts & a line as near it as possible has been taken occupying in some instances the very heads of the streams & in others points as far up them as furnished material and fuel and water & were in due communication with the other posts." As a matter of fact, the Marcy road carried little emigrant travel, although the trans-

With two lines of forts guarding the frontier of settlement and a third policing the international boundary, Smith turned in 1854 to a fourth designed to guard the road from San Antonio to El Paso. This route had been pioneered by army engineers in 1849 and in the early 1850s carried mounting emigrant, freight, and mail traffic. From Devil's River to the Limpia (Davis) Mountains Kiowas and Comanches menaced it, and between these mountains and El Paso Mescalero Apaches from New Mexico preyed on it. In the autumn of 1854 Smith toured this remote corner of his department. After visiting newly reactivated Fort Bliss at El Paso, he personally selected the site for Fort Davis in the Limpia Mountains. In 1855 he added Fort Lancaster near the crossing of the Pecos, and his successors filled in the chain with Camp Hudson (1857) at the crossing of Devil's River, Fort Quitman (1858) where the road touched the Rio Grande ninety miles below El Paso, and Fort Stockton (1859) at Comanche Spring, intersection of the El Paso Road with the Great Comanche War Trail to Mexico. All these posts were manned by infantry—elements of the 1st and 8th—and although they gave travelers some security they did not noticeably discourage the Indians from depredating on the road.[25]

While the Army struggled manfully but in vain to make the elaborate defense system work, officials of the Indian Bureau sought peaceful solutions to the problems. Managing the effort on the scene, except for the brief Whig interlude from 1849 to 1853, was that political rarity, an able and incorruptible Indian agent. Veteran of the Texas Revolution, Major Robert Simpson Neighbors served the Republic, the State, and the United States as Indian agent. He repeatedly journeyed to the Southern Comanche camps high on the Brazos and Colorado and talked earnestly with such chiefs as Old Owl, Sanaco, Ketumseh,

continental stagecoaches of the Butterfield Overland Mail followed substantially this route between 1858 and 1861. See also Richardson, *Frontier of Northwest Texas*, pp. 67-73.

25 For Smith's tour, during which his escort fought a rousing battle with Apaches, and the founding of Fort Davis see Smith to Cooper, Sept. 30, Oct. 9, Oct. 14, 1854, RG 94, NARS. For a discussion of the evolution of the Texas defense system see W. C. Holden, "Frontier Defense, 1846-1860," *West Texas Historical Association Year Book*, 6 (1930), 35-65. Detailed descriptions of all the forts will be found in Martin L. Crimmins, ed., "Freeman's Report on the Eighth Military Department [1853]," *Southwestern Historical Quarterly*, serially in 13 parts from 51 (1947-48) to 54 (1950-51); and Crimmins, ed., "Col. J. K. F. Mansfield's Report of the Inspection of the Department of Texas in 1856," *ibid.*, serially in 3 parts in 42 (1938-39).

Buffalo Hump, and Yellow Wolf. There he also met chiefs of the wilder bands of Comanches from the north. All had signed treaties with the United States—the Southern Comanches on the Brazos in 1846 and the Northern Comanches on the Arkansas in 1853. In both treaties they had promised to quit warring on the whites and give up their captives and stolen property. Neighbors tried to persuade them to keep their promises, but he came to appreciate that it was not that simple. Young warriors had always raided, and they would not stop even on those rare occasions when the chiefs tried to compel them to stop. Now, moreover, with the whites relentlessly cutting down the Indian hunting ranges, there were motives for raiding other than mere plunder. The nomadic way of life itself stood in imminent peril. To arranging an accommodation that would end the shedding of his countrymen's blood at the same time that it secured rights and property to the Indians, Neighbors dedicated himself with tireless energy.

As Neighbors and his superiors saw it, the solution lay in guaranteeing land to the Indians. At first the idea was to draw a line separating the settlements from the Indian country—the old idea of a permanent Indian frontier. The Indians would be compelled to stay on one side, the whites on the other. As the impossibility of imposing such a restriction became increasingly apparent, this solution gave way to another: set aside reservations for the Indians and let the oncoming settlements flow by, leaving behind islands of Indians in a sea of whites. On the reservations the Indians would be taught to support themselves as farmers rather than as huntsmen, and the federal Intercourse laws would protect them from white rapacity. Neighbors repeatedly urged this plan, but the federal government could do nothing until Texas made available the land. This the legislature finally did, after six years of federal prodding, early in 1854. The act of February 6 authorized federal officials to survey no more than twelve leagues (53,136 acres) of unclaimed state land for occupancy by the Indians of Texas.

Neighbors and Captain Marcy explored the headwaters of the Brazos the following summer and marked out two reservations. One, on the upper Clear Fork of the Brazos, was for the Southern Comanches. Genuinely alarmed by the approach of the settlements and influenced over the years by the counsel of Neighbors, they professed readiness to settle down and try their hand at farming. The other reservation, on the Salt Fork of the Brazos just below Fort Belknap, was for the Anadarkos, Caddos, Tawakonis, Wacos, and Tonkawas. Semisedentary and loosely confederated tribes, they had been caught in a tightening vise of settlements on the one side and roving Comanches on the other. They greeted the innovation with relief and brought to it a considerably firmer grounding in agriculture than the Comanches. By the middle of 1855 both reservations, each with its own agent under the supervision of Neighbors, were in operation and exhibiting encouraging results. On the Brazos Reservation lived nearly eight hundred Indians, on the Comanche Reservation nearly three hundred. Fort Belknap guarded the former, newly erected Camp Cooper the latter.[26]

This was a very small beginning, and its efficacy remained to be proved. Moreover, thousands of Northern Comanches and their Kiowa allies continued to play havoc on the Texan and Mexican frontiers. Not until they, too, were confined to reservations did Neighbors foresee relief for the settlements. The military authorities viewed the Texas reservations with sympathy and optimism, but in their opinion not until Texas received enough troops to carry the war north of Red River would there be much relief for the frontier. Neither, it turned out, was entirely correct.

[26] This phase of Texas Indian history is treated in depth in a series of articles by Kenneth F. Neighbours: "The Marcy-Neighbors Exploration of the Headwaters of the Brazos and Wichita Rivers in 1854," *Panhandle-Plains Historical Review*, 27 (1954) 26–46; "Robert S. Neighbors and the Founding of the Texas Indian Reservations," West Texas Historical Association *Year Book*, *31* (1955), 65–74; and "Chapters from the History of the Texas Indian Reservations," *ibid.*, *33* (1957), 3–16. See also Neighbors' annual reports in the CIA, *Annual Report* (1848 through 1859); Richardson, *Comanche Barrier*, pp. 211–32; and Harmon, "United States Indian Policy in Texas."

FIVE

Occupying the Southwest

O<small>N</small> August 15, 1846, General Stephen Watts Kearny climbed to the top of a flat-roofed building on the east side of the plaza of Las Vegas, the first New Mexican town occupied by the invading Army of the West. The Mexican populace crowded the plaza below. His soldiers came in peace, the general announced, and would not disturb the persons, property, or religion of the inhabitants. New Mexico now belonged to the United States, and henceforth its people would live under American law and enjoy the benefits of American citizens. Their new condition, Kearny promised, entitled them to protection from the ravages of hostile Indians. "From the Mexican Government you have never received protection. The Apaches and Navajos come down from the mountains and carry off your sheep, and even your women, whenever they please. My government will correct all this. It will keep off the Indians."[1] At Tecolote, San Miguel, and finally Santa Fe, Kearny repeated this promise. New Mexico fell in a bloodless conquest.

What passed through the minds of the people of Las Vegas as they stood quietly listening to Kearny transform them into U.S. citizens is not recorded. For many years they had heard similar fine pronouncements from their governors and at the same time had known poverty and the oppression of despotic rulers. Of still more consequence to their daily lives, they had known the terrible insecurity of existing always at the mercy of the Indians.

---

[1] Quoted in William H. Emory, *Notes of a Military Reconnaissance, from Fort Leavenworth . . . to San Diego . . .* , Senate Ex. Docs., 30th Cong., 1st sess., No. 7, p. 27.

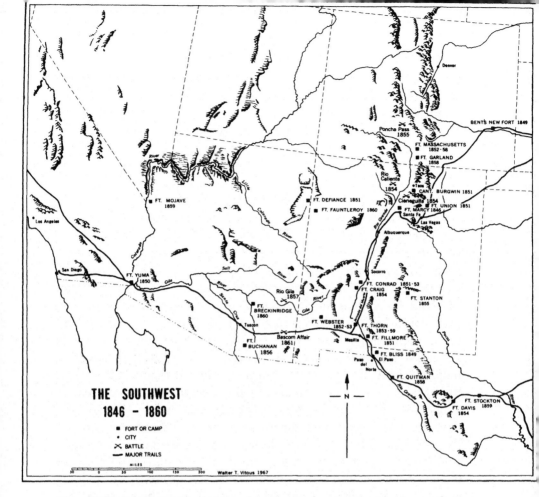

THE SOUTHWEST
1846 - 1860

■ FORT OR CAMP
● CITY
✕ BATTLE
━ MAJOR TRAILS

MILES

Walter T. Vitous 1967

New Mexicans had no love for the gringos upon whom they had grown dependent through two decades of commercial intercourse, but it is a safe guess that if the general's words raised any emotion at all, it was a hope that the Americans could indeed make their lives secure from the Indians.

As Kearny had learned a great deal about New Mexico from the veterans of the Santa Fe trade in his entourage, he probably understood that the rooftop guarantee engaged his government to protect some sixty thousand former Mexican nationals scattered in tiny mud hamlets along the Rio Grande from Taos to El Paso del Norte, a distance of nearly four hundred miles, and in outposts like Las Vegas and Cebolleta on either side of the great valley that contained most of the population. He could not have foreseen the added burdens imposed on this army by the flow of gold-seekers over the very trails that his California-bound columns were soon to blaze, by the commitment to block Indian raids into Mexico that American diplomats would make two years later at the peace table of Guadalupe Hidalgo, and by the business, commercial, and agricultural enterprises of five hundred or so of his countrymen who were to make homes on the Rio Grande in the postwar years. The promise voiced by the American general in the dusty Las Vegas plaza that August morning in 1846 was not to be fulfilled for thirty years.

After five years of military government, New Mexico finally became an organized territory of the United States as part of the Compromise of 1850. With the Gadsden Purchase of 1853, the territorial boundaries embraced roughly the present states of New Mexico and Arizona together with a small portion of Colorado. Within these boundaries resided an Indian population of about forty thousand people.[2] Scarcely more than half, however, could be counted as a threat. Of the rest, some had reached an accommodation with their alien rulers. Such were the docile Pimas and Papagos of the lower Gila River, who extended a helpful friendship to travelers on the emigrant road to California. Such, too, were the sedentary Pueblos scattered in picturesque adobe villages along the middle Rio Grande. A few of them had participated in the revolution of 1837–38, and Taos rose against the Americans in 1847, but these were not so much interracial conflicts as political rumblings in which Indian and Mexican made common cause. Other groups, more belligerent, had neither accommodated nor in recent years clashed with the outsiders because their country remained virtually unviolated. Such were the Yumas, Mojaves, Yavapais, and Hopis—all inhabitants of the extreme western and northwestern reaches of the territory. There remained, then, the three tribes that constituted the Indian menace to the people of New Mexico in the 1850s—Ute, Navajo, and Apache.

Although the Utes blanketed most of the Colorado Plateau and the Great Basin, two bands, the Capote and Moache, ranged the San Luis Valley of present Colorado (then part of New Mexico) and its bordering mountains. Through intermarriage, they had formed close ties with the Jicarilla Apaches on the south. Superb horsemen, the Utes shared with the Shoshonis the

[2] Contemporary estimates range from thirty to sixty thousand. The figure of forty thousand has been reached by a study of population on estimates given by officials during the 1850s together with those in Swanton, *Indian Tribes of North America.*

distinction of being the most warlike of the plateau tribes. In 1855 the Capote and Moache bands numbered about two thousand people, including some five hundred warriors.[3] Long warfare with the tribes of the High Plains on the east and the Navajos on the west had worked its ravages. Despite the Jicarilla alliance, the Utes of New Mexico were troublesome only until they seriously tested conclusions with the U.S. Army.

Far more formidable than the Utes, the Navajos crowded the Rio Grande settlements from the west. Ranging between the San Juan and Little Colorado Rivers, they had spread westward as far as the Hopi mesas. When the Americans took over New Mexico, the Navajos were nearing the apex of their power as an independent people. They were farmers and herders as well as hunters, and they boasted a material wealth, counted principally in horses and sheep, unsurpassed by any southwestern tribe. Americans marveled at their handsome buckskin clothing, fine woven blankets, leather belts, and well-constructed horse trappings. The Navajo shepherd, dwelling semipermanently in a log-and-brush hogan and tending his sheep, corn, and fruit trees, seemed inappropriately cast as the fierce warrior who ravaged the Pueblo and Mexican populations on his eastern borders. But such he was. His war complex resembled that of the Plains tribes. War consisted mainly of lightning raids by small mounted parties armed with bow and arrow, lance, and shield; and war expeditions, picking a tortuous course amid narrowly circumscribing taboos, proceeded under a mantle of elaborate religious ritual. With a population close to 12,000, a fighting force of some 2,500 men, a skill in warfare sharpened by long hostility with Spaniards, Mexicans, and other Indians, and a swollen tribal egotism fortified by self-evident cultural superiority over their neighbors, the Navajos acknowledged no masters and accommodated themselves to no aliens.[4]

Half as numerous and considerably less organized than their Navajo kinsmen, the Apaches scourged every settled portion of the Territory of New Mexico. Jicarillas and their Ute allies infested the Sangre de Cristo Mountains east of the Rio Grande from Santa Fe and Las Vegas to the north of Taos. Mescaleros

[3] CIA, *Annual Report* (1855), p. 188.

[4] Excellent tribal histories are Ruth Underhill, *The Navajos* (Norman, Okla., 1956); Clyde Kluckhohn and Dorothea Leighton, *The Navaho* (Cambridge, Mass., 1946); and Katherine Luomala, *Navaho Life of Yesterday and Today* (Berkeley, Calif., 1938).

haunted the Sierra Blanca and the Sacramento Mountains to the south. West of the Rio Grande Gila Apaches, loosely divided into Mimbres, Copper Mine, Warm Spring, and Mogollon groups, ranged the Continental Divide from the Datil Mountains southward to Lake Guzman in Chihuahua. Still farther west, in what is now eastern Arizona, Coyotero (or White Mountain), Pinal, and Aravaipa Apaches claimed the middle Gila and the upper reaches of the Salt, while to the south Chiricahuas roamed the mountains of the same name straddling the emigrant road to California. Altogether, there were probably no more than eight thousand Apaches in the 1850s, but the havoc they created was out of all proportion to their population.[5]

Cunning, courage, endurance, fortitude, and skill in the aboriginal forms of warfare characterized the Apache as it did warriors of most other North American tribes. What stamped the Apache as the most formidable antagonist the Americans encountered in the march across the continent was an unsurpassed ability to turn to his advantage every feature of a hostile landscape combined with a prudence so well developed as to discourage combat except under the most favorable circumstances. With a constancy maddening to their enemies, the Apaches fought only on their own terms. "To rob and not be robbed; to kill and not be killed; to take captive and not be captured, form the sum of an Apache's education and ambition," remarked one of the keenest students of their ways. "Twenty Apaches will not attack four well armed and determined men, if they keep constantly on their guard and prepared for action. In no case will they incur the risk of losing life, unless the plunder be most enticing and their numbers overpowering, and even then they will track a small party for days, waiting an opportunity to establish a secure ambush or effect a surprise."[6]

[5] The population is from Swanton, *Indian Tribes of North America*, p. 330, Apache groupings have inspired much confusion. Although the standard history is Frank C. Lockwood, *The Apache Indians* (New York, 1936), this breakdown is drawn from intensive studies of Albert H. Schroeder for the Indian Land Claims Section of the Lands Division, U.S. Department of Justice. His findings are incorporated in a mimeographed report entitled *A Study of the Apache Indians* (5 vols.; Santa Fe, N. M., 1960–63). One other group should be mentioned. In the late 1860s and early 1870s, as settlers and soldiers found their way into the Prescott country of central Arizona, a tribe commonly labeled Tonto Apache gave much trouble. Schroeder's researches suggest, however, that no such group existed and that these Indians were in fact Yavapais, or Apache-Mojaves, a Yuman rather than Apachean people.

[6] John C. Cremony, *Life among the Apaches* (San Francisco, Calif., 1868), pp. 86–87.

The country of the Apaches offered a bare subsistence in game and such edible flora as mescal, agave, and berries; and long ago these people had discovered that economic necessity fortified a natural inclination to take from the scarcely less poverty-ridden Mexicans what the land denied. Thievery had become a way of life, and the guerrilla warfare at which the Apaches excelled was but a means to this end. With predictable regularity, Apache raids desolated not only New Mexico but also Coahuila, Durango, Chihuahua, and Sonora. Stolen sheep and cattle helped to dispel the spector of starvation. Stolen horses and mules furnished transportation as well as a mobile commissary. And captives, readily assimilated into the tribe, slowed the steady decline in population decreed by centuries of war and famine.

Navajo raids were grounded less in economic imperatives than Apache raids—wealth, distinction, adventure, and retaliation offering more powerful incentives—but for the victims, those of New Mexico and those of the states to the south, in old Mexico, the distinction was academic.[7] In two and one half centuries they had made their adjustment to the harsh condition of life imposed by Navajo and Apache. Paralyzed by fear and futility, they rarely resisted. In meek submission lay a ray of hope of escaping death, for sometimes the Indian appreciated the investment in the future represented by a live Mexican, who would raise more stock for next month's or next year's raid. For many Mexicans this discovery had given rise to another. The raiders admitted to their homeland traders willing to barter such scarce items as arms and ammunition for stock and captives seized in their raids. It was a lucrative and widespread commerce that could, by ignoring certain obvious flaws of reasoning, be rationalized as humanitarian.

There was still another side to the relationship. For Mexicans all was not passivity. Frequently they banded together to scour the Apache or Navajo country. These were not so much punitive expeditions as raids cast in the mold of those from which they themselves suffered. The objectives were stock, plunder, and captives who could be sold as slaves in Mexican households. The methods of combat, once contact was made, rivaled in barbarity those employed by the victims. Such invasions, falling on guilty and innocent alike, inevitably provoked reprisals that also fell

[7] There is no satisfactory term for Americans of Spanish or Mexican descent. Although inaccurate, "Mexican" was the term most commonly used during the period under consideration and will be used throughout this volume.

on guilty and innocent, and as often as not the reprisal in turn set off a counter-reprisal. For the Mexicans, then, the response to the Apache and Navajo menace was passive defense coupled with savage offense.

The strands of Mexican and Indian life had in truth become tightly interwoven in a fabric of unique and partly cynical relationships. Navajos and Apaches robbed, terrorized, enslaved, and butchered Mexicans. On a lesser scale Mexicans robbed, terrorized, enslaved, and butchered Indians. Mexicans supplied arms and ammunition to the Indians, who used them in slaughtering other Mexicans and paid for them with the proceeds gained in the process. The pattern was fixed by generations of practice, and it was not to be easily broken by either party. For the American newcomers, this heritage from Spain and Mexico raised one of the most stubborn obstacles to an effective attack on the Navajo and Apache problem. And they themselves, holding their conquered subjects in contempt and in turn earning a cordial and well-merited dislike from them, injected a further complicating factor into a situation already smothered with complications.[8]

Not for five years after General Kearny's bloodless seizure of New Mexico was any positive and comprehensive approach to Indian affairs devised along either military or civil lines. From 1846 to 1848, while the armies of Scott and Taylor decided the outcome of the Mexican War on fields far to the south, Missouri Volunteers held New Mexico. Kearny had promulgated a code of civil law and left Charles Bent as governor, but Bent perished in the bloody Indian-Mexican revolution at Taos early in 1847, and after its decisive suppression by Colonel Sterling Price military government in fact ruled New Mexico. The Treaty of Guadalupe Hidalgo only aggravated the political uncertainty, for the acquisition of New Mexico and California set off the momentous constitutional debate over slavery in the territories and delayed for another three years the organization of a territorial government in the wake of the Compromise of 1850. The

[8] The relationship here sketched is a constant theme in the official military and civil correspondence of New Mexico during the 1850s. It emerges most clearly in the documents contained in Abel, *Official Correspondence of James S. Calhoun.* See also testimony of various officials of long residence in Santa Fe taken there in 1865 and printed in "Condition of the Indian Tribes," Senate Reps., 39th Cong., 2d sess., No. 156, pp. 325–37. A particularly bitter commentary was authored by the outspoken Captain John Pope; see Utley, "Captain John Pope's Plan of 1853 for the Frontier Defense of New Mexico," pp. 162–63.

end of the war, therefore, only substituted regular army governors for the volunteer governors. Brevet Lieutenant Colonel John M. Washington assumed the executive authority in October 1848, followed a year later by Brevet Colonel John Munroe.[9]

Although a restive Mexican population and multitudes of bitterly contending political factions spawned by the prolonged constitutional crisis in Washington preoccupied the military governors, they could not, of course, ignore the Indian problem. As commanders of the regular soldiery assigned to New Mexico after the war, they were also responsible for holding back the Indians. The Regulars reached New Mexico, newly styled the 9th Military Department, by detachments throughout 1848 and 1849. By 1850 twenty-one companies of infantry and dragoons, numbering slightly more than a thousand rank and file, had taken station in the department. Posted in the principal towns of the Rio Grande Valley from Taos to El Paso, and at Las Vegas, Abiquiu, and Cebolleta on either side, their mission was to protect the settlements and travel routes from Indian raiders.[10]

To the Indian aggressions that fell on the settlements in the spring of 1849 these troops responded with surprising vigor. Augmented by five companies of New Mexican Volunteers called into federal service by Colonel Washington, they thrust at the Jicarillas and Utes on the north and the Mescaleros and Gilas on the south. Small-unit combats flared all along the perimeter of settlement. Washington himself led a strong column into the Navajo country, skirmished with some warriors who resented the intrusion, killed an important chief, and ended by signing a treaty with two more chiefs at the mouth of Canyon de Chelly. It was an active season but barren of lasting benefit.[11]

Washington's successor, Colonel Munroe, proved less ener-getic. He detested New Mexico and particularly its climate. Reputed to be the ugliest man in the Army, the colonel, according to one observer, "would brew his pitcher of toddy at night, and take the first drink of it at noon next day, after which hour he would not attend to any official business."[12] And his mornings

[9] This period is treated in Ralph E. Twitchell, *The Military Occupation of New Mexico, 1846–1851* (Denver, Colo., 1909).

[10] SW, *Annual Report* (1849), pp. 182–84; (1850), table following p. 116.

[11] *Ibid.* (1849), pp. 104–15. For the Washington reconnaissance see Frank McKnitt, ed., *Navaho Expedition: Journal of a Military Reconnaissance from Santa Fe, New Mexico, to the Navaho Country. Made in 1849 by Lieutenant James H. Simpson* (Norman, Okla., 1964).

[12] Espinosa, "Memoir of a Kentuckian in New Mexico," p. 7.

were largely occupied with political headaches. Some of his field officers, notably veteran Captain Enoch Steen in the south and fatherly old Captain William Grier in the north, displayed extraordinary zeal on scout and in pursuit.[13] But by the close of 1850 the Indians were obviously coming more and more to have their own way in New Mexico.

Two tragedies, widely publicized in the East, dramatized this condition to authorities in Washington. In October 1849 allied Jicarilla and Ute warriors fell on the J. M. White train at Point of Rocks on the Santa Fe Trail, killed White, and made off with his wife and daughter. Captain Grier's dragoons, guided by Kit Carson, caught up with the Indians a month later, but Mrs. White was slain before she could be rescued. Although Congress appropriated $1,500 to ransom the little girl, she was never found. In May 1850 warriors of the same tribes ambushed and wiped out the east-bound mail party, consisting of eleven men, at Wagon Mound, also on the Santa Fe Trail. Reporting this atrocity, Lieutenant Ambrose E. Burnside penned a vivid description of the massacre site that stirred a sensation in Santa Fe and Washington.[14] Against this background, bluff old Bull Sumner relieved scholarly John Munroe in July 1851.

Lieutenant colonel of the 1st Dragoons, Edwin V. Sumner assumed command of the 9th Department in his brevet rank of colonel. Like General Persifor Smith, who went to the 8th Department at the same time (see p. 73), Sumner carried instructions to root out the old order and institute a new one. He was to get the troops out of the towns, which Secretary of War Conrad regarded as iniquitous and enervating, and station them in a network of posts designed to protect the settlements of New Mexico, to block Indian incursions into old Mexico, and to exploit the countryside for forage, fuel, and food. The soldiers would build their own forts, gather their own forage, chop their own wood, and grow much of their own ration, thus permitting a vast reduction in civilian employment. Sumner was also to organize campaigns against the Navajos, Utes, and Apaches and "inflict upon them a severe chastisement."[15] Firm-

[13] SW, *Annual Report* (1850), pp. 67–75.
[14] For the White Massacre see Edwin L. Sabin, *Kit Carson Days: Adventures in the Path of Empire* (2 vols.; New York, 1935), 2, 618–22; and W. W. H. Davis, *El Gringo, or New Mexico and Her People* (New York, 1856), pp. 44–46. Official documents concerning both events are in Abel.
[15] SW, *Annual Report* (1851), pp. 125–26.

ness in defense, vigor in offense, and a stringent economy founded on self-support were the incompatible goals set for the 1,388 officers and men of the 9th Department. Confidently, Sumner attacked the problem with a will. He failed, of course, but in the process he sketched the broad outlines of a defense system that endured without basic change for forty years.

At once the new commander ordered nearly the whole headquarters garrison and all the department quartermaster stores out of Santa Fe, "that sink of vice and of extravagance," and located them on the prairies a hundred miles to the east. Here, near the junction of the Mountain and Cimarron branches of the Santa Fe Trail, Fort Union sprang to life and ultimately became the largest installation in the Southwest and the supply and ordnance depot for the department. In August 1851, less than a month after his arrival, Sumner marched off to the west at the head of seven companies, grimly determined to conquer the Navajos. "He went, and saw, and left," was the cryptic verdict of the *Santa Fe Gazette*.[16] But behind him five companies of soldiers fixed their presence on the heart of the Navajo country. In a pleasant valley at the mouth of Canyon Bonito, the post took shape with the brave name of Fort Defiance.

In the autumn of 1851, after his return from the Navajo campaign, Sumner turned his attention to the south. Withdrawing the garrisons from El Paso, Doña Ana, and Socorro, he founded three more posts. Fort Conrad rose on the Rio Grande at the northern end of the dreaded Jornada del Muerto, focus of raids by Mescalero and Gila Apaches as well as Navajos. A hundred miles to the south, Fort Fillmore watched over the river crossing of the California Trail, attempted to intercept Indian expeditions to Mexico, and guarded the string of river towns from Doña Ana through El Paso to San Elizario. And a hundred miles northwest of Fort Fillmore, Fort Webster was erected at the old Spanish copper mines in the midst of jumbled mountains inhabited by Gila Apaches.

The following summer, 1852, Sumner rounded out the defense system by establishing two posts in the northern part of the territory. Cantonment Burgwin occupied a mountain valley in the Jicarilla Apache country ten miles south of Taos. And on the northeastern edge of the San Luis Valley, nestled

---

16 Feb. 26, 1853.

at the foot of towering Blanca Peak, Fort Massachusetts watched over the Utes.

Subsequent years brought changes in the system, as new responsibilities became apparent and as old sites, for one reason or another, proved undesirable. In 1854 Fort Conrad gave way to Fort Craig eight miles down the river. Fort Massachusetts was moved six miles southward in 1858 and renamed Fort Garland. Fort Webster was abandoned in 1853 and reestablished the next year on the Rio Grande as Fort Thorn. Fort Bliss was reactivated at El Paso in 1854. Fort Marcy in Santa Fe and the Post of Albuquerque alternated in prominence as department headquarters moved back and forth between them. Fort Stanton was planted in the midst of the Mescaleros of the Sierra Blanca in 1855, and after the Gadsden Purchase Fort Buchanan (1856) and Fort Breckinridge (1860) extended military occupation to southern Arizona. That neither these nor still later changes fundamentally altered the framework testified to the general soundness of the defense scheme laid out by Colonel Sumner in 1851–52.[17]

The civil system of Indian management emerged even more tardily than the military. Officials of the new Indian Bureau in the Department of the Interior knew almost nothing about the tribes thrust upon them by the territorial acquisitions of the Mexican War. In the summer of 1849 James S. Calhoun, appointed Indian agent for New Mexico by President Taylor, arrived in Santa Fe to appraise the problem. Appalled by its magnitude and complexity, he lost no time in appealing for help. Not until 1851, however, did Congress respond by providing for four agents, one each for the Utes, Jicarillas, Navajos, and southern Apaches. By this time Calhoun had ascended to the territorial governorship, which embraced also the office of Superintendent of Indian Affairs. First as agent, then as superintendent, this idealistic, sensitive, and somewhat visionary man laid the foundations for the civil approach to the New Mexican Indians.[18]

Treaties were signed with representatives of the various

[17] Sumner to Jones, Oct. 24, 1851, in Abel, pp. 416–19. Same to same, Jan. 1, 1852, Fort Union LS, RG 98, NARS. Frazer, *Mansfield on the Condition of Western Forts,* introduction and chap. 1.

[18] Calhoun's tenure in New Mexico is well documented in Abel, *The Correspondence of James S. Calhoun.*

tribes, then promptly broken by both sides. Agencies were established as centers for those scattering tribesmen who could be lured by paltry rations and a few presents to foreswear the old life and for a time try their hand at farming. The governor's agents were few and inexperienced if not also incompetent and corrupt. His appropriations were niggardly. His charges had always raided and, though professing change of heart, could not bring themselves to throw off the cultural commitment. The civilian population resisted any policy tinged with humanitarianism. The Indian Intercourse Act of 1834, setting up stringent controls on trade in the Indian Country, remained ambiguous in its application to the new territories because of the impossibility of clearly defining the Indian Country. Washington was a long way off and its officials only spasmodically interested in the problems of New Mexico. And above all, the Army refused to cooperate. In Colonel Munroe's regime, civil-military relations grew cool and often irritating. In the Sumner regime they broke down altogether.

Openly contemptuous of civil officials, Sumner tormented and hamstrung them in many ways—from bold usurpation of executive authority to such petty harassments as withholding transportation and military escorts. Calhoun broke under the strain, departed the territory in the spring of 1852, and reached the eastern terminus of the Santa Fe Trail in a coffin that with prophetic foresight he had brought along. Sumner sprang into the executive chair in Santa Fe, suffered a War Department rebuke for exceeding his authority,[19] and in the autumn petulantly moved his headquarters to Albuquerque rather than face the ceremonial obligation of welcoming Calhoun's successor to the capital. Governor William Carr Lane found that even the national flag that flew over the plaza had, in a calculated affront, been packed off to the new seat of military power.[20] Lane stood up to the colonel more sternly than Calhoun, but there was constant friction. Sumner also maintained a running feud with the citizens of the territory, climaxed with his offi-

19 Conrad to Sumner, Dec. 23, 1852, SW LS, 34, pp. 38–39, RG 107, NARS.
20 When Lane courteously requested the flag's return, Sumner icily replied that he "was not authorized by the government to furnish him with government stores." Sumner also reproved the commander at Santa Fe for firing an artillery salute at Lane's inauguration. Ralph E. Twitchell, Historical Sketch of Governor William Carr Lane (Santa Fe, N. M., 1917), p. 10.

cial recommendation, echoed in all seriousness by Secretary Conrad in his annual report, that the United States abandon New Mexico altogether.[21]

At last another Secretary, Jefferson Davis, heeded the outcry against "The Big Bug at Albuquerque" and wisely withdrew him. Brevet Brigadier General John Garland, who assumed command in July 1853, and Governor David Meriwether, who supplanted Lane shortly afterward, laid the groundwork for civil-military cooperation. Garland commanded the newly re-named Department of New Mexico for nearly five years and proved capable and efficient as well as popular with the citizenry. During this time the Army scored some notable triumphs over the Indians.

[21] SW, *Annual Report* (1852), pp. 6, 23–24.

SIX

Pacific Outpost

WITH 125 dragoons, General Stephen Watts Kearny crossed the Colorado River near the mouth of the Gila on November 25, 1846. Bloodlessly he had conquered New Mexico, and reportedly California had already fallen to Captain John C. Frémont's Bear Flag insurgents and Commodore Robert S. Stockton's U.S. naval forces. At the Battle of San Pascual on December 6, Kearny learned to his costly surprise that the reports were premature. By January 1847, however, the half-hearted resistance of the Californians had collapsed, and at once the general discovered in the intrigues of Stockton and Frémont a source of far more pain than the two lance wounds he had taken at San Pascual. These two opportunists declined to recognize his authority, derived from the President himself, and enormously complicated the task assigned him of pacifying the province newly seized from Mexico and erecting a government for it. By June, however, he had accomplished the mission and headed east, ultimately to face the vindictive wrath of Frémont's powerful father-in-law, Senator Thomas Hart Benton.

Behind him, Kearny left a handful of dragoons under Colonel Richard B. Mason to symbolize the attainment of President Polk's principal war aim and the fulfillment of the expansionist vision of the North American republic as a continental nation. To the north no soldiers symbolized U.S. sovereignty over the Pacific Northwest, but the Oregon Treaty of 1846 and the burgeoning American settlements in the Willamette Valley made it nonetheless real.

Neither in California nor in Oregon had the Indian population intruded very seriously on the thoughts of settlers. Unlike New Mexico, the pastoral calm of Spanish and Mexican California had seldom been shaken by an Indian menace. The settlements hugging the coast and spilling into the Central Valley had by about 1820 pushed the original native occupants back into the mountains or rendered them harmless. Much the same thing had happened in Oregon's Willamette Valley, although in 1847 the massacre at Marcus Whitman's mission, across the Cascade Mountains to the east, made Oregonians for a time acutely aware of Indian dangers.

This pleasant condition was not to last for long. A great many Indians called California and Oregon their home, and when James Marshall spotted flecks of gold in a millrace on American River in January 1848, he unleashed forces that were to bring these people into conflict with the Atlantic nation whose western border now rested on the Pacific.

Unlike the sterile Southwest, or even the Great Plains with their millions of buffalo, California and the Pacific Northwest contained vast areas rich in attractions for primitive people. Range upon range of towering mountains overspread with forests of cedar, spruce, and redwood yielded a profusion of game animals, sheltered many varieties of berries, and afforded sturdy building material for dwellings. Upland prairies nurtured edible roots. Swift alpine streams and broad rivers draining to the ocean swarmed with salmon, sturgeon, and lamprey and webbed the twisted topography with travel corridors. On the whole the climate was mild. Nowhere west of the Missouri River did nature favor its native population with such bounty, and nowhere west of the Missouri did the land support such a large native population.

At the midpoint of the nineteenth century, the onset of the American period, California contained about one hundred thousand Indians. Except for the Yumas and Mojaves on the southeastern margins (treated in chapter 8), the Californians possessed only the most rudimentary political organization. Loosely associated in ethnic groups bearing almost unpronounceable names, they owed allegiance to no single tribe or leader, as these terms are applied to other Indians of the continent.[1] On

[1] A. L. Kroeber, *Handbook of the Indians of California*, Bureau of American Ethnology Bull. 78 (Washington, D.C., 1925), pp. 830–33. This is the most authoritative and comprehensive treatment of the California Indians.

this score alone, their numbers availed them little against the Americans who swarmed over the Sierra Nevada and the Central Valley after the gold strike of 1848. Beyond this, many groups had been declining for a century as contact with the Spanish introduced new diseases, new diet, and new and enforced customs. Between 1800 and 1850, the California Indian population dropped from 260,000 to 100,000, and in the half-century after the Americans arrived it fell to scarcely more than 15,000.[2] Only in northern California were there Indian groups that put up enough resistance to the white flood to require very serious attention from the Regular Army.

These Indians, a congeries of small groups displaying much the same characteristics, occupied the watersheds of the Trinity, Klamath, and Pit Rivers in California, the Rogue and Umpqua of Oregon, and the coastline by which these streams found outlet in the ocean. The more important included the Yurok, Karok, Tolowa, Hupa, Wintun, Shasta, and Klamath. Culturally almost identical though politically unconnected, they exhibited few traits to make differentiation meaningful. To the whites they were usually known by their locale—the Rogue River or Scott's Valley Indians; or by their leaders—Old John's or Old Jake's band.

The Yuroks, centered at the junction of the Klamath and Trinity Rivers, set the cultural pattern for these Indians. Among them the distinctive culture traits were most sharply delineated. Among their neighbors, and their neighbors' neighbors, the traits recognizable by non-Indians faded in proportion to the distance from the Yurok fountainhead. Living in habitations made of planks, the Yuroks subsisted comfortably on acorns, salmon, game meat, berries, seeds, and roots. No formal social or political ties united them beyond the family or extended family group. Such bonds as existed stemmed from kinship, with the wealthiest man exercising a weak sort of leadership over his kinsmen. Organized religious societies did not exist. Female shamans served as medical practitioners and spiritual leaders in a religion featuring deities that represented natural forces.

The most distinctive manifestation of the adaptation of the Yuroks and their neighbors to the natural bounty of their homeland was an all-consuming pursuit of wealth. It motivated

[2] C. Hart Merriam, "The Indian Population of California," *American Anthropologist*, n.s. 7 (1905), 594–606.

and directed nearly every form of human endeavor. "Every injury, each privilege or wrong or trespass, is calculated and compensated," writes A. L. Kroeber. "The Yurok concerns his life above all else with property. . . . He schemes constantly for opportunity to lodge a claim or evade an obligation. No resource is too mean or devious for him to essay in this pursuit."[3] Intergroup clashes occurred wholly within the framework of economic compensation for injuries inflicted. Settlement could be arranged only through compensation, with the winner, having suffered less loss or injury, yielding forth the larger compensation. The war of extermination waged by the white man came as an appalling shock to these people. They could not understand it, and lacking meaningful political organization they could not cope with it.

Northeast of the Sierra, in the lava-strewn country surrounding the Klamath lakes, roamed a related group exhibiting characteristics perceptibly different from those of their kinsmen to the west. The Modocs inhabited a country more hostile to man than the mountains on their west, and they were also somewhat influenced by tribes to the east and north. Although resembling the distinctive Californians in loose political ties, the Modocs nonetheless acknowledged some tribal solidarity and rendered allegiance to chiefs possessing a shadow at least of political authority. They also earned a reputation for warlike inclinations foreign to the California Indians. Horses obtained from northern Indians in exchange for slaves seized from southern Indians made them formidable foes. The Modocs proved hostile to parties of whites that occasionally strayed into their country in the 1850s, and ultimately, in the 1870s, they severely tested the mettle of the U.S. Army.[4]

In the Pacific Northwest—present Oregon, Washington, and most of Idaho—contemporary estimates place the Indian population in the middle of the nineteenth century at slightly less than 25,000.[5] Like the Californians, the coastal people west of the Cascade Mountains gathered in loose family or extended family groups that easily fell prey to the acquisitive whites

---

[3] *Handbook of California Indians*, p. 2.
[4] *Ibid.*, pp. 318–32.
[5] Alban W. Hoopes, *Indian Affairs and Their Administration, with Special Reference to the Far West, 1849–1860* (Philadelphia, Pa., 1932), pp. 6–7.

who rolled over their mountains and valleys in the 1840s. They, too, had been declining for half a century under the paternal but nonetheless exploitive overlordship of the British North West Company and its successor the Hudson's Bay Company. One example is the fate of the Chinookans who lived at the Cascades of the Columbia. The leaders of their stock, they were almost wholly obliterated by disease and dissipation in a few decades.[6]

Although the Indians east of the Cascades may be grouped in tribes more readily than those nearer the coast, the term even here is not wholly satisfactory. Deliberate intermarriage so mixed them that precise categorization is often misleading.[7] A standard breakdown of the two major stocks, Sahaptin and Salishan, has nevertheless been developed to permit a convenient identification of the people who so boldly challenged the U.S. Army in 1855 and 1858. Of the Sahaptins, extending from the middle Columbia to the middle Snake, those who figured most notably in the wars of the 1850s were the Yakima, Klikitat, Palouse, Umatilla, and Walla Walla; the Sahaptin Nez Perces cast their fortunes with the whites and only later, long after their brethren had been overwhelmed, found themselves arrayed against their former friends. Of the Salishans, residents of northern Washington and northern Idaho, the principal combatants were the Spokane, Coeur d'Alene, Pend d'Oreille, and Flathead.[8]

Occupying territory between the coastal groups on the west and the Plains tribes on the east, the Sahaptin and Salishan people bore similarities to both. Exogamy led to those on the west more nearly resembling their neighbors beyond the Cascades; those on the east had fallen heavily under Plains influence. Most were horse Indians and had imbibed the Plains war complex freely enough to make worthy fighters. Political, social, and religious institutions, though lacking the strength

---

[6] Curtis, *North American Indian, 8,* 86.

[7] Leslie Spier, *Tribal Distribution in Washington* (Menasha, Wis., 1936), pp. 2–3.

[8] Sketches of these tribes appear in Curtis, *North American Indian, 7* and *8.* Excellent syntheses of recent but scattered studies emerge in Alvin M. Josephy, Jr., *The Nez Perce Indians and the Opening of the Northwest* (New Haven, Conn., 1965); and Robert Ignatius Burns, S.J., *The Jesuits and the Indian Wars of the Northwest* (New Haven, Conn., 1966).

and elaboration found east of the Rockies, were well enough developed to create a potential for group action impossible for the people oriented toward Yurok or Chinook. Not unexpectedly, tribes of Sahaptin and Salishan stock led a seminomadic existence reflecting a meeting of influences from east and west. Each band claimed as home territory some sheltered valley where it passed the winter. In the spring and autumn the tribes converged on common fisheries in the larger rivers, and in the summer they spread out over the mountains to dig roots and gather berries. Parties of Nez Perces conducted annual excursions to the buffalo plains east of the Rockies, sometimes remaining several years before returning home; their western neighbors made similar journeys with less frequency and regularity.

All the Sahaptin and Salishan tribes had been introduced to the white men long before threatened with white invasion. Hudson's Bay Company traders had worked the Columbia and Snake drainages for decades, and their trading posts dotted the Inland Empire. From them the Indians obtained muskets and ammunition and learned much about the ways of the whites. Firm in discipline and strong in influence, the company sought no Indian land and disturbed few basic cultural values or institutions. Both Catholic and Protestant missionaries had also come among these tribes as early as the 1830s. DeSmet, Whitman, Spalding, and their associates had sprinkled missions all over the Sahaptin and Salishan country and had indeed disturbed some basic values. By the 1850s many of the tribes had split into progressive and conservative factions, the former professing Christianity and favoring subservience to the whites, the latter clinging to the ancient "earth mother" religion and avoiding so far as possible all dealings with the whites. This factionalism often complicated relations with the Indians but also, by preventing them from forming a united front, often aided the Americans in attaining both military and civil goals.

War Department orders late in 1848 named Brevet Major General Persifor F. Smith, colonel of the Regiment of Mounted Riflemen, to head the newly constituted Third or Pacific Division of the Army. Embracing California and Oregon as well as what is now Idaho and Nevada, the Pacific Division was subdivided by the northern boundary of California into the

10th and 11th Departments. The courtly and sociable old general, veteran of the Seminole War and a hero of Contreras, sailed from New York and reached San Francisco in February 1849.[9]

General Smith stepped from the boat to find the Pacific Coast racked by the turmoil of the gold rush and grappling, in addition to consequent political, economic, and social ills, with an Indian problem created by the explosion of miners into inland valleys and canyons hitherto known only to Indians and a scattering of white mountain men. The feverish quest for gold, littering the western slopes of the Sierra with mining camps from the Feather River on the north to the Merced River on the south, shattered the placid existence of the hunters and fishermen who claimed these mountains. Some were ruthlessly dispossessed or exterminated before they could even think of resistance. Others fought back.

Not yet the scene of spectacular gold discoveries, Oregon nevertheless felt shock waves from the California strikes. Abandoning their homes on the Willamette and Columbia, Oregon settlers streamed southward to California and converted old pack trails into well-traveled pathways. Traffic over the Calapooya and Siskiyou Mountains gave way to settlement as gold was discovered here early in 1850. Mining camps blossomed among the forested heights drained by the Rogue and Umpqua Rivers of southern Oregon and the Klamath and Trinity of northern California. Unrest spread among the Rogue, Shasta, and related peoples of this region. Farther north, although surrounded by relatively weak and inoffensive Indians, Oregon settlers who stayed at their hearths in the lower Willamette Valley felt as much menaced as their California neighbors. They carried fresh memories of the brutal Whitman Massacre, which had occurred in the Walla Walla Valley east of the Cascades in 1847. The Cayuse murderers of the zealous Presbyterian missionary and his wife and associates remained at large despite a campaign by Oregon Volunteers in 1848. With so many men gone to the mines, Oregonians looked anxiously

---

[9] Smith brought with him his wife and a retinue of servants, all but one of whom promptly deserted to the gold fields. The faithfulness of his Negro servant Isaac so impressed Smith that he was wont to doff his hat to any Negro met on the streets, explaining that the Negroes were the only gentlemen in California. *Memoirs of William T. Sherman* (Civil War Centennial ed., Bloomington, Ind., 1957), pp. 63, 66.

to the federal government not only to exact retribution east of the Cascades but also to prevent a repetition of the tragedy west of these mountains.

The Pacific Division could not cope with the large demands on it. Like other major commands, it suffered a crippling shortage of troops. For California, the War Department let General Smith have the 2d Infantry, which arrived by ship in April and July 1849. With units of the 1st Dragoons and 3d Artillery, this gave him fifteen companies for the 10th Department. The lieutenant colonel of the 2d Infantry, rough-hewn Bennet Riley, took command of the 10th Department in his brevet grade of brigadier general.[10]

For the 11th Department, Oregon, only a token force could be spared. In the spring of 1849, after a six-month sea voyage from New York by way of Hawaii, Brevet Major John S. Hatheway disembarked two companies of the 1st Artillery on the lower Columbia River. One company settled in shabby log quarters, christened Columbia Barracks, erected at the Hudson's Bay Company post of Fort Vancouver, on the Columbia River; the other, in August, went to Puget Sound and founded Fort Steilacoom. Hatheway marked time until autumn. In October the new department commander, Lieutenant Colonel William W. Loring, reached the Columbia River after leading the Regiment of Mounted Riflemen on its historic march from Fort Leavenworth (see chapter 4). The one-armed colonel had with him but four companies of the regiment; the rest garrisoned the Oregon Trail at Forts Kearny and Laramie and at Cantonment Loring near old Fort Hall. With the rainy season closing in and the artillery crowding Columbia Barracks, Loring crossed the river to Oregon City and rented the homes of citizens who had rushed off to the California mines.[11]

From 1849 until 1853 the Pacific Division rarely counted a thousand officers and men, and in one year, 1851, the number fell to less than six hundred.[12] Enormously aggravating the

[10] SW, *Annual Report* (1849), pp. 185, 188E. A former shoemaker, Riley had risen from the ranks. The story is told that, shortly after receiving general officer brevet, he was approached by a man who offered to obtain a coat-of-arms for him. Riley responded: "Clear out; because, sir, I never had a coat of any kind until I was twenty-one years old." Maury, *Recollections of a Virginian*, p. 43.

[11] SW, *Annual Report* (1850), pp. 284–88. Clark "Military History of Oregon," pp. 22–24. Brigadier General T. M. Anderson, "Vancouver Barracks—Past and Present," *Journal of the Military Service Institution of the United States*, 35 (1904), 269–70.

[12] SW, *Annual Report* (1851), pp. 209–11; (1853), pp. 122–23.

sparsity of assigned units was a soaring desertion rate. The lure of the mines made it impossible to keep the companies at more than skeleton strength; indeed, they were laden with men who had enlisted with the intention of deserting as soon as the government transported them to the gold fields. Captain Erasmus D. Keyes had a typical experience. Assigned a company of 86 newly arrived men at San Francisco, he lost two-thirds by desertion within a few weeks. One night the whole guard, including the corporal, stole away. Keyes sent an officer in pursuit. "He overtook them some fifteen miles on the road to San José, shot a couple, but brought back only one wounded soldier, as all his escort joined the deserters."[13] Aware of this danger, Lieutenant William T. Sherman, aided only by six officers, pursued another group of deserters and captured 24.[14] A special casualty return for the 10th Department covering eighteen months, July 1848 to January 1850, tersely noted: total deaths, 60; total desertions, 716.[15] By autumn 1849 General Riley could find only 539 officers and men present for duty in California.[16]

In Oregon Colonel Loring experienced similar trials. In February 1850, 120 Mounted Riflemen, half the force at Oregon City, deserted in a body and made for the mines. Loring was absent on Puget Sound and the less resolute Captain Charles F. Ruff made a show of pursuing. Learning of the defection by express, Loring hastened back to the Columbia and organized another expedition. Through snow-choked canyons and over frozen mountains judged by experienced trappers to be impassable in winter, Loring kept up the chase. Perseverance won out, and after a march of nearly a thousand miles he returned to Oregon City with all but thirty-five fugitives. Of those who escaped, a few reached the mines, but most froze to death. Loring's achievement, declared General Smith, demonstrated that "the shot which, at the garita of Belen, took off a limb, in nowise diminished his spirit or even his strength."[17]

Besides keeping units undermanned, desertion complicated

[13] Keyes, *Fifty Years Observation of Men and Events*, p. 228.

[14] Sherman, *Memoirs*, pp. 71–72. Five of the seven became Civil War generals: Sherman, Nelson H. Davis, E. R. S. Canby, Alfred Gibbs, and Alfred Sully.

[15] April 19, 1850, R119/1850, RG 94, NARS.

[16] SW, *Annual Report* (1849), p. 188E.

[17] Loring to McDowell, March 6, 1850, L89/1850. Smith to McDowell, May 25, 1850, S363/1850. Both in RG 94, NARS. Clark, "Military History of Oregon," p. 23.

in another way the task of preventing trouble between Indians and whites. The danger spots were usually where the diggings at the moment held most promise, and these were the very places that troops could not be sent without inviting them to shed the blue and disappear into the hills. For this reason alone, General Smith made his familiarization tour of the mining region in 1849 without the protection of an escort. General Riley thought the difficulty might be overcome by concentrating the troops in the mining districts and furloughing them a contingent at a time to try their hand at prospecting. "The mania for gold hunting," he reasoned, "would exist in its most exaggerated form at points the most remote from the placers, for experience in the hardships of gold digging speedily dispels many of its illusions." But desertion kept the units so depleted that he never had enough men to test this thesis.[18]

In both departments the mining boom confounded commanders with staggering logistical problems. Soaring prices made quartermaster allowances, meager at best, wholly inadequate for the subsistence and supply of troops. Rations, forage, stock, fuel, building material, civilian labor, transportation—everything, indeed, on which an army depends for its existence —commanded an exorbitant outlay when obtainable at all. "Everything," declared General Smith, "from the price of a broom to the building of a ship, costs at least *ten* times what it does in the Atlantic States." And this, he added, was a "moderate computation." Harried by a quartermaster general under congressional mandate to hold down military costs, commanders on the Pacific repeatedly discovered their plans circumscribed, delayed, or altogether canceled by logistical factors.[19] The same economic forces worked severe hardship on officers and men whose pay and allowances fell far short of meeting the inflated prices of even the most essential personal wants —a condition eased but little when Congress authorized a slight increase in pay for service in California and Oregon.[20]

California won statehood as part of the Compromise of 1850,

[18] SW, *Annual Report* (1849), pp. 160–61, 173–77.
[19] *Ibid.* (1850), pp. 111–12, 245–90. Smith to Freeman, Oct. 29, 1850, S633/1850, RG 94, NARS.
[20] For officers an additional $2 a day, for enlisted men an amount equal to ordinary pay to be held until honorable discharge. 9 Stat. 508 (Sept. 28, 1850).

and the Army was relieved of the heavy burden of military government it had borne since 1847. But for General Smith and his successors statehood was not an unmixed blessing, for it resulted in a civil government that expressed popular attitudes even more savagely hostile to the Indian than in New Mexico. In the mining camps the dominant sentiment favored extermination of all Indians who failed to get out of the way fast enough, and the origins of nearly every Indian disturbance could be traced clearly to undisguised white aggression. Elsewhere an Indian war could usually be defended with real or imaginary justifications, and it was ordinarily conducted with some concession to humanitarian considerations. In California and Oregon rationalizations were rarely contrived; the Indians were simply annihilated.[21] The civilian attitudes thrust on the Army a hard dilemma. Either the troops fought Indians with whom they sympathized or in protecting them incurred the wrath of outraged citizens.[22]

As a consequence of the Army's reluctance to abet schemes of extermination, the citizens took matters into their own hands. Volunteer companies sprang up in any mining camp with an Indian problem and quickly exhibited to the Army how a war of extermination ought to be conducted. But the Volunteers naturally wanted compensation for doing what they believed the soldiers should be doing. The Regulars, Governor John McDougal informed President Fillmore in March 1851, were not only too few to protect Californians from the savages, but also unfit for "desultory mountain warfare." The whole trouble could be quickly resolved if the governor had discretionary authority

[21] General E. A. Hitchcock, Smith's successor, recorded in his diary on July 31, 1852, that he had called on a Methodist clergyman in San Francisco "who had the audacity to say that Providence designed the extermination of the Indians and that it would be a good thing to introduce the small-pox among them!" *Fifty Years in Camp and Field: The Diary of Major General Ethan Allen Hitchcock*, W. A. Croffut, ed. (New York, 1909), p. 395. In later years General George Crook, a lieutenant in northern California in the 1850s, recalled: "It was of no unfrequent occurrence for an Indian to be shot down in cold blood, or a squaw to be raped by some brute. Such a thing as a white man being punished for outraging an Indian was unheard of. It was the fable of the wolf and the lamb every time." Crook, *Autobiography*, p. 16.

[22] General Hitchcock noted in 1852: "The whites go in upon Indian lands, provoke the Indians, bring on collisions, and then call for protection, and complain if it is not furnished, while the practical effect of the presence of troops can be little else than to countenance and give security to them in their aggressions; the Indian, meanwhile, looking upon the military as their friends, and imploring their protection." SW, *Annual Report* (1852), p. 30.

to muster Volunteers into state service and call on the federal government for their pay and arms. But as General Smith wrily noted, the governor planned to pay the privates of his militia army more than any regular officer in the division except the commanding general. Secretary of War Conrad properly replied that the President had neither authority nor inclination to aid the governor in this way, especially to meet difficulties produced by the aggressions of lawless white men.[23] But as in Texas, the dispute tormented military authorities throughout the decade, and California was indeed eventually reimbursed almost a million dollars for expenses "in suppressing Indian hostilities."[24]

General Smith early faced the necessity of reorienting the military system on the Pacific to the new conditions created by the gold rush. Upon reaching California, he found the troops positioned at the Presidio of San Francisco, Sonoma, and Monterey—stations chosen before the gold rush converted the Army's mission from occupation of a conquered province to protection of a population moving into Indian country. The general extended this pattern to the south in April 1849 by establishing a garrison at San Diego. In the same month he founded the division quartermaster depot at Benicia.[25]

A proponent of roving columns, Smith resisted General Riley's proposals to station troops in the interior, where they could police the miners and Indians. "Small scattered posts," he declared, "are the graves of activity and enterprise." Nevertheless, in the summer of 1849 he advanced detachments into the Central Valley to erect two posts, one near Stockton and the other near Sutter's Fort. Both proved short lived.[26] Of greater permanence were Fort Yuma, planted in January 1850 on the Colorado River at the mouth of the Gila to meet threatened trouble with the Yuma Indians (see chapter 8), and Fort Miller, erected in the Sierra foothills at the head of the San Joaquin in May 1851 to control Indians aggravated to violence by an influx of prospectors.[27] In the 11th Department Smith author-

23 Ibid., (1851), pp. 37–42.
24 10 Stat. 582–83 (Aug. 5, 1854).
25 SW, Annual Report (1849), pp. 185, 188E. Francis Paul Prucha, Guide to the Military Posts of the United States (Madison, 1964), pp. 60, 92, 106, 108, 150.
26 SW, Annual Report (1849), pp. 159–60.
27 Prucha, Guide to the Military Posts, p. 91.

ized a post at The Dalles of the Columbia, where the Oregon Trail touched the river. In May 1850 Colonel Loring called in the Rifle companies that had wintered on Snake River and placed three at The Dalles to establish Camp Drum, later named Fort Dalles.[28] This post, Fort Steilacoom, and Columbia Barracks, which took the name of Fort Vancouver in 1853, formed the rudiments of the Oregon defense system.

Like Texas and New Mexico, the Pacific Division came under the scrutiny of President Fillmore's Secretary of War, Charles M. Conrad, early in 1851, and as part of the shakeup in the high command that resulted Smith gave way to a successor. Polite, cheerful, of beardless and benign countenance, Brevet Brigadier General Ethan Allen Hitchcock, colonel of the 2d Infantry, possessed a solid military reputation and undoubtedly the finest intellect in the Army—one, however, so obsessed with metaphysical speculations that philosophy had become his vocation, military science his avocation.[29] Much of each day he devoted to studying the writings of the great thinkers of history and filling volume after volume of his diary with endless reflections on the nature of man and the universe. That he ably discharged his military duties as well testifies to uncommon attainments. Hitchcock's orders, like those reassigning Smith to Texas and Sumner to New Mexico, required a reorganization of Pacific defenses aimed at getting the troops into the Indian country and cutting down the cost of their maintenance.[30]

No more than Smith and Sumner did Hitchcock reduce expenses, but he did shift most of the troops from the coast to the interior. Oregon claimed his attention first, for the thin defenses sketched there by Smith had all but vanished. The Rifle Regiment got off to a bad start with the citizens as commanders lined out military reservations that swallowed the land claims of settlers, officers "held high carnival with the Hudson Bay people and a roistering frontier set at Oregon City," and

28 *Ibid.*, p. 113, SW, *Annual Report* (1850), p. 116E. Cantonment Loring, near old Fort Hall in what is now Idaho, had proved unsuitable as a military location; it was difficult to supply, there was no natural forage in the winter, and the Indians did not need watching anyway. Hatch to Porter, Oct. 3, 1849, encl. to Loring to Freeman, April 28, 1850, L106/1850. Porter to Jones, Jan. 22, 1850, P126/1850. Both in RG 94, NARS.

29 See assessment of editor W. A. Croffut in *Fifty Years in Camp and Field*, p. 188.

30 SW, *Annual Report* (1851), pp. 42-43.

enlisted men "became an absolute terror to the pious people of the Willamette Valley."[31] The citizens clamored for the removal of the regiment, and in Congress Oregon's Delegate Samuel Thurston contended that the citizens, if armed by the government, could defend themselves. The War Department lost no time complying. In 1851 the regiment was broken up, to be reconstituted in Texas, and the privates used to bolster the desertion-riddled ranks of the 1st Dragoons in California.[32]

No sooner had the regiment been withdrawn than the Indians rose against the growing population of miners and farmers in southern Oregon. In June 1851, en route to California, Brevet Major Philip Kearny and two companies of the 1st Dragoons, recently formed from the Rifle Regiment, paused to aid the beleagured settlers. Near the looming landmark of Table Rock, on Rogue River near present Medford, they won two quick victories, and "the people made up their minds that frolicking soldiers were preferable to murdering red devils."[33] Governor John P. Gaines called for a return of the Regulars, and former Governor and Delegate Joseph Lane put the matter succinctly: "Our people will go to the mines and they must have protection."[34] General Hitchcock came up in August, looked over the situation, read Spinoza, and paid seventy-five cents for a haircut in Portland.[35] The result was Fort Orford, established on the coast in September by Lieutenant August V. Kautz. Lieutenant Colonel Silas Casey and a mixed force scraped together in California arrived in October, dealt a damaging blow to the nearby Coquille Indians, and sailed back to their stations in the south.[36]

The troubles in southern Oregon were but part of a larger problem with the myriad similar groups of Indians who peopled the gold-rich mountains on both sides of the California-

[31] Anderson, "Vancouver Barracks," p. 271.

[32] Clark, "Military History of Oregon," pp. 23–24.

[33] Anderson, "Vancouver Barracks," pp. 272–73. Hoopes, *Indian Affairs*, pp. 89–90, gives an account of Kearny's operations. See also Ray H. Glassley, *Pacific Northwest Indian Wars* (Portland, Ore., 1953), pp. 54–55.

[34] SW, *Annual Report* (1851), pp. 144–45. In February 1852 Lane touched off a debate in the House of Representatives by introducing a resolution requesting the President to send the Rifle Regiment back to Oregon. Only after long and acrimonious debate and a promise of the Secretary of War to assign mounted troops to Oregon did he consent to table the motion. *Cong. Globe*, 32d Cong., 1st sess., pp. 507–10, 517–23 (Feb. 9–10, 1852).

[35] Hitchcock, *Fifty Years in Camp and Field*, p. 387.

[36] Prucha, *Guide to the Military Posts*, p. 96. SW, *Annual Report* (1851), pp. 148–49. Glassley, *Pacific Northwest Indian Wars*, pp. 56–60.

Oregon boundary. The mining boom here created a situation in which Indians and whites needed nearly constant protection from each other. In the next two years General Hitchcock established a network of forts in this region. Fort Orford turned out to be misplaced—the Coast Range cut off access to the scene of conflict—and Fort Lane was established in Rogue River Valley near Jacksonville in the autumn of 1853. To the south, in California, Fort Reading was erected at the head of the Sacramento River in May 1852 and Fort Jones in Scott's Valley six months later. Fort Humboldt, founded in January 1853, guarded the California coast.[37]

Such was the basic framework of the defense system of the Pacific Division—renamed the Department of the Pacific in 1853, when the 10th and 11th Departments were dissolved. Ad ditions to the system came as consequences of the hostilities that flared later in the decade. Brevet Major General John E. Wool, Hitchcock's successor, authorized construction of seven new forts in Oregon and newly created Washington Territory —Fort Cascades in 1855 as a defense for the Cascades of the Columbia in the Yakima War; Forts Bellingham and Townsend in 1856 to watch over Indians pacified by the campaigns of the Yakima War; and Forts Hoskins, Umpqua, and Yamhill in 1856 to guard reservations created after the Rogue River War. In California Wool founded Fort Tejon in 1854 adjacent to the Tejon Indian Reservation, and General Newman Clarke filled in the northern California defenses in 1857 with Forts Bragg and Crook. In northeastern Washington General Harney built Fort Colville in 1859 to guard the Colville mines against the Indians subjugated in the Spokane War of 1858.[38]

While the Army laid out a defense system, the Bureau of Indian Affairs erected its own apparatus and initiated civil relations with the Indians of the Pacific. In California the military government appointed civilian Indian agents as early as 1847, but not until 1852 did Congress authorize a Superintendent of Indian Affairs, the able Edward Fitzgerald Beale. In Oregon the first territorial governor, Joseph Lane, held the concurrent position of Superintendent of Indian Affairs until an act of Congress in 1850 provided for a separate superinten-

37 Prucha, *Guide to the Military Posts*, pp. 82, 84, 101, 191.
38 *Ibid.*, pp. 60, 62, 65, 67, 69, 108, 111, 113, 114, 118.

dent and three agents. Anson Dart drew the first appointment
to head the Oregon superintendency.

The principal and most urgent mission of the civilian officials was to clear the natives from the areas coveted or already
possessed by the immigrants streaming into California and
Oregon. Not only the mineral districts were involved. In the
early 1850s the mining fever began to abate and disillusioned
prospectors turned to farming. Agricultural settlements stabil-
ized and gave permanence to the mining camps, they took root
in increasing numbers in the great Central Valley of California, they overspread much of Oregon's Willamette and lower
Columbia Valleys, and they fingered northward toward the expanding population center on Puget Sound. In Oregon the task
of the Indian Bureau was rendered the more urgent by the
Oregon Donation Land Law of 1850, which stimulated agricultural growth by providing free land to homesteaders—without regard to Indian title.

To make way for both miners and farmers as quickly as
possible, Congress in 1850 authorized the appointment of two
three-man commissions to negotiate treaties of territorial cession with the Indians of the Pacific. In Oregon the object was
to move all the Indians west of the Cascades to new homes east
of the mountains, in California to move all those in the Sierra
to reservations in the Central Valley. Between them, the two
temporary commissions and the regular appointees concluded
a total of twenty-seven treaties in 1851. Providing for the cession of most of California and Oregon, they also promised
rations and other annuities in return. Not one was ratified. Californians objected to setting aside good agricultural land for
Indians, and Congress objected to the cost of feeding Indians
even when deprived of their customary means of subsistence.

Later in the decade Congress consented to a series of treaties that placed relations with the Oregon Indians on a formal
footing. These people steadfastly declined to move east of the
Cascades; they loved their homeland, needed its economic resources, and feared the warlike tribes beyond the mountains.
A few reservations were staked out in the Coast Range bordering the Willamette Valley, and on them most of the Indians east of the Cascades were ultimately colonized. For the
Rogue River people, however, it took a military conquest to
bring about the removal. No formally ratified treaties sancti-

fied the eviction of the California natives, but Superintendent Beale finally gained grudging acceptance of a reservation system. He and his successor, Thomas J. Henly, established five small reservations in the coastal ranges and the Central Valley and settled some of the refugee groups, but a commentary on their success is Kroeber's remark that "the Indians kept running away even faster than they could die."[39]

[39] *Handbook of California Indians*, p. 890. A thorough study of Indian affairs in California and Oregon for this period is Hoopes, *Indian Affairs and their Administration*. See also William H. Ellison, "The Federal Indian Policy in California, 1846–1860," *Mississippi Valley Historical Review 9*, (1922), 37–67. The annual reports of the CIA, 1848–60, are also unusually full for the Oregon and California superintendercies.

Rise of the Plains Indian Barrier, 1854-61

As the midpoint of the 1850s neared, the 7,760 officers and soldiers of the frontier army could look back on a half-dozen years of intense activity and considerable accomplishment. They had advanced the thin line of eight forts that in 1848 picketed the eastern edge of the Great Plains all the way to the Pacific and transformed it into a network of fifty-two forts that covered half a continent. It was a thin covering, to be sure, but the flag that floated over each post brought the appearance and in places the substance of U.S. authority to an empire that a short decade earlier had owed allegiance to four separate flags.

Charged primarily with protecting their countrymen from hostile Indians, the blueclad frontiersmen conferred other benefits of large importance on the burgeoning western population. They provided a market for local goods and services and more often than not the indispensable foundation of the civilian economy. They explored and mapped great sweeps of imperfectly known mountain, plain, and desert and thus helped stimulate further immigration as well as federal programs for improving transportation and communication. They built new and improved old roads that bore civilian as well as military traffic.

But in discharging its primary mission, the frontier army had made a disappointing beginning toward bringing security of life and property from Indian aggression to the settled and traveled parts of the West. The fifty-two forts of 1854 brought a large measure of security to a small radius around each and

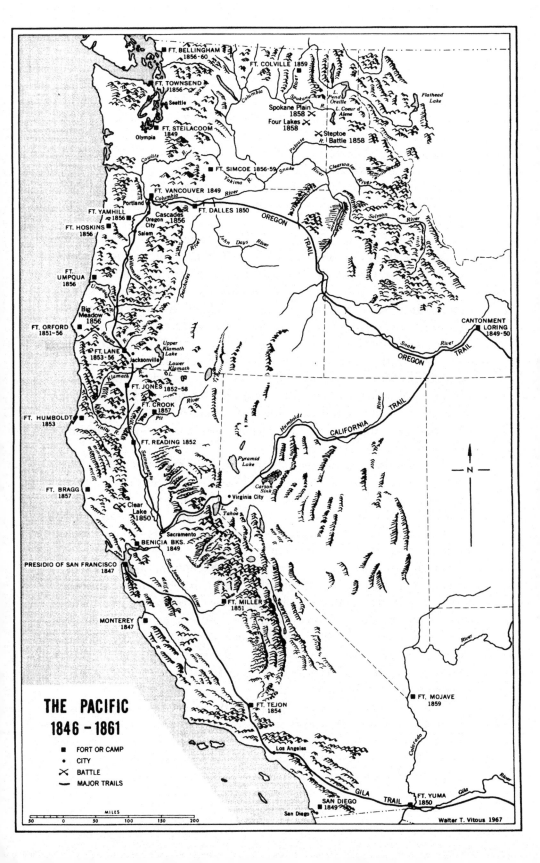

THE PACIFIC
1846 – 1861

■ FORT OR CAMP
● CITY
✕ BATTLE
— MAJOR TRAILS

MILES
50 0 50 100 150 200

Walter T. Vitous 1967

a small and ephemeral security to the very large territory
beyond. For such security as they enjoyed, however, most westerners had to rely mainly on their own arms, on luck, and on
the ever changing and uncertain temper of the Indians. With
a kernel of justice they could blame the Army for lethargy or
stupidity, and with considerably more justice the Army could
point to fiscal policies that severely circumscribed the militarily possible. Yet there was another, less easily recognized di-
mension to the problem.

The soldier who marched west to conquer the Indians and
make the frontiers safe for settlement and exploitation discovered that he could not function as a conquerer at all. A conquerer must have a definable enemy to conquer, and rarely
could any tribe or band be clearly defined as the enemy. On
the contrary, during the 1850s most tribes entered treaty arrangements with the federal government that explicitly defined them
as friend rather than foe. Constant Indian aggressions in Texas
and New Mexico and sporadic hostilities elsewhere belied the
formal definition, but as they were usually the work of warrior
groups acting without the sanction (though not always without the tacit approval) of tribal authority they provided insuffi-
cient excuse for a redefinition.

The would-be conquerer found himself cast instead in the
role of policeman, patrolling his sector in an effort to detect
the presence of "criminals" and giving chase when "crime" had
been committed, assailed by westerners for not treating all
Indians as criminals and by easterners and agents of the Indian
Bureau for inflicting punishment without clear evidence of
criminal guilt. With an occasional exception, however, the
Army embraced this essentially defensive strategy for the
first few years of its western experience—patrolling, scouting,
escorting, pursuing, and always the endless work of building
and maintaining the little forts that multiplied across the face
of the West. Even the few clearly offensive operations of these
years could usually be placed in a defensive context of specific
response to specific provocation.

It was dismal, frustrating duty. Boredom, low pay, coarse
food and shabby quarters, harsh discipline and cruel punishment, constant labor of an unmilitary character, field service
marked by heat and cold, rain and snow, mud and dust, hunger and thirst, deadening fatigue—these were to be expected.

But they were unaccompanied by the prospect of meaningful combat and the opportunity for distinction that ordinarily make the terms of military life more endurable. Against an adversary "everywhere and yet nowhere," recognizable as such only on those rare occasions when caught in an act of aggression or in possession of evidence of aggression, the frontier policemen had proved disappointing in their effectiveness. By the middle 1850s, however, with the basic defense systems of the West defined and laid out, they began to think and act like soldiers as well as like policemen.

Deeply frustrated by the futility of trying to secure half a continent against a shadow enemy, commanders began to take an increasingly harder view of the opponent. If a tribe or band could not keep its members from raiding white people, ran the argument, then the whole group should be held responsible and punished accordingly. Although the theory ignored the realities of Indian social and political organization, it was quite consistent with the established constitutional principle that tribes were "domestic dependent nations" and with the practice of negotiating treaties with tribal leaders erroneously assumed to possess all the authority of a European monarch.

For the Army the theory had definite advantages. It enabled commanders to define and recognize an enemy, to wage something resembling war on him, and even on rare occasions to engage in a conflict that might be called a battle. It offered the prospect of functioning as conquerer after all, for it raised the hope that severe enough punishment of the group, even though the innocent suffered along with the guilty, might indeed produce true group responsibility and end the menace to the frontiers.

Not that the troops ceased to be mainly policemen or that the conditions of frontier military service changed fundamentally. The same monotony of garrison life and fatigue labor relieved at long intervals by profitless patrols and pursuits still characterized duty at the isolated forts. But now in the late 1850s there were more and larger offensive operations, directed at tribes or bands instead of a handful of raiders, and even on occasion leading to a confrontation that might be called a "war."

Now, if Yakima warriors protested the invasion of their homeland by killing some gold-seekers, the Army would react against the whole tribe and its allies as well. If Apaches driven by hunger and the plundering forays of New Mexicans stole sheep and killed settlers who got in their way, the Army would sweep their ranges and attack any ranchería that could be found. If Kiowa and Comanche warriors persisted in raiding the Texas frontier, the Army would seek out and destroy the villages from which they came. And if a green lieutenant got himself and his men killed trying to bully an entire Sioux band for harboring a warrior who had butchered an emigrant's straying cow, the Army would crush the band and intimidate the whole Sioux confederacy.

The chain of events set off by the emigrant's cow revealed a pattern emerging all over the West. On the Great Plains, it was the first stirring in the rise of a Plains Indian barrier to westward expansion that would take nearly forty years to destroy.

In marked contrast to their attitude toward Texans, the Kiowas and Comanches gave little offense to the whites along the Arkansas River before the middle 1850s. Their Sioux and Cheyenne neighbors to the north displayed similar restraint. With the Indians quiet and the cost of supporting cavalry beyond the frontier drawing increasing fire from congressmen, all the mounted force had been withdrawn from the Plains by 1851. Even the Rifle Regiment, authorized and created specifically for Oregon Trail service, had gone to Texas. There were proposals, motivated by economy, to abandon Forts Kearny, Laramie, and Atkinson altogether.[1] These went unheeded, but after 1851 only one company of the 6th Infantry held each of the posts.

Agent Thomas Fitzpatrick perceived the situation with a clarity born of thirty years' intimate experience with the red men. In Fort Atkinson he saw "a small insignificant military station, beneath the dignity of the United States, and at the mercy and forebearance of the Indians." Fort Laramie prompted a similar judgment. "There is not a single day that passes in which the Indians could not, if disposed to do so, strip and deprive these posts of all their resources, murder the different fatigue parties in detail, and drive off all the horses and stock

[1] Cf. General Scott in SW, *Annual Report* (1851), pp. 161–62, who based his proposal on economy grounds; and General Twiggs, whose remarks in April 1849 preceded the establishment of Fort Laramie as a military post, in Merrill J. Mattes, *Fort Laramie and the Forty-Niners* (Estes Park, Colo., 1949), p. 12.

belonging to the post." Laramie and Atkinson, he asserted, should be installations "such as are to be respected and feared" —vital ingredients, the old mountain man knew, in any confrontation with the Indians—and each should boast a garrison of three hundred men.[2] But such was impossible until Congress voted more cavalry.

The junior officers of the 6th Infantry at Fort Laramie did not let the Tetons wait for Congress. Each summer, in anticipation of the annual annuity issue, the Brule, Oglala, and Miniconjou Sioux tribes gathered near the fort in numbers that included at least a thousand fighting men. Far from adopting the prudence that such a force suggested, the officers at Laramie conceived it their duty to assert the authority of the United States whenever opportunity offered.

A portent occurred in June 1853, as the tribes began to gather on the Platte for the annual issue. A Miniconjou warrior, who may or may not have had good reason, took a shot at the soldier-operator of a skiff used as a ferry across the Platte. The post commander, First Lieutenant Richard B. Garnett, sent Second Lieutenant Hugh Fleming with twenty-three men to arrest the offender—always a dangerous undertaking even for experts. Fleming marched resolutely into the Sioux village. Firing broke out, six Indians dropped, and the lieutenant retired without his prisoner. By great exertion the chiefs kept their people from massive retaliation, but by September, when Fitzpatrick arrived to hand out the annuities, they were still in an ugly mood. The fort, they told the agent, had been placed on the Platte for their protection—so apparently someone had informed them—"but now the soldiers of the Great Father are the first to make the ground bloody." The Indians demanded the removal of the fort. Fitzpatrick calmed them, but in less than a year the ground was to be still bloodier.[3]

By the next summer, 1854, Garnett had gone and Lieutenant Fleming, two years out of West Point, commanded. His subordinate, John L. Grattan, West Point 1853 and still a brevet second lieutenant awaiting a regimental vacancy, eagerly looked for an occasion to teach the Sioux how U.S. sol-

[2] SI, *Annual Report* (1851), pp. 33, 335–36.
[3] CIA, *Annual Report* (1853), p. 367. LeRoy R. Hafen and W. J. Ghent, *Broken Hand: The Life Story of Thomas Fitzpatrick, Chief of the Mountain Men* (Denver, Colo., 1931), p. 257. Hyde, *Red Cloud's Folk*, pp. 70-71, and *Spotted Tail's Folk*, p. 48. Bandel, *Frontier Life in the Army*, p. 24.

diers fought. He could crush the whole lot of them, he boasted, with a handful of infantry and a howitzer. When a Mormon emigrant came to the fort on August 18 to report that an Indian from one of the camps down the Platte had butchered a straying cow, Grattan saw his opportunity and pressed Fleming for permission to arrest the Indian, a young Miniconjou living in the Brule camp. Conquering Bear, head chief of the Brules by U.S. appointment, urged Fleming to defer action until the agent arrived with the annuities, when restitution could be made as provided by the Treaty of 1851. But Grattan was not to be denied, and he persuaded an indecisive Fleming to authorize the expedition.

The next day, with twenty-seven privates, two noncommissioned officers, and an Indian-hating French interpreter, Grattan marched boldly into Conquering Bear's camp and trained a 12-pounder howitzer and a 12-pounder mountain gun on the tepees. A forty-five minute parley with the chief failed to produce the culprit, who sulked in the entrance to his lodge and declared his wish to die honorably. Grattan lost patience and ordered his men to fire. Conquering Bear fell, mortally wounded. Grattan signaled the artillery to open, but the pieces were set too high and the canister charges harmlessly shredded the tepee tops. There was not time to wonder at the enemy's failure to flee in panic. Sioux swarmed over the handful of infantry and scattered them in disorganized rout. Joined by the Oglalas, the Brules raced about the valley shooting down the fleeing soldiers. A lone survivor ultimately reached the fort, but he died several days later.[4]

The enraged Indians pillaged the warehouses of P. Chouteau and Company, talked for a time of wiping out the feeble garrison of Fort Laramie, then withdrew northward from the Platte to await developments. Two companies of infantry marched up from Fort Riley to strengthen Laramie, and a mature officer, Major William Hoffman, assumed command from Fleming.

Shock and outrage swept the Nation, but it did not produce a unanimous demand for revenge. Reports from the upper Platte disclosed that the officers at Laramie had blundered. The Indian Bureau promptly embraced this view, and opponents of the bill

[4] Lloyd E. McCann, "The Grattan Massacre," *Nebraska History*, 37 (1956), 1–26, is a careful reconstruction based on all evidence, but see also Hyde, *Spotted Tail's Folk*, pp. 48–53, for a graphic account.

to increase the Army made much of it on the floors of the Senate and the House.[5] But Secretary of War Davis expressed the military position when he labeled the Grattan disaster "the result of a deliberately formed plan" to plunder the trade and annuity stores.[6] This was not true, but the conclusion to which it pointed was nevertheless sound. The young Sioux warriors had wiped out Grattan's command with surprising ease, and now they turned to the rich possibilities for further plunder offered by the emigrant road. Petty thefts, mostly of horses, occurred throughout the winter. In November a small Brule war party waylaid the Salt Lake stage, killed three men and wounded a fourth, and made off with a strongbox containing $10,000 in gold. Security of the Platte demanded retaliation for the loss of Grattan if such raids were not to multiply.

To direct operations against the Sioux, Secretary Davis summoned Colonel William S. Harney home from Paris, where he was enjoying leave of absence, and assigned him to the command in his brevet rank of brigadier general. A big, powerful man with personality and convictions to match, Harney went at any task with an inflexible dedication undiluted by hesitation or self-doubt. Reaching St. Louis in April 1855, he set about concentrating a command at Fort Kearny. When finally organized in July, it numbered about six hundred men —portions of the 2d Dragoons (Harney's own regiment), the 6th and 10th Infantry, and the 4th Artillery. Major Albemarle Cady led the foot soldiers, and the horsemen rode behind the Army's foremost cavalry expert, Lieutenant Colonel Philip St. George Cooke. In the Black Hawk and Seminole Wars Harney had decided that one deals with Indians by whipping them soundly before consenting to any peace talk, and as he rode forth from Fort Kearny at the head of his column on August 24 he declared, "By God, I'm for battle—no peace."[7]

The Indian Bureau was trying desperately for peace. The new agent, Thomas S. Twiss, sent runners into the Sioux country to summon all who wished to be considered friendly

---

[5] CIA, *Annual Report* (1854), pp. 16–17. The Grattan affair, said Representative Thomas Hart Benton, was "a heavy penalty for a nation to pay for a lame runaway Mormon cow, and for the folly and juvenile ambition of a West Point fledgling." *Cong. Globe*, 33d Cong., 2d sess. (Appendix), p. 339 (Feb. 27, 1855).

[6] SW, *Annual Report* (1854), p. 5.

[7] Quoted in Bandel, *Frontier Life in the Army*, p. 31.

to camp near the fort. Those who remained north of the Platte would be treated as hostile. About half the Sioux who had been on the Platte in past summers came in, making a sprawling camp of about four hundred lodges but the Brules and Miniconjous, those who had been implicated in the Grattan affair, stayed north of the deadline. One group, headed by Little Thunder, successor to the dead Conquering Bear, resided on Blue Water Creek practically within sight of the emigrant road at Ash Hollow. Little Thunder regarded himself as peaceful, but in his village were the young men responsible for the winter's depredations on the Platte road. He had received Twiss's summons but had not heeded it, and he had been warned that soldiers were coming up the Platte.[8]

Harney knew Little Thunder's position several days before reaching Ash Hollow. His skilled guide, Joe Tesson, assured him that the Brules were hostile, and reports from travelers met along the way confirmed that the Indians had been menacing the road. As the troops descended into Ash Hollow on the evening of September 2, they could see the Indian village across the river in the distance. Little Thunder knew of Harney's proximity, too, for the old fur trapper Louis Vasquez brought in a message from the chief stating that Harney could have peace or war, whichever he wished.[9]

A night march on September 2–3 placed Cooke with his two companies of dragoons and two of mounted infantrymen on Blue Water Creek above the Indian village. Harney and the five foot companies under Major Cady advanced up the creek valley below the village. At daybreak the Brules at last awoke to their peril, struck their lodges, and began to move up the valley—toward Cooke. Little Thunder and his headmen came out under a white flag for a talk. The general wasted no time coming to the point. If Little Thunder were peaceful, as he professed, he could give up the warriors who had caused the trouble. Otherwise, "the day of retribution had come," and if he did not want to get hurt he had better get out of the way. The chief and his party hastened back to their people and the infantry resumed the advance.

8 Hyde, *Spotted Tail's Folk*, pp. 58–59.
9 John B. S. Todd, "The Harney Expedition against the Sioux: The Journal of Capt. John B. S. Todd," Ray H. Mattison, ed., *Nebraska History, 43* (1962), 110–11. Captain Todd commanded Company A, 6th Infantry.

When within range the troops opened fire. The sound carried up the valley and signaled Cooke to charge from above. Caught from two sides, the Indians turned up a ravine opening into the valley from the east. The infantry rushed to the edge of the ravine and poured a murderous volley into the compact mass below, then the cavalry plunged down the opposite slope. Dropping their baggage, the Brules scattered in wild retreat. The cavalry followed, cutting down fleeing fugitives. When Harney's bugler sounded recall, the horsemen were beyond hearing and gave up the chase only after a run of five to eight miles. "There was much slaughter in the pursuit," observed Cooke. Most of the 85 dead and 5 wounded suffered by the Brules fell in this pursuit, and another 70 women and children were made prisoners. Less than half the 250 people in the village escaped. Harney sustained losses of 4 killed, 7 wounded, and 1 missing. Searching the campsite and abandoned baggage, the troops discovered papers stolen from the Salt Lake mail (but not the $10,000, which was never found), the scalps of two white women, and the clothing of some of Grattan's men.[10]

Sending the captives down to Fort Kearny, Harney proceeded to Fort Laramie, where the bands that had declared for peace by moving south of the Platte greeted his arrival apprehensively. He spoke curtly to them, serving notice that the men guilty of waylaying the mail coach would have to be surrendered before he would talk peace. Two weeks later he formed his command and struck off to the northeast. Penetrating the heart of the Sioux country, he flung a challenge at the bands that had scorned the ultimatum to move south of the Platte. They gave him a wide berth. The column skirted the Black Hills and dropped down White River along the edge of the Badlands. Not an Indian showed himself.[11] Harney reached the Missouri River at the old fur trading station of Fort

[10] Harney's official report appears in SW, *Annual Report* (1855), pp. 49-51, and in Rodenbough, *Everglade to Cañon*, pp. 527-28. Cooke's report, printed in response to congressional inquiry, is in Senate Ex. Docs., 34th Cong., 3d sess., No. 58, and in Rodenbough, pp. 181-82. Contemporary accounts appear also in *Missouri Republican* (St. Louis), Oct. 20, 1855, and in *Missouri Gazette* (St. Louis), Oct. 26, 1855. A detailed account is in Todd, "The Harney Expedition," pp. 111-14. See also Richard C. Drum, "Reminiscences of the Indian Fight at Ash Hollow, 1855," *Collections of the Nebraska State Historical Society*, 16 (1911), 143-51. A brief documented synthesis is in Bandel, *Frontier Life in the Army*, pp. 29-36.

[11] The march is covered in Todd, "The Harney Expedition," pp. 116-25.

Pierre on October 20. In preparation for his operations, the government had bought the rundown post from P. Chouteau and Company, and during the summer five companies of the 2d Infantry had come up the Missouri to take possession. The combined forces went into winter quarters while the general continued to intimidate the Tetons.

They stood ready to do exactly as he commanded. The Blue Water catastrophe, fear of what might happen to the women and children held at Kearny, the psychological effect of the invasion of their ranges north of the Platte, and Harney's suspension of the Indian trade combined to make any sacrifice seem worth the price. On October 25, five days after he reached Fort Pierre, Spotted Tail, Red Leaf, and Long Chin, the perpetrators of the mail coach massacre, rode into Fort Laramie to surrender themselves. (They were held at Fort Leavenworth for a year and then released; Spotted Tail returned so impressed by what he had seen that he consistently counseled peace with the white man for the rest of his life.)[12] Moreover, when the chiefs received orders during the winter to report at Fort Pierre for a treaty council on March 1, 1856, they made preparations to obey even though it required a hard winter journey.

All the Teton tribes, even the aloof Hunkpapas, sent representatives to Fort Pierre early in March. For five days they talked, then ended by signing, as the price of peace, a treaty that Harney himself had drafted and cleared with the War Department. Besides promising to refrain from hostilities in the future, the Indians agreed to a system of tribal government designed to centralize authority in chiefs and subchiefs whom Harney appointed and whom the United States would hold accountable for the actions of their people.[13]

In assuming treaty-making powers, Harney invaded the preserve of the Indian Bureau. Agent Twiss recognized this when Harney sent the summons to the chiefs during the winter. The new agent had already become deeply embroiled in profiteering on Indian goods, and he correctly foresaw a threat to his illicit operations if the Army gained control of Indian affairs

---

[12] This experience convinced Spotted Tail that the Indians could not hope to win a war with the whites, and as a prominent war leader and later as chief he threw his influence against war. In 1864–65, however, the decision went against him, and he dutifully took up arms. See below, p. 300. Hyde, *Spotted Tail's Folk*, chronicles his attitude and role in Sioux history.

[13] Council proceedings are in House Ex. Docs., 34th Cong., 1st sess., No. 130.

on the upper Platte. When he began to obstruct Harney's treaty plans, Major Hoffman, commanding at Laramie, assembled some impressive evidence of Twiss's malfeasance and sent it to Harney, who thereupon instructed Hoffman to suspend him. The general possessed no shadow of authority for such an order, but he had the strength to enforce it, and Twiss left for Washington to seek redress. Commissioner of Indian Affairs George W. Manypenny, already upset over the Blue Water attack, was furious at Harney's encroachment on Bureau prerogatives, and he conspired with Twiss to block ratification of the treaty by the simple expedient of demonstrating with inflated figures the cost of carrying it out. Although Harney had whipped the Sioux, he came off second in the contest with the Indian Bureau. The Senate rejected the treaty, and Twiss returned to the upper Platte for another five years.[14]

The formidable command that wintered on the Missouri broke up in the summer of 1856 and scattered to new assignments, Harney packing off to Florida to war once more on his old antagonists the Seminoles. The new post of Fort Randall replaced Fort Pierre as the Army's frontier bastion on the upper Missouri. The old trading post had proved unsatisfactory, and the troops who served there with Harney—four companies of dragoons and ten of infantry—would long remember the miserable winter of 1855–56. "Oh, we don't mind the marching, nor the fighting do we fear," they sang, "but we'll never forgive old Harney for bringing us to Pierre."[15]

Nor would the Teton Sioux ever forgive, or forget, old Harney. For Blue Water they named him "The Butcher," for the invasion of their stronghold "The Hornet," and for the councils at Laramie and Pierre "The Big Chief Who Swears." Untroubled by considerations of justice and humanity, he had cowed them as no other commander would do in future years. The Teton Sioux had not begun this war, but without a Harney to stop them they would have been quite willing to expand it into a

[14] Harry H. Anderson, "Harney v. Twiss; Nebraska Territory, 1856," *Westerners Brand Book* (Chicago), 20, (1963), 1–3, 7–8. Uncritical of Twiss is Alban W. Hoopes, "Thomas S. Twiss, Indian Agent on the Upper Platte, 1855–1861," *Mississippi Valley Historical Review*, 20 (1933), 353–64.

[15] Official correspondence relating to Fort Pierre during 1855 and 1856 is reproduced in *South Dakota Historical Collections*, 1 (1902), 381–440. A graphic account of the winter hardships is Meyers, *Ten Years in the Ranks*, Pt. 4.

conflict of costly proportions. As it was, the specter of Harney restrained them for nearly a decade.

Now the Cheyennes were to test the power of the white invaders. In the first years after the Mexican War they were uniformly regarded as among the most tractable of the Plains Indians. But in the middle 1850s the Army began to survey new roads through the heart of their domain—a warning of things to come. The chiefs found it more and more difficult to restrain their restive young men. Ignoring the Treaty of 1851, the Cheyennes continued to raid their old enemies the Pawnees in the neighborhood of Fort Kearny. This raised the danger of incidents on the emigrant road, and in the spring of 1856 General Harney sent word to the Cheyenne and Arapaho chiefs to leave the Pawnees alone or he would "sweep them from the face of the earth." He even laid plans to attempt it, but the slavery uproar in "Bleeding Kansas" kept his troops tied down throughout the summer of 1856.[16]

Both the Army and the Cheyennes shared blame for the trouble that broke out along the Platte during the travel season of 1856. In April a small band of Cheyennes came to Upper Platte Bridge to trade. In a dispute over ownership of a horse, Captain Henry Heth tried to arrest three Indians. One was killed and another imprisoned. The frightened Cheyennes abandoned their lodges and rushed off to the Black Hills, killing an innocent trapper on the way. In June some Cheyennes searching for Pawnees killed an emigrant below Fort Kearny, then rode boldly into the fort. Captain Henry W. Wharton tried to seize three as hostages, but they escaped amid a volley of musket balls. In August another party out after Pawnees flagged down the mail coach from Salt Lake to beg tobacco. The scared driver drew his pistol, lashed his horses, and raced into Fort Kearny with an arrow in his arm. Captain Wharton sent Captain George H. Stewart and a company and a half of the 1st Cavalry to run down the offenders. The troopers discovered a camp of about eighty Cheyennes on the Platte above the fort and attacked, killing ten Indians, wounding as many more, and seizing assorted stock and other baggage. All along the emigrant road the Cheyennes struck back, and within a month

[16] Berthrong, *Southern Cheyennes*, pp. 127–33. SW, *Annual Report* (1856), pp. 32, 111.

about a dozen travelers had been killed, wounded, or carried off as captives.

With the conflict escalating swiftly toward a state such as had called down the wrath of Harney on the Sioux, a delegation of Cheyenne chiefs went to Upper Platte Agency to talk over the matter with Agent Twiss. The trouble, they said, had been caused by the soldiers at Platte Bridge and Fort Kearny, and now the young warriors were "hot for the warpath." Twiss agreed that the Army was to blame, but he made the chiefs promise to withdraw from the Platte and cease depredations. In his opinion the conferences had smoothed over the difficulties, but the military authorities thought otherwise. The new commander of the Department of the West, General Persifor Smith, had already informed Washington that the Cheyennes must be "severely punished" and had announced his determination to mount an offensive in the spring of 1857. Secretary Davis promptly issued the authorization.[17]

During the winter the Cheyennes brooded over their wrongs, and by the spring the young men had grown even hotter for the warpath. At Fort Leavenworth a worthy antagonist also prepared to take the warpath with two formidable columns. Colonel Edwin Vose Sumner had returned to the Plains after an unhappy interlude as commander of the Department of New Mexico. With white hair and beard and a large, powerful frame, he was a tough old frontier dragoon who loved a fight. A musket ball glancing from his skull at Cerro Gordo had earned him the sobriquet "Bull," which his men, awed by his booming voice, lengthened to "Bull o' the Woods." In 1855 Sumner, then lieutenant colonel of the 1st Dragoons, had won the coveted colonelcy of the new 1st Cavalry.[18]

During late May and June Sumner's columns swept along the edges of the Cheyenne country. Sumner himself led two com-

---

[17] Berthrong, *Southern Cheyennes*, pp. 133–36. Grinnell, *Fighting Cheyennes*, pp. 111–16. SW, *Annual Report* (1856), pp.106–12. CIA, *Annual Report* (1856), pp. 87–103. Hoopes, "Thomas S. Twiss," p. 362.

[18] Characterizations of Sumner are in Peck, "Recollections," p. 485; Maury, *Recollections of a Virginian*, p. 37; and J. Manuel Espinosa, "Memoir of a Kentuckian in New Mexico, 1848–1884," *New Mexico Historical Review, 13* (1937), 8. For another view see Percy G. Hamlin, ed., *The Making of a Soldier: Letters of General R. S. Ewell* (p.p. Richmond, Va., 1935), pp. 60–61. Ewell called Sumner "the greatest martinet in the service." "Old Sumner has had one good effect on us," he wrote from the Rio Grande in 1847. "He has taught some of us to pray who never prayed before, for we all put up daily petitions to get rid of him."

panies of the 1st Cavalry and two of the 2d Dragoons up the Platte, while Major John Sedgwick marched up the Arkansas with four companies of the 1st Cavalry. A third column, consisting of four companies of the 1st Cavalry and two of the 6th Infantry under Lieutenant Colonel Joseph E. Johnston, had been assigned the impossible dual mission of surveying the southern boundary of Kansas and cooperating with Sumner. Johnston accomplished the first but found no occasion to participate in Sumner's operations. No Cheyennes showed themselves either on the Platte or on the Arkansas, although Major Sedgwick encountered a stampeding herd of buffalo that might have wrecked his command had not the able Captain Samuel D. Sturgis promptly assumed command and formed a wedge of carbines that split the charging mass. Sumner lost his dragoons, ordered to join Harney's expedition moving on Utah to coerce the Mormons, but picked up three companies of the 6th Infantry at Fort Laramie. Early in July Sumner and Sedgwick rendezvoused on the South Platte near present Greeley, Colorado. Cutting loose from the supply train, the entire force turned eastward to scour the heart of the Cheyenne homeland.[19]

On the morning of July 29 scouts brought word of Indians in the front, and, leaving the infantry and four howitzers to follow, Sumner pushed ahead with the cavalry. This was the usual pattern. Even with superior numbers, Indians rarely stood up to so many soldiers unless surprised. With a swift dash, the quarry might be overtaken before scattering. But this time the Cheyennes had every intention of fighting. They had washed their hands in a magic lake whose waters, promised the medicine men, would render the cavalry firearms harmless.[20] Secure in this conviction about three hundred warriors (Sumner's estimate) drew up in mounted line of battle to await the attack of an equal force of cavalrymen. The left of the line rested on the timbered

[19] Official correspondence of the expedition is set forth in LeRoy R. and Ann W. Hafen, eds., *Relations with the Indians of the Plains, 1857–1861* (Glendale, Calif., 1959), pp. 21–48. Sedgwick's march is covered in R. M. Peck's account in *ibid.*, pp. 97–140, and in *Transactions of the Kansas State Historical Society*, *8* (1904), 484–507. The journal of Sumner's wagonmaster, P. G. Lowe, narrates the activities of the wagon train in *Five Years a Dragoon*, pp. 256–98, reprinted in Hafen and Hafen, *Relations with the Indians*, pp. 49–96. For the Johnston column see Bandel, *Frontier Life in the Army*, pp. 121–214; and Nyle H. Miller, ed., "Surveying the Southern Boundary Line of Kansas: From the Journal of Col. Joseph E. Johnston," *Kansas Historical Quarterly*, *1* (1931), 104–39.

[20] CIA, *Annual Report* (1857), p. 141.

bank of the Solomon River, the right on the bluffs bordering the valley on the north.[21]

For perhaps the only time in the long history of Indian warfare, the contending forces acted their parts according to the script that a later generation of motion picture and television writers would enshrine in the folklore of the West. The command formed in a line of three squadron columns. Sumner delivered a few brief words of inspiration, then, "Bugler, sound the advance." Later, echoing a second call, the captains commanded, "Trot—march." As the three columns swept down the slopes into the valley, carbines at the ready, the Cheyenne line sprang to life and surged forward. Then, to the surprise of his men, Sumner shouted: "Sling—carbine. Draw—saber." "Now," recalled Trooper Peck, "came the command in the well-known roar of 'Old Bull,' 'Gallop—march!' and then immediately 'CHARGE!' and with a wild yell we brought our sabers to a 'tierce point' and dashed at them."[22]

Sight of the flashing blades dissolved the supernatural armor of the Indians. The magic waters acted on firearms, not sabers. Hesitating in surprise, then turning in confusion, they fled to the river and splashed across. For seven miles the cavalrymen galloped after them. A few warriors mired in the quicksands of the Solomon and fell beneath the sabers; others were cut down in the pursuit on the other side. Cornered Cheyennes fought savagely, knocking ten enlisted men from their saddles, largely with arrows that inflicted ugly wounds and for two soldiers death. One Indian put a pistol ball in the chest of Lieutenant J. E. B. Stuart; the surgeon saved him for a more illustrious death seven years later. So precipitous was the retreat that Sumner could report only nine Indians killed, but it was a psychological victory of major proportions.

Leaving a company of infantry in an earthen fortification with the wounded, Sumner set out on the Indian trail two days later. Fifteen miles south of the battlesite he found the Cheyenne village, which had been hastily abandoned. Destroying the lodges

---

[21] Sources for the battles are cited in n. 19, above. R. M. Peck's account is detailed and graphic, as is David S. Stanley's in *Personal Memoirs* (Cambridge, Mass., 1917), pp. 43-46. See also Berthrong, *Southern Cheyennes*, pp. 138-40; Grinnell, *Fighting Cheyennes*, pp. 117-21; and Lavender, *Bent's Fort*, pp. 331-33. Lieutenant J. E. B. Stuart's account, penned the next day, is in Rodenbough and Haskin, *Army of the United States*, p. 212.

[22] Peck, in Hafen and Hafen, *Relations with the Indians*, p. 122.

and their contents, he proceeded southward to the Arkansas, then turned upstream to Bent's Fort. Here he found a badly frightened Indian agent with the annual annuities, including arms and ammunition, destined for the Cheyenne and other Plains tribes. Agent Robert Miller had received word from the Cheyennes that they would take their share by force. William Bent, concluding that they meant it, refused to allow the goods within his walls and finally compromised by turning over the fort to Miller and moving up the river to another location. Sumner's action on the Solomon probably discouraged the Cheyennes from making good the threat. The other Plains tribes got the Cheyenne share of the presents, but Sumner confiscated the guns and ammunition and threw most of them in the Arkansas.[23]

Sumner intended to keep after the Cheyennes, but early in September he received orders to end the campaign and send most of his command to join the expedition to Utah. He regretted the premature suspension of operations, for, as he informed the adjutant general, the Cheyennes were "now more hostile than they were before they were punished, and it will require another severe blow to bring them to sue for peace."[24] This was only partly true. Angry war parties had indeed retaliated. They promptly attacked the sod fort on the Solomon where the infantry company guarded Sumner's wounded, forcing the defenders at first opportunity to make their painful way across the prairies to Fort Kearny. They also ranged up and down the Platte playing havoc with Harney's supply lines to Utah and again spotlighting the inability of infantry garrisons to run down mounted raiders. The depredations on the Platte revived some old antagonisms as General-in-Chief Scott reflected on Harney's competence, Harney criticized Scott and Scott's protege Sumner, and Sumner, drawing an obvious parallel between his battle on the Solomon and Harney's on the Blue Water, righteously observed in his report that he had not harmed a single woman or child—none of whom, of course, was present.[25]

But Sumner after all had prosecuted an effective campaign. With the coming of winter the Cheyennes gathered in their camps and began to reflect on the ease with which the soldiers

[23] Hafen and Hafen, *Relations with the Indians*, pp. 30–43. Lavender, *Bent's Fort*, pp. 332–33.
[24] Sept. 3, 1857, in Hafen and Hafen, *Relations with the Indians*, p. 47
[25] *Ibid.*, pp. 141–57.

had routed them and destroyed quantities of valuable property. The following July Agent Miller, handing out the 1858 presents, took the measure of their conclusions: "Colonel Sumner has worked a wondrous change in their dispositions towards the whites!" he wrote. "They said they had learned a lesson last summer in their fight with Colonel Sumner; that it was useless to contend against the white man."[26] That they were sincere became apparent as, this same summer, hundreds of gold-seekers made their way unmolested through the Cheyenne and Arapaho country to the new diggings in the foothills of the Rocky Mountains. The burgeoning mining camps at and around Denver, the new Smoky Hill travel route across Kansas that they called into being, and the increase in traffic on the Platte and the Arkansas subjected the Cheyennes and Arapahoes to unprecedented pressures, but not until provoked beyond toleration six years later did they again rise in armed protest.

Harney had temporarily humbled the Sioux and Sumner the Cheyennes, but the Kiowas and Comanches, whose offenses far overshadowed any charged to their northern neighbors, had yet to suffer a damaging blow. They continued to ravage the Texas frontier without letup, and General Smith's undermanned defenses seemed powerless to cope with them. On the Arkansas River, in another military department and Indian superintendency, these same Indians enjoyed comparatively harmonious relations with the white man on the Santa Fe Trail and each summer collected from the agent of the Great Father $10,000 worth of presents, including guns and ammunition, due them under the Fort Atkinson Treaty of 1853. It was a curious situation; $10,000, Agent Neighbors pointed out in the autumn of 1855, would not pay for the property these Indians had stolen in Texas during the previous three months.[27] And a later Texas commander confessed his inability to understand a policy that armed Indians on the Arkansas for raids in Texas. "I do not complain of it," he wrote resignedly, "but think it strange that such things are."[28]

Such things continued to be for the balance of the decade, but

[26] Miller's report from Bent's Fort, Aug. 17, 1858, in CIA, *Annual Report* (1858), p. 98.

[27] *Ibid.* (1855), p. 179.

[28] SW, *Annual Report* (1858), pp. 249–50.

beginning in 1856 the Kiowas and Comanches paid a mounting price in casualties for the stock, plunder, and scalps wrested from the Texas settlers. For one thing, a new and more energetic breed of Regulars manned the Texas defenses from 1856 to 1861 and, like Harney and Sumner to the north, began to think and act offensively. For another, increasing numbers of Texas Rangers were mobilized for Indian duty, and they, too, on occasion carried the war to the homes of the marauders. The Kiowas and Comanches were not conquered, nor did their raiding activity diminish, but their aggressions now brought penalties unknown in the past.

Late in December 1855 the newly organized 2d Cavalry, 750 strong, reached Fort Belknap after an overland march from Jefferson Barracks. With a well-chosen officer complement and horses purchased in Kentucky without regard for the usual price ceilings, the 2d swiftly became a crack outfit. Its able and dignified colonel, Albert Sidney Johnston, himself a Texan, assumed command of the department from General Persifor Smith and distributed the regiment by squadrons along the outer cordon of defense posts. The 2d Cavalry replaced the Rifle Regiment, ordered to New Mexico, and thus effected no increase in the troops assigned to Texas; but it went about its mission of defending the frontier with such zeal that by the autumn of 1856 Agent Neighbors, who was not given to undeserved praise of the Army, could write from the Brazos Agency: "Our frontier has, for the last three months, enjoyed a quiet never heretofore known. This state of things is mainly attributable to the energetic action of the 2d Cavalry, under the command of Colonel A. S. Johnston."[29]

Although the Comanches shattered the quiet that autumn, Neighbors had accurately detected a new aggressiveness that was to characterize the conduct of military affairs so long as the 2d remained in Texas. Johnston's field officers were Robert E. Lee, William J. Hardee, and George H. Thomas, and his line officers included Earl Van Dorn, Edmund Kirby Smith, George Stoneman, Kenner Garrard, William B. Royall, Nathan G. Evans, Fitzhugh Lee, and John B. Hood. These future generals of blue and gray led hundreds of scouts, patrols, and pursuits with a

---

[29] CIA, *Annual Report* (1856), pp. 174–75. See also Charles P. Roland, *Albert Sidney Johnston, Soldier of Three Republics* (Austin, Tex., 1964), chap. 11.

skill and vigor that added the spice of real danger to the hitherto rather tame plundering expeditions of the Kiowas and Comanches. In the next four years, elements of the 2d Cavalry engaged in forty small-unit combats with hostile Indians and nearly always exacted a slight toll in casualties.[30]

Behind the engagements were countless days of weary and usually fruitless trailing in a land hostile to man and beast, where rocks, sand, and thorny vegetation in profusion covered the landscape, where widely scattered and unmapped pools of brackish water made thirst a greater concern than Indians, and where summer heat and winter cold seemed more extreme than anywhere else in the West. For every conflict there were a dozen profitless scouts that netted nothing but thirst, hunger, and fatigue.

Although the 2d Cavalrymen compiled a laudable record, they were still too few, even when aided by mounted contingents of the 1st, 3d, and 8th Infantry, to screen the frontier from Red River to the Rio Grande. Since 1846 Texans had championed the use of state rangers to make up the deficiency. Petitions from all parts of the frontier poured in on a succession of governors for the recruitment of companies for local defense, but only in the gravest of emergencies could the governors bring themselves to call up such units without a guarantee of federal money for their support. And only in the gravest emergencies could the federal commanders bring themselves to ask for state rangers in federal service; they usually made good Indian fighters but, like all frontiersmen, tended to go their own way with supreme disregard of federal authority, plans, and objectives. And, as General Brooke remarked as early as 1849, their "general and natural hostility to the Indians . . . would be very apt to bring about what we wish to avoid—a general war."[31]

In Hardin R. Runnels, who took office as governor in 1857, the ranger advocates at last found an executive who could be prodded into sanctioning a sizable state force operating independently of the U.S. Army and relying on the Texas congressional delega-

[30] For the organization of the 2d Cavalry and its service in Texas see George F. Price, *Across the Continent with the Fifth Cavalry* (New York, 1883), chaps. 1–6. The 2d Cavalry became the 5th Cavalry in 1861.

[31] SW, *Annual Report* (1849), p. 143, For correspondence between the governors and their petitioners see Dorman H. Winfrey, ed., *Texas Indian Papers, 1846–1859* (Austin, Tex., 1960), passim. The evolution of the Texas Rangers in the 1850s is treated in Webb, *Texas Rangers*, pp. 130–31, 140, and passim.

tion in Washington to secure reimbursement for its expenses. With four companies already in service, Runnels won authority from the legislature in January 1858 to raise an additional contingent of a hundred men to be employed offensively. The command went to Captain John S. (Rip) Ford, a veteran of more than a decade of intermittent ranger service against the Indians and a frontiersman who knew how to handle the individualistic volunteers. Commented the *Austin Intelligencer:* "What with the Utah War and Kansas, the United States fails to afford Texas the protection necessary to save the scalps of our citizens. Let us, therefore, protect ourselves, and charge the bill to Uncle Sam."[32]

The federal commander was also beginning to think offensively. Colonel Johnston had retained command of the department only until May 1857, when he was summoned to Washington and entrusted with leadership of the army that General Harney was having trouble getting across the Plains to subjugate the Mormons of Utah. Johnston's successor was David Emanuel Twiggs—"Old Davey, the Bengal Tiger"—one of the Army's three full brigadiers, who commanded until 1861 in his brevet grade of major general. Most associates recoiled from his ill temper, cold personality, and occasionally vindictive treatment of subordinates. But a six-foot frame surmounted by a cherry-red face wreathed in flowing white hair and beard gave the sixty-seven-year-old veteran of the War of 1812 a commanding presence, and of all the prewar Texas commanders he was the only one to launch a determined and successful offensive against the Kiowa and Comanche raiders from the north.

As Rip Ford organized his ranger command and marched it toward the northern frontier in the early spring of 1858, General Twiggs moved to cooperate. He stripped Fort Mason and Camps Verde, Colorado, and Cooper of all cavalry that could be spared and ordered a concentration at Fort Belknap.[33] In April, however, orders arrived for the entire 2d Cavalry to rendezvous at Fort Belknap for a march to Kansas preparatory to joining its colonel in Utah. By the time the concentration had been completed in July, the orders had been rescinded, but it was too late to cooperate with the state troops.[34]

[32] Winfrey, *Texas Indian Papers,* pp. 270–77. SW, *Annual Report* (1858), pp. 253–54.

[33] SW, *Annual Report* (1858), pp. 253–54. Winfrey, *Texas Indian Papers,* pp. 275–77.

[34] Price, *Across the Continent,* p. 66

Captain Ford had already led his hundred rangers and an equal force of Indian auxiliaries from the Brazos Agency in an invasion of the Comanche range north of Red River. On May 11 he had surprised a large Comanche village on the Canadian River near Antelope Hills. In a seven-hour conflict, his men put 300 warriors to rout, killed a reported 76, and destroyed the camp with all its contents. A week later Ford was back at Fort Belknap.[35]

In the Battle of Antelope Hills the Comanches were badly hurt by the whites for the first time. Far from discouraging them from frontier aggressions, it served only to inflame them. Gathering on the Arkansas in July for the annual giveaway, they and the Kiowas put on a show of unaccustomed belligerence. Even as Agent Robert Miller prepared to hand out the presents, a party of warriors attacked a freight train on the Santa Fe Trail within sight of his camp. The instigator was the irascible old Southern Comanche chief Buffalo Hump, who had scorned the Texas reservation and gained considerable stature among his northern brethren. His village on the Canadian had escaped Ford's blow in May, but his heart was black. Insolently Buffalo Hump boasted of his hostility toward the "white men of the south." They had surprised his people and won a temporary success, he told the agent, but as soon as the presents were distributed he planned to lead his own warriors and part of the Northern Comanches against the Texas settlements.[36]

But first there was another matter to attend to. In June and July some parties of young Comanches, seeking replacements for the horses seized by Ford's rangers at Antelope Hills, had raided the peaceful Choctaws, Chickasaws, and Wichitas in the neighborhood of Fort Arbuckle. Unwilling to incur the wrath of these Indians, Buffalo Hump and several other Comanche chiefs journeyed to the Wichita village at Rush Spring to return the horses and make amends. While there in late August they entered into discussions with Captain William E. Prince at Fort Arbuckle, some thirty miles to the southeast, and exchanged professions of friendship with him.[37]

35 John S. Ford, *Rip Ford's Texas*, Stephen B. Oates, ed. (Austin, 1963), pp. 223-36. Webb, *The Texas Rangers*, pp. 151-58, W. J. Hughes, "Rip Ford's Indian Fight on the Canadian," *Panhandle-Plains Historical Review*, *30* (1957), 1-26.

36 CIA, *Annual Report* (1858), pp. 98-99.

37 *Ibid.*, pp. 157, 131-32; (1859), pp. 217-18. SW, *Annual Report* (1858), pp. 419-21.

At this same time the Regulars in Texas were preparing to follow up the success of Ford's rangers. All ten companies of the 2d Cavalry had gathered at Fort Belknap only to have the orders for Utah cancelled. General Twiggs thought it a good opportunity to use the regiment in something more than platoon or company strength. "For the last ten years we have been on the defensive," he wrote to General Scott on July 6. Now it was time to abandon this policy, invade the Indian homeland, "and follow them up winter and summer, thus giving the Indians something to do at home in taking care of their families, and they might possibly let Texas alone." Twiggs wanted Scott to order the campaign because of the probability that the column would cross into the Department of the West, but army head-quarters, reluctant perhaps to assume such responsibility, replied that Twiggs already had ample authority. If he thought that Texas could best be defended by offensive operations, it was up to him to do it that way.[38]

Originally Twiggs had planned to send eight companies in two columns into the field, but in the end he settled for one of four companies and returned the rest to defensive duties along the frontier. The striking column consisted of Companies A, F, H, and K, 2d Cavalry, about 225 men, a detachment of the 1st Infantry for camp guard, and 135 Indian auxiliaries from the Brazos Reservation under the agent's twenty-year-old son, Law-rence S. (Sul) Ross, home on vacation from college. Twiggs designated the senior captain of the 2d Cavalry, scrappy little Earl Van Dorn, to lead the expedition in his brevet grade of major.[39]

The "Wichita Expedition" marched out of Fort Belknap on September 15, 1858, and arrived on Otter Creek, in the shadow of the Wichita Mountains, on the twenty-third. Here the troops threw up a log stockade, christened Camp Radziminski in honor of a recently deceased lieutenant of the 2d Cavalry, and prepared to scout the country for signs of the enemy. On September 29 the Indian scouts brought word that the tepees of a sizable body

[38] SW, *Annual Report* (1858), pp. 258-60.
[39] *Ibid.*, p. 258. Price, *Across the Continent*, pp. 67-68. Major Thomas was the ranking officer of the 2d Cavalry in Texas. His biographer, who was a company commander in the 2d at this time, says that Twiggs nursed an old grudge against the future Rock of Chickamauga and kept him at Belknap with the regimental staff and band while his junior directed the operations of 1858-59. R. W. Johnson, *Memoir of Maj. Gen. George H. Thomas* (Phila-delphia, Pa., 1881), pp. 32-34.

of Comanches were standing next to the grass lodges of the
Wichitas near Rush Spring. This was Buffalo Hump and his
people, still making friends with the Wichitas secure in the belief
that the recent talks with Captain Prince at Fort Arbuckle had
set matters right with the soldiers for a time. But Van Dorn
knew nothing of this. He mounted his cavalrymen and set forth
in the direction indicated by the scouts.

Shortly after daybreak on October 1, Van Dorn crested the
ridge west of the valley of Rush Creek. The Comanche tepees
could be dimly seen rising above a low-lying morning fog. Placing Captain Nathan G. Evans with his company and the Indian
allies on the left with orders to seize the horse herd, Van Dorn
formed the other three companies in line at intervals of a hundred yards. The bugler sounded the charge, and the cavalry
raced down the slope. The surprise was complete. Startled Comanches awoke to find bluecoats among the tepees and the horses
driven beyond reach. Their families endangered, the men fought
ferociously. With the battlefield cut up by ravines and obscured
by fog and carbine smoke, the conflict fragmented into individual
encounters, often featuring hand-to-hand duels between saber-
swinging troopers and warriors armed with lance, tomahawk,
and knife.

Sul Ross and a few of his Indians, joined by Lieutenant
Cornelius Van Camp and a soldier, went in pursuit of a group
of escaping Comanches. They turned out to be women and
children, but the whites were cut off. A knot of warriors charged
them, dropping Van Camp and the private with arrows. Scooping
up the soldier's carbine, a Comanche shot Ross in the side and
advanced on him with a scalping knife. Ross fumbled for his
pistol but discovered himself paralyzed by the wound. At this
juncture a squad of troopers opportunely came to the rescue,
and the warriors scattered. But not before Lieutenant James
Majors put a charge of buckshot between the shoulders of Ross's
assailant.

The fight raged for about an hour and a half before the
Comanches disengaged themselves and fled the battlefield. They
had suffered grievously. Dead on the battlefield were 56 warriors
and 2 women, and another 25 or so escaped with wounds that
later proved fatal. The troops burned 120 lodges and appropriated
or destroyed their contents of food, ammunition, and camp
equipage. The captured horse herd numbered 300 animals. The

attackers had sustained some casualties too. Van Dorn himself was down, an arrow in his stomach and another through his wrist. Lieutenant Van Camp was dead with an arrow in his heart. Two privates had been killed and a third was missing, presumed dead. A sergeant was mortally wounded and another nine enlisted men out of action with serious injuries. Sul Ross lay with dangerous wounds, and the sutler, J. J. Ward, who had assisted Ross in leading the Indian allies, had also received a wound.

Captain Charles J. Whiting took command and summoned supplies and medical aid from Fort Arbuckle. The surgeon removed the arrow from Van Dorn's abdomen, but no one expected him to live. The wounded soldiers were sent down to Arbuckle, but the major insisted on accompanying his command back to Camp Radziminski. Within five days he was well enough to dictate and sign an official report of the battle, and within five weeks he was in the saddle once more.[40]

A week after the Battle of Rush Spring, but before the official reports reached San Antonio, General Twiggs picked up a copy of the *Washington Star* bearing a September date. In it appeared a letter, mailed from Fort Arbuckle in August, telling of a treaty concluded between the officers there and a band of Comanches. "At that time," he reported to army headquarters, "I was fitting out an expedition against those Indians. There ought to be some concert of action. One of us has made a serious blunder—he in making the treaty, or I in sending out a party after them."[41]

Although no treaty had been concluded, the intercourse between Captain Prince and the Comanche chiefs at Fort Arbuckle in August cast a shadow on Van Dorn's triumph and spotlighted the absence of communication between the Department of the West and the Department of Texas. Van Dorn and his men received fulsome praise from Scott and Twiggs, but no one could quite deny that the Comanche victims had been played falsely. Not that they were innocent of raiding in Texas. As we have seen, Buffalo Hump announced to Agent Miller in July his intention of leading a war party into Texas. Now he had

[40] SW, *Annual Report* (1858), pp. 268–76. Price, chap. 4. W. S. Nye, *Carbine and Lance: The Story of Old Fort Sill* (Norman, Okla., 1943), pp. 18–26. J. W. Wilbarger, *Indian Depredations in Texas* (2d ed. Austin, 1935), pp. 327–32.

[41] SW, *Annual Report* (1858), p. 267.

motives of revenge as well as plunder. For the rest of the year Texas settlers paid dearly for the victories of Ford and Van Dorn. As one unhappy frontiersman complained to Governor Runnels in November, "I think ever since Van Dorn routed them and dismounted so maney they have bin down to get more horses and I think he will drive them down on us."[42]

Twiggs and Van Dorn had every intention of keeping up the pressure on the Indians north of Red River. The veterans of Rush Spring spent the winter at Camp Radziminski while their commander plotted his next campaign. To avoid a repetition of the Rush Spring misfortune, he urged that General Scott be asked to publish an order declaring the Comanches at enmity with all troops of the Army. Otherwise, "it might possibly occur that whilst a squadron of cavalry from this department are pursuing a party of murderers and marauders of the families and property of the citizens of Texas, they are smoking in quiet security on the parade ground of some military post in a neighboring department, the invited guests of the commanding officer."[43] Scott did not publish such an order, but he moved to reduce the chance of further mischief from Fort Arbuckle. A squadron of the 1st Cavalry strengthened the post, and Major William H. Emory assumed command with directions to take orders from General Twiggs as well as from his own superiors in the Department of the West.[44]

Throughout the winter of 1858–59 Van Dorn's scouting parties laced the High Plains drained by the Canadian, Red, and Brazos Rivers but could find no fresh Indian sign. The Comanches were giving him a wide berth. Some had probably gone north to the Arkansas. Others—seven to eight hundred—were reported wintering in Chihuahua. Still others kept the Texas settlements in constant turmoil. And a few remained on the frontiers of Arkansas and Missouri, where patrols of the 1st Cavalry from Fort Arbuckle collided with small war parties in February 1859.[45]

By late April the grass had freshened enough for Van Dorn to take the field again. Twiggs had reinforced him, and on April 30, with six companies of the 2d Cavalry, nearly 500 officers

[42] Winfrey, *Texas Indian Papers*, p. 309.

[43] SW, *Annual Report* (1859), pp. 356–57.

[44] *Ibid.*, (1858), p. 276.

[45] *Ibid.* (1859), pp. 356–57, 381–85. Twiggs to Thomas, Feb. 5, 1859, RG 94, NARS. *Daily Missouri Republican* (St. Louis), March 28, 1859.

and enlisted men, and a newly recruited contingent of 58 Indians from the Brazos Reservation, Van Dorn marched out of Camp Radziminski. He believed that Comanches would be found near the Arkansas, and the column pointed almost due north. The major had guessed correctly. Four days out flankers captured a Comanche boy who reported that part of the luckless Buffalo Hump's people were camped on a small tributary of the Cimarron about fifteen miles south of abandoned Fort Atkinson. Planting a supply base on the Canadian thirty miles below the Antelope Hills, Van Dorn forced the captured boy to lead the command to the village.

Soaked by constant rain driven by a chilling north wind, the cavalrymen plowed through thick mud to the Cimarron and beyond. On May 13, on Crooked Creek (Van Dorn erroneously called it the Nescutunga), they paused early in the afternoon to rest the horses. Pickets spied two Comanches, and the major sent Lieutenant William B. Royall with thirty men in pursuit. Across a ridge, about three miles distant, Royall overhauled a band of nearly one hundred Indians, both men and women, trying to get clear of the soldiers. They took refuge in a deep, brush-choked ravine with precipitous sides. Sending a messenger to summon Van Dorn, Royall expertly separated the Comanches from their horses and bottled them up in the ravine.

The rest of the command came up promptly, but getting at the enemy proved a real problem. Mounted troops were placed on the hills above the ravine to pin down the Indians and seal off their escape route, while the bulk of the command went in as dismounted skirmishers to sweep down the ravine through rain-soaked brush. The Indians had taken positions behind fallen trees and fought savagely. As Van Dorn wrote in his report, there was no "clank, clash, and glitter of steel"; the cavalrymen "*felt* for the danger they were called on to encounter." Working through the thickets, they never knew when they might come face to face with a Comanche warrior. Captain E. Kirby Smith, his spectacles clouded by the rain, walked by a log that sheltered a Comanche and caught a pistol ball in the thigh. Another warrior rose from behind a log and drove an arrow into Lieutenant Fitzhugh Lee's breast with a force that left it protruding from his back. With the arrow in flight, Lee's pistol flashed and sent a ball squarely between his assailant's eyes.

The Comanches were trapped and they knew it. They "fought without giving or asking quarter until there was not one left to bend a bow," wrote Van Dorn. This was no exaggeration. Not a Comanche escaped. Forty-nine warriors were slain and five wounded; thirty-two women and five men fell prisoners to the troopers. The victory cost Van Dorn the two officers badly wounded, two men killed, nine wounded, and two Indian allies killed and two mortally wounded. Encumbered with wounded and prisoners, Van Dorn turned back to Camp Radziminski, where he arrived on May 30.[46]

Van Dorn was summoned to San Antonio, and his jubilant troopers remained under Kirby Smith at Camp Radziminski. They did not launch another campaign in 1859, however, for during the summer the services of two full squadrons were required in Texas, where, paradoxically, they were called on to protect Indians from white settlers.

Affairs on the Texas reservations had taken an ominous turn. By 1858 the Brazos Reservation contained 1,112 members of the confederated tribes and the Comanche Reservation 371 people, principally followers of the docile old Southern Comanche chief Ketumseh.[47] All the reservation Indians had been making progress in the arts of the white man's civilization that impressed observers. The Comanches found it a hard road to follow because they had so recently been nomads and because their northern brothers kept them stirred up and often incited the young men to join in raids on the frontiers of Texas and Mexico. Still, most of them tried conscientiously to make a success of the new life, and the very real advances exhibited by the residents of both reservations amply justified the optimistic predictions that Robert S. Neighbors, now Superintendent of Indian Affairs for Texas, had made back in 1855.

But pressures had steadily built up against the reservations. In 1855 and 1856 the settlers on the frontier of northwestern Texas had accepted the reservation Indians as neighbors and viewed the experiment with friendly interest. In 1857 and 1858,

[46] Van Dorn to Withers, May 13 and 31, 1859, RG 94, NARS. Joseph P. Thoburn, "Indian Fight in Ford County in 1859," *Kansas Historical Collections*, 12 (1911–12), 312–29. Price, *Across the Continent*, pp. 79–80. Camp Radziminski actually occupied three successive locations on Otter Creek during 1858 and 1859. See Nye, *Carbine and Lance*, pp. 24–25.

[47] CIA, *Annual Report* (1858), p. 173.

however, their attitude changed to suspicion and then to open and lawless hostility. The man largely responsible was John R. Baylor, a disgruntled former agent dismissed from the service on Neighbors' recommendation. By early 1859 he had large numbers of whites convinced that the reservation Indians, not the wild bands to the north, were chiefly responsible for the continuing thefts and murders along the frontier. That some of the young Comanches probably had participated in an occasional raid did not justify the mob action that Baylor incited against the reservation Indians in 1859.

For four years the aim had been to move these Indians out of Texas and settle them north of Red River. In 1855 the government negotiated a treaty with the Choctaws and Chickasaws leasing in perpetuity all their land west of the ninety-eighth meridian for a reservation on which to establish the Texas Indians and the Wichitas living near Fort Arbuckle. This was the heart of the Kiowa and Comanche homeland, and Neighbors hoped that these wild tribes, the real scourge of the Texas frontier, could be induced to settle down too. The only thing holding up the move was the Army's delay in erecting a military post to guard the agency. Now, with Texas settlers murdering Indians found off the reservation and ominously threatening to clean out the reservations themselves, Neighbors appealed repeatedly and urgently for authority to lead his charges out of Texas.

The crisis came in May 1859. Baylor had organized some three to four hundred self-styled rangers and got himself elected captain. Neighbors said that most of them were newly arrived settlers who were not sustained by the older residents, and he likened them to the freebooters who had terrorized Kansas in recent years. The announced intention was to rid the frontier of alleged thieves and murderers, but the partisans seem to have been more interested in plundering the Indians of stock and other property. They regarded all Indians off the reservations as fair game. As the Indian stock grazed without reference to boundaries, this worked a real hardship on the hapless victims, most of whom lost horses and mules and some of whom lost their lives, to say nothing of the demoralization suffered by all as a consequence of the danger. Governor Runnels, fearing to antagonize a part of the electorate, confined his intervention to appeals for order. General Twiggs, imploring the governor to take firm action, cautioned officers on the scene to avoid a collision with citizens at all costs.

Baylor forced the issue on May 23 by leading about 250 "rangers" against the Brazos Agency, home of the very Indians who had so ably served Ford and Van Dorn in the northern campaign. Only ten days earlier, in fact, fifty-eight of them had fought bravely beside the 2d Cavalrymen at Crooked Creek. Captain J. B. Plummer, who commanded two companies of the 1st Infantry at the agency, ordered Baylor to clear out, but that defender of the frontier, forming his men for an attack, served notice that if the federal troops sided with the Indians he would fight them too. As Plummer disposed his men for defense, Baylor's resolution wavered and he began to withdraw. Some fifty to sixty reservation Indians swarmed on his flanks and, after an eight-mile chase, forced him to fort up at an abandoned farmhouse, where he was held under siege until nightfall.

Early in June Major Thomas pulled four companies of the 2d Cavalry down from Camp Radziminski to guard the Comanche Reservation and reinforce the infantry at the Brazos Agency. The vigilantes did not again attempt to bully the Regulars, but they continued to run down any Indians found off the reservation, to appropriate their stock to themselves, and to indulge in a great deal of noisy and belligerent talk that, sooner or later, was sure to nerve them for another assault on the reservation. At last, early in July, Neighbors received the long-sought authority to take his Indians to their new homes. Late in June Elias Rector, head of the Southern Superintendency at Fort Smith, had journeyed to the Leased District and selected a site for an agency on the Washita River, forty-five miles northeast of the Wichita Mountains. Early in August, under an escort of cavalry and infantry commanded by Major Thomas, the Texas Indians began the march to their new homes—forced, in the haste of departure, to leave nearly all their possessions to their tormenters. On the eighth Neighbors sat down in his tent and wrote to his wife:

I have this day crossed all the Indians out of the heathen land of Texas and am now out of the land of the Philistines.

If you want to have a full description of our Exodus out of Texas —Read the "Bible" where the children of Israel crossed the Red Sea. We have had about the same show, only our enemies did not follow us to R River. If they had—the Indians would have—in all probability sent them back without the interposition of Divine Providence.[48]

After turning over his charges to the new agent at the Wichita Agency, the disillusioned Neighbors rode back to Texas, heading for his San Antonio office to close out his accounts with the Indian Bureau. In the town of Fort Belknap a man named Ed Cornett, supposedly inflamed by the passions aroused before the removal, stepped from behind a house and fired a shotgun into the superintendent's back. He died within twenty minutes, thus rewarded for nearly two decades of service to Texas and the United States.[49]

In the autumn of 1859 the War Department finally got around to authorizing the long-promised army post in the Leased District. Major Emory, commander of Fort Arbuckle, toured the Wichita Mountains in September and selected a site at the junction of Pond Creek and the Washita River, twelve miles west of the Wichita Agency. Here Fort Cobb was built and garrisoned with elements of the 1st Cavalry. Camp Radziminski was then abandoned.[50]

Although an order of August 19, 1859, transferred all the military posts in Indian Territory west of the Arkansas River to the Department of Texas, the Texas Indian Superintendency was abolished and the new Wichita Agency placed under the Southern Superintendency at Fort Smith. Superintendent Rector favored a pacific approach to the Comanches aimed at enrolling them at this agency. They had been treacherously handled at Rush Spring, he felt, but if given liberal quantities of presents and persuaded that Van Dorn's attack was an unhappy mistake, they might settle down there. Presents were much cheaper than war, he noted, for in the overall view it cost a lot of money to kill one Comanche. Agent William Bent, who dealt directly with these

[48] The quotation, from the Neighbors Papers in the University of Texas Archives, is printed in Webb, *The Texas Rangers*, pp. 171-72. For official correspondence concerning the abandonment of the Texas reservations, see CIA, *Annual Report* (1859), pp. 165-66, 215-334; SW, *Annual Report* (1859), pp. 365-74; Winfrey, p. 312 passim. See also Kenneth F. Neighbours, "Indian Exodus out of Texas in 1859," West Texas Historical Association *Year Book*, 36 (1960), 80-97; and Richardson, *Comanche Barrier*, pp. 211-59.

[49] Kenneth F. Neighbours, "The Assassination of Robert S. Neighbors," West Texas Historical Association *Year Book*, 34 (1958), 38-49.

[50] Sw, *Annual Report* (1859), p. 386.

Indians on the Arkansas rather than from an office in distant Fort Smith, had another assessment. Forced northward by the campaigns based in Texas, the Kiowas and Comanches threatened to winter on the Arkansas and play havoc with the Santa Fe Trail. Bent believed it essential to meet this threat by erecting two permanent forts on the Arkansas, one at the mouth of Pawnee Fork and the other at Big Timbers.[51]

Far from agreeing with Superintendent Rector, top military authorities heeded Van Dorn's suggestion that the Comanches be placed "at enmity with all troops of the Army wherever found." On March 10, 1860, carrying out War Department instructions, army headquarters issued a general order directing three columns to take the field during the coming summer and operate independently of one another against the Kiowas and Comanches. One was to be organized at Fort Cobb, one at Fort Riley, and one at Fort Union, New Mexico.

The summer campaign of 1860 was the most comprehensive operation yet directed at these tribes, but in results it proved the most sterile. Major Sedgwick led the Fort Riley column—four companies of the 1st Cavalry and two of the 2d Dragoons—in an exhausting and profitless scout south of the Arkansas to the Antelope Hills, then in July marched up the Arkansas to the foot of the Rockies. North of Bent's Fort Captain William Steele and Lieutenant J. E. B. Stuart skirmished with a small party of Kiowas, killed two men, and captured sixteen women and children, but this was the only action anyone in the Sedgwick column saw.

Captain Samuel D. Sturgis with six companies of the 1st Cavalry struck northward from Fort Cobb on June 6. Early in July the command overhauled a large band of Kiowas on Solomon's Fork, Kansas. Several hundred warriors dropped back to screen the flight of their families. Sturgis reported twenty-nine of them slain, but exhausted horses prevented him from bringing on a decisive engagement.

Six companies of the Regiment of Mounted Riflemen composed the Fort Union column. First under Major Charles F. Ruff, then under Captain Andrew Porter, the Riflemen scoured the Plains country east of the Canadian River. Beyond the capture of a hastily abandoned Comanche village, they accomplished nothing but the breakdown of their horses.

[51] CIA, *Annual Report* (1859), pp. 138, 166.

And finally, Major Thomas collected a force of 2d Cavalry-men from the posts of northern Texas and marched to the head of the Concho and Colorado Rivers, where he encountered eleven Comanches and killed one, who, however, wounded five enlisted men and put an arrow into Thomas' chest before succumbing. As Superintendent Rector had said, killing one Comanche was an expensive proposition. The campaign of 1860 proved that beyond question.[52]

There was one concrete result of the operations—the strengthening of the Santa Fe Trail defense system along the lines recommended by William Bent a year earlier. Brevet Major Henry W. Wessels with two companies of the 2d Infantry had wintered at the junction of Pawnee Fork with the Arkansas River and in the summer set about erecting Fort Larned. In August 1860 orders reached Major Sedgwick, then campaigning on the Arkansas, to found another post, named Fort Wise, at Big Timbers. At the conclusion of the summer offensive against the Kiowas and Comanches, therefore, the Santa Fe Trail gained two strongly held bastions. Four companies of cavalry and two of infantry under Sedgwick garrisoned Fort Wise, while two dragoon and two infantry companies under Wessels garrisoned Fort Larned.[53]

By the close of the fifteen-year period between the Mexican and Civil Wars, neither the Army nor the Indian Bureau could boast much progress in neutralizing the menace to travel and settlement represented by the large tribes of the Great Plains. In contending with the Kiowas and Comanches, the Army could point to a truly imposing network of forts in Texas, Indian Territory, and along the Arkansas and to battlefield triumphs at Rush Spring and Crooked Creek; the Indian Bureau could point to treaties that engaged these Indians in theoretically peaceful relations with the United States and to the beginnings of a reservation system designed to clear them from the paths of westward expansion. But the hard truth remained that in the last years before the Civil War the Kiowas and Comanches visited greater devastation on the Texan and Mexican frontiers than in the first

[52] Official correspondence and reports are in SW, *Annual Report* (1860), pp. 13-25, 56-60. Additional official documents, together with private diaries and letters, are in Hafen, *Relations with the Indians*, pp. 191-254.

[53] Hafen, pp. 257-81. William E. Unrau, "The Story of Fort Larned," *Kansas Historical Quarterly*, 23 (1957), 257-80.

years after the Mexican War, and that in addition they now posed a danger to the Santa Fe Trail almost wholly absent in earlier years.

Farther north, the Army could take satisfaction in sharp, short, and decisive offensives against the Sioux and Cheyennes and the Indian Bureau in seemingly successful treaty and agency relations with the nomads of the central and northern Plains. But the Army bore much of the responsibility—unadmitted, it is true— for the events that provoked the hostilities of 1855 and 1857. The Sioux and Cheyennes had not forgotten this, nor had they forgotten the blows they had suffered from the soldiers in the course of the ensuing operations. Events were to prove how illusory was the harmony that seemed to prevail among these tribes in 1860.

By the early 1860s Sioux, Cheyenne, Arapaho, Kiowa, and Comanche presented a wall of open or suppressed opposition to the white man that extended from Canada to Mexico. The Army alone had not produced it, but the soldiers had played their part along with emigrants, settlers, traders, and government officials. The tribes had not acted in concert to resist the invasion and never would—although on occasion they would all be hostile at the same time. For this reason the barrier analogy may not be wholly exact. But to the actors in the drama of westward expansion, it surely seemed that in the decade of the 1850s there had risen a Plains Indian barrier that for a quarter of a century slowed the advance of the American frontier.

EIGHT

Rio Grande Campaigns, 1854-61

As on the Great Plains, the middle and late 1850s featured a rising military aggressiveness against the tribes of the southwestern deserts and mountains. But there were differences of enemy and terrain between the two regions that made offensive operations in the Southwest more difficult and less productive.

Apache and Navajo proved more elusive than the Plains Indians. Less often did they congregate in numbers large enough to come to grips with. Less often did they stand and fight. Less often were they careless about allowing their camps to be discovered, much less surprised. And even more than their brethren of the Plains, they possessed a combination of skill and instinct that made them extremely difficult to take at a disadvantage. As a pastoral and agricultural people, the Navajos had points of vulnerability that the Apaches did not, but for both the character of their homeland was an almost unconquerable ally. It confronted the troops with vast distances, tangled terrain, and sparsity of water and forage that speedily exhausted the heavily equipped soldiers on grain-fed horses while aiding the Indian inhabitants who in several generations of adaptation had come to terms with it.

The southwestern commanders mounted nearly a dozen major offensives between 1854 and 1861. Two netted positive and lasting results, but the rest turned out to be inconclusive. These operations showed that the southwestern Indians could easily elude a single or even several strong columns marching through their country and that, unless lucky, the troops usually succeeded mainly in wearing themselves out. It remained for a later commander to draw the obvious conclusion: the character of both enemy and terrain promised greater success to many small columns than to a few large ones. To this approach, however, the Rio Grande campaigns of the 1850s were a not wholly unproductive prelude.

Except for occasional banditry, the Utes and Jicarilla Apaches had been quiet since the massacres of 1849 and 1850 on the Santa Fe Trail (see p. 86). Mainly this resulted from the efforts of Governors Calhoun and Lane to bring them into a system of civil management. In the winter of 1852–53 Lane instituted a program for moving all the Indians east of the Rio Grande to new homes west of the river, where they were to be settled in fixed locations and taught to support themselves by farming. Many Utes and Jicarillas had already been relocated and attached to agencies at Taos and Abiquiu when, early in 1853, Commissioner of Indian Affairs George W. Manypenny learned of the operation. Pointing out that Lane had no authority to bind the government to feed these people while they were learning to feed themselves, the Commissioner ordered the program suspended. Lane struggled to terminate the rations gradually rather than abruptly, but even this could not conceal from the Indians that they had been played falsely.

Taking office as governor and Superintendent of Indian Affairs in August 1853, David Meriwether inherited an actively discontented lot of Indians in the northern part of the Territory. After only five weeks in office, he reported thirteen citizens murdered, ten to fifteen wounded, and a property loss by theft of $10,000 to $15,000. "Unless these Indians be whipt or fed," he warned, "the territory will soon be in a sad condition even if it is not so already."[1] For the time being, feeding was out of the question, but two incidents roused General Garland to try Meriwether's alternative.

Bands of Jicarillas and Utes had once more begun to threaten the Santa Fe Trail east of the Canadian River, and one of them

---

[1] Greiner to Lane, Dec. 1, 1852, encl. to Lane to Lea, Dec. 31, 1852, N82/1853; Lane to Lea, Feb. 24, 1853, N107/1853; Manypenny to Lane, April 9, 1853, OIA NM Field Papers; Steck to Lane, May 20, 1853, encl. to Lane to Manypenny, May 21, 1853, N128/1853; Lane to Manypenny, May 30, 1853, N127/1853; Meriwether to Manypenny, Sept. 17, 1853, N176/1853; same to same, Nov. 28, 1853, N197/1853; same to same, Dec. 29, 1853, 209/1853. All in RG 75, NARS.

ran off some cattle from a herd belonging to the Fort Union beef contractor. The fort's commander, Lieutenant Colonel Philip St. George Cooke, sent out a thirty-man platoon of the 2d Dragoons under Lieutenant David Bell. On March 5, 1854, in the breaks of the Canadian fifty miles southeast of the fort, the dragoons overhauled the quarry, an equal number of Jicarillas under Lobo Blanco (White Wolf), third ranking chief of the tribe and leader of the party that had massacred the White family five years earlier. In a brief but sharp action, the troops cut up the war party, and Bell himself felled Lobo with several pistol balls. But "the ravisher of Mrs. White" clung to life, and, as Colonel Cooke explained laconically, "a man got a great rock and mashed his head."[2]

The second episode occurred three weeks later. Learning of Apaches behaving suspiciously on the road from Taos to Santa Fe, the commanding officer at Cantonment Burgwin, Major George A. H. Blake, dispatched Lieutenant John W. Davidson and his company of the 1st Dragoons to investigate. On March 30, in the Embudo Mountains twenty-five miles south of Taos, Davidson rode into an ambush set up by Chacón, first chief of the Jicarillas, who was probably intent on revenge for the death of Lobo. Outnumbered four to one and caught at a disadvantage, the dragoons fought desperately for three hours to extricate themselves. Through firm leadership, the lieutenant saved the command from annihilation, but even so he left 22 dead on the field and reached Taos with 36 wounded. Only two men emerged from the Battle of Cieneguilla unhit by arrow or bullet.[3]

General Garland, though en route to El Paso, reacted decisively. In response to the report of Lieutenant Bell's action, he had already sent reinforcements to Fort Union for Santa Fe Trail duty. Now, learning by express of the Cieneguilla debacle, he hastened to Santa Fe and ordered Colonel Cooke to take the field with his whole available force. "Give them neither rest or quarter until they are humbled to the dust," he instructed. Cooke was already on the march. He heard of Davidson's defeat by messenger on the morning of March 31 and by noon was leading two hundred dragoons and an artillery company serving as riflemen

[2] Bell to Cooke, March 7, 1854, encl. to Garland to Thomas, March 29, 1854, G177/1854, RG 94, NARS. Cooke, "Personal Recollections," in Rodenbough, *Everglade to Cañon*, pp. 176–78.

[3] Blake to Nichols, March 30, 1854, encl. to Garland to Thomas, April 1, 1854, G178/1854, RG 94, NARS. Sabin, 2, 660–62.

out of Fort Union. Pausing at Taos on April 3 and 4, he added a mixed force of thirty-two Pueblo and Mexican "spies and guides" to the column, engaged Ute agent Kit Carson to show the way, and plunged into the snow blanketed wilderness west of the Rio Grande.[4]

The scouts quickly picked up Chacón's trail and pursued it so tenaciously that the Apaches finally turned. On April 8, amid a jumble of boulders on a cliff fronted by the snow-fed Rio Caliente, 150 warriors concealed themselves for another ambush. Captain James Quinn's Pueblos unmasked the trap and charged pell-mell across the icy stream against the enemy positions. The riflemen rushed to their support, Captain George Sykes cheering them "from a limping walk into a sort of run"—they had marched for five days in constant snow-showers. Bell's dragoons dismounted and spread up the slope to seize a rocky ledge flanking the Apache line, and Cooke, Blake, and Lieutenant Samuel D. Sturgis hurled the rest of the command at the center. Lieutenant Joseph E. Maxwell hastened to cut off the pony herd. The Indians broke and scattered into the mountains, leaving Cooke with one dead and one wounded. The Battle of Rio Caliente was over so quickly that Chacón could later acknowledge casualties of only five killed and six wounded. In their flight the Jicarillas abandoned nearly all their camp equipage and ponies, which Cooke seized and appropriated or destroyed, and lost track of seventeen women and children who wandered among the wintry mountains until they perished from exposure.[5]

For five days Cooke's men pursued through a tangle of mountains before losing the trail and wearily retracing their steps to Abiquiu, on the Chama. For the rest of April and into May, scouting detachments combed the Jicarilla country, keeping the enemy on the run but unable to close in combat. Late in May, however, Brevet Major James H. Carleton led a hundred troopers of the 1st Dragoons and Quinn's Pueblo-Mexican trailers in a probe to the north and east of Taos. Kit Carson went along as guide.

[4] Garland to Cooke, April 7, 1854, Dept. NM LS, Vol. 9, pp. 158–59, RG 98, NARS. Cooke, p. 178. SW, *Annual Report* (1854), pp. 33–34. Messervy to Manypenny, April 29, 1854, N269/1854, RG 75, NARS.

[5] Cooke, in Rodenbough, *Everglade to Cañon*, pp. 178–80. Sabin, *Kit Carson Days*, 2, 660–64. James H. Quinn, "Notes of Spy Company under Colonel Cooke [diary]," Rich Collection, Bancroft Library. Cooke to Nichols, April 8, 1854, G202/1854; and same to same, May 24, 1854, encl. to Garland to Thomas, May 30, 1854, G269/1854, both in RG 94, NARS.

Quinn's scouts picked up a trail, and on the morning of June 4, nearing the base of Fisher's Peak in the Raton Range, Carson alerted Carleton that the quarry would be overtaken by two o'clock. If true, promised the flint-eyed dragoon officer, he would buy Kit a new hat in New York City. At two o'clock that afternoon the column fanned out and crashed down a mountainside to jump a Jicarilla camp of twenty-two lodges hidden in a forested glen. The Apaches resisted briefly, lost a few men, then faded into the trees and escaped. They left behind all their possessions, including thirty-eight ponies. Months later a box arrived at Taos addressed to the Ute agent. It contained a fine hat lettered in gilt on the inside band: "At 2 o'clock, Kit Carson from Major Carleton."[6] The friendship and mutual respect cemented on the slopes of Fisher's Peak bore fruit eight years later when these two veteran frontiersmen again teamed up, with notable consequences, against the southwestern tribes.

No conclusive event marked the close of the Jicarilla war. During the summer of 1854 there were occasional depredations and at least one skirmish with soldiers—a hand-to-hand fight near Fort Union in which Lieutenant Joseph E. Maxwell went down bristling with arrows. But most of the Jicarillas had lost their enthusiasm for engaging dragoons. A peace delegation came to Santa Fe in July but was turned away, and in the autumn Chacón began to assemble his people on the Chama to do as the white man instructed. Some renegades stayed out and drifted northward to ride with the Utes, but never again was the Jicarilla tribe to rise against its conquerors.

Stirred up by Jicarilla renegades and disturbed by new white settlements on the east and south, the Utes were growing more and more restive as 1854 drew to a close. On Christmas Day a combined Ute and Jicarilla war party of about a hundred swooped down from the Sangre de Cristos and smashed the fledgling settlement of Pueblo, on the Arkansas River. They slaughtered fifteen men, wounded two more, carried a woman and two children into captivity, and made off with two hundred horses. In subsequent weeks Ute warriors, reinforced by Jicarilla refugees, killed travelers and stole more than a thousand sheep,

[6] Carleton to Cooke, June 5, 1854, encl. to Cooke to Nichols, June 7, 1854, RG 98, NARS. Quinn. Sabin, *Kit Carson Days*, 2, 664-65.

goats, and horses from settlers on the upper Arkansas and Rio Grande. General Garland acted promptly. Calling up five companies of territorial Volunteers under the veteran trapper and trader Céran St. Vrain, commissioned lieutenant colonel for the purpose, he ordered Colonel Thomas T. Fauntleroy to organize an invasion of the Ute homeland. The Ute tribe was to be crushed. The general, his adjutant advised Fauntleroy, "does not recognize the principle urged by the peace establishment men, that we can wage war upon one part and not the whole of a nation."[7]

At the head of five hundred men (two companies of the 1st Dragoons, two of the 2d Artillery serving as infantry, and St. Vrain's Volunteers), Fauntleroy pushed north from Fort Union in mid-February 1855. Basing himself on Fort Massachusetts, he marched and countermarched in the frozen bleakness of the San Luis Valley and its bordering mountains. A skirmish on March 19 felled eight Utes, but there was nothing more to show for two months of hardship and exposure when, late in April, the column put in at Fort Massachusetts to refit. Here Fauntleroy divided his command. Part, under Colonel St. Vrain, rode into the Sangre de Cristos to the east, while the rest, under Fauntleroy, turned once more to the San Luis Valley.

On April 28 Fauntleroy's division, two companies of Regulars and two of Volunteers, picked up a hot trail and pressed on in the blackness of night to the approaches of Poncha Pass. Blanco and his Utes, estimated at 150 warriors, had dropped all security precautions as they whirled in a wild war dance around a leaping bonfire. The soldiers dismounted and crept forward in skirmish line on two sides of the camp. They had approached to within 150 yards when Indian dogs began to bark. The colonel gave the command to open fire, and a crescent of flame, "almost eclipsing the illumination" of the dance fire, "swept the enemy like chaff." Forty Indians fell in the fusillade, and the rest scampered up the mountainside in panic. They abandoned all their possessions, which the troops piled on the fire and burned. In the next few days the command skirmished several times with small war

<hr />

[7] Meriwether to Manypenny, Jan. 31, 1855, M386/1855, RG 75. SO 12, Hq. Dept. NM, Feb. 5, 1855, SO and GO, Hq. Dept. NM, Vol. 27, RG 98. Nichols to Fauntleroy, Feb. 6, 1855, Dept. NM LS, Vol. 9, pp. 292–93, RG 98. All in NARS. SW, *Annual Report* (1855), pp. 56–57.

parties and killed or wounded another half-dozen warriors; but the Battle of Poncha Pass had knocked all the belligerence out of the Utes and they displayed no will to stand and fight.[8]

St. Vrain, too, had won success. Crossing the Sangre de Cristos, he descended to the plain east of the mountains. On April 25 his troops jumped 60 Jicarillas on the Purgatorie, killed 6, captured 7, destroyed all the camp equipage, and seized 31 horses.[9]

The campaign brought about a collapse of Ute resistance that was no less real for its informality. Fauntleroy and St. Vrain had ended forever the armed hostility of the Capote and Moache Utes and the unreconciled remnant of the Jicarilla Apaches. The operation was unusual in several ways. The troops had cornered the adversary on a half-dozen occasions, they had inflicted heavy casualties and logistical losses, and they had crushed the enemy for all time. Moreover, the Volunteers and Regulars had worked together effectively and with little friction. St. Vrain and his men won high praise from both Fauntleroy and Garland. This in itself was notable, for Regular officers rarely found anything favorable to say about Volunteers. When mustered out of federal service at the close of the summer, the Volunteers of Mexican descent had dramatically disproved the common Anglo charge that they would not fight.

General Garland could take special satisfaction in the conquest of the Utes, for it was achieved simultaneously with success, equally creditable if less enduring, on another front. Trouble with the Mescalero Apaches, perhaps not wholly unrelated to the unrest among their Jicarilla kinsmen, erupted just as the Utes taxed Garland's limited resources to make up Fauntleroy's column.

The Mescalero tribe probably numbered no more than nine hundred people, divided into seven bands that led a precarious existence among the mountains of southern New Mexico, western Texas, and northern Chihuahua. In their attitude toward the whites, the band chiefs varied from the pacifism of Palanquito to the implacable hostility of Santa Anna. Occasionally a chief

[8] SW, *Annual Report* (1855), pp. 62–69. Pertinent sources are analyzed and summarized in Morris F. Taylor, "Action at Fort Massachusetts: The Indian Campaign of 1855," *Colorado Magazine*, 42 (1965), 292–310.

[9] Whittlesey to Sturgis, May 1, 1855, Fort Union LS, RG 98, NARS. SW, *Annual Report* (1855), pp. 63–64, 70–71.

visited officials in Santa Fe or at the Rio Grande forts. Occasionally, too, a war party committed depredations against the river settlements, waylaid travelers on the Jornada del Muerto, and, while en route to or returning from Mexico, attacked wagon trains on the road across West Texas to El Paso. Twice in 1854, under orders from General Garland, Brevet Lieutenant Colonel Daniel T. Chandler, 3d Infantry, campaigned from Fort Conrad to the Sierra Blanca, favorite resort of these Apaches, but accomplished no more than to learn a great deal about a hitherto obscure country.[10] The mounting tempo of Mescalero raids during 1854, partly a response to Chandler's saber-rattling, inspired the campaign of 1855.

Troops from the Department of Texas participated. General Persifor Smith, touring the western part of his department in October 1854, had seen first-hand evidence of Mescalero depredations on the San Antonio-El Paso road, and his escort had tangled with a band in a canyon of the Sierra Diablo.[11] Returning to San Antonio, Smith ordered Major John S. Simonson, based on Fort Davis, into the field. General Garland sent another column, commanded by his son-in-law, Major James Longstreet, out from Fort Bliss to cooperate. During the first two months of 1855, Simonson and Longstreet searched the mountains and deserts of the Trans-Pecos but failed to close with the elusive Apaches.[12] It remained for other troops, operating under Garland's direction, to bring the Mescaleros to terms.

Late in December 1854, learning of the theft of 2,500 sheep from a ranch on the Pecos, Garland ordered two forces, one from Fort Fillmore and one from Los Lunas, to go after the Mescaleros in their home country. One column, 80 men of the 1st Dragoons under the bald-headed little eccentric Richard S. Ewell, marched to and down the Pecos, then turned into the Capitan Mountains. On January 13 Captain Ewell met the Fort Fillmore column, 50 infantry and 29 dragoons under Captain Henry W. Stanton. Four days later the expedition reached the Peñasco, a pleasant alpine stream draining toward the Pecos plains below. That night the Mescaleros showered the camp of the invaders with arrows and bullets and tried to burn it out. Throughout

10 Chandler to Nichols, Jan. 24, 1854, encl. to Garland to Thomas, March 27, 1854, G183/1854, RG 94. Chandler to Nichols, Aug. 10, 1854, Fort Craig LB Vol. 95, RG 98. All in NARS.

11 Walker to Gibbs, Oct. 6, 1854, RG 94, NARS. See p. 75n.

12 SW, Annual Report (1855), p. 52.

the next day, as the column plodded up the valley of the Peñasco, they contested the march, forcing Ewell to keep skirmishers in advance to clear the way. The effort cost the Indians fifteen men dropped from their mounts by the dragoons and infantrymen. Late in the afternoon Ewell halted at an abandoned Apache camp and sent Captain Stanton with a dozen men to investigate another in an adjoining valley about five hundred yards distant. Stanton rode into a trap. Pressed by mounted warriors, his little detachment fell back, the captain himself covering the withdrawal with a Sharp's carbine until a bullet smashed his head. A dragoon private, his horse shot, was also cut off and lanced by a party of Apaches. The Indians had accomplished their purpose of delaying Ewell while their families escaped. Now they scattered, leaving no trail to follow. Saddened by the death of Stanton, the command made its way back to the Rio Grande.[13]

On January 16, only two days before Ewell's collision with Mescaleros in the Capitans, another Mescalero party, numbering about a dozen men, got badly cut up not far to the north, along the eastern foot of the Manzanos. These warriors had hit the Eaton Ranch in the Galisteo Basin near Santa Fe, raped the women, shot two herders, and run off 75 horses and mules. Lieutenant Samuel D. Sturgis with eighteen dragoons and six civilians took the trail that night. Three days later, 175 miles southeast of Santa Fe, he came up with the marauders, who stood in front of the stolen stock and shouted peace overtures. "Well, men, I do not understand a word they are saying," exclaimed the lieutenant; "haul off and let them have it." At a range of one hundred yards the dragoons opened with musketoons and pistols. The Indians broke for some nearby timber. The day was bitterly cold, and the hands of the soldiers grew too numb to reload. Sturgis led the detachment in a saber charge. One Indian, afoot, raised his lance against Private Katon, who parried it with his saber. The lance pierced the dragoon horse. The warrior tried to duck under the horse to save himself. "But Katon was too quick for him," Bugler Drown recorded in his diary, "and took off nearly all one side of his head, just as he was in the act of stooping, and that finished his mutton." Sturgis' men killed three and wounded four of the raiders and recovered all of Eaton's stock. Three dra-

13 *Ibid.*, pp. 59–61.

goons and Eaton himself were wounded. One of the wounded, Private Pat Rooney, was packed on a mule all the way back to Santa Fe with an arrow buried two and a half inches in his skull; there he died a week later.[14]

The Mescaleros were appalled by the military activity their raids had stirred up—Simonson and Longstreet in the Guadalupes, Ewell and Stanton in the Capitans, and now Sturgis in the Manzanos. They were disheartened, too, by the casualties of the day-long fight with Ewell. Most important, one of these happened to be Santa Anna, the strident champion of war. His death strengthened the hand of Palanquito, and early in March a delegation of peace emissaries appeared at the Fort Thorn agency to bargain with Agent Michael Steck, who referred the overture to Garland.[15] The general responded by ordering Lieutenant Colonel Dixon S. Miles and three hundred men of the 3d Infantry to sweep through the Mescalero country once more. On April 2, in forbidding Dog Canyon of the Sacramentos, Miles came up with nearly the whole tribe. Under a white flag the chiefs sued for peace. The colonel was sorely tempted by the opportunity to inflict one last punishment. "There are about 400 warriors here," he wrote to Agent Steck with some exaggeration; "what a beautiful chance for a fight. The troops will never get such another. But they have met me in faith trusting to my honor," and he could not quite ignore that. The conference ended with his promise to take up the matter with the department commander.[16]

Garland was not satisfied that the Mescaleros had been humbled, but he could not justify continued war on a people so unanimously imploring an end to bloodshed. Conclusion of the campaign came in May 1855, when Governor Meriwether negotiated a treaty with the Mescaleros at Fort Thorn. Although not ratified in Washington, it had the effect of bringing the tribe into formal if somewhat tenuous civil relations with the United States. Now and then these Apaches drew rations at Fort Thorn, and later in the decade a few even tried their hand at the plow.

[14] William Drown, "A Trumpeter's Notes," in Rodenbough, pp. 199–203. Meriwether to Manypenny, Jan. 31, 1855, M386/1855, RG 75, NARS.

[15] Steck to Meriwether, March 8, 1855, OIA NM Field Papers, RG 75, NARS. Steck to Garland (draft), March 6, 1855, Steck Papers, University of New Mexico.

[16] Miles to Steck, April 3, 1855, Steck Papers. "Minutes of a 'Talk' Held at Dog Cañon on the 3d of April 1855 between Col. Miles and . . . Chiefs or Captains of the Apache Nation. . . ." N440/1855, RG 75, NARS.

More important in influencing their behavior was a new fort in the heart of the Mescalero homeland. In April, shortly before the signing of the Meriwether treaty, General Garland toured the theater of operations. In the Capitan Mountains, at the confluence of the Bonito and Ruidoso, he rode into the camp of Colonel Miles's soldiers. "They are here," recorded a dragoon in the commanding general's escort, "for the purpose of building a fort to be called Fort Stanton. . . . General John Garland selected the site for the fort today. The Officers all got drunk."[17] Subsequent events proved the Mescalero peace none too substantial, but Garland's fort on the Bonito kept them under a measure of restraint for five years.

The Mescalero treaty was but one of six that Governor Meriwether concluded in 1855 as part of a comprehensive program, authorized by the Indian Bureau, of regulating relations with the New Mexican tribes by extinguishing their land claims and bringing them into an incipient reservation system. Congress swallowed the commitment to ration Indians while they learned to farm but balked at paying for vast blocks of territory they claimed to own. All the treaties went unratified, thus disrupting a program to which the tribes, somewhat tentatively, had engaged themselves.

Another of the Meriwether treaties was with part of the Gila Apaches. Agent Steck had lined up an impressive array of Gila chiefs to participate with the Mescaleros in the treaty ceremonies at Fort Thorn in May, but they were busy on a raid in Mexico and did not turn up until June, when some Mimbres chiefs put their marks to paper. With the Jicarilla, Ute, and Mescalero hostilities ended, the Mimbres treaty marked a shift of military and civil attention to the Apaches west of the Rio Grande.

The Gila Apaches inhabited the rugged mountains that give rise to the Gila River. Taking its name from the principal range of these mountains, the Mogollon tribe, except for periodic raids against the ranches and towns of the middle Rio Grande, remained untouched by the white advance. The rest of the Gila tribes—Copper Mine, Mimbres, and Warm Spring —lived in the southern foothills of the mountain mass. The

---

[17] Brooks and Reeve, *Forts and Forays*, p. 66. SW, *Annual Report* (1855), pp. 63–64.

California Trail edged their domain, El Paso and the Mesilla Valley towns lay less than a hundred miles to the southeast, and the old Spanish copper mines in the heart of their homeland beckoned prospectors who suspected that the surrounding peaks hid deposits of gold. Thus the southern Gilas had early come into contact with the Americans—in fact had parleyed with General Kearny in 1846. They continued to raid in Mexico and now and then struck at the Rio Grande settlements. But, in contrast to the Mogollons, they were always ready to sit down and talk friendship with American officials. Already they had signed two ineffective treaties with the United States, and for a time in 1853 some had settled around short-lived Fort Webster.

The Meriwether treaty of 1855, carrying the promise of rations, lured some three hundred Mimbres Apaches under Cuchillo Negro and lesser chiefs to take up farming under the paternal guidance of Agent Steck. Another five hundred or more of the remaining southern Gilas, principally Copper Mine and Warm Spring, occasionally drew rations at Thorn but stayed on the upper Gila and its tributaries to plant corn.

These people followed the lead of the powerful Mangas Coloradas. Captain John C. Cremony, who knew him well, labeled Mangas "the greatest and most talented Apache Indian of the nineteenth century." Shrewd, crafty, and sagacious, "he combined many attributes of real greatness with the ferocity and brutality of the most savage savage."[18] Throughout the 1850s Mangas Coloradas was the scourge of Chihuahua and Sonora. With the Mexicans, he bluntly informed Captain Steen in 1850, "it was and ever would be war to the knife,"[19] and he kept his word. With the Americans he pursued an ambiguous course, at times bristling with hostility, at other times displaying a desire for friendship and cooperation.

During most of 1855 Mangas was too busy conducting his private war against Mexico to fit very well into Steck's agricultural program. It was a bad year anyway, with game so scarce that the Gilas had difficulty finding enough to eat. From Albuquerque to El Paso, the Rio Grande settlements supplied the deficiency. Most of the raids were the work of the Mogollons, whose remote homeland afforded excellent refuge from

18 Cremony, *Life among the Apaches*, pp. 176–78.
19 Steen to McLaws, Sept. 3, 1850, S23/1850, Dept. NM LR, RG 98, NARS.

pursuit, but the southern Gilas ran off their share of stock, too. Visiting Fort Thorn in December, General Garland appraised the situation. Recognizing that hunger, combined with the aggressions of "a lawless band of our Mexican population," had set off the acceleration of Gila raids, he nevertheless concluded that relief for the settlements demanded a punitive blow at the marauders.[20]

Early in March 1856 two columns of infantry and dragoons, numbering about a hundred men each, took the field from Forts Craig and Thorn. One, under Colonel Chandler, penetrated the Mogollon Mountains from the north, while the other, under Brevet Lieutenant Colonel John H. Eaton, marched in from the south. The two forces joined on the upper Gila and fell under Chandler's command. In the Sierra Almagre the troops smashed a Mogollon rancheria, killed or wounded several Indians, and recovered 250 stolen sheep. On the Mimbres River, returning to the Rio Grande, Chandler picked up another stock trail, which led to a large Apache camp. The column at once spread out and attacked. Several women and children were felled by musketry before one of the chiefs, under a white flag, induced Chandler to sound the recall. The Indian explained that these were Delgadito's friendly Mimbres Apaches who had assembled to watch the troops march by and to confer with Agent Steck, who accompanied the expedition. Chandler made some embarrassed apologies, offered indemnity, and hastily marched off to Fort Craig. The Indians generously accepted the explanation, but Steck loosed on Chandler a verbal offensive whose shock waves, to the colonel's discomfiture, rolled all the way to Washington and back. With this inglorious finale, the campaign drew to a close.[21]

Chandler and Eaton had led troops into the Mogollon Mountains for the first time, but the Mogollon Apaches disregarded the portent. During the summer and autumn of 1856 they stole thousands of sheep on the Rio Grande without provoking any greater military response than the usual ineffectual pursuit. Then,

[20] Garland to Thomas, Jan. 31, 1856, N22/1856, RG 94, NARS.

[21] Chandler to Nichols, April 12, 1856, C12/1856, RG 94. Chandler to Nichols, April 27, 1856, C14/1856, Dept. NM LR, RG 98. Steck to Meriwether, April 6, 1856, encl. to Meriwether to Manypenny, April 30, 1856, N100/1856, RG 75. Garland to Thomas, April 30, 1856, N66/1856, RG 94. SI McClelland to SW Davis, May 31, 1856, N105/1856, filed with J28/1856, RG 94. Davis to McClelland, Sept. 25, 1856, W182/1856, RG 75. All in NARS.

in November, the able and popular Navajo agent, Henry L. Dodge, disappeared while hunting deer near Zuñi Pueblo. The Mogollons promptly fell under suspicion. Agent Steck enlisted Mangas Coloradas and his relatives to seek out and ransom Dodge from the Mogollons, but after a month's efforts they could report only that he had probably been slain. In February a detachment from Fort Defiance found the body, but already Dodge's fate had so dramatized the offenses of the Mogollons that the acting department commander had drawn up plans to punish them.[22]

General Garland had gone on leave for seven months in October 1856. The temporary commander, colonel of the 3d Infantry, was no longer the dashing captain whose unorthodox western adventures had thrilled the readers of Washington Irving's prose. To his subordinates, Benjamin L. E. Bonneville—"Old Bonny Clabber"—was a hulking bag of wind in his dotage. But the colonel planned to lead the Mogollon expedition in person. From all over the territory, in the spring of 1857, he concentrated troops at Albuquerque and Fort Fillmore. The Northern Column he placed under the one-armed colonel of the Mounted Rifles, William W. Loring. Consisting of three companies of his own regiment, two of the 3d Infantry, and a detachment of Pueblo trailers, the column entered the Mogollon Mountains from the north early in May 1857. The Southern Column Bonneville assigned to red-nosed Dixon S. Miles, lieutenant colonel of the 3d Infantry. This command consisted of three companies of the 1st Dragoons, two of the Mounted Rifles, a two-company battalion of the 3d Infantry, and another of the 8th Infantry. Accompanied by Bonneville himself (Garland had resumed command in Santa Fe), the Southern Column moved westward in two wings and established a supply base on the upper Gila River.

The campaign got off to an inauspicious start. Loring cut through the Mogollon heartland and on May 18 reported to Bonneville at Rio Gila Depot that he had flushed none of the enemy. Confusion and indecision held sway. Acid-tongued Captain Ewell swore that he would rather be raising potatoes and

[22] Kendrick to Nichols, Nov. 26, 1856, encl. to Meriwether to Manypenny, Dec. 31, 1856, N216/1856, RG 75, NARS. Steck to Meriwether, Jan. 3, 1857, Steck Papers. Bonneville to Thomas, Jan. 31, 1857, Dept. NM LB, Vol. 10, pp. 72–73, RG 98, NARS. Carlisle to Kendrick, Feb. 17, 1857, encl. to Bonneville to Thomas, March 1, 1857, N37/1857, RG 94, NARS.

cabbages than "chasing a parcel of Indians about at the orders of men"—Bonneville and Miles—"who don't know what to do or how to do it if they knew what they wanted."[23] Infantry Lieutenant Henry M. Lazelle pronounced an even more biting indictment of a campaign "originating in the bombastic folly of a silly old man . . . and thus far conducted with a degree of stupidity almost asinine."[24] Both spoke prematurely. Although Bonneville disturbed few Mogollons, the proclaimed enemy, he loosed two blows that fell heavily on other Apaches whose misfortune it was to get in his way.

Mimbres chieftain Cuchillo Negro, for three years a pillar of Steck's agricultural experiment, had chosen an unpropitious moment to enter the zone of operations with a herd of more than a thousand stolen sheep. Bonneville's scouts picked up the broad trail in late May, and at once Colonel Loring and his Mounted Riflemen were hot in pursuit. On May 25 they surprised the fugitives in a rocky mountain valley some seventy miles northeast of the supply depot. A half-dozen warriors fell in the attack and the rest scattered up the mountainside, abandoning the sheep and all other property to the attackers. Among the slain was the wayward Cuchillo Negro. His loss proved serious for Steck's civilization program at the Fort Thorn agency.[25]

Meanwhile, Bonneville had launched Miles down the Gila in what Ewell termed a "solumn"—a solid column of six hundred men that the dragoon captain, commander of the right wing, gave no chance of catching any Indians. It turned up no Mogollon camps, but along the Gila, in the shadow of Mount Graham, a large camp of Coyotero Apaches reposed in fancied security. Their surprise and panic could not have been more complete when, late in the afternoon of June 27, they suddenly found Ewell and the right wing of Bonneville's "solumn" in the midst of their camp. The fight was short and sharp and all but over when the left wing, Bonneville and Miles urging their burdened mounts at its head, reached the battlefield. Victory was total. Scarcely an Apache escaped. Nearly 40 warriors were killed

23 Ewell to Dear Mother, June 10, 1857, in Hamlin, *Making of a Soldier,* pp. 82–83.
24 Reeve, "Puritan and Apache," p. 288.
25 Loring to Bonneville, June 2, 1857, encl. to Bonneville to Nichols, July 3, 1857, Dept. NM LR, B18/1857, RG 98, NARS.

or wounded and 45 women and children taken captive. Bonneville's losses were 2 officers and 7 enlisted men wounded.[26]

The largest share of the credit went to diminutive Baldy
Ewell, whose achievement Bonneville freely acknowledged, but
after the Battle of Gila River no one called the Gila Expedition Bonneville's Folly. General Garland, suspending the
campaign because of trouble with the Navajos, praised the colonel's energy, and the territorial legislature passed an effusive
resolution of thanks. True, a few voices suggested that the
Coyoteros may have been guilty of no greater offense than getting in Bonneville's line of march, but these fell silent when
Agent Steck turned up evidence that the Coyoteros had committed depredations on the California road and had harbored
some Mogollons, including the murderer of Agent Dodge. This
man, Steck learned, had in fact died in Ewell's assault on the
Coyotero camp.[27] Paradoxically, Bonneville had wound up the
Mogollon campaign by killing but one Mogollon for certain
—the one who had started the whole thing.

Bonneville's campaign carried him into the western half of
the Territory of New Mexico, within seven years to become the
Territory of Arizona, and into contact with a segment of the
Western Apaches. These were the Coyotero, or White Mountain, Apaches of the upper Gila, numbering about 2,500 people; the Chiricahuas in the mountains directly to the south,
numbering about 600; the Aravaipas on the lower San Pedro,
numbering about 200; and the Pinals on the middle Gila north
of Tucson, numbering some 500. The Western Apaches were
but dimly known to American officials in the middle 1850s.
They regularly preyed on Sonora and western Chihuahua but
had not seriously tampered with traffic on the California road.

Bonneville's Gila Expedition was but one of several developments that focused attention on the Western Apaches in the
late 1850s. Ratification of the Gadsden Treaty in 1854 added
some thirty thousand square miles to the United States south
of the Gila and presented the military and civil authorities of
New Mexico with new Indian responsibilities. These were ac-

[26] Official reports of Garland, Aug. 1, 1857; Bonneville, July 14; Miles,
July 13; and Ewell, July 13, in SW, *Annual Report* (1857), pp. 136–41.
[27] Steck to Bonneville (draft), Sept. 3, 1857, Steck Papers.

cented by a surge of mining activity in the mountains around
Tubac, by an influx of Anglo adventurers into sleepy Mexican
Tucson, and by the launching of John Butterfield's overland
stage service on the southern route to California in 1858. Late
in 1856 General Garland extended the New Mexican defense
system into the Gadsden Purchase when Major Enoch Steen
led two squadrons of the 1st Dragoons to Tucson. The adobe
village proved wholly unsuited for a military installation, and
early in 1857, after camping a few months on the Santa Cruz
near the new international boundary, he erected Fort Buchanan
in the verdant Sonoita Valley, fifty miles southeast of Tucson.[28]

Steen's dragoons had little trouble with the Coyoteros and
Chiricahuas. Although the most powerful of Apache tribes,
the former relied more heavily on agricultural pursuits than
their brethren. Less mobile, they were thus more vulnerable
to attack, and the Battle of Gila River was an object lesson not
soon forgotten. The Chiricahuas, too, seemed disposed to leave
the Americans alone and in fact enjoyed cordial relations with
the attendants of the Butterfield stage station in Apache Pass.
Coyotero and Chiricahua warriors may have been guilty of occasional depredations in the neighborhood of Tucson and Fort
Buchanan, but the evidence pointed overwhelmingly to the Pinals
as chiefly responsible for the wave of robbery and murder that
rolled over the Santa Cruz and Sonoita Valleys in 1858 and 1859.
First under Major Steen, then under Captain Ewell, the dra-

---

[28] Benjamin Sacks, "The Origins of Fort Buchanan, Myth and Fact,"
Arizona and the West, 7 (1965), 207–26. Much to the relief of embarrassed
U.S. diplomats and military officials, the Gadsden Treaty also cancelled
Article 11 of the Treaty of Guadalupe Hidalgo, which engaged the United
States to keep Indian raiders out of Mexico. Between 1848 and 1853, the
records and newspapers of Tamaulipas, Nuevo Leon, and Coahuila disclose
casualties of 385 citizens killed, 221 wounded, and 113 carried into captivity.
They also report raids that produced uncounted additional losses. Chihuahua
suffered much more than any of its eastern neighbors but provided no statistics. Sonora, where the impact was fairly well documented, recorded human
losses of 840 killed, 97 wounded, and 89 taken prisoner. To make up for the
American failure, Mexico, beginning in 1848, laid down a chain of eighteen
military colonies along the boundary from the Gulf of Mexico to the Pacific
and manned them with some 2,500 soldier-settlers charged with colonizing
the frontier and defending it against Indians. The troops did some good
service, but poverty, epidemics, and national political unrest aborted the program. General Persifor Smith estimated that, to honor Article 11, six hundred cavalry and four hundred infantry would be required on the line of
the Gila alone. SW, *Annual Report* (1850), pp. 75–81. The Mexican side of
the story is summarized in J. Fred Rippy, "The Indians of the Southwest
in the Diplomacy of the United States and Mexico, 1848–1853," *Hispanic-
American Historical Review*, 2 (1919), 363–96.

goons at Fort Buchanan tried without success to defend the settlers.

Meanwhile, officials of the Indian Bureau moved to embrace the Arizona Apaches in the civil system. An agent, John Walker, took up residence in Tucson in 1857, but he concerned himself mainly with the sedentary Pimas and Papagoes. The initiative came instead from Agent Steck, spurred in turn by the Superintendent of Indian Affairs in Santa Fe, James L. Collins. (The posts of governor and superintendent were separated in 1857, when Abraham Rencher succeeded David Meriwether as governor.) In December 1858 Steck visited the Coyoteros and Chiricahuas, distributed rations and agricultural implements, and received convincing promises of good behavior. Some Pinals sat in on the talks and witnessed the white man's generosity.[29] Two months later, as Captain Ewell was organizing an offensive into the Pinal homeland, two chiefs appeared at Fort Buchanan to make peace overtures. Late in March, at Canyon del Oro, twenty-five miles north of Tucson, Ewell and Steck met nearly the whole tribe, patched up a peace, and handed out an array of presents.[30]

How faithfully the Pinals observed the accord concluded at Canyon del Oro is difficult to assess. The plundering expeditions to Mexico continued, and doubtless some of the raiders paid scant attention to the international boundary. But Arizonans had become adept at exaggerating the proportions of the Apache menace in order to stampede the Army into ordering more troops, and thus larger supply contracts and payrolls, into the region. With or without good reason, they won partial victory. Colonel Bonneville, once more commanding in Santa Fe, authorized a punitive expedition against the Pinals in the autumn of 1859, and Brevet Lieutenant Colonel Isaac V. D. Reeve, 8th Infantry, organized a command at Fort Buchanan. Steck and Superintendent Collins both protested that these Indians had not given sufficient offense to warrant such action and predicted that Reeve's small expedition—176 rank and file of the 1st Dragoons and the Rifle Regiment—would throw all the Western Apaches into open hostility without really punishing any.[31]

[29] Steck to Collins, Feb. 1, 1859, Steck Papers.
[30] Same to same, April 8, 1859, *ibid.*
[31] Collins to Greenwood, Oct. 2, 1859, C184/1859, RG 75, NARS. Steck to Collins, Nov. 30, 1859; Collins to Steck, Dec. 11, 1859, Steck Papers.

The Army ignored the appeal. Establishing a supply depot on the San Pedro sixty miles northeast of Fort Buchanan, Colonel Reeve led a fifteen-day scout through the Pinal country in November and succeeded in capturing 1 warrior, 2 women, and 17 children. A second sweep, in December, lasted 21 days and featured a skirmish in which, at the cost of a slight wound in Captain Ewell's hand, 8 Indians were slain, 1 wounded, and 23 made captive. It was not a bad accomplishment, but Colonel Fauntleroy, filling in for Bonneville as department commander, labeled the campaign an "entire and utter failure." With Fauntleroy and Reeve exchanging acrimonious missives, the command disbanded and the Mounted Riflemen marched back to their stations on the Rio Grande.[32] The Pinals, however, were thoroughly alarmed by the military onslaught, and early in 1860, with Agent Walker as intermediary, they made their peace with Captain Ewell at Fort Buchanan.[33]

The Pinal campaign pointed up the inadequacy of the Arizona defenses, and Colonel Reeve urged that they be expanded. That Fort Buchanan was not well located strategically had become apparent to Major Steen and his officers as early as 1858, when Steen endorsed Captain John W. Davidson's recommendation that a new post be built on the lower San Pedro. From there the mail route could be more effectively guarded and a major Apache war trail interdicted. Colonel Bonneville reached the same conclusion during an inspection tour in the spring of 1859.[34] What was needed, he recognized, was a chain of posts along the Gila to keep the Indians at home. Despite the noisy demands of Arizonans for such a plan, the Department of New Mexico simply lacked the troops to man an elaborate network of forts. As a consequence of Reeve's recommendations, however, the Army authorized a sister post for Fort Buchanan, and in the spring of 1860 Fort Breckinridge was erected on the San Pedro River near the site of Reeve's old supply depot.

[32] Reeve to Wilkins, Nov. 27, 1859, encl. to Fauntleroy to Thomas, Dec. 11, 1859, N110/1859, RG 94, NARS. Fauntleroy to Thomas, Feb. 10, 1860, with enclosures, N22/1860, RG 94, NARS.

[33] Walker to Collins, Jan. 4, 1860, OIA NM Field Papers, RG 75, NARS. Walker to Steck, March 4, 1860, Steck Papers.

[34] Davidson to Lord, March 20, 1858, encl. to Bonneville to Thomas, July 15, 1859, N57/1859, RG 94, NARS.

Fort Breckinridge was a token expression of Colonel Bonneville's concern for the exposed condition of the overland mail route. For three years, 1858 to 1861, John Butterfield's stagecoaches, plying twice monthly between St. Louis and San Francisco, provided the nation with its first transcontinental mail and passenger service. To Americans the enterprise was an object of wide interest and a source of deep pride, but to military authorities it was a cause of profound worry. From the Brazos to the Colorado of the West, the line cut across one Indian raiding trail after another. East of El Paso the Texas defense network afforded at least the appearance of protection; west of El Paso passengers rarely saw a blue uniform until, 610 miles and 7 days later, they reached Fort Yuma, on the Colorado. The founding of Fort Breckinridge in 1860 provided some small comfort, but upon the uncertain temper of Gila, Coyotero, Chiricahua, and Pinal Apaches the company mainly depended for the security of its coaches and chain of relay stations.

As a matter of fact, the Apaches gave the Butterfield people little serious trouble, contenting themselves instead with plundering northern Mexico and, less regularly, the Santa Cruz and Sonoita settlements of Arizona. Company and military officials knew that at any moment the Apaches might turn on the stage line with devastating effect, but not until early in 1861, on the eve of the Civil War, was a Butterfield coach impeded by the Apaches. And on the Army itself rested the responsibility for this incident.

In October 1860 Coyotero raiders hit the ranch of John Ward in the Sonoita Valley. They ran off some oxen and made a captive of Ward's six-year-old stepson, mixed-blood offspring of an Apache warrior and Ward's Mexican wife, a former captive of the Apaches. (Under the name Mickey Free the boy later became a prominent Arizona character.) Ward trailed the war party to the San Pedro, then hastened to tell his story to Lieutenant Colonel Pitcairn Morrison, who commanded two companies of the 7th Infantry at Fort Buchanan. The culprits, Ward mistakenly asserted, were the Chiricahua Apaches who resided in Apache Pass and owed allegiance to Cochise, a leader whom future generations of writers would fix in the pantheon of American Indian chiefs.

Colonel Morrison did not question the accuracy of Ward's

indictment of Cochise. He was new in Arizona and seemingly ignorant of the amicable relations existing between the Chiricahuas and the Butterfield employees in Apache Pass. In January 1861, when Morrison finally had troops to spare, he instructed Lieutenant George N. Bascom to mount a company on mules, ride over to Apache Pass, and demand the return of Ward's boy and the stolen oxen, using such force as proved necessary.

The command reached Apache Pass on February 4. Accompanied by his brother, two nephews, and a woman and child, Cochise appeared at the military camp. Bascom preferred his charge and Cochise denied it. Firing broke out when the lieutenant tried to seize the Indian delegation as hostages. Cochise himself escaped, but his five companions fell prisoner to the soldiers. Cochise responded by capturing a Butterfield employee, James F. Wallace, and two hapless travelers found in the pass. If he thought this might induce a more reasonable attitude in his antagonist, he was mistaken. In a dramatic confrontation near the mail station, Bascom refused to exchange prisoners unless Ward's boy and the oxen were included in the trade.

Furious, the chief lashed back. During the ensuing week, while the troops remained barricaded in the depot corral, he blocked Apache Pass. At the crest of the pass he stopped a small train, bound the teamsters to wagon wheels, and set fire to the wagons. Nearby, in the black of night, he attacked the eastbound stagecoach; after a stirring chase the passengers forted up in the station with the troops. He ambushed the troops themselves while they watered their mules within sight of the station. And finally, he executed Wallace and the other hostages before clearing out for Mexico. On February 10 Surgeon Bernard J. D. Irwin and a small detachment made it through from Fort Buchanan, and four days later two companies of dragoons arrived from Fort Breckinridge. When a scouting party found the butchered remains of the white hostages high in the pass, the officers decided to retaliate. Three of the Chiricahua hostages and three Coyoteros captured by Irwin on the way from Fort Buchanan were hanged from a scrub oak over the graves of the murdered whites.[35]

[35] Pertinent evidence bearing on this confusing and controversial event is summarized and analyzed in Robert M. Utley, "The Bascom Affair: A Reconstruction," *Arizona and the West*, 3 (1961), 59–68; and Benjamin H. Sacks, ed., "New Evidence on the Bascom Affair," *ibid.*, 4 (1962), 261–78.

The Bascom affair plunged Arizona into twenty-five years of hostility with the Chiricahua Apaches. Cochise had been wrongfully accused and the wrong compounded by the hanging of his relatives. He responded in traditional Apache fashion. If Colonel Morrison had been less peremptory in his orders, or if Lieutenant Bascom had possessed the judgment to adapt them to circumstances, the war would surely have broken out over some other incident. But it was the one in Apache Pass that Cochise remembered with unrelenting bitterness, and it is Lieutenant Bascom whom history, not altogether justly, holds individually responsible for the consequence.

West of Tucson, beyond the domain of the Apaches, all the southern overland trails drew together in a single strand to cross the Colorado River at the mouth of the Gila. The Yuma Crossing was the southern gateway to California, and its strategic importance became evident as soon as the gold rush got underway in 1849. The Colorado River Valley was remote from the headquarters and principal areas of operation of both the Department of New Mexico and the Department of the Pacific, but it fell to the latter as a zone of responsibility.

The Yuma Indians, mustering about three hundred warriors, inhabited the valley in the neighborhood of the crossing. Although not openly hostile, they were an unpredictable and often troublesome people who bore watching if the flow of traffic into California were not to be impeded. The Yumas operated a ferry across the Colorado in 1849 when the first waves of the gold rush hit the crossing. Observing the lucrative possibilities, a gang of about a dozen white adventurers moved in and dispossessed them. The Yumas bided their time until the aggressors dropped their guard one night and got drunk. Vengeful warriors swarmed over the camp and butchered all but three, then resumed the operation of the ferry. The alarm created in San Diego subsided when full reports demonstrated that the victims had got what they deserved, but the massacre underscored the need for a military post at Yuma Crossing to insure the security of emigrants and freighters.

Although hard pressed for troops, the Pacific commander, General Persifor Smith, scraped together three companies of the 2d Infantry, placed them under Brevet Major Samuel P. Heintzelman, and sent them overland from San Diego. In November

1850 the major established Fort Yuma on the California shore of the river. Separated from San Diego by 160 miles of mountains and utterly barren desert, the fort proved almost impossible to supply by land, and in fact the garrison had to withdraw altogether late in 1851. Troops returned early in 1852 and thereafter depended almost entirely on water communication with higher headquarters. Coastal vessels transported supplies and personnel from San Francisco and San Diego to the mouth of the Colorado, where river steamers took over for the journey up the treacherous stream to the crossing. Thus supported, Fort Yuma kept the Yuma Indians in check, succored countless destitute emigrants, and watched over the Yuma Crossing for forty years.[36]

Upstream from the Yumas lived the Mojaves, a kindred people with a population of about fifteen hundred. The California migration touched them only peripherally until 1858, when it looked as if another emigrant route might be opened through the center of their range. This route was pioneered by Lieutenant Edward F. Beale, U.S. Navy, using some of Jefferson Davis' camels, in 1857. It cut across northern New Mexico from Albuquerque on a line later adopted by the Santa Fe Railroad, and struck the Colorado just below the place where Hoover Dam now holds back the river. Such travelers as used the new road in subsequent years still found it necessary, for topographical reasons, to bear southward and ford the Colorado at Yuma Crossing, but in 1858 Beale's Route and Beale's Crossing were widely expected to form a major corridor of the westward movement.

The first sizable emigrant party to try Beale's Route, in the spring of 1858, encountered hostile Mojaves, endured a costly siege, and ended by retreating all the way back to Albuquerque. To open the road and control the Mojaves, Secretary of War Floyd ordered General Newman Clarke, commanding the Pacific Department, to establish a fort at Beale's Crossing.

In December 1858 Lieutenant Colonel William Hoffman, escorted by a company of dragoons, rode across the Colorado Desert from Los Angeles to make a preliminary reconnais-

[36] The story of Fort Yuma's founding and early years is well told in Arthur Woodward, *Feud on the Colorado* (Los Angeles, Calif., 1955); and Woodward, ed., *Journal of Lt. Thomas W. Sweeny, 1849–1853* (Los Angeles, Calif., 1956). See also Frazer, ed., *Mansfield on the Condition of Western Forts*, pp. 107–10, 146–49.

sance of the country around Beale's Crossing. The Mojaves, triumphant over their repulse of the emigrant train, harassed the march and finally, on January 9, 1859, provoked a brief skirmish in which they lost nearly a dozen warriors. Hoffman returned to the coast and, under orders from General Clarke, assembled seven companies of the 6th Infantry. Two companies marched overland while the rest went by water. Rendezvousing at Fort Yuma in March 1859, the expedition pointed northward during the early weeks of April.

The belligerence of the Mojaves vanished as soon as they saw the column of seven hundred infantrymen winding up the valley. The chiefs came in for a talk. "They said the country was mine," reported Hoffman, "and I might do what I pleased with it." To make sure they remembered, the colonel left behind two companies of infantry and some artillery. Under Brevet Major Lewis Armistead, they erected Fort Mojave on the east bank of the river. For the next two years the fort guarded a nervous tribe of Indians and a little-used emigrant road.[37]

Fortunately for the overtaxed military establishment in New Mexico, the hostilities with Jicarillas, Utes, Mescaleros, and Gilas occurred at a time of relative quiet among the Navajos. Part of the explanation lay in the presence of Fort Defiance, legacy of Colonel Sumner's otherwise abortive expedition of 1851, in the midst of the Navajo country. Part lay in the good sense of Brevet Major Henry L. Kendrick, post commander from 1853 to 1857. But the largest credit for the unprecedented security enjoyed by the Mexican settlements west of the Rio Grande went to Henry L. Dodge, appointed Navajo agent in 1853. A frontiersman of unusual ability, this strange scion of a distinguished Iowa family served the Navajo nation as devotedly as his father and brother, both U.S. senators, served the American nation. Taking an Indian wife and traveling constantly to remote corners of the tribal homeland, Henry Dodge attained an influence over the Navajos that held them in check for three years.[38]

[37] Correspondence covering the Mojave expedition and the founding of Fort Mojave is in SW, *Annual Report* (1859), pp. 387–413. See also Bandel, *Frontier Life in the Army*, pp. 57–62, 247–78.

[38] An excellent assessment of Dodge's significance is in McKnitt, ed., *Navaho Expedition*, pp. 181–211. This section of McKnitt's epilog to the Simpson journal of Washington's 1849 expedition contains a well-documented

Not that Navajo raids ceased altogether. Throughout Dodge's tenure an occasional theft or murder kept settlements as far east as Albuquerque on guard. But these were the work of a few outlaws—*ladrones*—not sanctioned by the propertied elements that made up the tribal power structure. Because Navajo political organization featured a form of democracy bordering on anarchy, the tribal leadership could not control the *ladrones*. In this lay the seeds of endless trouble with the Americans, who insisted on holding the chiefs responsible for the behavior of all Navajos. Also, like other tribes, the Navajos had a war party, which resisted any accommodation to U.S. authority and approved the raids of the *ladrones*. By the early 1850s, however, no Navajo could deny that the Americans had come to stay, and most of the tribe unquestionably favored peaceful co-existence—so long as it involved no serious compromise of deep-rooted tribal customs.

Another treaty, the first in which the Navajos engaged at all willingly, affirmed the new spirit of accord. In the summer of 1855 Governor Meriwether and General Garland met Navajo leaders at Laguna Negra to sign one of the six Meriwether treaties that Congress declined to approve. Among the treaty provisions was the definition, for the first time, of a boundary between the Navajo and New Mexican populations. More significant, the treaty bound the Navajos to surrender tribesmen guilty of depredations for punishment under the white man's law—something the Navajos no less than the Sioux could seldom steel themselves to do. Neither party in fact paid more than lip service to the Treaty of Laguna Negra, and the influence of Agent Dodge continued to form the shaky foundation on which the peace rested.[39] Twice during his regime, moreover, the foundation nearly crumbled.

The first incident occurred in October 1854, before the Laguna Negra council, when a Navajo killed a soldier near Fort Defiance and Dodge and Kendrick demanded the murderer. The chiefs temporized mightily but at last acquiesced. The man was delivered with an arrow in his groin, and on the spot,

---

history of the tribe from 1849 to 1857. See also Frank D. Reeve, "The Government and the Navaho, 1846–1858," *New Mexico Historical Review, 14* (1939), 82–114.

[39] SW, *Annual Report* (1855), pp. 71–72. McKnitt, *Navaho Expedition*, pp. 194–200. Lynn R. Bailey, *The Long Walk: A History of the Navajo Wars, 1848–68* (Los Angeles, Calif., 1964), pp. 65–71.

Dodge reported, he was "hung until he was *dead dead dead*."
Regretting such peremptory justice, Governor Meriwether nonetheless conceded its favorable effect on the Navajos. This may
have been more apparent than real, for his successor as Indian
superintendent cited evidence that the chiefs had duped the
Americans by substituting an Indianized Mexican for the
guilty Navajo.[40]

The second incident proved far more serious and registered
a significant shift in Navajo attitudes. In the spring of 1856,
in a shattering attack on Peralta, a Navajo band killed
some Mexicans and stole either four or eleven thousand sheep,
depending on whose report is credited. The perpetrators were
not outlaws but the youthful offspring of leading members of
the tribe. This time the chiefs, after briefly temporizing, defi-
antly refused to turn over the guilty Indians as required by
the Treaty of 1855. Only the scarcity of troops prevented General Garland from responding at once with a full-scale campaign. The affair was at length smoothed over as the chiefs
reconsidered their hasty action and adopted a more concilia-
tory demeanor. Although they did not give up the offenders,
they saw to it that, for the time being, their unruly sons stayed
at home. As Garland could not put a command in the field
capable of doing more than advertise his weakness, he and the
governor chose to accept at face value the Navajo professions
of contrition.[41]

The aftermath of the Peralta raid left Navajo leaders with
fresh contempt for American ability to enforce an ultimatum
and with less inclination to discourage the time-honored custom of stealing sheep. It also left officials in Santa Fe with a
bad taste in their mouth and an unfulfilled ambition to make
an ultimatum stick. The death of Henry Dodge at the hands of
Mogollon Apaches in November 1857 (see p. 155) stilled a
powerful voice of moderation that might have averted an open

[40] Garland to Thomas, Oct. 31, 1854, G447/1854, RG 94. Meriwether to
Manypenny, Nov. 30, 1854, enclosing Dodge to Meriwether, Nov. 13, 1854,
N349/1854, RG 75. All in NARS. CIA, *Annual Report* (1858), p. 190.
[41] Garland to Thomas, April 30, 1856, enclosing Kendrick to Nichols,
April 21, 1856 (2 letters), N66/1856, RG 94. Meriwether to Manypenny,
May 31, 1856, enclosing Dodge to Meriwether, May 16, 1856, N118/1856,
RG 75. Garland to Thomas, June 30, 1856, enclosing Kendrick to Nichols,
June 2 and 13, 1856, N96/1856, RG 94. Garland to Thomas, July 31, 1856,
N111/1856, RG 94. All in NARS. CIA, *Annual Report* (1856), p. 182. Bailey,
The Long Walk, pp. 73-75.

rupture. The next incident found neither side disposed to conciliation.

Early in July 1858 a Navajo warrior rode into Fort Defiance to do some trading. He had recently come off second in a quarrel with his wife, and his heart was black. According to Indian custom, this sanctioned drastic action against anyone who got in his way. The luckless individual happened to be a Negro youth, servant of Brevet Major W. T. H. Brooks, post commander. As the boy walked across the parade ground, the Navajo shot an arrow into his back and galloped out of the fort, his heart free of the domestic cloud. The slave tried to pull out the arrow but broke the shaft, leaving the point buried in his lung. He died four days later.

The usual demand for the culprit's surrender elicited the usual excuses for delay. General Garland perceived how the negotiations would likely end. In August he scraped together enough units to form an expedition and sent them to Fort Defiance under Lieutenant Colonel Miles. Alarmed, the tribe on September 8 produced a corpse alleged to be that of the murderer, but no one was fooled by this second attempt to sacrifice a Mexican captive to the strange demands of the white man's justice.

The next day Colonel Miles formed his column and set forth to the northwest. It numbered 307 rank and file—three companies of the Mounted Rifles, two of the 3d Infantry, and a company of "Mexican guides and spies" under Captain Blas Lucero. The first day out the flankers snared a Navajo warrior. Miles questioned him, concluded that "it was embarrassing us too much to retain him," and had him shot as a spy. On the third day the command dropped into Canyon de Chelly at its head and marched the full length of this awesome chasm, long dreaded as an impregnable stronghold of the Navajos. Warriors gathered on both edges of the sheer cliffs, six hundred to a thousand feet high, to shoot arrows and drop boulders on the troops, but produced no casualties. From the canyon down the west flank of the Defiance Plateau, the column beat off harrassing thrusts by angry Navajos. Both sides suffered minor damage. Back at Defiance on September 15, Miles could count more than a dozen enemy casualties as the accomplishment of his march.

Throughout October and November the colonel kept up the

pressure. On October 10 Major Brooks clashed with about a hundred Navajos near Bear Spring, on the road to Albuquerque, and may have killed as many as twenty-five. On the twentieth Captain George McLane broke up a herd camp and captured four hundred sheep, only to lose them in a counterattack that panicked his Zuñi auxiliaries. On the twenty-fourth, twenty-five miles south of Defiance, Lieutenant George W. Howland and Captain Lucero fell on a Navajo camp and captured all the occupants, twenty people, before they could organize a resistance. Early in November Miles led a powerful force in another sweep through the country west of the fort. Only a few Indians were slain and some stock seized, but the Navajos were now convinced that they had better try to pacify the aggressive old colonel who kept their homeland teeming with soldiers.

On Christmas Day 1858 Superintendent Collins and Colonel Bonneville, commanding in Santa Fe since September, when ill health forced Garland's return to the States, sat down with Navajo leaders at Fort Defiance and drew up peace terms. The Indians agreed never to approach closer to the settlements than a line drawn about twenty-five miles east of the fort, to indemnify owners of stolen property, to release all prisoners, to appoint a head chief answerable for the whole tribe, and to concede the tribe's responsibility for the actions of its members. On the crucial issue, however, the chiefs managed to persuade the officials from Santa Fe that the man who shot Major Brooks' slave had fled the country and that the demand for his surrender should therefore be dropped.[42]

Bonneville was convinced that the Navajos sincerely desired peace, as of course they did, but he was not inclined to hail the Christmas accord as a millennium in Navajo relations. He retained twenty-one prisoners as hostages, beefed up the Defiance garrison to four companies of the 3d Infantry, and placed an additional six companies of infantry and Mounted Riflemen on the Rio Grande line with responsibility for supporting Defiance. The next summer, to underscore the new firmness with the Navajos, he dispatched strong "exploring" columns to range the country west of the Defiance Plateau and Chuska Moun-

[42] Official reports covering the 1858 operations are in SW, *Annual Report* (1858), pp. 309–13; (1859), pp. 258–77. See also Bailey, *The Long Walk*, chap. 5, and J. P. Dunn, *Massacres of the Mountains: A History of the Indian Wars of the Far West, 1815–1875* (New York, 1886), pp. 228–36.

tains and remind the inhabitants of the recent unpleasantness.[43] These measures paid off in a year of near tranquillity. As 1859 drew to a close, however, the tribe grew increasingly restive under the restraints imposed by the troublesome fort at Canyon Bonito, and the war party gained sufficient strength to commit the tribe to a policy of open aggression.

In mid-January 1860 a strong force of warriors jumped a supply train en route to Fort Defiance. For three days, as the wagons continued the journey, the escort of forty infantrymen repulsed one determined strike after another. On February 8 an estimated five hundred Navajos attacked a herd guard of twenty-eight men seven miles north of Fort Defiance. The sergeant in charge kept his men well in hand and fell back in good order until reinforced. Ten Navajos were reported slain and another twenty wounded. Then, shortly before dawn on April 30, close to a thousand Navajos launched an assault on Fort Defiance itself. Three assault columns struck from different directions and gained some of the outbuildings before Brevet Major Oliver L. Shepherd could form his three companies of the 3d Infantry and close off the penetration. For two hours the predawn gloom flashed with musketry. Then, with sufficient light to permit maneuver, Shepherd sallied from the fort, drove the enemy to the nearby slopes, and finally cleared the area of Indians. For all the firing, casualties were slight —one soldier killed and two wounded, perhaps a dozen Navajos killed or wounded—but here was a monstrous challenge that had to be met.[44]

Colonel Fauntleroy, department commander since October 1859, forwarded Major Shepherd's report to army headquarters in New York, where General Scott, long since shorn of control over the field commanders, endorsed it to the Secretary of War with the note that the defense of Fort Defiance reflected great credit on Shepherd and his command. Secretary Floyd moved at once. "Active operations will be instituted against the Navajoes as soon as the necessary preparations can be made," he wrote on July 9, 1860, and they should be made "*with infantry.*" To give substance to the authority, he

[43] SW, *Annual Report* (1859), pp. 276–77, 316–23.
[44] Official reports are in *ibid.* (1860), pp. 52–56, 203–4. "Dick" [Captain William Dickinson], "Reminiscences of Fort Defiance, 1860," *Journal of the Military Service Institution of the United States, 4* (1883), 90–92. Bailey, *The Long Walk,* pp. 16–22.

ordered the first meaningful reinforcement of the Department of New Mexico since the Regulars took over in 1848. From Utah, where the Mormon threat had proved largely illusory, came the entire 5th and 7th Infantry regiments, together with three companies of the 10th and two of the 2d Dragoons. To organize and direct the offensive Fauntleroy chose Major Edward R. S. Canby, 10th Infantry, who would command in his brevet grade of lieutenant colonel. Beardless, colorless, he fully deserved his biographer's characterization of "prudent soldier."[45]

Colonel Canby organized his command at Fort Defiance in September. Available for field service were nine foot companies of the 5th and 7th and six mounted companies of the 2d Dragoons and Rifle Regiment—more than six hundred men—together with a large force of Ute auxiliaries and Blas Lucero's "guides and spies." These Canby formed into three columns, one under Brevet Major Henry H. Sibley, one under Captain Lafayette McLaws, and the third under his own direct command. In November, with the garrisons of Fort Defiance and newly established Fort Fauntleroy, thirty miles to the south, guarding the rear, Canby's columns moved west. All three scoured the Chuska Mountains and the expanse of red rock and sand beyond. The Utes, operating between the columns, preyed on Navajo flocks and planting grounds. But the region was locked in its second season of drought. Water holes were dry and forage sparse. The cavalry horses broke down. Supplies came through irregularly. And Navajo warriors hung on the flanks and rear of the columns, always harrying but never closing in decisive combat. After a month of this torture, Canby returned to Fort Defiance.

The operation had not been a complete failure. The Navajos had lost nearly three dozen warriors, a thousand horses, and seven thousand sheep. This damage, combined with the insecurity produced by so many soldiers roaming about the countryside, had already impelled some of the chiefs to sue for peace, and there had been open intratribal fighting between the

---

[45] Official documents covering the campaign through October 1860 are in *ibid.*, pp. 59-69. For the remainder of the operations I have relied on Max L. Heyman, Jr., "On the Navaho Trail: The Campaign of 1860," *New Mexico Historical Review*, 26 (1951), 44-63. The same subject matter is treated by Heyman in *Prudent Soldier: A Biography of Major General E. R. S. Canby, 1817-1873* (Glendale, Calif., 1959). See also Bailey, *The Long Walk*, chap. 7.

war and peace factions. But until the peace party could deliver an ironclad guarantee to eliminate or control the *ladrones*, Canby turned down all overtures, and Colonel Fauntleroy sustained him.

So did Secretary Floyd, who now ordered a winter campaign and seized the occasion to lay down some precepts for conducting it. The striking force, he decreed, should be largely if not wholly infantry, which could operate less cumbersomely than cavalry, and it must comport itself in a humanitarian way. The troops, that is, "should have for their object to inspire them"—the Navajos—"with fear, by a few decisive blows for the destruction of life; and not impoverish them, by wantonly destroying their flocks and herds." The Secretary thus exposed his ignorance of the realities of Indian fighting. Cavalry had difficulty enough closing with the elusive Navajos; infantry had almost none at all. "Humanitarian" warfare, moreover, had rarely brought Indians to bay in the past and rarely would in the future. Only by impoverishing them could the troops force the adversary to give up. "To seize and destroy the crops of the Navajos" had been the mission Fauntleroy set for Canby in September. It was the means by which the Navajos would be crushed three years later.

No one on the frontier took the Secretary's instructions very seriously. It was a long way from Washington to Fort Defiance, and anyway Mr. Floyd, before his departure from the Cabinet in January 1861, was more preoccupied with the secession crisis than with a remote war with the Navajos. Canby did adopt a different course, however, and he did make large use of infantry. Establishing a network of strong points in the Navajo country, he kept patrols constantly in the field destroying crops, seizing stock, and keeping the Navajo people always on the run. By January 1861 the tribal leaders were begging for relief, and by February they were willing to sit down and discuss how the peace faction might team up with the soldiers to subjugate the war faction.

Complicating the problem throughout the winter were bands of self-styled New Mexican volunteers overrunning the area of operations. These had tried to get enrolled in the federal service in the autumn, but, recognizing them as mere predators, Fauntleroy had refused and had even instructed Canby to keep them out of the Navajo country. This proved impossible, and the "volunteers" rode about killing and stealing with supreme disregard of the plans of federal officers. Their actions grew particularly troublesome after Canby began to separate the peace and war factions and to play one against the other, for the irregulars never discriminated between the two. Indeed, on one occasion they killed and scalped a Navajo scout employed by the Army and wearing military insignia.[46]

By April 1861 Canby's program gave some promise of ultimately bringing the Navajos under control. In February he had granted a three-month armistice and was working quietly but effectively with the peace leaders to undermine and isolate the proponents of continued war. While still considerably short of this goal, which indeed may have been unattainable, Canby had to hasten to Santa Fe to shore up a military department shaken to its foundations by the firing on Fort Sumter. By the summer of 1861 the Navajo threat had receded to insignificance compared to the threat from the south. A full brigade of Texans was organizing to invade New Mexico. Canby's job was to stop it. At its head rode a recent subordinate in the Navajo campaign—Henry H. Sibley, now brigadier general, C.S.A.

"My government will correct all this. It will keep off the Indians." New Mexicans of 1861 recalled General Kearny's bright words with a touch of irony. The toll of lives exacted by these Indians in the fifteen years since his seizure of New Mexico ran somewhere between two and three hundred, and property loss, principally in sheep, cattle, mules, and horses, approached a million dollars.[47] At the moment, three thousand soldiers and five Indian agents were striving mightily to make Kearny's promise come true, but the end was nowhere in sight and the toll was not only mounting but accelerating.

Not that the military and civil effort of the 1850s was bereft

[46] See, in addition to sources cited in note 28 above, House Ex. Docs., 36th Cong., 2d sess., No. 24.

[47] H. H. Bancroft's estimate (History of Arizona and New Mexico [San Francisco, Calif., 1889], p. 659), which is as good as any considering the character of the evidence. In 1865 the Territorial Secretary of State wrote that records in his office covering the years 1846 to 1856 disclosed 244 citizens reporting the loss of 150,231 sheep, 893 horses, 761 mules, and 1,234 cows, for a total sworn value of $502,986.68. No records were kept thereafter until 1862, but damages during this period were thought to have exceeded half a million dollars. Arny to Legislative Assembly, Dec. 16, 1865, CIA LR NM, A33/1865, RG 75, NARS.

of lasting results. Because of the conquest of the Utes and the Jicarilla Apaches, residents of the upper Rio Grande enjoyed a security hitherto unknown, and on the New Mexico end of the Santa Fe Trail traffic moved with little apprehension of Indian attack. Elsewhere, although no other tribes had been brought to heel with any degree of finality, both the Army and the Indian Bureau had intruded into the heart of their ranges, had fought and negotiated with them, had fed and taught them, and had planted such forts as Stanton, Defiance, Buchanan, and Breckinridge in their very midst. These inconclusive contacts of the past were necessary preludes to the conclusive contacts of the future. But they had also stirred up the Indians and, together with a growth of settlements and a rise of travel that heightened the opportunities for plunder, produced the unhappy situation in which the territory found itself at the turn of the decade.

The onset of the Civil War collapsed the military and civil assault on the Indian problem. Requiring the mobilization of the territory's entire military resources to head off the Confederate invasion, it withdrew all restraints from the Indians. The tribes took full advantage of the white man's weakness. Yet because of the Civil War, this weakness soon turned to a strength that within three years brought the downfall of some of the most troublesome of the New Mexican Indians.

NINE

Operations in the Pacific Northwest, 1855-60

I AM a commanding general without troops!" lamented the Pacific Division's General Hitchcock late in 1851; "my adjutant general in arrest, no aide de camp, and this evening's mail brings me a letter from the U.S. Quartermaster General, Jesup, complaining of the officers of his department in this division and saying that he may be obliged to refuse payment of their drafts and cease to send further funds here!"[1] The general's frustrated outburst partly explains why the Regular Army figured unimportantly for nearly five years in the confrontation between Indians and whites brought on by the California gold rush. It simply lacked the resources.

General Persifor Smith, Hitchcock's predecessor, had begun his assignment determined to mete out quick retribution to such Indians as resisted U.S. authority. In September 1849, near Goose Lake in northeastern California, Pit River Indians ambushed an army exploring expedition and killed Captain William H. Warner of the Topographical Engineers. At the same time, Indians in the neighborhood of Clear Lake, some fifty miles north of San Francisco, grew restive and throughout the winter murdered an occasional prospector. In the spring and summer of 1850, Smith sent a force of dragoons and infantry against both offending groups. Contentious, tyrannical Captain Nathaniel Lyon led the expedition first to Clear Lake, where some four hundred Indians had taken refuge on an island. Crossing by boat, Lyon drove them into tule-studded swamps and shot down

[1] Hitchcock, *Fifty Years in Camp and Field*, p. 391.

between sixty and one hundred. He then marched over the divide to Russian River and proceeded downstream some twenty miles, where another four hundred or so natives had also fortified on an island. Surrounding them, the troops closed in and made the position "a perfect slaughter pen." Lyon placed the dead at not less than 75 and perhaps as high as 150. A second expedition in July penetrated the Pit River country and clashed with the slayers of Captain Warner, though less decisively than at Clear Lake and Russian River.[2]

Lyon's two campaigns, like Phil Kearny's almost accidental collision with the Rogue River Indians and Silas Casey's brief offensive against the Coquilles (see p. 104), formed no part of a coherent approach to the mission assigned the Pacific Division. Lack of troops, an escalating desertion rate, prohibitive logistical costs, War Department economy strictures, and a deepening disgust at unprovoked or indiscriminate white aggression combined to prevent Smith and Hitchcock from exerting a meaningful influence on the Indian situation. Meanwhile, transitory volunteer and militia companies rampaged over much of the Sierra and expeditiously solved the Indian problem for all time.[3] Only in the mountains of northern California and southern Oregon did the natives defy extermination long enough for the Regulars to become involved. The troop buildup of 1853–54, though nominal, at last permitted the Army to advance into this troubled country and try to keep the Indians and whites from slaughtering one another.[4]

Since 1850, when miners first began to overrun these mountains, relations between Indians and whites had steadily

[2] William H. Goetzmann, *Army Exploration in the American West, 1803–1863* (New Haven, Conn., 1959), pp. 251-53. Smith to Freeman, Feb. 27, 1850, S167/1850. Lyon to Canby, May 22, 1850, L105/1850. Smith to Freeman, Sept. 27, 1850, S591/1850. All in RG 94, NARS.

[3] A thorough account of how the volunteers went about this, presented from the viewpoint of the miners, is A. J. Bledsoe, *The Indian Wars of the Northwest* (San Francisco, Calif., 1885).

[4] The 3d Artillery and 4th Infantry were assigned to the Department of the Pacific in 1853. The 2d Infantry was disbanded, to be reconstituted in New York, and its personnel used to build up understrength units already on the Pacific. SW, *Annual Report* (1853), p. 93. In December 1853, off Cape Hatteras, disaster overtook the steamer *San Francisco*, bearing the 3d Artillery to its new station, and two hundred of the six hundred aboard were drowned. Reconstituted in New York, the 3d shipped again for the Pacific in 1854. William A. Ganoe, *The History of the United States Army* (New York, 1924), p. 235. By the close of 1854, the Department of the Pacific counted 1,198 officers and men. SW, *Annual Report* (1854), p. 63.

"Cavalry Charge on the Southern Plains." Rarely did the troopers get close enough to the adversary for such a charge to take effect, but it happened often enough to inspire Frederic Remington's classic painting and to fix the scene indelibly in the motion picture and television image of the Old West. *(Courtesy Metropolitan Museum of Art)*

"Prairie Indian Encampment." The Plains Indians—Sioux, Cheyenne, Arapaho, Kiowa, Comanche, and others—lived in portable skin lodges and followed the buffalo herds. With no fixed abode, they presented the Army with a formidable task simply to find them. Contrary to popular belief, however, once found they were not difficult to take by surprise. *(From a painting by John Mix Stanley, courtesy Detroit Institute of Arts)*

"The American Soldier, 1847." The uniform worn by the armies invading Mexico in 1846–47 persisted into the early 1850s. Shown here is an infantry lieutenant and, mounted, a dragoon private. *(From a painting by H. Charles McBarron, courtesy Department of the Army)*

"The American Soldier, 1855." The military attire of the middle 1850s appeared more ornamental than its undistinguished predecessor but was usually supplanted in the field by clothing selected for durability and practicality. Here a quartermaster officer in dress uniform confronts a first sergeant of light artillery as a light battery passes in the background. *(From a painting by H. Charles McBarron, courtesy Department of the Army)*

"2nd U.S. Cavalry, 1855–61." The new cavalry regiments organized in 1855 were given distinctive uniforms characterized by the celebrated "Jeff Davis" or "Hardee" hat, and within five years the pattern had been adopted for the entire Army. From left to right: musician, company officer, private in fatigues, corporal in full dress. *(From a plate by Colonel Frederick P. Todd, reproduced by permission of Colonel Todd and the Company of Military Historians)*

Military attire on the eve of the Civil War owed much to the patterns adopted for the new cavalry regiments in 1855. Basic features of this uniform remained regulation until after the Civil War, but as usual the troops—especially the wartime Volunteers—adopted more serviceable attire. H. A. Ogden here represents the period 1858–61 with (left to right) lieutenant colonel of the Mounted Rifles, lieutenant colonel of the 2d Dragoons, captain of the 5th Infantry, infantry private and dragoon sergeant. *(Courtesy Library of Congress)*

"Indian Warfare," by Frederic Remington, depicts Plains warriors in typical harassment of an army supply train. Such "attacks" rarely did much damage to either side, but when a warrior chanced to be killed or wounded his comrades went to any length, no matter how great the peril, to prevent him from falling into the hands of the bluecoats. Such a rescue is portrayed here. *(Courtesy Thomas Gilcrease Institute of American History and Art, Tulsa, Oklahoma)*

Edwin Vose Sumner laid out the New Mexico defense system in 1851–52 and commanded the 1st Cavalry in the Cheyenne campaign of 1857. A skull thick enough to deflect a musket ball gave "Bull" Sumner his sobriquet and also enclosed a mind full of frontier and military lore but often obtuse in applying it. *(Courtesy National Archives)*

General Persifor F. Smith. Widely held in affection and esteem, the veteran colonel of the Mounted Rifles sketched the framework of the California and Texas defense systems in the late 1840s and early 1850s. Ill health, draining his vigor and dimming his faculties, ended in death in 1858. *(Courtesy National Archives)*

General David Emanuel Twiggs. "Old Davey, the Bengal Tiger" ably commanded the Department of Texas from 1857 to 1861, but his hasty surrender of federal property to Texas secessionists earned him dismissal from the Army and from loyalist officers the epithet of "Traitor Twiggs." *(Courtesy National Archives)*

"By God, I'm for battle—no peace," declared General William S. Harney as he marched forth on the Sioux campaign of 1855. By word and deed, "The Big Chief Who Swears" fired the Sioux with a fear and hatred that still burned two generations later. *(Courtesy National Archives)*

Although a high-pitched nasal voice made his commands sound unmilitary, Philip St. George Cooke enjoyed a reputation as the Army's leading expert on the employment of mounted troops. "He lived and probably died in the unshakable belief that the mounted sabre charge was the crowning event of a cavalryman's life," writes his biographer, Otis Young. The contrasting reality of Indian campaigning never dimmed his stirring vision of the U.S. Cavalry. *(Courtesy National Archives)*

Fort Laramie looked like this to a passing emigrant-artist in the summer of 1849. This same summer the Army bought it from the American Fur Company for use in guarding the Oregon-California Trail. Divested of its battlements and greatly enlarged, Fort Laramie served as the most important post on the northern Plains until its abandonment forty years later. (*Courtesy State Historical Society of Wisconsin*)

Fort Defiance, New Mexico. Founded by Colonel Sumner in 1851, this outpost on the edge of the Navajo country was the principal base of operations for the Navajo campaigns of 1858–61. In 1864 Kit Carson built Fort Canby on its site and from here mounted the expeditions that ended the Navajo wars. (*From a painting by Seth Eastman based on a sketch by Lieutenant Colonel J. H. Eaton, Courtesy National Archives*)

Cheyenne warrior. Ranging in northern and southern divisions, the Cheyennes were to be found on the Platte and the Arkansas, frequently allied with the Sioux against the invading whites. *(Courtesy National Archives)*

Comanche family. "The most warlike people we have on the continent," said Colonel Jesse H. Leavenworth of the Comanches. "There are no better horsemen in the world." These "Lords of the South Plains" ranged south from the Arkansas to the Texas plains, regularly raided the Texas frontier and settlements of northern Mexico. *(Courtesy National Archives)*

Little Spaniard, Comanche warrior painted by George Catlin in 1834. *(Courtesy Smithsonian Institution)*

Close friends of the Cheyennes, the seven tribes of Teton Sioux roamed the northern plains between the upper Missouri and the Platte. This is Steep Wind, painted in 1832 by George Catlin. *(Courtesy Smithsonian Institution)*

Navajo Warrior. Proud, sensitive, skilled in crafts, agricultural and pastoral pursuits, and warfare, the powerful Navajos scourged New Mexican settlements for two centuries until rounded up by Kit Carson and exiled by General Carleton to a reservation distant from their homeland. *(Courtesy State Historical Society of Wisconsin)*

Apache warriors. Superb skill in guerrilla warfare combined with the hostile character of their mountain-and-desert homeland made the Apaches the most formidable Indians the Army encountered. *(Courtesy National Archives)*

The Battle of Gila River, June 27, 1857. With advance elements of Colonel Bonneville's Gila Expedition, Captain "Baldy" Ewell stormed into a Coyotero Apache ranchería and all but annihilated its inhabitants before the obese colonel and his wornout mule could reach the scene. *(From a contemporary drawing by Joseph Heger, courtesy Arizona Pioneers Historical Society)*

Benjamin Louis Eulaile Bonneville. Little about the gouty old colonel of the 3d Infantry recalled the dashing captain of Washington Irving's adventure, but the Battle of Gila River turned the Gila campaign of 1857 from "Bonneville's Folly" into a triumph that won him a vote of thanks from the New Mexico Territorial Assembly. *(Courtesy Denver Public Library Western Collection)*

Combative little General John E. Wool feuded incessantly with civil authorities and his own superiors while conducting a two-front war in Washington and Oregon in 1855–56. Secretary of War Jefferson Davis finally relieved him from command of the Pacific Department, but failed to tarnish a bright reputation earned in the Mexican War. *(Courtesy National Archives)*

worsened. Shastas, Rogues, Umpquas, Klamaths, and related groups reacted predictably to the invasion with petty thievery and an occasional murder. Citizens fought back, rarely discriminating between guilty and innocent. Mutual suspicion and hatred, intensified by the language barrier, led periodically to open warfare, as in 1851 when Major Kearny helped local forces suppress a Rogue River uprising. Again in August 1853 violence flared, this time as transient Shastas from California committed depredations near Jacksonville, Oregon, provoking the citizens to retaliate against the innocent Rogues. This resulted in a combination of bands that seriously threatened Jacksonville and prompted a hurried call for help to Fort Jones, across the state line in Scott's Valley.[5]

Captain Bradford R. Alden could muster but ten men of his company of the 4th Infantry, but with them and such arms and ammunition as his magazine yielded he marched northward. At Yreka he enrolled a volunteer company and at Jacksonville three more. Joseph Lane, newly elected territorial delegate to Congress, placed himself at the head of the force and, with Alden as second in command, went after the hostiles high in the Cascades. A sharp fight with two hundred warriors on August 24, 1853, led to a truce and ultimately, on September 8–10, to a treaty conference at Table Rock. Here Lane and Superintendent of Indian Affairs Joel Palmer negotiated the Table Rock Treaty, which bound the Rogues and their allies to cede all their territory and settle temporarily on a hundred-mile-square reservation until a permanent home could be selected. Promptly ratified in Washington, this treaty formally accomplished what had been intended by its predecessor in 1851. Two weeks after the Table Rock negotiations, Captain Andrew Jackson Smith established Fort Lane near Jacksonville, and in the neighborhood of Table Rock the Indian Bureau marked out a reservation for the Indians party to the treaty.[6]

The Table Rock Treaty brought the Rogue River War of 1853 to a close, but it solved few problems. During the ensuing year Superintendent Palmer concluded similar treaties disposses-

---

[5] The causes of the conflicts in the Rogue River country are analyzed with rare clarity and perception by Agent S. H. Culver, July 20, 1854, in CIA, *Annual Report* (18ˑˑ), pp. 292–97.

[6] SW, *Annual Report* (1853), pp. 37–43. Hoopes, *Indian Affairs*, pp. 98–99. Glassley, *Pacific Northwest Indian Wars*, pp. 71–76. The treaty is in Kappler, *Indian Affairs: Laws and Treaties*, 2, 603–5.

sing Umpquas, Shastas, and Calapooyas. To provide them a haven until a permanent reservation could be found, he engaged the Table Rock signatories to another treaty opening their reservation to these refugees.[7] None of the bands liked this arrangement, but no serious trouble erupted between them because few Indians paid any attention to the reservation boundaries. Instead they located wherever inclination suggested. The whites tended to view any Indian off the reservation as up to no good and a fair target for execution. The Indians in turn frequently lived up to this reputation.[8]

In this situation the Army steered a tortuous course. At Fort Lane Captain Smith and his company of the 1st Dragoons and at Fort Jones Captain Henry M. Judah and his "Forty Thieves" of the 4th Infantry alternated between protecting innocent Indians from slaughter by angry settlers and joining with improvised volunteer units to run down Indians accused of robbery or murder. That the Regulars aided the Indians at all infuriated the settlers, and relations between the Army and the civilians it had been sent to protect deteriorated dangerously.

Further irritating the situation was the attitude of the new commanding general on the Pacific. Brevet Major General John E. Wool, senior of the Army's two full brigadiers, took command from Hitchcock early in 1854. A stiff-necked professional of forty-two years' service, the diminutive general possessed a contentious temperament that overshadowed a piety somewhat unusual in the Regular Army. He reposed great confidence in his own judgment and tended to regard anyone who differed with him as a scoundrel controlled by impure motives. In this category he placed the citizens of the Northwest and their political officials, who insisted on appropriating all the Indian's land and killing him if he objected. In the larger sense, of course, Wool was right, but in the context of the times his inability to understand the other point of view as well cost him needed civilian support and deepened the bitterness already engendered by field commanders who now and then sided with the Indians. Intemperate public utterances insured wide circulation of the general's views.

In the remote northeastern corner of General Wool's depart-

---

[7] Kappler, *Indian Affairs*, 2, 654-60.

[8] House Ex. Docs., 34th Cong., 1st sess., No. 93, pp. 62-65. The settler, remarked Agent Ambrose, "would about as soon shoot an Indian as eat his supper."

ment, Indian relations suddenly grew dangerous. This "Inland Empire" east of the Cascades supported much more numerous and warlike groups than those in the Rogue and Klamath country. For many years they enjoyed cordial relations with Hudson's Bay Company traders and, less uniformly, with the missionaries that began arriving in the 1830s; but the campaign of the Oregon Volunteers in 1848, aimed at the Cayuse murderers of the Whitmans yet falling heavily on innocent groups as well, left a legacy of bitterness and distrust. Late in May 1855 part of these people were summoned to a great treaty council in the Walla Walla Valley, near the site of the martyred Whitman's burned-out mission. From northeastern Oregon came the Walla Wallas, Umatillas, and Cayuses. From the area drained by the Yakima River and cradled by the great bend of the Columbia came the Yakimas. Palouses rode down from their country north of Snake River, and the Nez Perces, both Upper and Lower, arrived from the western foothills of the Rockies beyond the Snake. Some five thousand Indians gathered to hear what the Great Father's emissaries had to say. These were Superintendent Palmer of Oregon and Governor and Superintendent Isaac I. Stevens of Washington Territory.

A West Point graduate, a man of varied attainments and firm opinions, Stevens had resigned from the Army at the age of thirty-five, in 1853, to accept the post of territorial governor of Washington, newly carved from Oregon north of the Columbia. En route to his capital, Stevens had conducted one of the War Department's Pacific Railway Surveys. In the short time since his arrival, the governor had become an enthusiastic promoter of the Pacific Northwest and a vigorous champion of a transcontinental railway following the northern route that he had marked out. Now his objective was to clear the whole Northwest of Indian land titles, concentrate the natives on reservations, and teach them how to farm.[9] As a first step, he concluded three treaties with the Puget Sound tribes in late 1854.[10] In the spring of 1855, anticipating the day when settlers would spill over the Cascades to the east, he set forth to try his hand with the tribes beyond the mountains.

It was an exciting meeting. The Indians had no desire to give up their land, and some of the chiefs could express them-

[9] CIA, *Annual Report* (1854), pp. 247–48.
[10] Kappler, *Indian Affairs*, 2, 661–64, 669–77.

selves quite as forcefully as Governor Stevens. Leading the opposition were the brothers Kamiakin and Skloom, offspring of a Spokane-Yakima union who had married Yakima women and acquired commanding influence in the Yakima tribe; Owhi, chief of the Kittitas and acknowledged leader of the upper Columbia Salishans; and the Walla Walla Peo-Peo-Mox-Mox, long a friend of the whites and once a guide for Frémont. These and most other chiefs resisted Stevens' proposals. The conservative Lower Nez Perces, under Old Joseph and Looking Glass, echoed this defiance, but the missionized and somewhat opportunistic Lawyer, chief of the Upper Nez Perces, worked tirelessly in behalf of the treaty. After the governor had argued relentlessly for nearly two weeks, the chiefs gave in and signed —"some," remarks Curtis, "in good faith, but most in a spirit of sudden, reckless desire to have the business over, at any cost, and get rid of this persistent annoying commissioner."[11]

On June 16 Stevens and his party set forth to the northeast, intending to negotiate additional treaties with the Spokanes, Coeur d'Alenes, Pend d'Oreilles, and even with the Flatheads and Blackfeet on the upper Missouri. Although the Walla Walla treaties had not been ratified, and would not be for four years, newspapers promptly published Stevens' announcement opening the country east of the Cascades to settlement. Actually it had been open since 1850, when the Oregon Donation Land Law sanctioned homesteading without regard to Indian title, but less than a dozen pioneers had ventured beyond the Cascades to take up residence in the Walla Walla Valley. Now the Stevens treaties coincided with the discovery of gold in the neighborhood of the Hudson's Bay Company post of Fort Colville, high on the Columbia near the Canadian boundary. The rush got underway in the summer of 1855. Over the Cascade passes or up the Columbia hurried the prospectors. By either route they crossed the heartland of the Yakimas.

[11] Josephy, *Nez Perce Indians*, chap. 8, gives an excellent account of the proceedings based on deep research and rare insight. Curtis, *The North American Indian*, 7, 14–16, is also outstanding. For Stevens' side see Hazard Stevens, *Life of General Isaac I. Stevens* (2 vols.; New York, 1901), 2, 54 ff. Hoopes, *Indian Affairs*, pp. 103–15, gives a standard account. Actually, there were three treaties signed at the Walla Walla council, one with the Walla Walla, Cayuse, and Umatilla tribes; one with the Yakima, Klikitat (who were not even there), Palouse, and associated Salishan tribes, all of whom were to be considered one tribe under Kamiakin as head chief; and the third with the Nez Perce. See Kappler, *Indian Affairs*, 2, 694–706.

To these people the invasion exhibited an unbecoming haste to possess land that the Stevens treaty said they would no longer own. But the paper had not been approved by the Great Father, reservations had not been marked out, and anyway few intended to give up their land and way of life for a crowded reservation. For some time Kamiakin had agitated war against the aggressive "Bostons," so unlike the "King George men." Now conditions seemed ripe for involving his own and neighboring tribes in a fight to preserve the old order.

In the Yakima country the Indians had been moved to take the first stand against the encroachment of the white man. In the Rogue country they were about to make their last stand. In the autumn of 1855 hostilities broke out in both places. Civil and military officials alike saw in the simultaneous explosions a pre-arranged concert between Yakimas and Rogues. Although no evidence supports such an improbability, General Wool undeniably had a two-front war on his hands.

For the most part, the original tenants of the temporary Table Rock Reservation—those who for convenience may be labeled Rogue Rivers proper—had kept aloof from the pilferage and sporadic homicide that so enraged the settlers of Rogue River Valley. Although Old John agitated persistently for a general uprising against the whites, principally at fault were the disparate bands from elsewhere in southern Oregon that had been attached to the reservation at the beginning of 1855.[12] Even had discrimination between guilty and innocent been possible, however, the settlers had long since lost any inclination to draw it.

Early in October 1855 Captain Smith took the measure of the citizens' temper and sent word to Sambo and Old Jake, camped a few miles from Fort Lane, that prudence suggested a move to the security of the fort. The men responded at once, leaving the women and children to follow in a few days. The delay proved fatal. At dawn on October 8, a volunteer company from Jacksonville under Captain James Lupton stormed into Old Jake's camp and left twenty-three women, children, and old men dead, though in the melee Lupton fell with a mortal wound. Volunteers also fired on Sambo's camp and attacked still a third suspected of harboring "vicious and ill-disposed

12 House Ex. Docs., 34th Cong., 1st sess., No. 93, pp. 62–65.

Indians."[13] Next day, in retaliation, a war party swept the length of the valley killing, plundering, and burning; by evening twenty-seven settlers had paid with their lives for the massacre of Old Jake's people.[14]

As the citizens mobilized for defense, the Indians chose sides. About three hundred—principally Rogue River followers of Sam, Elijah, and Sambo—hastened to Fort Lane to claim the protection of the dragoons. Another five hundred, mustering some one hundred and fifty warriors, took to the mountains under Old John, George, Limpy, and others. These were mainly Shastas, Scotans, Klamaths, Grave Creeks, Umpquas, and Cow Creeks, but including perhaps one hundred Rogues. "There is no alliance," reported Agent Ambrose, "but the simultaneous hostility of all produces much the same result."[15]

"These inhuman butchers and bloody fiends must be met and conquered," cried the Portland *Oregonian*, "vanquished—yes, EXTERMINATED."[16] On October 15 Governor George Curry called up two battalions of Volunteers for service in southern Oregon.[17] Organizing at Roseburg, one of the battalions elected as major William J. Martin, who promptly issued instructions that "in chastising the enemy you will use your own discretion provided you take no prisoners."[18] Captain Smith's two dragoon companies at Fort Lane and the handful of troops at Fort Orford were too few to exert much influence on the situation. At once the war passed largely into the hands of the Volunteers.

Throughout the winter the Volunteers, ultimately numbering fifteen companies, swarmed over the countryside, skirmishing at times with roving bands of Indians, more often marching and countermarching in cold, rain, snow, and sleet. The Regulars participated at times, as on October 31 when Smith concentrated some 250 Regulars and Volunteers against a party of between 75 and 150 warriors well posted on Hungry Hill, between Grave and Cow Creeks. The dragoon captain pressed the attack all day without dislodging the enemy. Next

13 *Ibid.*, pp. 68, 93–94.
14 Glassley, *Pacific Northwest Indian Wars*, pp. 81–82.
15 House Ex. Docs., 34th Cong., 1st sess., No. 93, pp. 88–90.
16 Quoted in Clark, "Military History of Oregon," p. 30.
17 Senate Ex. Docs., 34th Cong., 1st sess., No. 26, pp. 8–10.
18 Harvey Robbins, "Journal of the Rogue River War, 1855," *Oregon Historical Quarterly, 34* (1933), 345.

day the Indians counterattacked, but they, too, were thrown back. The battle ended a draw, but with 9 whites dead and 25 wounded.[19]

At other times Smith shielded unoffending Indians from the fury of the Volunteers. Through much of the winter his post harbored several hundred tribesmen who wished to be counted out of the war. To him late in December came a group of women and children, hands and feet frozen, with the report that again Old Jake had fallen prey to the Volunteers. Two camps of his band had been attacked fifteen miles from Fort Lane and all the men slain. Late in February the dragoons formed to escort four hundred of these refugees through the hostile whites to Port Orford for ultimate concentration on Superintendent Palmer's new Coast Reservation. But still the war went on. "It has become a contest of extermination by both whites and Indians," observed General Wool.[20]

Although faced with two wars in his department, the Pacific commander had not reacted vigorously. He sailed to Fort Vancouver in November to look over the situation and found a number of circumstances combining to delay a serious effort on either front until spring. Throughout the winter, moreover, Wool focused his preparation on the Yakima War. The Rogue River War would be a sideshow to the main effort north of the Columbia, and it would be conducted with such units as could be spared from the Yakima campaign.

Early in March 1856, his plans matured, General Wool again embarked by steamer for the Columbia, pausing at Fort Humboldt to set the Rogue River forces in motion. To direct the campaign he selected Brevet Lieutenant Colonel Robert C. Buchanan, major of the 4th Infantry, whom a subaltern remembered as "particularly elated at his own importance, and his fitness for the duties assigned him."[21] The plan of action called for the simultaneous movement of three columns toward the lower Rogue River—Buchanan from Fort Humboldt with three companies of the 4th Infantry and Captain Edward O. C. Ord's company of the 3d Artillery, Captains Christopher C. Augur and John F. Reynolds with their companies of the 4th Infan-

---

[19] House Ex. Docs., 34th Cong., 1st sess., No. 93, pp. 11–14, 93–94. Glassley, *Pacific Northwest Indian Wars*, p. 85.

[20] House Ex. Docs., 34th Cong., 1st sess., No. 93, pp. 48–49.

[21] Crook, *Autobiography*, p. 9.

try and 3d Artillery from Fort Orford, and Captain Smith with his company of the 1st Dragoons downstream from Fort Lane. All were to converge at the mouth of Rogue River.[22]

Most of the hostiles had drifted into the mountains around the Big Bend of the Rogue, and the "Southern Army" of Oregon Volunteers under Brigadier General John K. Lamerick had formed a screen that discouraged them from returning to the wide stretch of the valley occupied by Jacksonville and other mining towns.[23] Moving inland from the coast, Buchanan was to hound the hostiles into surrendering and taking up new homes on the Coast Reservation. Many in fact had already given up and, in growing encampments at Port Orford and the mouth of the Rogue, awaited transportation to the north. Others, notably George and Limpy, were wavering. But Old John remained adamant; the whites had resolved to kill him and his people, he said, and he might as well die fighting.[24]

For the better part of two months, Buchanan's command accomplished little or nothing except to keep itself supplied and to march futilely among the cold, damp mountains as the Volunteers had been doing all winter. Smith had skirmished with the hostiles while marching down Rogue River, and Ord fought sharp actions on March 20 and April 26 and 29. Early in May, the weather moderating, Buchanan marched his entire command up the Rogue to the mouth of Illinois River. From here he sent Indians as emissaries to invite the hostiles to talk with him. On May 21 Old John, George, and Limpy appeared. The last two seemed inclined to give up, but Old John vowed never to leave his homeland. The conference ended with George and Limpy promising to bring their people to Big Meadows, on the north bank of the Rogue above the Big Bend, in three days and surrender to Captain Smith.[25]

But Old John coerced George and Limpy into going back on their promise. From other disaffected bands down the river, he enlisted two hundred warriors and laid plans to give Smith a warm reception at Big Meadows, then one at a time to knock off Buchanan's companies, now scattered on packtrain and road-

[22] Captain T. J. Cram, "Topographical Memoir of the Department of the Pacific," House Ex. Docs., 35th Cong., 2d sess., No. 114, pp. 48–49.
[23] House Ex. Docs., 34th Cong., 1st sess., No. 118, pp. 24–25.
[24] SW, Annual Report (1856), p. 149.
[25] Cram, "Topographical Memoir . . . ," p. 50. CIA, Annual Report (1856), p. 214. Glassley, Pacific Northwest Indian Wars, pp. 104–5.

building detail. Smith reached Big Meadows on May 25 with his fifty dragoons, thirty infantry under Lieutenant Nelson B. Sweitzer, and a howitzer. Next day, the appointed date, no Indians appeared, but as heavy rains had fallen the captain reasoned that muddy roads had caused a delay. That evening, however, two Indian women came to his camp with a warning that old John would attack next morning. At once Smith moved his camp from the meadow to a nearby elliptical mound about 250 by 20 yards dividing two creeks that flowed into Rogue River. During the night, as the men laid out defenses, a courier rode out to summon help from Colonel Buchanan.

At ten o'clock next morning Old John's warriors surrounded Smith's knoll and launched an attack from all sides. While some posted themselves on neighboring elevations and opened a long-range fire, others worked their way up the hillside and tried to break through the defenses. The thirty infantrymen and the howitzer crew bore the brunt of the fighting, for the musketoons of the dragoons took effect only when assault parties approached close to the lines. During the night, as the warriors kept up a steady sniping fire, the troops dug rifle pits and erected breastworks.

On the morning of the twenty-eighth the battle resumed. Old John could be heard shouting, cursing, and exhorting his men to greater effort. His words were translated for Smith by the two Indian women who had alerted him to the impending attack. Warriors waved ropes in the air, taunting the beleaguered soldiers with the fate that had been planned for them. In the afternoon, with a third of the command dead or wounded, ammunition running low, and water gone since early morning, the defenders saw the Indians mass for a major assault on two sides. They had started up the hill when Smith glimpsed help on the way—Augur's infantry company advancing at double time. The dragoons and the infantrymen leaped from their positions and poured down the slope just as Augur's men struck from the rear. In fifteen minutes the warriors had fled to the hills, dragging their dead and wounded with them.[26]

For Smith it had been a near thing. He had lost nine killed and seventeen wounded, and Augur counted two killed and three wounded in his company. But the Battle of Big Mead-

---

[26] Cram, "Topographical Memoir . . . ," pp. 51–53, gives a detailed account. See also CIA, *Annual Report* (1856), pp. 214–15.

ows, coupled with the movement of Lamerick's Volunteers from the east, convinced nearly all the hostile leaders that the game was up. George and Limpy surrendered to Buchanan and Superintendent Palmer on May 30, and the bands on the lower Rogue that had helped Old John at Big Meadows laid down their arms during the first week of June. Not until June 29, however, after several brushes with the Volunteers, did Old John finally submit to the inevitable.[27]

The Rogue River War and its aftermath stripped southern Oregon and northern California of most of the native population. During June and July more than twelve hundred Indians were conducted from Port Orford by steamer to the Coast Reservation.[28] Buchanan's soldiers went along, as much to protect the Indians from citizens as to prevent defections. In California, more than one hundred Shasta refugees, collected at Fort Jones by Captain Judah to save them from annihilation, were colonized on the Nome Lackee Reservation.[29] The Army abandoned Forts Orford and Lane and erected Forts Hoskins, Yamhill, and Umpqua to seal off the approaches by which Volunteers might gain access to the Coast Reservation, whose establishment had kindled angry resentment among Oregonians.[30] Two years later, in 1858, Fort Jones was also abandoned.

The Rogue River War lasted nine months, and except for the concluding phases it was principally a contest between Volunteers and Indians. Although Buchanan's troops played an important role in bringing about the final surrender, the result had been produced mainly by Governor Curry's citizen-soldiers. They operated under orders to take no prisoners, and they rarely distinguished between neutral and hostile. General Wool and Superintendent Palmer contended that such harsh tactics, ethical considerations aside, prolonged the war by driving submissive bands into the hostile ranks. Whether the "Southern Army" lengthened or shortened the war, it undeni-

[27] CIA, *Annual Report* (1856), p. 222. Old John stirred up so much trouble on the reservation that he was sent to Alcatraz Island for several years, then was returned to the Coast Reservation to live out his life in resigned bitterness.

[28] SW, *Annual Report* (1856), pp. 155-57, 167. CIA, *Annual Report* (1856), pp. 217-21.

[29] House Ex. Docs., 34th Cong., 1st sess., No. 93, pp. 37-42.

[30] Palmer was censured in a petition of both houses of the Oregon Legislature to President Pierce in January 1856. He was accused of "foolish and visionary acts and movements," particularly in colonizing Indians on the Coast Reservation so near the Willamette settlements, and of sacrificing his Democratic principles on the altar of "perfidious" Know-Nothingism. *Ibid.*, pp. 99-102, 133-35.

ably would have ended it without the participation of the Regulars. In the final reckoning, perhaps the most important service Colonel Buchanan rendered was to save twelve hundred Indians from the slaughter that almost certainly awaited them had he not been there to receive the surrender.

Even as Governor Stevens passed the summer of 1855 negotiating his way across the Rockies from one tribe to another, the seeds planted at the Walla Walla council in early June took root. Yakimas, Walla Wallas, Cayuses, Umatillas, Palouses, and Upper Columbia Salishans brooded over the treaties they had universally opposed but to which they had nonetheless been persuaded to agree. The Klikitats, once lords of the Willamette Valley but now restricted to the White Salmon drainage near The Dalles, were doubly wrathful, for even though they had refused to send representatives to the council, they yet found themselves listed as parties to the Yakima Treaty. The summer's stream of gold-seekers to the upper Columbia nurtured the growing conviction that something had gone dreadfully wrong.

At last the inflammatory words of the proud Kamiakin, long the most powerful native leader of the Columbia Basin, fell on receptive ears. Now the dangers of which he had warned, heretofore pleasantly remote, lay bare for all to see. The Yakima chief's proposal was simple: kill all white men who ventured onto Indian land, including the soldiers who would come to exact punishment. His emissaries of war radiated in all directions and in all tribes aroused interest if not prompt commitment. Even the Squaxon, Nisqually, and Puyallup of Puget Sound, victims of similar treaty proceedings engineered by Stevens late in 1854, looked on the plan with favor. Owhi, chief of the Kittitas, held out; he had made a promise and hoped to keep it. But Kamiakin knew his wife's uncle and neighbor to the north. "I will double up my legs and let the soldiers pass to Kittitas," he boasted, "and let Owhi fight them." This he adroitly maneuvered by enticing Owhi's son Qualchin into murdering two gold-hunters, and resignedly, for he could not turn his back on his son, Owhi brought the Upper Columbia Salishans into the formless alliance.[31]

[31] Curtis, *North American Indian*, 7, 21–22, 39; 9, 16–17. Acknowledged authority on the Yakima War is W. N. Bischoff, S. J.: "The Yakima Indian War, 1855–56" (Ph.D. Dissertation, Loyola University, 1950); "Yakima Indian

The murders committed by Qualchin were the first acts of violence. Others followed. In mid-September 1855 A. J. Bolon, red-bearded agent to the Yakimas, set forth from The Dalles to investigate the killings and try to reason with Kamiakin. Four Yakima warriors waylaid him. While one held him, another pushed back his head and slit his throat.[32] Early in October a Deschutes chief brought word from Kamiakin that no "Bostons" would be allowed in his country. The Yakimas had killed Bolon, and they would kill anyone else who tried to enter.[33]

At once Major Gabriel J. Rains, district commander, ordered a demonstration in force to intimidate the Yakimas. With two companies of the 4th Infantry and a howitzer, Brevet Major Granville O. Haller marched north from Fort Dalles on October 3. Three days later, on Toppenish Creek, he ran head-on into Kamiakin and Owhi with more than five hundred warriors. Beseiged on a ridgetop for two nights and a day, the infantrymen finally broke free and fought a three-day rearguard action back to Fort Dalles. Besides the howitzer and packtrain, abandoned in the retreat, Haller's police operation cost five men killed and seventeen wounded. Meanwhile, Lieutenant William A. Slaughter and fifty men, sent from Fort Steilacoom to cooperate with Haller, had crossed the Cascades at Naches Pass, found the Yakima Valley crawling with Indians, and hastily fallen back to White River.[34]

Haller's defeat emboldened the hostiles and spread the war fever to uncommitted tribes. West of the Cascades it decided the Puget Sound groups. South and east of the Columbia it stirred up the Walla Wallas, Cayuses, Palouses, and even some of the Nez Perces. "The volcano is about ready to break forth," warned the Walla Walla agent on October 12.[35] Panic swept the settlements of Washington and Oregon. Major Rains called

---

War, 1855–1856, A Problem in Research," *Pacific Northwest Quarterly*, *41* (1950), 162–69; and "Yakima Campaign of 1856," *Mid-America*, *31* (1949), 169–208.

[32] Curtis, *North American Indians*, 7, 23. Glassley, *Pacific Northwest Indian Wars*, p. 113. H. Dean Guie, *Bugles in the Valley: Garnett's Fort Simcoe* (Yakima, Wash., 1956), pp. 29–30. CIA, *Annual Report* (1855), pp. 192–95.

[33] House Ex. Docs., 34th Cong., 1st sess., No. 93, p. 56.

[34] Curtis, *North American Indians*, 7, 24. CIA, *Annual Report* (1855), pp. 192–95. SW, *Annual Report* (1855), pp. 80, 88–89. Theodore N. Haller, "Life and Public Services of Colonel Granville O. Haller," *Washington Historian*, *1* (1899–1900), 102–4.

[35] House Ex. Docs., 34th Cong., 1st sess., No. 93, p. 78.

on the two territories for Volunteers, four Oregon companies and two Washington companies. With Governor Stevens still beyond the Rockies, Acting Governor Charles H. Mason responded at once. Governor Curry refused, explaining that Oregon troops would not serve under federal officers, then promptly called up a mounted regiment, eight companies of one hundred men each, to operate under exclusively territorial control. James W. Nesmith, brigadier general of the Oregon Militia, repaired to The Dalles to organize his command and "subdue the enemy country."[36]

Major Rains planned the same thing. At Fort Dalles he assembled 350 Regulars of the 4th Infantry, 3d Artillery, and 1st Dragoons together with three howitzers and two Washington companies. Much to the disgust of his officers, Rains proudly assumed the rank of brigadier general of Washington Volunteers conferred on him by Acting Governor Mason. General Nesmith, now serving in the more modest and appropriate grade of colonel, decided to accompany "General" Rains with three Oregon companies. Altogether, the column that plunged confidently into the Yakima country on October 30 numbered about eight hundred. To cooperate with Rains, Captain Maurice Maloney started a column of one hundred Regulars and a volunteer company (one of four more Mason had mobilized on Puget Sound) toward Naches Pass to drop into the Yakima homeland from the rear.[37]

Lieutenant Philip H. Sheridan said the Regulars regarded Rains as incompetent.[38] General Wool judged him honest and conscientious but unfit to conduct large-scale operations.[39] The result of the Yakima Expedition gave color to such indictments. Following brief, indecisive skirmishes at the crossing of the Yakima and upstream at Union Gap, the column marched up Ahtanum Creek to Father J. Charles Pandosy's Catholic mission, which stood deserted. Finding gunpowder buried in the garden, some soldiers erroneously concluded that the Father had been supplying the hostiles and burned the mission to the

[36] *Ibid.*, pp. 4–5, 8–9, 15–19. SW, *Annual Report* (1855), pp. 81–85.
[37] House Ex. Docs., 34th Cong., 1st sess., No. 93, pp. 11–14. For accounts of the expedition see *Personal Memoirs of P. H. Sheridan* (2 vols.; New York, 1888), *1*, 54–69; Curtis, *North American Indians*, 7, 24–25, 67; *Message of the Governor of Washington Territory* (Olympia, 1857), pp. 163–64; House Ex. Docs., 34th Cong., 1st sess., No. 93, pp. 15–19, 123–24.
[38] Sheridan, *Personal Memoirs*, *1*, 54.
[39] House Ex. Docs., 34th Cong., 1st sess., No. 93, pp. 33–34.

ground. With snow showers hinting of approaching winter and the Indians declining to fight, Rains led the dispirited command back to Fort Dalles in mid-November. "Almost everyone connected with the expedition voted it a wretched failure," declared Lieutenant Sheridan.[40]

Captain Maloney had also failed to close with the Yakimas and in fact had found Naches Pass, gateway to the Yakima country, blocked with snow. In his absence, moreover, the Squaxon, Nisqually, Puyallup, and other Puget Sound groups had risen against the whites and driven them into Seattle, Olympia, and Steilacoom, where they erected blockhouses to defend themselves. A party of 150 to 200 Indians moved up White River to greet the returning Maloney. At a river crossing they collided with an advance detachment of Volunteers and Regulars from Maloney's command and, after losing thirty warriors in an all-day exchange of musketry, broke contact in the night.[41]

On November 15 General Wool arrived at Fort Vancouver and remained until early January. At once he prepared plans for meeting the Yakima crisis, not by chasing Indians through the mountains in the Rains-Nesmith fashion, but by occupying their hunting grounds and fisheries with fixed garrisons. Available, not counting the Oregon regiment, were 702 Regulars and 280 Washington Volunteers. More Regulars would be needed, he had informed General Scott before leaving California. Other circumstances also counseled delay. As a result of Governor Curry's "private war" against the Indians, transportation and forage costs had soared as territorial purchasing officers bought up quantities of supplies with depreciating script. Wool had to order horses, mules, and forage from California. Then early in December winter set in with a vengeance, freezing the Columbia as far down as the Willamette and prompting Wool to throw off all thought of an offensive before spring.[42]

West of the Cascades, Wool's decision assumed that the

---

[40] Sheridan, *Personal Memoirs*, *1*, 68. Captain Ord preferred charges against Rains, and Rains responded with countercharges. Ord also published a blistering indictment of Rains in the New York *Herald*, Feb. 17, 1856: "So much for fogey field officers," he concluded, "and, dear people, you have got hardly any others." Quoted in Guie, *Bugles in the Valley*, pp. 37–38.

[41] *Message of the Governor of Washington Territory*, pp. 185–86. House Ex. Docs., 34th Cong., 1st sess., No. 93, pp. 11–14, 186–87.

[42] SW, *Annual Report* (1855), pp. 88–89. House Ex. Docs., 34th Cong., 1st sess., No. 93, pp. 10–11, 15–19, 25–28, 42–44.

Puget Sound settlements could be defended by the garrison at Fort Steilacoom and the U.S. naval forces that had gathered in the Sound in October. East of the mountains it assumed that the Indians of the Colville mining district and the sparsely settled Walla Walla Valley would remain peaceable and that Governor Stevens, still somewhere in or beyond the Rockies, could make his way to safety or descend the Missouri to return by way of the eastern States.

On Puget Sound, with the aid of four Washington volunteer companies, the defenses held, although not without bloodshed. On the night of December 4 Klikitat warriors under Kanaskat from east of the Cascades quietly surrounded the fog-shrouded camp of Lieutenant Slaughter's company of the 4th Infantry near the confluence of Green and White Rivers, fired one volley, and hastily withdrew, leaving the lieutenant and three soldiers dead and a fourth wounded.[43] A month later a party of Yakimas came over the mountains, joined with some coastal warriors, and on January 26 attacked Seattle. Moored on the Sound behind the tiny log hamlet, the U.S. sloop-of-war *Decatur*, Commander Isaac Sterrett, opened with her guns and put 120 sailors and marines ashore to reinforce the town's 55 defenders. Rifle and cannon fire held the attackers to the forest edge, and at nightfall they withdrew.[44] Captain Erasmus D. Keyes kept patrols from Fort Steilacoom probing the wet forests throughout the winter, but the Indians stayed clear of them.[45]

East of the Cascades the Colville mines remained secure, but the tribes in and around the Walla Walla Valley were not left to decide the question of peace or war for themselves. Although they had talked of joining the hostiles, they had made no overt move. To restrain them, however, Governor Curry, heeding advice of their threatening behavior, advanced most of the Oregon volunteer regiment into the valley early in December. Under Lieutenant Colonel James F. Kelly, the Volunteers skirmished with angry Walla Walla, Cayuse, Umatilla, and Palouse tribesmen, and during a parley they seized Peo-Peo-Mox-Mox and four other leaders. On December 7, while allegedly trying to escape, the haughty chief of the Walla

[43] Extracts from Keyes' diary in Keyes, *Fifty Years Observation*, pp. 252–53.
[44] Curtis, *North American Indians*, 7, 26. Truman R. Strobridge and Bernard C. Nalty, "And Down Came the Indians: The Defense of Seattle, 1856," *Pacific Northwest Quarterly*, 55 (1964), 105–10.
[45] House Ex. Docs., 34th Cong., 1st sess., No. 93, pp. 20–21.

Wallas was shot and killed; his ears and scalp were cut off and sent down the river for display in the Oregon settlements. After several days of desultory combat, the Indians drew off and scattered beyond the Snake.[46] In March 1856 Kelly's successor, Colonel Thomas Cornelius, led the Volunteers in a sweep north of the Snake as far as Palouse River but flushed no Indians.[47]

Wool did not hesitate to express his conviction that the Oregon troops had pushed the tribes of the Walla Walla country into hostility.[48] Governor Stevens had other views. Late in October, shortly after striking west from the Missouri, he had learned of the Yakima outbreak. An apprehensive dash across the Rockies had brought him on December 20 to the welcome safety of Kelly's troops in the Walla Walla Valley.[49] In the opinion of Stevens, Kelly's movement to Walla Walla not only broke up a hostile alliance intent on uniting with the Yakimas, but it also saved the governor and his party from massacre after General Wool had abandoned them to this fate by discharging the federalized Washington Volunteers and pulling the Regulars into Fort Vancouver for the winter. And now the general pursued a course of majestic inactivity waiting for spring when he should be out conquering Indians. In a speech to the Washington legislature, Stevens excoriated the "gallant and war-worn veteran."[50] And of Secretary of War Davis he demanded the general's removal from command for "utter and signal incapacity" and "criminal neglect of my safety."[51] Underscoring his loss of confidence in Wool, Stevens in February 1856 mobilized a regiment of Washington Volunteers, to act exclusively under territorial authority.[52] Oregon echoed Washington's indignation. In January the legislature adopted a memorial denouncing Wool, and early in April Governor Curry demanded his dismissal.[53]

For his part, Wool convinced himself that "the two war gov-

---

[46] *Ibid.*, pp. 99–102, 121–23. J. F. Santee, "Pio-Pio-Mox-Mox," *Oregon Historical Quarterly, 34* (1933), 175.

[47] House Ex. Docs., 34th Cong., 1st sess., No. 118, pp. 25–31.

[48] House Ex. Docs., 34th Cong., 1st sess., No. 93, pp. 25–28, 42–44.

[49] *Ibid.*, pp. 137–40.

[50] Special Message of Jan. 21, 1856, Senate Ex. Docs., 34th Cong., 1st sess., No. 66, pp. 23–27.

[51] *Ibid.*, pp. 3–9.

[52] *Ibid.*, pp. 29–31.

[53] Memorial of Jan. 30, 1856, *ibid.*, pp. 2–3. House Ex. Docs., 34th Cong., 1st sess., No. 118, pp. 44–47.

ernors" had deliberately ballooned some minor Indian troubles into a conflict of major proportions. "The object of the war has been, from the commencement, one of plunder of the Indians and the treasury of the United States, prompted by political and pecuniary considerations," he informed General Scott. California had won federal reimbursement for her volunteer expenses, and now these "would-be military chieftains," in order to "promote their own ambitious schemes and that of pecuniary speculators," intended to enrich Washington and Oregon from the federal coffers in a similar manner. In fact, they "appear to be running a race to see who can dip deepest into the treasury of the United States." "I have never doubted for a moment that as soon as the volunteers ceased their depredations and savage barbarities on the Indians, arrangements could be made satisfactory to all concerned. Nothing is required but common justice and the ordinary feelings of humanity to be extended to the Indians, to keep them quiet and to preserve the peace of the country." For this task the regular force was quite ample.[54]

While the war of words raged, Wool made ready for his offensive. In January his reinforcements arrived—all ten companies of the newly organized 9th Infantry, one of the four additional regiments authorized by Congress in 1855. The colonel was George Wright, a muscular veteran of 34 years service with a leathery, beardless face, a thatch of unruly white hair, and a quietly competent manner that inspired confidence and respect in subordinates. The lieutenant colonel, Silas Casey, boasted a bright war record, a proficiency in higher mathematics, and a tactical skill that would soon make *Casey's Tactics* a standard army textbook. Wool sent two companies of the 9th with Casey and Major Robert S. Garnett to Fort Steilacoom. The remaining eight he posted under Wright at Fort Vancouver. As soon as weather permitted, Casey was to pacify Puget Sound and Wright to occupy the Yakima and Walla Walla Valleys, forcing all hostiles to come to terms.

[54] SW, *Annual Report* (1856), pp. 153-55, 185-86. Senate Ex. Docs., 34th Cong., 1st sess., No. 66, pp. 50-51, 56-61. House Ex. Docs., 34th Cong., 1st sess., No. 93, pp. 25-28, 42-44, 45-47. That his expressions were not confined to official communications is indicated by the protest of the Oregon legislature that Wool had openly censured the governor and people of Oregon. Memorial of Jan. 30, 1856, in Senate Ex. Docs., 34th Cong., 1st sess., No. 66, pp. 2-3.

And the less either officer had to do with Stevens, Curry, and their Volunteers, the better for the service.[55]

The war on Puget Sound quickly spent itself. Only twice did the hostiles fight in force. On March 1 about two hundred struck Kautz's company of the 9th Infantry on White River. Casey sent Keyes' company of the 3rd Artillery to his aid. The two units joined and, storming a hilltop position, scattered the warriors. In the assault, two men were killed and eight, including Kautz, wounded. Shortly before this engagement, Keyes had captured the notorious Kanaskat, the Klikitat chief responsible for Lieutenant Slaughter's death the previous November. He had been shot in the spine but struggled furiously and shouted for help. Keyes tried unsuccessfully to silence him, then Corporal O'Shaughnessy "placed the muzzle of his rifle close to the chieftain's temple, blew a hole through his head, and scattered his brains about."[56]

After a fight with Volunteers on March 8, the hostiles appeared no more in strength west of the mountains. Thereafter, in Governor Stevens' words, the Puget Sound conflict became "emphatically a war of blockhouses."[57] Thirty-three such fortifications, manned by Volunteers and Regulars, protected the settlements and commanded the travel routes, while the U.S. steamer Massachusetts and several lesser warships lay on the Sound to back up any population center that might be threatened.[58] Minor skirmishes occasionally took place, but by July 11 Casey could report that "the war in this district has ceased."[59]

Through the first weeks of March 1856, Colonel Wright forwarded supplies and troops up the Columbia to Fort Dalles. They were transported by steamboat to the lower end of the rock-studded Cascades, portaged six miles around the rapids, then embarked on other steamers for the remainder of the

---

[55] Senate Ex. Docs., 34th Cong., 1st sess., No. 66, pp. 62–64.
[56] Keyes, Fifty Years Observation, pp. 254–60.
[57] Senate Ex. Docs., 34th Cong., 1st sess., No. 66, pp. 27–29.
[58] Ibid., pp. 31–37.
[59] SW, Annual Report (1856), pp. 173–74. Later in the year Indians from Canada dropped down to Puget Sound and committed depredations. Commander Samuel Swartwout pitted the Massachusetts against them in the novel spectacle of a warship vs. hostile Indians. The ship's cannon and rifle fire from a landing party killed 27 warriors and wounded 21. The survivors, 87 in number, then surrendered and were towed in their canoes by the Massachusetts to a point opposite Victoria and released. Message of the Governor of Washington Territory, pp. 124–29.

journey to Fort Dalles. Wool had intended for Wright to advance simultaneously into the Walla Walla and Yakima Valleys, establishing permanent posts in both places. But Wright now planned to march on Walla Walla before turning to the Yakima country—a course adopted, Wool hinted darkly, under the influence of Governor Stevens. The result, whatever the motivation, was to leave Wright's supply line exposed to the Yakimas, whose warlike spirit now awoke with the approach of spring.[60]

On the morning of March 26, as Wright marched his 250-man column east from Fort Dalles, about one hundred Yakima, Klikitat, and Chinook warriors fell on the Cascade settlements. They gained the Lower Cascade landing and besieged the Upper Cascades and a blockhouse, manned by a sergeant and eight men of the 4th Infantry, at the Middle Cascades. Word of the attack reached Forts Vancouver and Dalles that night. At the former Lieutenant Philip H. Sheridan scraped together forty soldiers and ascended the river by steamboat, while at the latter an express raced to halt Colonel Wright. On March 27 Sheridan retook the Lower Cascades and skirmished his way upstream toward the surrounded blockhouse. At the same time Wright, now back at Fort Dalles, embarked his command on two steamers and started down the river. On the morning of the twenty-eighth he landed his infantry at the Upper Cascades, quickly cleared the area, then advanced to unite with Sheridan and drive the Indians from the blockhouse. The Yakimas and Klikitats got away with slight loss, but Wright seized the local Chinooks who had participated in the fight, tried Chief Chenowith and eight men by military commission, and hanged all but one.[61]

For the better part of April Wright tarried at Fort Dalles, then on the twenty-eighth set out for the Yakima country. He took with him three infantry companies of the 4th and 9th, a company of the 1st Dragoons, and a company of the 3d Artillery. Brevet Lieutenant Colonel Edward J. Steptoe, a dark-eyed Virginian who was senior major of the 9th, was to follow with three companies, and another two, under Major Garnett, had been alerted for movement from Puget Sound to join

[60] SW, *Annual Report* (1856), pp. 153–55.
[61] Sheridan, *Personal Memoirs, 1,* 72–84. House Ex. Docs., 34th Cong., 1st sess., No. 118, pp. 1–12. SW, *Annual Report* (1856), p. 188; (1857), pp. 52, 53.

Wright's expedition. Naches River, bankful with the spring runoff, delayed the march for a month while the troops labored to erect a log bridge. Steptoe joined on May 29, swelling the force to ten companies.[62]

Across the river Indians came and went, and finally on June 9 Kamiakin, Owhi, and other of the hard-core hostile chiefs camped on the opposite bank. Observing five hundred soldiers swarming on the river's edge, building a bridge and throwing together a temporary supply depot, "Fort Naches," the chiefs at once fell to quarreling over whether it would be wise to fight so many bluecoats. Owhi spoke for conciliation and overcame the warlike counsels of Kamiakin. He and "old and timid" Tias swam the river and conferred with Wright. Kamiakin, reluctant to place himself in the power of the soldiers, sent "strongest assurances of friendship." The meeting ended with the chiefs promising to bring all the hostiles and surrender within five days.[63]

They failed to keep the appointment. Major Garnett had now arrived, and on June 18, leaving Colonel Steptoe with three companies to man Fort Naches, Wright crossed eight companies over the Naches bridge and pushed toward Kittitas Valley. For the next two months he worked his way methodically through the Yakima homeland—up the Yakima to Snoqualmie Pass, over the rugged Wenatchee Mountains to the river of the same name, down it to the Columbia, and back to Kittitas Valley. Everywhere he found the recent enemy calmly and peaceably harvesting the spring salmon crop. The war chiefs had vanished; unable to bring themselves to trust the soldiers by surrendering, they had drifted one by one across the Columbia to seek refuge with the Palouses or Spokanes. Those tribesmen who remained behind, principally Yakimas and Klikitats, meekly promised to comply with any instructions the colonel might give.

Aware that he could not hold so many Indians prisoner without exhausting his commissary, Wright designated locations, usually near favored fishing places, for each group to remain until further notice. With hostages from each, he made his way late in July back to Fort Dalles, convinced that the

[62] Wright's reports on the progress of the expedition, dated May 30, June 11 and 12, July 7, 9, 18 (2), 25, and 27, Aug. 3, 17, 24 (2), are in SW, *Annual Report* (1856), pp. 152, 160–63, 174–80, 186–93.
[63] Curtis, *North American Indians*, 7, 28–30.

Indians of the Yakima country had been pacified and would remain so if Kamiakin and his lieutenants did not come back to stir up trouble.

In Wright's view, to confine these Indians to a small reservation as contemplated by the Stevens treaties appeared foolish unless the government was prepared to furnish their entire subsistence. They should be allowed to retain the whole expanse of country between the Cascades and the northward sweep of the Columbia. "The Indians can subsist themselves if they have it," he said; "the mountains, the plains, and the rivers, each in turn affords them food. In the winter they are compelled to live in the valley, and one strong military post will insure their good behavior." This post Wright had left Major Garnett to establish; in the Simcoe Valley sixty miles northeast of Fort Dalles, two companies of the 9th Infantry erected and garrisoned Fort Simcoe. But the future of these people still hinged mainly on the unratified Stevens treaties, and this Wright could not control.

While Wright pursued his bloodless campaign, Governor Stevens bristled over the mismanagement of the war. Wright insisted on negotiating with the Yakimas instead of fighting them, and he had failed to occupy the Walla Walla Valley, where Stevens had argued from the first that the main thrust ought to be made. These blunders, together with the withdrawal of the Oregon regiment to The Dalles, prompted the governor to take matters into his own hands. Early in June he formed two volunteer forces, one to cross the Cascades and crush the Yakimas, the other to advance up the Columbia and replace the Oregon Volunteers.[64] Watch out for your double enemy—Indians in the front, whites in the rear—warned General Wool. If Wright discovered any territorial troops in his zone of operations, he was to arrest, disarm, and deport them.[65]

The Volunteers did cross Naches Pass into the Yakima country, but at Stevens' orders they proceeded to The Dalles to unite with the Walla Walla expedition. Under red-bearded Lieutenant Colonel B. F. Shaw, the combined force, four hundred men, marched to the Walla Walla Valley early in July. On the seventeenth, in Grand Ronde Valley, they encountered about three hundred Walla Walla, Cayuse, Umatilla,

[64] *Message of the Governor of Washington Territory*, p. 82.
[65] SW, *Annual Report* (1856), pp. 165–66.

John Day and Deschutes Indians. In a sharp engagement the Volunteers routed the Indians, killed forty, and destroyed a sizable village. His troops had broken up the hostile combination, declared Stevens. It now remained only to call a council and secure the submission of these tribes to the 1855 treaties.[66]

Wool did not discount the urgency of fixing a federal garrison on the Walla Walla Valley—not so much to restrain the Indians, whom he regarded as peaceable, as to protect them from the Volunteers. No sooner had Wright wound up the Yakima campaign early in August than he received instructions to advance at once on Walla Walla, establish a fort, and order Shaw's troops out of the district. "If they do not go immediately they will be arrested, disarmed, and sent out."[67] Still involved in arranging the disposition of the Yakimas, Wright decided to send Steptoe on the mission. He anticipated no trouble, for Stevens planned to go along, order in his troops, and hold a grand council with the tribes brought to heel by Shaw in July.[68]

An angry four thousand Indians representing nearly all the tribes between the Columbia and the Rockies—Walla Walla, Cayuse, Nez Perce, Coeur d'Alene, Spokane, and others—showed up for the council early in September. The events of the year, notably the aggressions of the Oregon Volunteers and Shaw's attack in July, had put them in an irritable frame of mind. Kamiakin appeared on the scene, adding to the discord. And Stevens started talking about unconditional surrender and compliance with the yet unratified 1855 treaties—topics that might better have been left for another time. The governor had released all but one company of Volunteers, and his danger suddenly dawned on him. Steptoe, building Fort Walla Walla seven miles east of the council ground, declined to furnish the troops that Stevens requested for protection; if the Indians intended violence it would be unwise to divide his small command. Instead, the conference should be called off and the governor's party united with the Regulars. On September 19 the chiefs lost control of their warriors. Some burned off the grass on which the dragoon horses depended, while others attacked Stevens, at last moving with his volunteer

---

[66] *Message of the Governor of Washington Territory*, pp. 42–46, 83–86.
[67] SW, *Annual Report* (1856), p. 169.
[68] *Ibid.*, pp. 190–92.

escort to join the military camp. Rushing a blockhouse to completion in two days, Steptoe left an infantry company to man it, then escorted Stevens as far back as the Columbia, where the horses could find grass.[69]

The fiasco set off angry recriminations. Stevens blamed Steptoe, who had assured the Indians that he came in peace, and Wright, whose "feeble" and "procrastinating" campaign had emboldened the tribes. Steptoe and Wright blamed Stevens for gathering so many unhappy Indians in one place at such an unpropitious time and affording them the opportunity to talk over their grievances. And Wool reprimanded Wright for not going to Walla Walla in person and for permitting Stevens, even though governor and Indian superintendent, to appear among the Indians. "Were you not yet persuaded of the fatality attending every act of Stevens?" he asked.[70]

Military and civil authority had met head-on in the Walla Walla Valley, and the statutes left unclear who should prevail. Wool had the armed might, and he prevailed. Steptoe returned in November to fix military occupation on the Walla Walla Valley, conciliate the Indian residents, and enforce the general's orders barring white settlement everywhere east of the Cascades except at the Colville mines. Stevens raged against this edict, issued by a "military officer in the plenitude of his power," that set aside an act of Congress—the Oregon Donation Land Law—and complained that the Indians, having escaped punishment, now "scorn our people and our flag" and "denominate us a nation of old women."[71]

On but one issue did the governor win, and that only partially. An act of Congress in August 1856 authorized a three-man commission to determine the expense "necessarily incurred" by Washington and Oregon in suppressing the Rogue and Yakima hostilities. The commissioners found that Oregon had mustered two regiments, 4,526 men, with about 2,500 in service at any one time; and that Washington had mobilized two regiments, 1,896 men, with about 1,000 on duty at a single time. For Oregon, "necessary expenses" came to nearly $5

[69] Correspondence between Steptoe and Stevens, Sept. 10 and 13, 1856, *Message of the Governor of Washington Territory*, pp. 177–79. SW, *Annual Report* (1856), pp. 197–200. Josephy, *Nez Perce Indians*, pp. 373–78.

[70] *Message of the Governor of Washington Territory*, pp. 87–93. SW, *Annual Report* (1856), pp. 197–98, 201–3.

[71] *Message of the Governor of Washington Territory*, pp. 12–13, 94.

million, for Washington nearly $1.5 million. Treasury Department auditors, however, instructed by the House of Representatives to recalculate the bill using regular army allowances as a guide, trimmed the claims to less than $2.5 million.[72]

The Yakima War satisfied no one. Colonel Wright's "pacification" ended hostilities but left the Indians disgruntled, uncertain of the future, and, lending weight to Stevens' charge, somewhat contemptuous of their recent adversaries. It left the people of Oregon and Washington dissatisfied with the vague terms of the peace, scandalized at the Army's apparent alliance with the Indians, and outraged over Wool's attacks on their integrity. And it left the Army with the thankless task of preserving the peace between unhappy Indians and unhappy whites. Two concrete results of the Yakima War were Fort Simcoe and Fort Walla Walla. They would provide Colonel Wright with bases from which to prosecute the next war, which would not end so inconclusively.

Wright, Steptoe, and Garnett, headquartered respectively at Forts Dalles, Walla Walla, and Simcoe, continued to represent the United States east of the Cascade Mountains, but a change in the top level of officialdom cleared the air of much of the rancor that had set military and civil policies on such divergent courses. Elected territorial delegate to Congress, Stevens headed for Washington in 1857 to promote the ratification of his treaties and fight for federal assumption of territorial military expenses. After three years of acrimony between strong-willed General Wool and strong-willed Jefferson Davis, the Secretary finally concluded that a change in the Pacific command was in order. In May 1857 Brevet Brigadier General Newman S. Clarke, colonel of the 6th Infantry, relieved Wool as commander of the Department of the Pacific. Also in 1857, Oregon and Washington were combined in a single Indian superintendency, and J. W. Nesmith, late brigadier general of the Oregon Militia, was appointed superintendent. Clarke and Nesmith, although disagreeing in some matters, indulged in no name calling and strove to present a common front to the Indians.

Throughout 1857, however, the Indians remained unsettled.

---

[72] House Ex. Docs., 35th Cong., 1st sess., No. 45, Jan. 25, 1858. Clark, "Military History of Oregon," pp. 48–50.

Gold-seekers still trekked up the Columbia to the Colville diggings. From the southeast, where the Mormons of Utah were challenging U.S. authority, came reports of Mormons inciting the Washington tribes to rebel again.[73] Colonel Wright had given the recent hostiles the impression that the past was to be forgotten, yet Nesmith and Clarke were arguing over whether the murderers of Agent Bolon should be demanded for criminal trial.[74] The officers at Forts Simcoe and Walla Walla assured them that the 1855 treaties were dead and that the whole matter would be renegotiated; yet, although on this Clarke and Nesmith agreed, a special agent investigating government operations, J. Ross Browne, told them that the treaties would most certainly be ratified and enforced.[75] In the Army's view, an attempt either to carry out the treaties or to apprehend Bolon's slayers would set off hostilities with all the tribes east of the Cascades, and, as General Clarke pointed out, "suspense is scarcely less likely to prove injurious."[76]

As the spring of 1858 opened, Colonel Steptoe laid plans to lead an expedition eastward on the Oregon Trail to examine more fully the reports that Mormons were tampering with the Indians. First, however, he felt it desirable to make a quick trip northward. The Palouses had recently run off some of his stock and also were said to have killed some miners en route to Colville. Steptoe wanted to investigate the temper of the Palouses and awe them with a show of force. He then intended to proceed to the Colville district, where the miners stood in need of a comforting glimpse of blue uniforms. Finally, the colonel hoped that he might meet some leaders of the Spokane tribe. These people, residing in three divisions along the Spokane River, had stayed out of the Yakima War. They had no unratified treaty to upset them, for their scheduled council with Governor Stevens three years earlier had been canceled by the Yakima uprising. Now, however, they shared in the gen-

[73] SW, *Annual Report* (1858), pp. 335–39.

[74] See correspondence between Nesmith and Clarke, July 1857, in SI, *Annual Report* (1857), pp. 612, 671–75; and between Mackall and Garnett, Feb. 1858, in SW, *Annual Report* (1858), pp. 339–40.

[75] SW, *Annual Report* (1857), pp. 331–33. SI, *Annual Report* (1857), pp. 603–13. Browne was a special agent of the Treasury Department charged with ferreting out fraud in federal operations on the Pacific. His report contains much of interest regarding Indian affairs. See House Ex. Docs., 35th Cong., 1st sess., No. 39. For Browne's activities see Richard H. Dillon, *J. Ross Browne, Confidential Agent in Old California* (Norman, Okla., 1965).

[76] SW, *Annual Report* (1858), pp. 332–33, 337–41.

eral unrest created by the Colville gold rush and the unresolved issues of the Yakima War, and Steptoe hoped for a
chance to reassure them of the government's friendly intentions. On May 6 Steptoe set forth from Fort Walla Walla at
the head of three companies of the 1st Dragoons and 25 infantrymen serving two mountain howitzers—a total of 6 officers
and 158 men. The small ammunition supply—about 40 rounds
per man—suggests that no one expected any trouble.[77]

Crossing the Snake in canoes provided by some friendly Nez
Perces, the column proceeded to Palouse River. On the morning of May 16, shortly after crossing Tohotonimme (now In-
gossomen) Creek, Steptoe suddenly found about a thousand
painted warriors on his front and flanks. Upper and Middle
Spokanes, Coeur d'Alenes, Palouses, and parties from other
northern tribes had gathered to block the march. During par-
leys that evening and the next morning, Steptoe sought to convince the chiefs that he came in peace. Some argued vehemently
for restraint, but the exhortation of others, combined with the
war ardor of the young men, prevailed. The colonel recognized
the futility of proceeding with so badly outnumbered a command, and on the morning of the seventeenth he turned back
to the south.

But the warriors continued to hover menacingly around the
troops. They raced over the hills brandishing weapons and
uttering war cries. At 8 A.M. the rear guard came under fire,
and within twenty minutes the enemy pressed the column on
all sides. A dragoon company shielded each flank and the rear
as the infantry, howitzers, and packtrain slowly pushed forward. Desperate fighting, frequently at close ranges, precariously preserved the formation. Lieutenant William Gaston and
Captain Oliver H. P. Taylor, commanding on the flanks, dropped
with mortal wounds. At noon, his dragoon companies un-
nerved by the death of two officers and by the inadequacy of
their musketoons, Steptoe deployed on a hilltop and unlimbered the howitzers to hold his assailants at bay. The Indians kept the position under heavy fire all afternoon and once
attempted an assault, which was beaten off.

[77] *Ibid.*, pp. 344–45. B. F. Manring, *Conquest of the Coeur d'Alenes,
Spokanes and Palouses: The Expeditions of Colonels E. J. Steptoe and George
Wright against the Northern Indians in 1858* (Spokane, Wash., 1912), chap. 6.

As night fell and campfires marked the native lines on the creek below, the officers took stock of the situation. The day's fighting had exhausted the troops, exacted a toll of six killed and twelve wounded, reduced them to three rounds of ammunition per man, and drained off all hope of averting massacre. Captain Charles S. Winder and Lieutenant David Gregg urged that the command try to cut its way through the circling lines. Steptoe favored a fight to the death on the hilltop, but finally consented to the escape plan. A reconnaissance party located a route free of Indians. Abandoning the howitzers and burying the dead, the soldiers quietly shouldered the wounded and stole down the hillside, around the sleeping enemy camp, and across the creek. Five days later, on May 22, the battered column limped into Fort Walla Walla.[78]

This time there would be no Volunteers to complicate the military plans. This time there would be no temporizing with the enemy. General Clarke arrived at Fort Vancouver in mid-June and at once plotted his strategy. Colonel Wright would thrust northward from Fort Walla Walla, following Steptoe's route through the Palouse range into the Spokane homeland, thence around the lake named for the Coeur d'Alenes who lived on its shores. Major Garnett would strike up the Columbia from Fort Simcoe. "You will attack all hostile Indians," Clarke directed, "with vigor; make their punishment severe, and persevere until the submission of all is complete." The terms of submission were surrender of the Palouses who had murdered the miners in April, surrender of the warriors who had engineered the attack on Steptoe's command in May, and restoration of the howitzers abandoned in Steptoe's dash for safety. Moreover, Kamiakin and Qualchin, believed to have figured conspicuously in fomenting the present trouble, were to be captured or driven away, and no accommodation was to be made with any tribe that sheltered them.[79] Also, Clarke bluntly served

[78] SW, *Annual Report* (1858), pp. 346–48. Manring, chaps. 6–11, gives a detailed account with extensive quotation of original sources. Curtis, *North American Indians*, 7, 57–59. Steptoe reported that the Indians acknowledged 9 killed and 40 to 50 wounded, many mortally, but that he knew this to be an underestimate. He also reported one man, 1st Sergeant Edward Ball, missing. Ball had got lost during the night march but made his way safely to the fort. Commissioned during the Civil War, he died a major in the 7th Cavalry in 1884.

[79] SW, *Annual Report* (1858), pp. 363–65.

notice on the Hudson's Bay Company that all sale of ammunition to Indians at Fort Colville must cease,[80] and he won the ready consent of the priests at Coeur d'Alene Mission to attempt to persuade their charges of the futility of resistance.[81]

Garnett drew first blood. His mission was to hunt out some twenty-five warriors, mostly Palouses, known to have participated in killing the miners on Palouse River in April and who had scattered among the Yakimas west of the Columbia. With three companies of the 9th Infantry and one of the 4th, Garnett left Fort Simcoe early in August and marched northward. On the fifteenth, on Yakima River, Lieutenant Jesse Allen and a fifteen-man detachment fell on a Yakima camp harboring some of the suspects. In the uncertain dawn light Allen was killed by a shot from one of his own men. The Yakimas, about seventy in number, surrendered, and the soldiers singled out and executed five of the murderers. On the upper Wenatchee a week later, Lieutenant George Crook, with the aid of Yakima informants, identified another five of the fugitives and summarily shot them. But the chief culprits—Kamiakin, Owhi, Qualchin, and Skloom—remained at large, and Garnett extended his march nearly to the British line before dropping back down the Columbia. By now, reported the badly frightened Yakimas, the murderers had all fled east of the Columbia and joined the Spokanes. Late September found the command back at Fort Simcoe.[82]

During early August Colonel Wright forwarded troops and supplies from Fort Walla Walla to the crossing of the Snake, where a rock fortification was being built to serve as a supply base. Here he organized a striking column. It numbered about six hundred men—a four-company battalion of the 1st Dragoons under Brevet Major William N. Grier; a four-company battalion of the 3d Artillery, serving as infantry, under Captain Erasmus D. Keyes; a two-company battalion of the 9th Infantry under Captain Frederick T. Dent (whose brother-in-law, Captain U. S. Grant, had resigned his commission five years earlier); and an artillery company serving two 12-pounder

[80] *Ibid.*, pp. 366–69.

[81] *Ibid.*, pp. 361–63, 327–28. See also Robert I. Burns, ed., "Pere Joset's Account of the Indian War of 1858," *Pacific Northwest Quarterly*, 38 (1947), 285–314.

[82] SW, *Annual Report* (1858), pp. 371–72, 379–80. Crook, *General George Crook*, pp. 58–68.

mountain howitzers. Lieutenant John Mullan, whose road-building project between the Missouri and the Columbia had been interrupted by the outbreak, commanded thirty Nez Perce scouts proudly arrayed in new uniforms. Trailing a four-hundred-mule packtrain, the column set forth from Snake River on August 27.[83]

Success depended wholly on whether the enemy chose to fight or run. Wright knew he could whip them if they fought. But he also knew that he could march his unwieldy column to parched exhaustion if they ran. The colonel had good reason to hope that the rout of Steptoe had induced overconfidence. From Fort Colville came word of Indians exulting over Lieutenant Gaston's sword and Captain Taylor's blood-spotted saddle and boasting that they would kill all soldiers who ventured into their country. A priest from Coeur d'Alene Mission had brought Wright the reply to his peace feelers: the Indians were ready for war, and any soldier who crossed Snake River would not live to cross back. And the Nez Perce scouts reported the Spokanes, Coeur d'Alenes, Palouses, and even some Pend d'Oreilles assembling in large numbers around a cluster of prairie lakes southwest of where the city of Spokane now stands. Toward these lakes Wright pointed his column.

By August 30 the command had reached the northern edges of the Great Spokane Plain and began to descend a broken, pine-dappled landscape to a lower plain spotted with small lakes. Squads of Indians appeared on the hills, tantalizing the troops but keeping out of rifle range. Next day their numbers grew. At dusk an attempt to fire the grass and overwhelm the rear guard fouled on a smooth deployment of Keyes' foot soldiers. Dawn of September 1 revealed a large force of warriors atop a high, treeless hill directly in the line of march. Wright judged that the Indians were ready to fight.

Leaving two companies and a howitzer to guard the train, Wright pushed forward with Grier's dragoons and Keyes' and

[83] Sources for this expedition are unusually rich. The following account is based mainly on: Wright's official reports, dated Aug. 14, 19, and 31, Sept. 2, 6, 9, 10, 15, 21, 24 (2), 25, and 30 (3), in SW, *Annual Report* (1858), pp. 383–404. Lieutenant John Mullan, "Topographical Memoir of Colonel Wright's Campaign," Senate Ex. Docs., 35th Cong., 2d sess., No. 32. Diary of Lieutenant Kip in *Army Life on the Pacific*. Keyes, *Fifty Years Observations*, pp. 265–88, based on and quoting from a diary kept during the campaign. Curtis, *North American Indians*, 7, 32–33, 60–62, for the Indian viewpoint. Manring, *Conquest of the Coeur d'Alenes*, chaps. 12–16, reproduces much of this material and more. The most exhaustive and penetrating study of the campaign is in Burns, *Jesuits and the Indian Wars of the Northwest*, chaps. 7 and 8.

Dent's infantry and effortlessly seized the hilltop. Below, four lakes nestled amid rocky ravines, and beyond a vast plain stretched toward Spokane River. Around the lakes painted warriors decked in a colorful array of war trappings raced their ponies back and forth, brandishing bows, lances, and short trade muskets and shouting invitations to battle. Wright estimated their strength at four to five hundred, and he detected still more waiting in a pine forest edging the base of the hill on the right. Sending Dent's battalion of the 9th and a howitzer against the timber, the colonel ordered Keyes to advance his battalion of the 3d Artillery down the slope in skirmish formation. Grier's dragoons followed, leading their horses. The object was to prod the enemy out of the hills, gullies, and timber onto the plain, where the dragoons could get at them.

Keyes' skirmishers fanned out and advanced methodically against the horsemen. The Indian mass pulsed forward, knots of them making sharp sallies at the blue line, then swiftly pulling back. At six hundred yards the infantry, armed with the new 1855 rifle, opened fire and began to drop a warrior here and there from his mount. Under the steady fire of long-range rifles, the enemy slowly gave ground, unable to respond at such distances with bows and arrows and Hudson's Bay muskets. Dent closed on the timber. Howitzer rounds burst among the pine branches, and the infantry swept the Indians through the trees and onto the open plain beyond, where Dent aligned on Keyes' right flank.

With all the contending forces now on the plain, Major Grier mounted his four dragoon companies and shouted, "Charge the rascals!" The horsemen shot through the intervals between the footmen and piled into the Indians. For a brief few moments the dragoons laid about them with sabers and pistols. Lieutenant Gregg, veteran of the Steptoe humiliation, split the skull of one with his blade; Lieutenant Henry Davidson shot another with his pistol; and Sergeant Ball, unhorsing an opponent, calmly dismounted and dispatched him. The warriors broke under the impact of the assault and raced headlong in retreat. For a mile Grier pursued, but his wornout horses soon fell behind. By the time the infantry came up, only a few Indians could be seen on distant elevations, and the howitzer promptly scattered them.

Here ended the Battle of Four Lakes. Without a single casualty, either in dead or wounded, the troops had put the hostile alliance to flight and inflicted a loss in killed set first at eighteen to twenty but subsequently, on the basis of Indian admissions, raised to sixty, besides numerous wounded. This result Wright attributed largely "to the fact that our long-range rifles can reach the enemy where he cannot reach us."

After a three-day rest, the expedition again took up the march on September 5. Leaving the lakes behind, the column strung out over a plain fringed on the east by a strip of pine concealing rocky, ravine-scored slopes. From here some five to seven hundred warriors emerged to challenge the advance. Wright promptly closed up, obliqued toward the timber, and threw Keyes's battalion to the right and left in skirmish formation. The Indians fired the grass and, behind a wall of billowing smoke, curled around Wright's front and flank. Dashing through the flames, the riflemen again outgunned the attackers and drove them back to the timber. The artillery crew threw the howitzers into battery and shelled the trees. A bursting round sent a limb crashing down on Kamiakin, severely injuring the fugitive chief. Through the forested ravines the infantry advanced from one position to another for four miles, overcoming all resistance and driving the enemy once more into the open. Grier's waiting dragoons slammed into them with pistol and saber. The Indian force disintegrated into small groups that scattered over the plain and into the timber to continue harassing the column as it crawled toward Spokane River. Repeatedly Wright flung out a company or unlimbered the howitzers to break up a pocket of resistance or sweep a hill of a menacing gathering. That night he camped on the river bank below Spokane Falls, the fires of his adversary's camps plainly visible upstream.

The Battle of Spokane Plain, extending over a distance of twenty-five waterless miles, had been a grueling test of endurance. For the second time the Indians had been thrown back, although this time their loss was not estimated. One soldier was wounded, and all had neared the threshold of exhaustion; but all, too, took deep satisfaction in the damage inflicted on those who had routed Steptoe and so boldly challenged Wright.

Wright had knocked all the fight out of the hostile tribes. Within two days after the Battle of Spokane Plain he had received peace overtures. His response was uncompromising, and underscoring it he slaughtered nine hundred captured ponies belonging to a Palouse chief. For the next three weeks the expedition wound its way through the hostile country—up the Spokane, around Lake Coeur d'Alene, and down to the Palouse. Father Joseph Joset labored diligently among the Indians to bring about submission to U.S. authority. On September 17 Wright conferred with the principal chiefs of the Coeur d'Alenes, on the twenty-third with the Upper and Middle Spokanes, and during the last week of the month with the Palouses. Each tribe placed itself without reservation at the colonel's mercy. From each he singled out culprits accused of depredations and of inciting the attacks on Steptoe. Altogether, including four Walla Wallas considered trouble makers, Wright hanged fifteen men, and others he placed in irons.[84]

Kamiakin had almost been persuaded to give up, but at the last moment he wisely backed down and with Skloom lost himself in the Rockies. Not so fortunate were Kamiakin's brother-in-law Owhi and Owhi's son Qualchin. Never one of the fire-eating hostiles, Owhi came in to make his peace with Colonel Wright, whom he recalled favorably from the 1856 campaign. Wright seized him and forced him on penalty of death to summon Qualchin. When Qualchin appeared, he was summarily hanged. Later in the march, the embittered Owhi tried to escape. Lashing Lieutenant Michael R. Morgan across the face with a horsewhip, he made a dash for safety. Morgan lodged three pistol balls in his body, and Sergeant Ball put a fourth through his head.

After detaching a detail to clean up the Steptoe battlefield and recover the buried howitzers, Wright's victorious troops headed south, their mission accomplished beyond any shadow of doubt. On October 5 they marched into Fort Walla Walla and proudly paraded for Inspector General Mansfield. The next day the officers gathered for a "handsome collation" in honor of the visiting brass and of a campaign that would feed the fond reminiscences of its participants for the rest of their lives.

[84] Father Burns in chap. 8 of *Jesuits and Indian Wars* convincingly demonstrates the vital role played by Father Joset in bringing Wright and the chiefs to a mutually acceptable agreement. In the process, however, he minimizes the effect of their two military defeats on the willingness of the Indians to talk peace. Without detracting from the importance of Joset's services, I believe the evidence reveals the Indians to have been so thoroughly shaken by the ease with which Wright routed them that they were amenable to Joset's intervention as mediator.

Colonel Wright had organized and conducted the "Expedition against the Northern Indians" with a skill that stamped him as one of the Army's ablest regimental commanders and with an insight into Indian character that testified to lessons learned in the Yakima War. Contributing significantly to his triumph were an uncommonly superior officer corps of whom Keyes, Ord, Gregg, and Robert O. Tyler became Union major generals and Winder, Davidson, and Pender wore Confederate general's stars; an efficient quartermaster department presided over with rare competence by Captain Ralph W. Kirkham; the new rifled shoulder weapons, whose range and fire power came as an unhappy and costly surprise to the Indians; and above all the Indian decision to fight, which gave him two conclusive victories in place of an inconclusive tour of the Spokane country. Wright's peremptory treatment of the hostiles after their defeat in battle, especially the execution of Qualchin, exposed him to some criticism. But as the perceptive E. S. Curtis has remarked, "If in the march of civilization the Indians were to be dispossessed of their lands . . . decisive measures were more humane than the temporizing policy of the army in the trouble with the Yakima."[85]

A year later Delegate Isaac Stevens at last won ratification of the 1855 treaties, and all the tribes involved in the wars of 1856 and 1858 accepted the inevitable. Reservation life proved fully as unhappy as they had expected, but the memory of Colonel Wright hung over them, and never again did they try to deflect their destiny by force of arms. Twelve years later an agent of the Indian Bureau found Kamiakin living with a small band south of the new town of Spokane. He "is a large, powerful man, about fifty years old, and six feet high," wrote the investigator; "he is peaceable, but does not go much among the whites, and seems broken-hearted, having lost his former energy."[86] In him as in those he had led, the martial flame had been smothered by the heavy hand of Colonel Wright.

Military operations in the Pacific Northwest during the late 1850s, in contrast to those elsewhere in this period, were notably conclusive. The people against whom Colonel Buchanan campaigned suffered a disaster so final that they all but vanished

---

[85] Curtis, *North American Indian*, 7, 62.
[86] CIA, *Annual Report* (1870), p. 22.

as identifiable groups. Those on whom Colonel Wright made war met military defeat permanent in its effect. Never again would these Indians defy the alien force shaping their destiny. Never again would the settlers spreading over the fertile valleys west of the Cascades and the rolling plains of eastern Washington have cause to fear serious Indian trouble.

For this result the Regular Army could claim only partial credit. In the campaign of 1858 against the "Northern Indians," adequate manpower and logistical support combined with competent leadership had indeed contributed importantly. But in the earlier hostilities of 1855–56, which occurred closer to population centers, the Regulars never gained the initiative from volunteer forces expressing the attitudes of the passionately involved citizens and their political leaders. Unwilling to embrace extermination policies, unable to control the civilian forces that were, the federal military establishment played a secondary role in ridding western Oregon and Washington of the Indian menace.

And yet for the finality of their conquest the Indians themselves bore a large responsibility. Elsewhere Indian resistance was usually a rather diffuse, unplanned response to a threat only dimly perceived. A few raids and skirmishes took place, and even a battle if it could not be avoided, but rarely was there any inclination to resolve the issue by a formal test of arms. For the tribes of the Pacific Northwest, however, the threat was so real and so immediate that they perceived it with unusual clarity. They resorted to war consciously and with fairly well-defined aims. In its conduct they gravitated increasingly from the guerrilla-style harassment that so confounded their adversary to the open battlefield encounter that permitted his superior numbers, arms, and military organization to prevail. By fighting on the enemy's terms, they contributed significantly to the totality of their defeat.

Rarely would the U.S. Army again grapple with Indians willing to concede such advantages. But rarely, too, would the Army again have to conduct operations under such disadvantages of hostile public opinion and conflicting civil policy.

TEN

Fort Sumter and the Western Frontier

"NOTHING but secession talked of at the post," wrote Lieutenant John Van Deusen Du Bois in his diary at Fort Union, New Mexico, on February 11, 1861. And a month later: "I became involved in several bitter political discussions & threatened, if an effort was made to seduce my regiment from its allegiance I would assume command myself and fight it out."[1] From Fort Brown to Fort Steilacoom, the secession crisis of the winter of 1860–61 shook the frontier army to its roots. At nearly every post the officer complement was rent by deep and sometimes violent schisms such as engrossed Lieutenant Du Bois.

In Texas the gathering storm descended on the frontier army before the firing on Fort Sumter called North and South to arms. Texas seceded from the Union on March 4, 1861. But even earlier, on February 18, old General Twiggs, sympathetic with the South and unable to get a clear directive from Washington, had bowed to state demands for the surrender of federal property and withdrawal of federal troops. Evacuating the frontier forts, the garrisons concentrated at Indianola for embarkation. Some went with a defiant display of patriotism. Approaching San Antonio with the 3d Infantry in March, Major Oliver L. Shepherd received word that the temper of the citizens made it advisable to march quietly around the city.

Major Shepherd called a council of the officers [recalled a participant], the matter was laid before it, and without a dissenting voice

[1] Du Bois, *Campaigns in the West*, p. 110.

it was determined that the trunks and boxes should be opened, and full-dress uniform gotten out and put on, band instruments unpacked, and the regimental flags removed from their cases, and that we should march through San Antonio with everything that we possessed flying, floating, and beating; so that for awhile everything was in confusion, and the leeward side of every wagon in the train became an extemporized dressing room. I rode to the outskirts of the city in the direction from which our people were to come, and met them just as they entered, colors flying, band playing, drum-major nearly turning himself inside out with his baton, and every man and officer as fine as brass and bullion could make him.[2]

The 2d Cavalry and 3d Infantry got out of Texas, but most of the 8th Infantry, marching from distant Forts Lancaster, Stockton, Davis, Quitman, and Bliss, were seized as prisoners of war by Texas troops and later exchanged. To the north, the 1st Cavalry, evacuating Forts Smith, Gibson, Washita, Cobb, and Arbuckle, barely eluded a Texas force and concentrated at Fort Leavenworth. Far to the west, in the Gadsden Purchase tract of New Mexico, Forts Buchanan and Breckinridge were also abandoned and the garrisons withdrawn to the Rio Grande.

When the bombardment of Fort Sumter in April 1861 finally plunged the Nation into Civil War, the frontier army suddenly ceased to protect the frontier. Officers whose sectional loyalties drew them to the South resigned almost en masse, 313 relinquishing their commissions within a few months after the outbreak of war.[3] Most of those who remained soon found themselves in the East, organizing, training, and commanding the volunteer armies forming to save the Union. With few exceptions the enlisted men of the Regular Army never wavered in their Union loyalties.[4] But they, too, turned their backs on the frontier, as the scattered companies gathered, usually for the first time since the Mexican War, in battalion or regimental formation and marched eastward. A few regular units, notably

---

[2] Note by Major William H. Bell in *Journal of the Military Service Institution of the United States*, 4 (1883), 439.

[3] This represented about one-third of the officer corps in 1861. More than half, 184, were West Pointers; 182 became general officers in the Confederate Army. Upton, *Military Policy*, pp. 238–41.

[4] Only 26 out of about 15,000 are known to have defected to the South. *Ibid.*, p. 239.

the 5th and 9th Infantry and the 3d Artillery, spent the war years in the West, but most turned over their responsibilities to state or territorial volunteer regiments.

Authorization for raising a volunteer army was contained in a spate of legislation issuing from Congress in July and August 1861 that provided the basis for the federal military establishment erected over the next four years. Besides expanding the staff departments and bringing to them some long overdue reforms, these laws divided the army line into three major components—Regulars, Volunteers, and Militia.[5]

The Volunteers composed the great citizen armies that bore the brunt of the fighting. Organized by the state governors on requisition of the federal government, the volunteer regiments were mustered into the U.S. service for terms varying from six months to two years and employed, like the Regulars, wherever and however federal military authorities decreed. The officers of these regiments owed their appointments to the governors, and they served under general officers appointed in the volunteer service by the President. Militia resembled the Volunteers in that they were organized by the governors and could serve under federal authority when called, but unlike the Volunteers they could not be employed outside their home state or territory.

The Regular Army remained intact throughout the war. It was enlarged by nine regiments of infantry, one of cavalry, and one of artillery; and all mounted regiments were designated cavalry, thus eliminating the almost meaningless differentiation between cavalry, dragoons, and mounted riflemen.[6] Although the error of General Scott's resistance to dispersing the Regulars among the Volunteers as training cadre came to be recognized, measures to stimulate mixture of the two proved largely ineffective. The Regular Army fought with high distinction but dwindled rapidly because of inability to compete for recruits with the state regiments, which offered enlistment bounties and shorter terms of service. Too, most of the ambitious regular officers sooner or later, through a state appointment, entered the volunteer service with much higher rank than could be hoped for in the Regular Army. By the close of the war the

---

[5] 12 Stat. 268–71 (July 22, 1861); 274 (July 25, 1861); 279–81 (July 29, 1861); 287–91 (Aug. 3, 1861); 314 (Aug. 5, 1861); 317–18, 326 (Aug. 6, 1861).

[6] The 1st and 2d Dragoons became the 1st and 2d Cavalry, the Regiment of Mounted Riflemen the 3d Cavalry, the old 1st and 2d Cavalry the 4th and 5th Cavalry, and the new regiment organized in 1861 the 6th Cavalry.

Regulars were all but lost amid the mass armies of Volunteers.[7]

Between 1861 and 1865 more than two million Volunteers sprang to the defense of the Union and at last overwhelmed the Confederacy. But many of them discovered that they had volunteered for service in mountains, deserts, and plains remote from the wooded hills of Virginia or Georgia, and against enemies clad in breechclout and feathers rather than Confederate gray. For the national government could not and did not turn its back on the West while it dealt with the rebellious South. Texas, of course, had cast her fortunes with the Confederacy, and for the duration she could protect her own frontier. But in the rest of the West the war years brought new demands for military protection.

Paradoxically the pace of the westward movement hardly faltered as the Nation underwent its ordeal of Civil War. Breathtaking mineral discoveries opened new corners of the West to settlement. The Cherry Creek strikes of 1858 led to the founding of Denver and a proliferation of camps in the front range of the Rockies. On the eastern flank of the Sierra Nevada, discovery of the spectacular Comstock Lode in 1859 set off a rush that carried into the 1860s, gave rise to Virginia City, and sent prospectors north and south along the Sierra foothills. To the north, the Colville strikes of 1855 were followed in 1858 by the Fraser River rush. In 1860 gold-seekers pushed into the Nez Perce country and found wealth in the Clearwater River. Others who followed opened mines on the Salmon, the Boise, and the tributaries of Snake River heading in Oregon. At the same time, beginning in 1861, prospectors turned up riches on the headwaters of the Missouri, loosing a stampede that swelled Montana's population to nearly thirty thousand by 1864. Gold deposits on the lower Colorado River and in the mountains to the east brought miners flocking to the western reaches of New Mexico Territory.

A rapidly changing political map reflected the pulsing expansion of the mining frontier—Colorado Territory in 1861, Nevada Territory the same year followed by statehood in 1864, Idaho and Arizona Territories in 1863, and Montana Territory in 1864.

---

[7] For discussion of the 1861 legislation see Upton, *The Military Policy of the United States*, pp. 248–66, and Bernardo and Bacon, *American Military Policy*, chap. 8.

Although unrelated to the mining boom, Dakota Territory had been created in 1861.

Despite the war, the flow of emigration continued. From the Pacific Coast as well as the East, emigrants poured into the new territories over established travel routes and blazed new ones too. Transportation and communication took on mounting importance as the population grew and spread. The telegraph linked California to the Union in October 1861, putting the short-lived Pony Express out of business. Denied its southern route by the secession of Texas, the Butterfield Overland Mail moved northward, paralleling the telegraph wire on the overland route. For a time, by arrangement with Butterfield, Russell, Majors, and Waddell operated the coaches as far as Salt Lake. In 1862 Ben Holladay bought the entire enterprise and ultimately built a stagecoach empire that spanned the West and tapped the mining camps on each side of the trunk line as well. Stage lines also reached out from Leavenworth to Santa Fe and up the Smoky Hill to Denver. And with the opening of the Montana mines, steamboats in growing numbers ascended the Missouri River to Fort Benton, the head of navigation.

The energy and vitality with which Americans of the 1860s continued the task of subduing the wilderness intruded them more profoundly than ever before into the Indian world. Points of friction and violence between Indian and white multiplied, and the defense needs of the Indian frontier grew more pressing at the very moment when they could least be satisfied. Yet for reasons quite relevant to the war effort in the East, the voice of the West could not be ignored.

The administration of Abraham Lincoln fully appreciated the importance to the war effort of western gold and silver. Perhaps even more, it appreciated the importance of western political allegiance expressed in delegations to Congress that would support the administration and the war. Crucial to both was the assignment of enough troops to the West to keep open the emigrant routes, to maintain mail and telegraph service, and to provide security to the exposed new settlements. Also bearing on the government were the constant pressures from western businessmen and speculators who, sometimes sincerely, sometimes cynically, perceived Indian dangers that demanded troops—and the contracts to supply them. Thus, despite the need to throw every last military resource against the Confederacy, men and materiél in meaningful amounts had to be diverted to the Indian frontier.

As a matter of fact, for more than a year after the firing on Fort Sumter no grave threat arose to the settlements or travel routes. The Indians took some interest and an understandable satisfaction in the white men's quarrel, but except in New Mexico and northern California they let pass the opportunity afforded by the withdrawal of the Regulars to make serious trouble. Rumors flew that Confederate agents were tampering with the Indians and that the chiefs were plotting tribal alliances to make common cause against the whites, but these rested on ignorance of Indian ways and Confederate capabilities.[8]

By the middle of 1862 the critical period had passed. Volunteer regiments had filled in behind the Regulars. Indeed, as Major General Henry W. Halleck complained in 1863, "The number of troops now stationed in the frontier departments and Territories is much larger than in time of peace."[9] At the close of 1862 some fifteen thousand soldiers were available for Indian duty, about five thousand more than in 1860. And by 1865 the number approached twenty thousand.[10] The expansion of settlement, of course, created troop needs where none existed in 1860, but offsetting this was the disappearance of an obligation to defend the Texas frontier. Thus the bloody warfare that broke

[8] The Confederates recruited a brigade of Indian troops from among the Five Civilized Tribes which was employed in Arkansas and Indian Territory against the Federals. They also attempted to make peace with the Kiowas and Comanches, more to secure the Texas frontier than to form an offensive alliance against the Union settlements to the north. Undoubtedly, Confederate agents in Texas and Indian Territory tried to arouse the southern Plains tribes against the federals, but the effort was minor and of no consequence in the war that broke out on the Arkansas in 1864. Neither did the treaties secure the Texas frontier from Kiowa and Comanche raids, and Confederate units had to be diverted to meet them.

[9] Halleck to Carleton, Sept. 8, 1863, in *War of the Rebellion: Official Records of the Union and Confederate Armies*, series 1, vol. 26, part 1, p. 720. Hereafter cited as *O.R.*

[10] These figures are derived from an analysis of the departmental returns for the western commands printed at six-month intervals throughout the *O.R.* The number that may be considered available for Indian duty is approximate because in the command embracing the Great Plains the troops employed against Confederates and guerrillas in Missouri and eastern Kansas must be estimated and subtracted from the total. In other commands there is no such significant variable. From 1862 to 1865, the number assigned to the central plains fluctuated between 2,500 and 3,500, to the northern plains including Minnesota between 4,500 and 5,000, to the Southwest between 2,500 and 4,000, and to the Pacific Coast, Inland Empire, and Great Basin combined between 5,000 and 6,000.

out in Minnesota in 1862 and in the next three years spread over the Great Plains cannot be ascribed to an absence of troops on the frontier. At certain times and places there were still not enough men to meet the demand, but there were enough to mount a number of unprecedentedly strong offensives without significantly weakening the defenses.

In its human composition the frontier army that now faced the Indian excelled its prewar predecessor. The volunteer regiments tapped strata of society beyond the reach of peacetime recruiters, and the ranks filled with men of a physical and mental caliber unusual in the typical Regular unit before the war. If less amenable to discipline, they were also more highly motivated and more aggressive. Westerners predominated, and most of them claimed some experience with frontier life and Indian ways. Although many of their company and regimental officers were lamentably deficient, they served under a top command of more than ordinary knowledge and ability. The war swept the relics of 1812 into retirement and opened the way for officers of youth and vigor. With few exceptions, the ranking commanders boasted frontier experience, either in the Regular Army or a civilian pursuit, and they applied themselves with a zeal rare in earlier years.

The new frontier army also took a simpler, harder view of the Indian and the Indian problem than the regular force it replaced. The western Volunteers brought with them typical western attitudes toward the Indian, and the generals for the most part were men who firmly believed the Indian much more responsive to the sword than the olive branch. Absorbed with larger problems, the high command in Washington—Secretary of War Edwin M. Stanton, General Halleck (general-in-chief 1862–64 and chief-of-staff thereafter), and General Grant (succeeding Halleck as general-in-chief)—exerted little moderating influence. Less frequently now did the Army take the Indian side of a dispute, or discriminate between shades of guilt, or seek solutions other than armed might, or restrain tendencies toward barbaric excesses. The new militancy may well have provoked more hostilities than it quelled, but with the attitudes that shaped it came bolder and more effective fighters than the Indians had heretofore known.

For the Indians, the mounting tempo of westward expansion, the invasion of new areas of their homeland, the undefined but nonetheless unsettling effect of the white man's Civil War, and the sudden appearance of a larger and more warlike army of bluecoats combined to create new tensions and fears and new situations fraught with explosive possibilities. With the coming of the Civil War, many of the tribes entered a new and more traumatic phase of their relations with the white people. For the U.S. Army it was a phase characterized by operations more comprehensive in scope, more sweeping in objectives, more fruitful of combat, but with a few exceptions of no less doubtful result than those of earlier, less active times.

☆ ELEVEN ☆

The Army of the Pacific, 1861-65

O F the states and territories furnishing Volunteers for
western duty, California contributed the largest share.
More than seventeen thousand men enlisted in eight infantry
and two cavalry regiments, a "Native California" cavalry battalion, and a battalion of "California Mountaineers." Augmented
by volunteer units raised in New Mexico, Nevada, and Oregon,
these troops composed a loosely knit military entity that has
been labeled the Army of the Pacific.[1]

One full brigade of Californians organized to help meet the
Confederate thrust into New Mexico from Texas. Under
James H. Carleton, crusty dragoon veteran promoted colonel
and then brigadier general of Volunteers, the "California
Column" pushed across the southwestern deserts early in 1862.
It reached the Rio Grande too late to help Colonel Edward R. S.
Canby's Colorado and New Mexico troops turn back invading
Texans under Confederate Brigadier General Henry H. Sibley,
but for the next three years Carleton and his Californians, aided
by two regiments of New Mexico Volunteers, fought the Navajos
and Apaches of the Southwest.[2]

Another California command was organized by Colonel
Patrick Edward Connor, volatile Stockton businessman and
veteran of the Mexican War. These troops marched to Salt
Lake City and, buttressed by some Nevada units, assumed the
responsibility for policing the Overland Mail Route across Utah.

[1] Aurora Hunt, *The Army of the Pacific: Its Operations in California, Texas,
Arizona, New Mexico, Utah, Nevada, Oregon, Washington, Plains Region,
Mexico, Etc., 1860–1866* (Glendale, Calif., 1961).

[2] See chap. 13.

Californians also filled up a regiment of Washington Territorial Volunteers which, together with an Oregon cavalry regiment and a few companies of the 9th Regular Infantry, garrisoned the Pacific Northwest and the Inland Empire. Brigadier General Benjamin Alvord, lately a regular army paymaster, was elevated to this command.

Alvord, Connor, and briefly Carleton reported to the commanding general of the Department of the Pacific. In October 1861 this department fell to Brigadier General George Wright, conqueror of the Spokanes and Coeur d'Alenes in 1858.[3] For three years Wright superintended the organization of the volunteer regiments, strengthened the coastal defenses against the contingency of British intervention in the Civil War, maintained a precarious civil tranquility in California, and directed operations against Indians in the vast region between the Pacific Coast and the Continental Divide.[4]

Most critical of General Wright's farflung responsibilities was the security of the overland mail and telegraph route between Salt Lake City and Sacramento, for on this slender line California depended for speedy communication with the States. East of the Sierra Nevada the route, somewhat south of the Humboldt emigrant trail of earlier years, lay across a wild desert studded with range upon narrow range of barren mountains. Along the western segment a sparse, scattered population of

[3] Like nearly all general officers dealt with in this and succeeding chapters, Wright held his commission in the volunteer service, and it was thus temporary in nature, of practical effect only until the Volunteers were disbanded. Like all the Regulars commissioned in the Volunteers, he retained his regular commission as colonel of the 9th Infantry. Carelton, serving as a brigadier, remained a major in the Regular Army until 1866, when, mustered out of the Volunteers, he was promoted to lieutenant colonel and served in that rank. Alvord retained his paymaster majority while serving as a volunteer general. Further confusing the rank system was the continuing practice of awarding brevet rank, in both the regular and volunteer service, for heroism or other outstanding performance. At the close of the Civil War, for example, the celebrated George Armstrong Custer held a commission of captain in the Regular Army, a commission of major general of Volunteers, a brevet of major general of Volunteers, and brevets in the Regular Army of major, lieutenant colonel, colonel, brigadier general, and major general.

[4] Throughout this period the Department of the Pacific consisted with some variations of the Districts of Oregon, Utah, California (central California and Nevada), the Humboldt (northern California), and Southern California. Carleton replaced Canby in command of the Department of New Mexico in September 1862. This department retained its prewar boundaries until January 1865, when the recently organized Territory of Arizona was created a separate district and attached to the Department of the Pacific. For particulars see Thian, *Military Geography of the United States*, pp. 80–81, 86–87.

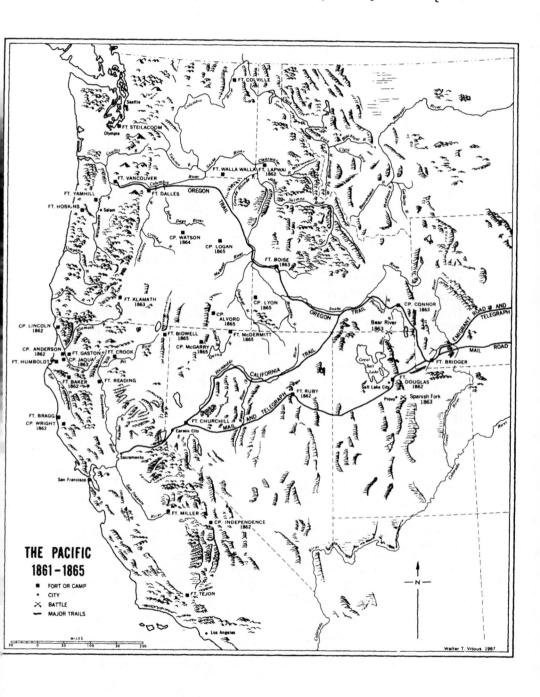

THE PACIFIC
1861-1865

■ FORT OR CAMP
• CITY
✕ BATTLE
— MAJOR TRAILS

Walter T. Vitous 1967

Western Shoshoni and Paiute Indians lived perpetually on the brink of starvation. In 1860, stirred by the mining boom that produced Virginia City, the Paiutes had briefly challenged the invaders, only to be crushed by a force of miners aided by arms, ammunition, and a handful of Regulars hastened over the Sierra from San Francisco.[5]

More powerful tribes inhabited the Utah division of the route. Northern Shoshonis and Bannocks ranged north of the mail road between the Snake and Green Rivers, and Utes occupied most of Utah south and east of Great Salt Lake. These groups had lived on fairly amicable terms with the Mormon settlers who spread out in all directions from Salt Lake City during the 1850s, but now and then they had committed depredations on the Oregon and California Trails. The 2,500 Regulars that General Albert Sidney Johnston assembled in the Salt Lake Valley in 1858 to assert U.S. authority over the Mormons had found themselves preoccupied with Indian troubles instead. Operating from Camp Floyd (renamed Fort Crittenden when Secretary of War Floyd defected), fifty miles southwest of Salt Lake City, detachments of Regulars had patrolled the two travel routes and had occasionally skirmished with Utes, Bannocks, and Shoshonis.[6]

To regarrison Utah and Nevada, Colonel Connor's 3d California Infantry and part of the 2d California Cavalry, more than a thousand strong, marched eastward by detachments during the summer and autumn of 1862. En route, Connor left a company of infantry and one of cavalry to man Fort Churchill, which had been erected in the Carson Valley at the time of the Paiute outbreak two years earlier. In eastern Nevada he paused to build Fort Ruby and left here two more infantry companies.

[5] SW, *Annual Report* (1860), pp. 69–143. Arthur W. Emerson, "The Battle of Pyramid Lake," in Potomac Westerners, *Great Western Indian Fights* (New York, 1960), pp. 73–81. Sketches of the Paiutes and Gosiutes are in Hodge, *Handbook of North American Indians*, *1*, 496–97; *2*, 186–88.

[6] SW, *Annual Report* (1859), pp. 176 ff; (1860), pp. 69–106. For sketches of Bannocks, Shoshonis, and Utes see Hodge, *Handbook*, *1*, 129–30; *2*, 556–58, 874–76. Tribal histories are Virginia C. Trenholm and Maurine Carley, *The Shoshonis: Sentinels of the Rockies* (Norman, Okla., 1964); Brigham D. Madsen, *The Bannock of Idaho* (Caldwell, Ida., 1958); and Wilson Rockwell, *The Utes, A Forgotten People* (Denver, Colo., 1956). Northern and Western Shoshonis bore little resemblance to each other. The former were buffalo-hunting Plains Indians, the latter horseless, nut-and-root-eating groups that whites usually dismissed contemptuously as "Diggers." Western Shoshonis were to be found in northwestern Utah, northern Nevada, southern Idaho, southeastern Oregon, and northeastern California. To the whites both divisions were more often known as Snake than as Shoshoni Indians.

Taking station in the Salt Lake Valley, the Californians briefly occupied Fort Crittenden, then moved to a shelf of the Wasatch foothills east of Salt Lake City and built Fort Douglas.[7]

In Connor the Indians as well as the Mormons discovered a man of fiery temper, firm opinions, and decisive action. For four years he feuded incessantly with the Mormons, whom he viewed as traitors seeking a favorable opportunity to revolt. Toward the Indians, his policies were clear before he left Nevada. Some Gosiutes (a band of Western Shoshonis) had wiped out a small emigrant train on the Humboldt, and Connor dispatched two companies to seek out and destroy them. If any were surrendered by friendlies, he instructed Major Edward McGarry, hang them and "leave their bodies exposed as an example of what evil-doers may expect while I command this district"—orders carried out in full.[8]

In Utah Connor found Shoshonis, Bannocks, and Utes in hostile array, the mail and telegraph route under attack east and west of Salt Lake, and the Oregon Trail from the Platte to the Snake all but closed. At once he turned his energies on the Shoshonis and Bannocks. A company marched over the Wasatch to garrison Fort Bridger. Major McGarry led another command northward to seek out a captive white boy held by Bear Hunter, one of the most militant Shoshoni leaders. In Cache Valley the troops clashed with a party of warriors and succeeded in inducing Bear Hunter to release the boy.[9] But almost immediately word reached Connor that these Indians were murdering an occasional prospector—the vanguard of the summer rush to the Montana mines—and he decided to strike a decisive blow.

In deep snow and bitter cold Connor set forth from Fort Douglas with nearly three hundred men, mostly cavalry, late in January 1863. Intelligence reports had correctly located Bear Hunter's village on Bear River about 140 miles north of Salt Lake City, near present Preston, Idaho. Mustering three hundred warriors by Connor's estimate, the camp lay in a dry ravine about forty feet wide and was shielded by twelve-foot embank-

[7] Hunt, The Army of the Pacific, pp. 187–92. Fred B. Rogers, Soldiers of the Overland: Being Some Account of the Services of Gen. Patrick Edward Connor and His Volunteers of the Old West (San Francisco, Calif., 1938), chaps. 4–7.

[8] O.R., ser. 1, vol. 50, pt. 2, p. 144. McGarry hanged four Indians and, in three separate instances of alleged attempts to escape, shot and killed a total of twenty more. Ibid., pt. 1, pp. 178–79.

[9] Ibid., vol. 50, pt. 2, pp. 182–83.

ments in which the Indians had cut firing steps. Hoping to surprise them, the troops marched only at night. But Bear Hunter probably had no intention of fleeing. When the soldiers appeared shortly after daybreak on January 27, the Shoshonis were waiting in their defenses.

About two-thirds of the command succeeded in fording ice-choked Bear River. While Connor tarried to hasten the crossing, Major McGarry dismounted his troopers and launched a frontal attack. It was repulsed with heavy loss. Connor assumed control and shifted tactics, sending flanking parties to where the ravine issued from some hills. While detachments sealed off the head and mouth of the ravine, others swept down both rims, pouring a murderous enfilading fire into the lodges below. Escape blocked, the Shoshonis fought desperately in their positions until slain, often in hand-to-hand combat. Of those who broke free, many were shot while swimming the icy river. By mid-morning the fighting had ended.

On the battlefield the troops counted 224 bodies, including that of Bear Hunter, and knew that the toll was actually higher. They destroyed 70 lodges and quantities of provisions, seized 175 Indian horses, and captured 160 women and children, who were left in the wrecked village with a store of food. The Californians had been hurt, too: 14 dead, 4 officers and 49 men wounded (of whom 1 officer and 6 men died later), and 75 men with frostbitten feet. Even so, it had been a signal victory, winning Connor the fulsome praise of the War Department and prompt promotion to brigadier general.[10]

Other Shoshonis and Bannocks took note. Connor kept them off balance. In May he planted a one-company post, Camp Connor, at the Oregon Trail landmark of Soda Springs, where a group of apostate Mormons called Morrisites had decided to settle. Patrols probed from here, Fort Douglas, and Fort Bridger throughout the summer and autumn of 1863, maintaining pressure and occasionally killing a few warriors. One after another the band chiefs begged for peace.[11]

Connor also dealt vigorously with the Utes and Gosiutes, who occasionally hit the mail road between Salt Lake and Fort Ruby. Mormon settlers, Connor believed, encouraged the Indians in their depredations and kept them informed of troop move-

[10] *Ibid.*, pp. 184–87. Rogers, *Soldiers of the Overland*, chap. 9.
[11] *O.R.*, ser. 1, vol. 50, pt. 1, pp. 226–28, 229, 527–30; pt. 2, pp. 479, 658–59.

ments. Whether wholly true or not, he could cite as evidence the spectacle of 150 male citizens of Pleasant Grove standing idly by while 100 Ute warriors besieged a squad of Californians in the very heart of town. Active patrolling, sometimes ending in a brief conflict, brought security to the mail road. On April 15, 1863, Lieutenant Colonel George S. Evans and about two hundred cavalrymen closed decisively with an equal number of Ute warriors in Spanish Fork Canyon, east of Provo. Supported by howitzers and attacking at close range with revolvers, the troops killed thirty, wounded many more, and pursued the rest up the canyon until they "scattered like quails." Like the Shoshonis and Bannocks, the Utes and Gosiutes were prompted to put out peace feelers.[12]

At a series of conferences during the summer and autumn of 1863, Connor and Superintendent of Indian Affairs James D. Doty made peace with nearly all the Indians of Utah. On each occasion the two officials spoke kindly but firmly, promising peace and just treatment to those who submitted, severe punishment to those who resisted. Shoshoni, Bannock, Gosiute, and Ute agreed to quit fighting and settle on reservations under the supervision of agents of the Indian Bureau. By October 1863 Connor and Doty could advise the Overland Mail Company that all Indians in the District of Utah were at peace and that "all routes of travel through Utah Territory to Nevada and California, and to the Beaver Head and Boise river gold mines, may now be used with safety."[13]

Westward from Fort Ruby the mail and telegraph route lay through Paiute country. Responsibility for this area fell to Major Charles McDermit, an able Californian who commanded Fort Churchill throughout the war years. At first part of Connor's district, western Nevada was detached in 1863 and made part of the District of California, which General Wright commanded concurrently with the Department of the Pacific. For the most part, the Fort Churchill troops engaged in patrolling the mail road

[12] *Ibid.*, pt. 2, pp. 198-99.
[13] CIA, *Annual Report* (1864), pp. 168-70, 173. O.R., ser. 1, vol. 50, pt. 2, pp. 479, 527-30, 658-59. SI, *Annual Report* (1863), pp. 512-16. Treaties that were ratified are in Kappler, *Indian Affairs*, 2, 848-52, 859-60. They were concluded with the eastern Shoshoni bands at Fort Bridger on July 2, the northwestern Shoshoni bands at Box Elder on July 30, the western Shoshoni bands at Ruby Valley on Oct. 1, the Gosiutes at Tooele Valley on Oct. 12, and mixed Bannocks and Shoshonis at Soda Springs (Camp Connor) on Oct. 14. The agreement with the Utes, at Spanish Fork on July 14, was oral.

and routinely policing the reservation Paiutes.[14] In 1862 a company marched southward to Owen's River Valley to aid a squadron of cavalry from Los Angeles in pacifying the Mono Paiutes, who had been tormented into hostility by white settlers. After some blood had been spilled on both sides, the Indians subsided into an uneasy complaisance, and from newly erected Camp Independence a company of Californians kept watch on them for two years.[15] In 1864 and again in 1865 McDermit, now a lieutenant colonel and commanding predominantly Nevada Volunteers, led wide sweeps to the north of Fort Churchill, where troubles were spilling over into Nevada from Oregon and Idaho. In August 1865, his term of service drawing to a close, McDermit was killed in an engagement on Quinn River.[16]

The Indian unrest in this area centered farther north, in General Alvord's District of Oregon. Besides garrisoning the posts established in Washington and Oregon during the 1850s, Alvord was charged with protecting the emigration on the Oregon Trail as well as the burgeoning mining camps on the Clearwater, Salmon, Boise, Owyhee, and Malheur Rivers. The influx of thousands of miners into this wilderness badly disturbed the Indians. The most powerful tribe, the Nez Perce, bowed to the inevitable. In June 1863 the peace chiefs signed a treaty that vastly reduced the reservation defined in the Stevens treaty of 1855 and bound them not to resist the white invasion. Earlier, in November 1862, at the request of the Nez Perces, Alvord had established Fort Lapwai near the confluence of the Snake and Clearwater Rivers to keep peace between miners and Indians.[17]

Not so compromising were the Western Shoshonis of southern Idaho. To end their depredations on the Oregon Trail, Alvord kept Colonel Reuben F. Maury and three companies of the 1st Oregon Cavalry patrolling the middle Snake between old Fort Hall and the Boise River during the travel seasons of 1862 and 1863, and in July 1863 he extended permanent military occupation to the area when Major Pinkney Lugenbeel and three companies of the 1st Washington Territorial Infantry founded Fort Boise on the Boise River forty-three miles from its mouth. To-

14 O.R., ser. 1, vol. 50, pt. 1, pp. 377–81, 403–12.

15 Ibid., pp. 46–49, 145–53, 210–13, 967–68. Hunt, The Army of the Pacific, pp. 254–60.

16 Hunt, The Army of the Pacific, pp. 277–78. O.R., ser. 1, vol. 50, pt. 2, pp. 1274–75, 1288–90. Effie Mona Mack, Nevada: A History of the State from the Earliest Times through the Civil War (Glendale, Calif., 1936), pp. 328–32.

17 O.R., ser. 1, vol. 50, pt. 1, pp. 156–58. Josephy, Nez Perce Indians, chap. 10. Kappler, Indian Affairs, 2, 843–48.

gether with Connor's operations farther east, these activities neutralized most of the Shoshonis. A few parties of irreconcilables, however, crossed the Snake into Oregon and joined bands of Northern Paiutes, commonly called Snakes, that resided there with Klamaths and Modocs.[18]

To oversee these tribes, Fort Klamath had been established in 1863 near Klamath Lake. In October 1864 J. W. P. Huntington, Oregon Indian superintendent, concluded a treaty with the Klamaths and Modocs, but this did not prevent some of the young men from making common cause with the intractable Snakes (Northern Paiutes) against the miners overspreading their country. "By dividing into small and prowling bands they are enabled to pounce at any moment upon remote settlements, isolated mining camps, or passing pack trains," lamented former Indian Superintendent J. W. Nesmith, now U.S. Senator. "Their stealthy presence is never indicated except by a consummated murder or robbery, while their parties are so small and so perfectly on the alert that pursuit is useless."[19]

Nevertheless, General Alvord sent elements of the 1st Oregon Cavalry to sweep through this country in the summers of 1864 and 1865, and Colonel McDermit led his Nevada cavalrymen northward from Fort Churchill to cooperate. They fought a few inconclusive actions and fixed military posts all over the region—Fort McDermit and Camp McGarry in northern Nevada, Fort Bidwell in California, Camps Watson, Alvord, and Logan in Oregon, and Camp Lyon in Idaho. But as Superintendent Huntington remarked: *"Ten good soldiers* are required to wage successful war *against one Indian.* Every Indian killed or captured has cost the government fifty thousand dollars at least." Such was the situation when the Volunteers turned their responsibilities back to the Regulars at the close of the Civil War.[20]

Across the Oregon boundary, in the tangled mountain wilderness of northern California, the Volunteers were more successful. Before returning to civilian pursuits they brought to a close nearly three years of constant warfare with Shasta, Klamath,

[18] *O.R.*, ser. 1, vol. 50, pt. 1, pp. 156–58, 214–25; pt. 2, pp. 172–74, 555, 579–80, 674–75, 763–64, 764–65.

[19] "Sub-Report of Hon. J. W. Nesmith," in Senate Reps., 39th Cong., 2d sess., No. 156, p. 4. See also letter of Lindsay Applegate, *ibid.*, p. 17; and Theodore Stern, *The Klamath Tribe: A People and Their Reservation* (Seattle, Wash., 1965), pp. 34–42.

[20] CIA, *Annual Report* (1865), p. 467. See also pp. 101–4, 466–74; *O.R.*, ser. 1, vol. 50, pt. 1, pp. 399–401, 403–8, 425–28; pt. 2, pp. 763–64, 837–38, 863–64, 877–78, 879–80, 1071–72, 1274–75.

Hupa, and related groups. These people, colonized on reservations after the Rogue River War of 1855–56, had not prospered. A hostile mining population abused and often slaughtered them, raped their women, kidnapped and sold their children into slavery, encroached on their land, and destroyed their crops and stock. A bewildering succession of agents gave little support, either material or moral. Sporadic retaliation gave way early in 1862 to open war as hundred of warriors, finally pressed too far, left the Nome Lackee, Mendocino, and Round Valley Reservations and gathered in roving bands to strike back.[21]

General Wright sent the entire 2d California Infantry against the marauders. Its colonel, Francis J. Lippitt, took command of the District of the Humboldt, with headquarters at Fort Humboldt, and scattered his regiment among stations all over the mountain region of northern California. A transplanted New Yorker, Lippitt was appalled at the injustices that had provoked the outbreak. The fugitives were to be rounded up by pacific means, he ordered, and any man who killed an Indian except in self-defense would be brought before a court-marital. The Indians failed to respond to this policy, and it lasted only a month; in April 1862 the colonel directed that quarter be granted only to those Indians who voluntarily surrendered. For seven months the troops campaigned relentlessly and clashed at least two dozen times with war parties. By October nearly a thousand prisoners had been gathered at Fort Humboldt and other posts. Conducted to the Round Valley Reservation, they promptly fled to the mountains.[22]

A thoroughly disillusioned Lippitt was now ready to let the miners handle the problem in their own way. General Wright agreed, and Governor Leland Stanford called for a battalion of local militia to replace the 2d California in the Humboldt District. Under Lieutenant Colonel Stephen G. Whipple, the 1st Battalion California Mountaineers garrisoned the posts in the Klamath, Trinity, Salmon, and Eel drainage. The battalion suffered from factionalism among the officers and an almost total absence of discipline among the men, but it sustained a war of attrition that gradually wore down the raiders. Colonel Henry M. Black took command of the district early in 1864, and companies of the 2d and 6th California bolstered the Mountaineers,

[21] CIA, *Annual Report* (1862), pp. 308–24. *O.R.*, ser. 1, vol. 50, pt. 1, pp. 803–4, 906–10, 982.
[22] *O.R.*, ser. 1, vol. 50, pt. 1, pp. 50–88, 169–77, 179–80, 798–99, 803–4, 906–10, 924, 992, 1012–13, 1133–34; pt. 2, pp. 50–51, 95–96, 149–50, 168–70.

but it was largely the aggressive persistence of Whipple and his men, wise in wilderness ways, that finally brought the uprising under control. The surrender of Big Jim and Seranaltin Jim in May 1864, followed a month later by the submission of Curley Headed Tom with fifteen survivors of his sixty-man band, foreshadowed the close of hostilities.[23]

Wright had long argued that Indian troubles in northern California could be ended only by removing the natives from the region and placing them on reservations in the southern part of the state or, better still, on one of the offshore islands. He went so far as to prepare Catalina Island for their reception. But the Indian Bureau demurred. The war leaders were imprisoned on Alcatraz Island or put to work on the defenses of San Francisco Harbor, but once more their followers were returned to reservations in the midst of an Indian-hating population, where their predictable fate was virtual extinction.[24]

For three years General Wright managed the Pacific Department with the quiet firmness and efficiency that had marked his long career. To his district commanders he was an ideal superior, granting considerable autonomy yet exerting leadership and according them full support. To the War Department he also gave satisfaction; unlike some of the western commanders, he rarely intruded unreasonably on the time and resources of a high command grappling with much larger affairs than he. Yet there had been complaints from factions disgruntled by his handling of California political issues—"the old granny with the patriotic buttons on his coat," one editor called him—and Secretary of War Stanton finally yielded to the extent of sending to San Francisco an officer of rank commensurate with the command. On July 1, 1864, Major General Irvin McDowell, in eclipse since his route at First Manassas in 1861, assumed command of the Department of the Pacific and relegated Wright to the District of California. General Grant, assessing McDowell as lacking the diplomacy requisite for California, judged this an unfortunate arrangement. If Army Chief-of-Staff Halleck could not be spared, he advised Stanton, Wright should be restored. But Stanton believed that McDowell deserved a chance, and the assignment stood.[25]

---

[23] *Ibid.*, pt. 1, pp. 188–89, 203–4, 230–31, 234–43, 246–307; pt. 2, pp. 293–94, 391–92, 392–96, 723–25, 733, 743, 746–47, 830–31, 841, 881–82.

[24] *Ibid.*, pt. 2, pp. 619, 637, 706, 947–49.

[25] *Ibid.*, pp. 886, 945, 949. Hunt, *The Army of the Pacific*, pp. 349–50.

On another personnel matter, however, Stanton deferred to the general-in-chief. Grant remembered General Alvord from their years together in the 4th Infantry. "I do not think he is fit for the command," he wrote, "and he ought to be called East." Stanton so decreed, and despite testimonials from McDowell and the governors of Oregon, Washington, and Idaho, Alvord took ship in the spring of 1865 for his New England home.[26]

General Wright bore the implied reflection on his administration without complaint, and after a year he rose once more to departmental command. A reorganization of June 1865 restored the old Division of the Pacific and, to supplant the District of Oregon, created the Department of the Columbia, to which Wright was assigned. On July 27, 1865, with his wife and staff, he boarded the *S.S. Brother Jonathan* for the voyage to Fort Vancouver. Two days later a gale swept the steamer against a rock off Crescent City. Of 300 passengers and crewmen, 281 drowned. As the vessel went down, on the quarter deck next to the captain stood General Wright.[27]

In its four years of service, the Army of the Pacific had spread itself thinly over a vast command embracing most of the Pacific watershed. To the areas pacified in the 1850s it had added Utah, most of Nevada, and northwestern California. The operations in these sectors had demonstrated what energetic, persistent troops could accomplish when well led and not too deeply troubled by humane instincts. The Army of the Pacific had also planted the flag permanently in sectors in the past only occasionally trod by a military column—Idaho, southeastern Oregon, northeastern California, and northern Nevada. In these new fields of mining activity, however, the Volunteers had only begun the fight; the postwar Regulars would not finish it for more than a decade. Finally, and perhaps most significant among its services, the Army of the Pacific, except for one brief interval, had kept open the overland mail and telegraph lines across California, Nevada, and Utah and had thus preserved intact the communications links that symbolized the unity of Pacific and Atlantic under the U.S. flag.

[26] *O.R.*, ser. 1, vol. 50, pt. 2, pp. 945, 949, 1146, 1166, 1194–95.
[27] Hunt, *The Army of the Pacific*, pp. 360–61.

TWELVE

The Army of the Southwest, 1862-65

ADVANCE elements of the "Column from California" reached the Rio Grande at abandoned Fort Thorn on July 4, 1862. Strung out on the old Butterfield mail road all the way to the Colorado River, the rest of the eighteen hundred California Volunteers were marching eastward by detachments according to a timetable based on the frequency and capacity of watering places. Without opposition, elements of the California Column on May 20 had retaken Tucson, evacuated two weeks earlier by the Confederate company that had held it since February. Except for a minor skirmish at Picacho Pass, north of Tucson, the Californians had encountered no Confederates.

Nor would they. The column commander, Colonel James H. Carleton, was still attending to logistical matters in southern California when General Sibley's brigade of Texans, pressing northward after the victory at Valverde in February, clashed on March 26–28 with Colorado Volunteers at Apache Canyon and Glorieta Pass, between Santa Fe and Fort Union. Here the Texans had victory snatched from them by a daring flanking operation executed by a Denver clergyman turned cavalryman. Major John M. Chivington's descent on the Confederate supply base doomed Sibley's grand design for the conquest of Colorado. Hastened by a rear-guard action with Colonel Canby at Peralta, the Texans retreated down the Rio Grande, passing Fort Thorn more than two months before the first of the Californians arrived.[1]

[1] For the New Mexico campaign of 1862, see official reports in *O.R.*, ser. 1, vol. 9, pp. 509–654; Martin H. Hall, *Sibley's New Mexico Campaign* (Austin, Tex., 1960); and William C. Whitford, *Colorado Volunteers in the Civil War: The New Mexico Campaign in 1862* (Denver, Colo., 1906). For the or-

By early August Carleton had brought the bulk of his column through to the Rio Grande, an achievement fully meriting General Halleck's tribute: "It is one of the most creditable marches on record. I only wish our Army here had the mobility and endurance of the California troops."[2] Since Tucson, Carleton had worn the shoulder straps of a brigadier. Canby, too, had won his star, and he had also, through his friend Halleck, contrived a transfer to the East. On September 18 General Carleton assumed command of the Department of New Mexico. Plagued by unprecedented Indian hostilities brought about by a full year in which federal forces had been diverted from the Indian frontiers by the Confederate invasion, the department now had at its head an officer grimly determined to rid it for all time of the Indian menace.

With Carleton's elevation to departmental command, leadership of the California Column fell to his successor as colonel of the 1st California Infantry, Joseph R. West, who gained promotion to brigadier general in October 1862. Although still reporting to Carleton, the Californians remained on the returns of the Department of the Pacific, and part of them actually served in the Pacific Department's District of Western Arizona. At the same time, Carleton created his own District of Arizona, embracing the Mesilla Valley and some territory on both sides, and assigned West to the command. On Carleton's petition to the War Department, these ambiguities were eliminated early in 1863 by the transfer of the California Column and the District of Western Arizona to the Department of New Mexico. First from Mesilla, later from Franklin (El Paso), Texas, General West commanded an enlarged District of Arizona that included all of New Mexico south of the Jornada del Muerto and west to the Colorado River. West held this command throughout 1863 as increasing friction with his superior in Santa Fe culminated at length in an open rupture and reassignment to the Eastern duty that he had sought from the first anyway. George Washington Bowie, colonel of the 5th California Infantry, succeeded to command of the District of Arizona early in 1864.[3]

---

ganization and march of the California Column, see *O.R.*, ser. 1, vol. 50, pt. 1, pp. 88–145; and Aurora Hunt, *Major General James Henry Carleton, 1814–1873; Western Frontier Dragoon* (Glendale, Calif., 1958), pp. 193–233.

[2] Quoted in *ibid.*, p. 236.

[3] Francis E. Rogan, "Military History of New Mexico Territory during the Civil War" (Ph.D. Dissertation, University of Utah, 1961), pp. 274–76, 289, 322–23, 418–20, 423–28.

To man existing forts, build new ones, and mount offensives, Carleton commanded the services of two cavalry regiments (the 1st New Mexico and 1st California) and four full or nearly full infantry regiments (the 1st and 5th California, the 1st New Mexico, and the 5th Regulars), together with a few companies from other regiments. The number of officers and men, fluctuating between 2,500 and 4,000, did not greatly exceed the department's strength in the years just before the war. But the Volunteers applied themselves with a zeal unknown to the prewar Regulars, who had never experienced anything like the forceful, almost overpowering leadership that now emanated from the office of the commanding general in Santa Fe.[4]

During the march across the desert, James Henry Carleton had won the respect of many of his troops, who honored him with the affectionate sobriquet of "General Jimmy."[5] Some of the Regulars of the old 1st Dragoons could have cautioned the Californians to withhold judgment for a time. They had known him as arbitrary, arrogant, tyrannical, and on occasion a cruel disciplinarian. A jutting chin flanked by whiskered jaws, piercing eyes sunk in dark sockets, and a high forehead fixed in perpetual frown gave him a visage that matched his abrasive temperament. Superintendent of Indian Affairs Michael Steck called him the "Great Mogul."[6] The appellation exactly captured the autocratic manner in which Carleton treated military subordinates or civil functionaries who crossed him. Captain Cremony welcomed the transfer orders that removed him "from under the nose of a commanding General, whose unscrupulous ambition and exclusive selfishness had passed into a proverb, despite his acknowledged ability and apparent zeal."[7]

Ability and zeal he possessed. Moreover, if the Army contained a career officer high or low who added to ability and zeal a deeper insight into the essential nature of Indian warfare, he left no evidence of the attainment. In 1855, in a classic pur-

[4] Strength and composition of the troops in New Mexico and that part of it that became Arizona in 1863 are in tabular form in *O.R.*, ser. 1, vol. 15, pp. 574, 725; vol. 26, pt. 1, pp. 612, 750, 901; vol. 34, pt. 2, pp. 208–10, 809–10; pt. 4, pp. 626–27; vol. 41, pt. 4, pp. 993–95; vol. 48, pt. 1, pp. 278–80, 703, 1043–44.

[5] Hunt, *Carleton*, p. 236. This biography is highly laudatory and wholly uncritical. None of the traits for which Carleton was so widely detested, and which are abundantly evident from even a cursory reading of his correspondence, emerge in this work.

[6] W. P. Baker to Steck, Nov. 15, 1863, Steck Papers: "Met the 'Great Mogul,' as you call C. yesterday. . . ." The term appears frequently thereafter in Steck's private correspondence.

[7] Cremony, *Life among the Apaches*, p. 198.

suit of Jicarilla Apaches with Kit Carson, Carleton had demonstrated the technique (see pp. 145–46). And in order after order
between 1862 and 1866 he revealed an understanding of the Indian's own method of war that stamped him as a master of guerrilla operations. Reprimanding a subordinate in 1863, Carleton
summed up the lessons of twenty-five years of careful observation and experience:

> The troops must be kept after the Indians, not in big bodies,
> with military noises and smokes, and the gleam of arms by day,
> and fires, and talk, and comfortable sleeps by night; but in small
> parties moving stealthily to their haunts and lying patiently in
> wait for them; or by following their tracks day after day with a
> fixedness of purpose that never gives up. . . . Some flour, bacon, a
> little coffee, and sugar, thrown on a pack-mule, with the men carry-
> ing, say, two or three days' rations in their haversacks, and it will
> surprise the country what a few resolute men can do. If a hunter
> goes after deer, he tries all sorts of wiles to get within gunshot of
> it. An Indian is a more watchful and a more wary animal than
> a deer. He must be hunted with skill; he cannot be blundered upon;
> nor will he allow his pursuers to come upon him when he knows
> it, unless he is stronger. . . . I once, in this country, with some good
> trackers under Kit Carson, followed a trail of Apaches for over a
> fortnight. I caught them. Others can do as well.[8]

In New Mexico Carleton found an old friend and associate
to whom these verities had become an instinct implanted by
thirty-three years as trapper, trader, army scout, and Indian
agent in the Rocky Mountain West. Christopher (Kit) Carson
had probably achieved no greater mastery of frontier lore than
any mountain man who had survived similar experiences. But
a capacity for leadership unusual in this individualistic breed
had carried him to the colonelcy of the 1st New Mexico Cavalry
and thus to a position allowing an application of his specialized
knowledge much wider than that which fell to any other mountain man. Yet Carleton's own leadership supplied the catalyst that
made the application effective, for it was the general's paternalistic manipulation—now prodding, now scolding, now lectur-
ing, now praising—that gave direction, energy, and success to
efforts that could easily have foundered in confusion and lassi-
tude. In return, the unlettered frontiersman accorded Carleton an
undeviating loyalty, admiration, and subordination that lent

[8] Senate Reps., 39th Cong., 2d sess., No. 156, p. 124.

color to charges that he was a pliable tool of the military despot in Santa Fe. Even so, the team of Carleton and Carson proved a winning combination.[9]

First to succumb to it were the Mescalero Apaches of south-central New Mexico. Subdued by the campaigns of Ewell, Sturgis, and Miles in 1855 and watched over by the troops at Fort Stanton (see pp. 148–52), they had lived precariously for six years on the slender game resources of their mountain home-land, supplemented by an infrequent issue of government rations, by sporadic and mostly unsuccessful efforts at farming, and by an occasional raid on the stock to be found near the settlements. Freed from military restraint by the abandonment of Fort Stanton in July 1861, the Mescaleros turned increasingly to the herds of the settlers for subsistence. In the process, reported their agent, during August 1862 alone they killed forty men and six children and carried others into captivity. "There is no security for life or property," he declared, "and unless the government takes immediate steps to stop these depredations the country will be stripped of every species of property it now contains."[10]

Carleton took the immediate steps late in September. Carson and five companies of the 1st New Mexico Cavalry were to reactivate Fort Stanton and operate against the Mescaleros, while Colonel West was to send two California companies under Captain William McCleave east from Mesilla and two more under Captain Thomas L. Roberts north and east from the Rio Grande below El Paso. Both Carson and West received the same uncompromising injunction: "There is to be no council held with the Indians, nor any talks. The men are to be slain whenever and wherever they can be found. The women and children may be taken as prisoners, but, of course, they are not to be killed." No field commander had authority to make peace. "If they beg for peace, their chiefs and twenty of their principal men must come to Santa Fe to have a talk here; but tell them fairly and frankly that you will keep after their people and slay them until you receive orders to desist from these headquarters."[11]

---

[9] This is my own assessment drawn from a study of the military and civil records of New Mexico during this period. The relationship has not been plumbed by Carson's biographers. It is instructive to note that Carson held an earlier military leader in similar awe—Lieutenant John C. Frémont.

[10] CIA, *Annual Report* (1862), p. 248.

[11] *O.R.*, ser. 1, vol. 15, pp. 579–80.

The Mescaleros had no more heart for a serious conflict with the soldiers in 1862 than in 1855. Many tribesmen fled south, to the Guadalupe Mountains, as soon as Fort Stanton came to life. Others made haste to sue for peace. One group met up with a scouting company under Captain William Graydon. The chiefs, Manuelito and José Largo, made peace signs, but the troops opened fire at once, dropping both chiefs, nine warriors, and a woman, and wounding others in the pursuit.[12] By the close of the first week of November a hundred Mescaleros were camped at Fort Stanton, and their chiefs, Cadete, Chato, and Estrella, were on the way to Santa Fe with Agent Lorenzo Labadi to ask Carleton for peace.[13]

While Carson, McCleave, and Roberts kept up the pressure on the Mescaleros, Carleton received the trio of chiefs in Santa Fe on November 24. He had just established a new post, he told them, in the midst of a stretch of timber on the Pecos River known as Bosque Redondo. Called Fort Sumner, it was a hundred miles northeast of Fort Stanton, well out of the zone of hostilities, and all Mescaleros who wanted peace must go there with their families. The Army would feed and protect them while warring on their brethren who remained at home. When the chiefs returned to Fort Stanton with word that rations awaited all who would surrender and go to Fort Sumner, most of the Mescaleros promptly complied. By the end of the year Carson had received 240 at Fort Stanton. Another one hundred reported on the way in he judged to be the last remaining at large. "I am happy to state," he informed Carleton on January 4, 1863, "that there no longer exists any reason why the prolific valleys of the Bonito, Pecos and their tributaries should remain uncultivated and the resources of this section of the country . . . remain undeveloped."[14]

[12] Senate Reps., 39th Cong., 2d sess., No. 156, p. 101. Sabin, *Kit Carson Days*, 2, 703-4. Graydon would appear to have been acting in the spirit of Carleton's orders. There is some indication, however, that through the instrumentality of one Charles Beach, a resident of Manzano, these Indians were treacherously lured into a trap. Carleton later ordered Carson to investigate and, if he found that the fight was "not fair and open," to return the captured stock to the survivors of Manuelito's band and to place Beach under arrest. Senate Reps., 39th Cong., 2d sess., No. 156, pp. 102-3.

[13] Carson to Cutler, Nov. 12, 1862, C66/1862, RG 108, NARS.

[14] Senate Reps., 39th Cong., 2d sess., No. 156, pp. 101-2, 104. Carleton to Updegraff, Dec. 20, 1862, Dept. NM LR, RG 98, NARS. Carson to Cutler, Jan. 4, 1863, C24/1863, and Jan. 17, 1863, C33/1863, RG 98, NARS. Other considerations governed the choice of a location for Fort Sumner: "It shut

The optimism was not fully justified. Although more than four hundred Mescaleros had been enrolled at Fort Sumner by the close of March 1863, perhaps another hundred defied all efforts at conquest. A party of twenty warriors that in March swooped down from the Sacramentos and massacred a train of Mexicans bound for the salt marshes gave notice that not all the Mescaleros had been humbled. While the bulk of the tribe sojourned at Bosque Redondo for the next three years, this handful of warriors made certain that the troops at Forts Stanton, Craig, and Sumner kept alert and active.[15]

Nevertheless, Carleton credited Carson with an impressive achievement in rounding up and deporting nearly the entire Mescalero tribe in little more than three months. And he took pride in his own achievement of devising a strategy that clearly separated friendlies from hostiles and insured that, the campaign ended, friendlies would not suddenly become hostile again. Moreover, enjoying regular meals for a change, the Mescaleros assured him of their satisfaction with conditions at Bosque Redondo even though, at his orders, soldiers stood by to shoot down any of them who tried to go back home. Busily laying plans for erecting a "pueblo" of peaceful Mescalero agrarians at Bosque Redondo and arranging with the Bishop of Santa Fe to make Christians of them as well, the general was already shaping plans for applying the same strategy of conquest by Carson and concentration at Bosque Redondo to the other hostile tribes of New Mexico. Next on the program were the Navajos.[16]

Carleton's grand design for the Navajos owed a considerable debt to ideas articulated by his predecessor a year earlier. Canby's military and diplomatic campaign of 1860–61 (see pp. 171–73) had been interrupted by the outbreak of the Civil War, but it had led him to conclude that new approaches to the Navajo question were essential. Most important, the deadly pattern of raid and retaliation in which Navajo and New Mexican had become locked by generations of practice had to be broken. Navajo raids could usually be attributed to the *ladrones*, yet New Mexican

---

the door through which the Kiowas and Comanches have hitherto entered New Mexico, and cut off a great thoroughfare northward of the Mescaleros." Also, the post opened good winter grasslands for pasturing wornout military stock.

[15] Senate. Reps., 39th Cong., 2d sess., No. 156, pp. 104, 106, 107, 248–49. Morrison to Bennett, March 29, 1863, M75/1863, RG 98, NARS.

[16] Senate Reps., 39th Cong., 2d sess., No. 156, pp. 106, 108.

retaliation usually fell on the peacefully disposed *ricos*, whose abundance of material possessions not only made them more profitable targets but also, advertising their whereabouts and hampering their mobility, more convenient targets as well. Progressive impoverishment transformed *ricos* into *ladrones*, and thus, through "the illegal acts of a few vicious individuals" among the New Mexican population, the Navajo peace party shrank while the war party swelled. "Recent occurrences in the Navajo country," concluded Canby on December 1, 1861, "have so demoralized and broken up that nation that there is now no choice between their absolute extermination or their removal and colonization at points so remote from the settlements as to isolate them entirely from the inhabitants of the territory."[17]

The recent occurrences prompting Canby's judgment stemmed largely from an incident in September at Fort Fauntleroy, the post established by Canby in August 1860 and soon, because of Colonel Fauntleroy's defection to the Confederacy, to be renamed Fort Lyon. Periodically Navajos gathered at the fort in large numbers to stage horseraces with the garrison of New Mexico Volunteers. Both Indians and soldiers wagered lavishly, the latter even staking government sheep from the fort corral. The race of September 13, 1861, ended in victory for the military entries. The Navajos cried foul. An Indian trying to enter the fort got into a scuffle with a sentry and a musket went off. Concluding that the fort was about to be attacked, the officer of the day ordered artillery into action. Five howitzer rounds burst among the crowds of Navajos, killing more than a dozen people.[18] Spurred by this outrage and by the abandonment of Fort Lyon in December as Canby pulled in his troops to meet Sibley, the Navajos lashed back with destructive raids on the settlements.

Rampaging Navajos still afflicted the Rio Grande settlements when General Carleton reached Santa Fe in September 1862. While Carson headed for the Mescalero country, the rest of his

[17] Canby to Governor of New Mexico, Nov. 22, 1861, encl. to Canby to AAG Western Dept., Dec. 1, 1861, N315/1861, RG 94, NARS.

[18] A detailed investigation report prepared in October by Captain A. W. Evans of the 6th U.S. Cavalry was only mildly critical of the post commander, Lieutenant Colonel J. Francisco Chavez, and pictured him as rushing from his quarters to stop the firing. In 1865, however, Captain Nicholas Hodt, a sergeant at the fort in 1861, alleged that Colonel Chavez had ordered the officer of the day to bring up the howitzers and fire on the Indians. Evans to AAG Dept. NM, Oct. 13, 1861, encl. to Canby to AAG Western Dept., Dec. 1, 1861, N315/1861, RG 94, NARS. Hodt in Senate Reps., 39th Cong., 2d sess., No. 156, pp. 313-14.

regiment, four companies under Lieutenant Colonel J. Francisco Chavez, marched to the borders of the Navajo country and, in the shadow of Mount Taylor, established Fort Wingate. This move, coupled with the peremptory treatment the Mescaleros were receiving, brought eighteen Navajo chiefs to Santa Fe in December 1862 to sound out Carleton on the possibility of making peace. Sending them home with the curt explanation that he "had no faith in their promises," Carleton laid plans to end the Navajo menace for all time in the manner suggested by Canby and already being applied to the Mescaleros.[19]

In April 1863 Carleton for the first time revealed to the Navajos the full magnitude of what he planned for them. Meeting at Cubero with two of the leading peace chiefs, Delgadito and Barboncito, he declared that a peace party could not be suffered to exist among the war party. Those who considered themselves friendly must move to the opposite side of the Territory, four hundred miles and more from their homeland, and settle at Bosque Redondo under the guns of Fort Sumner. Barboncito gave the predictable reply: he would not go so far from home. Two months later, on June 23, Carleton ordered Colonel Chavez to summon these two spokesmen of the *ricos* to Fort Wingate and repeat the ultimatum. "Tell them," he directed, "they can have until the twentieth day of July of this year to come in—they and all those who belong to what they call the peace party; *that after that day every Navajo that is seen will be considered as hostile and treated accordingly; that after that day the door now open will be closed.*"[20]

It was not an idle threat. Orders of June 15, 1863, set in motion a concentration at Fort Wingate of Kit Carson's entire regiment, nearly a thousand strong. With nine companies Carson was to march to Pueblo Colorado (Red Town) Wash, twenty-eight miles southwest of abandoned Fort Defiance, and establish a base of operations to be named Fort Canby. From here he was to "prosecute a vigorous war on the men of this tribe," while from Fort Wingate Lieutenant Colonel Chavez

[19] Senate Reps., 39th Cong., 2d sess., No. 156, pp. 98, 103. *O.R.*, ser. 1, vol. 15, p. 670. Fort Wingate was located at Ojo del Gallo, a spring on the site of present San Rafael. In 1868 it was moved 65 miles to the northwest and established at Ojo del Oso, the site of the Fort Fauntleroy-Lyon of 1860–61.

[20] Senate Reps., 39th Cong., 2d sess., No. 156, p. 116. Chavez to Collins, May 4, 1863, Steck Papers.

would keep two companies combing his sector at all times.
The Navajos would be given no respite "until it is considered, at these headquarters, that they have been effectually
punished for their long-continued atrocities."[21]

Cast in the mold of Canby's operations three years earlier,
Carson's campaign inflicted few casualties on the Navajos but
rather, through seizure of stock herds and destruction of crops,
raised the specter of starvation and undermined the will to
resist. While part of the command forwarded supplies and
built Fort Canby—actually located not at Pueblo Colorado but
at abandoned Fort Defiance—the rest formed a striking force
of nearly four hundred men that Carson led in a series of exhausting scouts through the Navajo country. Two such scouts,
in August, carried the invaders west nearly to the Hopi Mesas
and north around Canyon de Chelly. In September they marched
southwest eighty-five miles to the Little Colorado River and
returned. And in November they again struck west, beyond
the Hopi towns as far as the canyon of the Little Colorado.
At the same time, patrols from Fort Wingate probed south
and west as far as the Datil Mountains and the head streams
of the Little Colorado.[22]

For the Navajos, not only the soldiers were to be feared.
Other Indians—Utes, the Pueblos of Zuñi and Jemez, and
even the mild-mannered Hopis—had seized on the occasion
to renew old antagonisms. In December 300 Zuñi warriors
jumped a Navajo band in the Datil Mountains, killed Chief
Barboncito and 16 men, captured 44 women and children,
and appropriated 1,000 sheep. Utes served throughout as auxiliaries to the troops, but after they discovered that Carleton
had turned down Carson's petition for them to keep Navajo captives and stock, more and more ranged the Navajo
country on independent plundering expeditions. And finally,
the inevitable parties of citizen raiders mounted similar forays against the Navajos and their property. Although the
Navajos enjoyed considerable success in avoiding the troops

[21] Senate Reps., 39th Cong., 2d sess., No. 156, pp. 245–47.
[22] Carson's reports of July 24, Aug. 19, Aug. 31, Oct. 5, and Dec. 6, 1863,
in O.R. ser. 1, vol. 26, pt. 1, pp. 234–38, 250–57. For Fort Wingate see ibid.,
pp. 257–59, 315–16, and Senate Reps., 39th Cong., 2d sess., No. 156, pp. 251–55.
See also, for the August operations, Raymond E. Lindgren, "A Diary of Kit
Carson's Navaho Campaign, 1863–64," New Mexico Historical Review, 31
(1946), 226–46.

Quiet, competent, experienced, and well liked, George Wright organized the 9th Infantry in 1855 and led it against the "Northern Indians" of Washington Territory, then commanded on the Pacific Coast during the Civil War years. *(Courtesy Washington State Historical Society)*

An Indian patriot of high stature and ability, Kamiakin led the Yakimas and other Columbia Basin groups in the outbreak of 1855 and also figured prominently in the resistance that Colonel Wright crushed in 1858. Private Gustavus Sohon made this sketch from life, probably at the Walla Walla Council of 1855. *(Courtesy Washington State Historical Society)*

The U.S. Army leased Fort Vancouver from the Hudson's Bay Company and made it the command center for military activities in the Pacific Northwest. This view, made in 1859, looks across the Columbia River from the Washington to the Oregon shore. *(From a painting by J. M. Alden, courtesy Yale University Library)*

Fort Walla Walla, Washington. Planted in the Walla Walla Valley at the close of Colonel Wright's campaign of 1856, this post served as base for Colonel Steptoe's disastrous expedition in the spring of 1858 and Colonel Wright's punitive expedition the following autumn. This sketch was made in 1857 by Edward Del Girardin, a friend of Captain O. H. P. Taylor, who was killed in the Steptoe Battle. *(Courtesy National Archives)*

The Steptoe Disaster, 1858. This contemporary drawing by soldier-artist Gustavus Sohon represents Colonel Steptoe's dragoons trapped in hilltop positions in eastern Washington Territory. Although the colonel wanted to fight here to the last, his officers persuaded him to authorize an attempted escape under cover of night. It succeeded. *(Courtesy Library of Congress)*

Gustavus Sohon's sketch of the Battle of Spokane Plains, Washington, September 5, 1858, is a rare example of combat art of the Indian wars by a participant. Two skirmish lines with dragoon column between them advance against Indians, who have fired the dry prairie grass. Colonel George Wright and staff direct the advance from horseback in the center. *(Courtesy Smithsonian Institution)*

General-in-Chief Winfield Scott and part of his staff as sketched by A. R. Waud in the summer of 1861. Left to right: Lieutenant Colonel George W. Cullum, aide-de-camp; Lieutenant Colonel Schuyler Hamilton, military secretary; General Scott; Colonel Henry Van Rensselaer, chief of staff. *(Courtesy Library of Congress)*

"General Jimmy" Carleton locked Civil War New Mexico in the vise of a military dictatorship but got better results from his troops than any previous commander in the Southwest. *(Courtesy Museum of New Mexico)*

Surgeon Jonathan Letterman's observation that Fort Union, New Mexico, "presented more the appearance of a village . . . than a military post" applied to most of the frontier forts. Established by Colonel Sumner in 1851, Fort Union was a key link in the Santa Fe Trail defenses and supply base for the other New Mexico posts. Joseph Heger sketched this view from the bluffs to the west in 1859. *(Courtesy Arizona Pioneers Historical Society)*

Kit Carson. As colonel of the 1st New Mexico Cavalry, the old mountain man fought Apaches, Navajos, and Plains Indians with a success in large part the measure of General Carleton's paternalistic guidance. *(Courtesy Museum of New Mexico)*

Colossal ego and bombastic temperament kept General John Pope in trouble most of the time and tended to obscure his record of capable management as department and division commander of the plains frontier, 1862–66. Grant valued Pope's "subordination and intelligence of administration"—qualities not in abundant supply among Union generals in 1864. *(Courtesy National Archives)*

Pioneer fur trader and first governor of Minnesota, Henry Hastings Sibley improvised a volunteer army to suppress the Minnesota uprising of 1862, won a brigadier's star for an almost accidental victory at Wood Lake, and handled his brigade skilfully in the Dakota campaign of 1863. Excessive caution infuriated his superior, General Pope. *(Courtesy Minnesota Historical Society)*

Son of a noted painter, Alfred Sully dabbled in art himself. Ably leading formidable columns against the Sioux in 1863, 1864, and 1865, he emerged from the Civil War one of the Army's most experienced Indian campaigners, only to slip into eclipse in the postwar years. *(Courtesy Minnesota Historical Society)*

Colonel John Minton Chivington. "The Fighting Parson" often confused the dictates of ambition with those of God. Coloradoans applauded his butchery of Cheyennes at Sand Creek in 1864, but from the Arkansas to the Missouri Plains travelers and settlers suffered the penalty. *(Courtesy State Historical Society of Colorado)*

Fort Rice, Dakota Territory. Established by General Sully in 1864, this post was built on the west bank of the Missouri above the mouth of the Cannonball. For nearly a decade it was the principal military station on the upper Missouri. *(From a painting by Seth Eastman, courtesy Library of Congress)*

The Battle of Killdeer Mountain, Dakota Territory, July 28, 1864. Teton Sioux warriors fan out to screen their lodges from General Sully's infantry, advancing in a huge hollow square. With important aid from his artillery (far right), Sully put the Sioux to flight and destroyed their village. *(From a painting by Carl L. Boeckmann, courtesy Minnesota Historical Society)*

The Battle of Adobe Walls, November 25, 1864. A howitzer battery saved
Colonel Kit Carson's outnumbered command from defeat by Kiowas and
Comanches in the Texas Panhandle. *(From a painting by Nick Eggenhofer,
courtesy National Park Service, Fort Union National Monument)*

Officer group at Fort Laramie in 1864. Second from left, below, is Lieutenant Caspar Collins, youthful and popular son of the regimental commander of the 11th Ohio Cavalry. He died a year later at the Battle of Platte Bridge. *(Courtesy National Archives)*

One of the best of the citizen-soldiers, Grenville M. Dodge won the respect and admiration of Grant and Sherman before taking over the expanded Department of the Missouri late in 1864. After organizing the comprehensive but abortive plains campaigns of 1865, he left the Army to become chief engineer of the Union Pacific Railroad. *(Courtesy National Archives)*

A "fighting Irishman" who served an enlistment in the 1st Dragoons and commanded a Texas company in the Mexican War, Patrick Edward Connor was enjoying political and business prominence in California when the Civil War came in 1861. In Utah and on the Great Plains, 1862–66, the mercurial general commanded ably if noisily while carrying on a feud of historic proportions with the Mormons. *(Courtesy National Archives)*

and these impromptu allies, they sustained reported casualties in the last half of 1863 of 78 killed, 40 wounded, and 196 captured, as well as stock losses of more than 5,000 sheep, goats, horses, and mules.[23]

From his Santa Fe headquarters, General Carleton exercised a tight management of the campaign. He kept companies along the Rio Grande dashing frantically from one strategic point to another in a largely vain effort to stem the retaliatory raids that fell on the settlements, and he aimed at his subordinates at Wingate and Canby a barrage of admonitions touching large affairs and small: Lieutenant Colonel Chavez could not seem to understand that no Navajo peace party was to be recognized. "The whole tribe is a war party. The rule is a plain one, and needs no further correspondence to define its meaning." Chavez's officers were seen too often in Cubero. "They have no duties there." . . . They and their men were not doing their share of the fighting. "Shall the Indians *always* get the best of the Fort Wingate troops?"

Carson fared no better: make Major Morrison explain his long delay in moving. "That officer will be kept in the field until he has become an experienced Indian fighter." . . . Turn back no Navajos willing to surrender and kill none after in custody. Say to them: "Go to Bosque Redondo, or we will pursue and destroy you. There can be no other talk on the subject." . . . No, the colonel could not have a leave of absence in the midst of a campaign. . . . How could Carson be so lax as to let Navajo raiders get away with thirty-eight of his mules? "I sincerely hope we have had the last report of Indians running off stock in the Navajo country." . . . Lack of mules must not delay operations. The Army of the Potomac carried eight days' rations in haversacks; why could not Carson's men do the same? . . . And finally, on the last day of 1863, "*Now, while the snow is deep, is the time to make an impression on the tribe.*"[24]

Carleton's querulous prodding had sustained the momentum of the campaign for six months. Now, with the Navajos enervated by snow and cold, the time had come to strike at

[23] Senate Reps., 39th Cong., 2d sess., No. 156, pp. 128, 251–55. *O.R.* ser. 1, vol. 26, pt. 1, pp. 235–35, 315–16.
[24] Senate Reps., 39th Cong., 2d sess., No. 156, pp. 122–23, 125–26, 138, 139, 141, 146–47, 153–54.

their most forbidding citadel—Canyon de Chelly. Shadowed by sheer walls of red sandstone plunging six hundred to a thousand feet into the depths of the Defiance Plateau, the canyon floor had supported generations of Navajos in comparative abundance and security. Although Lieutenant Colonel Dixon S. Miles had marched its length in 1858, since Spanish and Mexican times commanders had understandably hesitated to penetrate a gorge that afforded such advantages to an enemy on the rims above. In place of a leave of absence Carson could have a trip to Santa Fe for consultation, but "it is desirable that you go through the Cañon de Chelly before you come."[25]

On the morning of January 6, 1864, Carson formed his striking force on the frosty parade ground of Fort Canby for the last major operation of the Navajo War. If the New Mexicans were in a singing mood, they joined in the verse that had recently been put to a traditional Irish song:

> Come dress your ranks, my gallant souls, a
>   standing in a row,
> Kit Carson he is waiting to march against the foe;
> At night we march to Moqui, o'er lofty hills of
>   snow,
> To meet and crush the savage foe, bold Johnny Navajo.
> Johnny Navajo! O Johnny Navajo![26]

Carson himself led a column of 389 officers and men in an exhausting march through drifted snow toward the west portal of Canyon de Chelly. At the same time an additional two companies made for the east entrance under Captain Albert H. Pfeiffer, a veteran frontiersman who had seen Apaches butcher his wife on the Rio Grande the previous summer and who had embarked with frightening singleness of purpose of a lifelong Indian-killing crusade.

Carson reached his destination on the morning of January 12. At the canyon mouth a patrol under Sergeant Andreas Herrera tangled with some Navajos and killed eleven. For three days the command scouted the canyon rims, probing fruitlessly for a safe passage to the bottom and searching with growing apprehension for Captain Pfeiffer. Back at the west end on the evening of the fourteenth, Carson found Pfeiffer

[25] *Ibid.*, p. 146.
[26] Quoted from *Rio Abajo*, Dec. 8, 1863, in Bailey, *Long Walk*, p. 159.

and his men resting at the base camp. They had marched the entire length of the canyon, thirty miles, without casualty or serious mishap. Although whooping, cursing Navajos gathered on both rims to rain arrows and rocks on the column, the soldiers carried less vivid impressions of this than of the scenic wonders and spectacular prehistoric Indian ruins observed in the course of the march. The next morning sixty Indians surrendered to Carson with the confession that "owing to the operations of my command they are in a complete state of starvation, and that many of their women and children have already died from this cause." Sending two companies under Captain Asa B. Carey to march through the canyon from west to east and destroy the hogans and peach orchards dotting the bottom of the gorge, Carson led the rest of the command back to Fort Canby.[27]

The Canyon de Chelly Expedition climaxed the Navajo campaign. Carson could report only twenty-three Indians killed and two hundred sheep seized besides the crops and orchards destroyed, but the effect on the Navajos was decisive. At no time or place, they now saw, could they or their property be safe from Carson's soldiers. In the six months before Canyon de Chelly, some two hundred had reached this conclusion and surrendered at Fort Canby or Fort Wingate for deportation to Bosque Redondo. After Canyon de Chelly this trickle swelled to a flood. Five hundred people surrendered to Carson on his return march, and within three weeks nearly three thousand were camped around the two forts awaiting transportation eastward. Thus the true significance of the Canyon de Chelly operation lay not in its destruction of life or property but in its impact as a symbol of Carleton's unshakable determination to keep Carson at his task until every Navajo had accepted one of two alternatives: Bosque Redondo or death.

Bereft of hope, they flocked to Canby and Wingate during

[27] Carson's report of Jan. 23, 1864, in *O.R.*, ser. 1, vol. 34, pt. 1, pp. 72–75. Canyon de Chelly takes the form of the letter Y, with the base representing the west entrance. The north leg is now called Canyon del Muerto, while the south leg and the stem form the main Canyon de Chelly. Carson, probing the south rim, had missed Pfeiffer because he passed through Canyon del Muerto. Carey's eastward march was through the main Canyon de Chelly. The Navajos lived in the canyon only in the summer, moving to the mesas above for the winter. Carleton and Carson both gave birth to the tradition, repeated ever since, that this was the first time whites had invaded the canyon in wartime. Actually both Spanish and Mexican troops had done so, as had Lieutenant Colonel Miles in 1858 and Captain John G. Walker in 1859.

the early months of 1864. By mid-March six thousand had surrendered. In a "Long Walk" replete with scenes of tragedy, pathos, and death, they were escorted in contingents of hundreds and sometimes thousands across the Territory to the remote Pecos. By late 1864 three-fourths of the tribe, more than eight thousand people, had been uprooted from their homeland and set down on the arid Pecos wastelands. "The exodus of this whole people," conceded Carleton's adjutant general, "men, women and children, with their flocks and herds, leaving forever the land of their fathers, was an interesting but a touching sight." Although some four thousand had fled westward, to the deserts scored by the great canyons of the Colorado River, Carleton had indeed substantially accomplished the isolation of the Navajos from the settlements that Canby had set as the only way to eliminate the Navajo menace.[28]

After Canyon de Chelly Carson left Captain Carey, the efficient Regular who had made up for the colonel's deficiencies in formal military learning, to manage the emigration of the surrendered Indians and conduct mopping-up operations. In Santa Fe Carson met a hero's welcome as well as lavish and not undeserved praise from a proud commanding general. Reporting the conquest of "the great fortress of the tribe since time out of mind," Carleton urged the adjutant general to see that Carson received "a substantial reward for this crowning act in a long life spent in various capacities in the service of his country in fighting the savages among the fastnesses of the Rocky mountains."[29] The reward, a brevet of brigadier general of Volunteers, was to come a year later—and by then Carson had conducted still another notable if less clearly successful campaign, this one against the Kiowas and Comanches (see below, pp. 297–99).

[28] The movement of the Navajos is summarized in the operations chronology in Senate Reps., 39th Cong., 2d sess., No. 156, pp. 258–64. See also Bailey, *The Long Walk*, pp. 163–68, and Underhill, *The Navajos*, pp. 124–26. The census of the Indian population at Bosque Redondo on Dec. 31, 1864 (Senate Reps., 39th Cong., 2d sess., No. 156, pp. 264–65), disclosed a total of 8,354 Navajos, more than a fourth of them adult males, possessing 3,181 horses and mules, 6,962 sheep, and 2,757 goats. In March a body of 2,400 Navajos was moved, losing 197 by death en route. Thompson to Cutler, April 15, 1864, encl. to Carleton to AG, April 24, N179/1864, RG 94, NARS. Carleton had estimated the tribal population at around five thousand, and the growing stream of people to Bosque Redondo forced him to reduce rations at all the New Mexico forts and take other stringent measures in order to feed so many people.

[29] Senate Reps., 39th Cong., 2d sess., No. 156, p. 157.

New Mexicans hailed Carleton as a deliverer who had won them freedom from a Navajo scourge of more than two centuries' duration. What he did with the Navajos at Bosque Redondo troubled them little. No doubts about the future troubled Carleton either. As he had informed the adjutant general back in September 1863, as Carson began to apply force:

The purpose now is never to relax the application of force with a people that can no more be trusted than you can trust the wolves that run through their mountains; to gather them together, little by little, on to a reservation, away from their haunts, and hills, and hiding-places of their country, and then to be kind to them; there teach their children how to read and write; teach them the arts of peace; teach them the truths of Christianity. Soon they will acquire new habits, new ideas, new modes of life; the old Indians will die off, and carry with them all latent longings for murdering and robbing; the young ones will take their places without these longings; and thus, little by little, they will become a happy and contented people, and Navajo wars will be remembered only as something that belongs entirely to the past.

Bosque Redondo was the ideal place—remote from the Navajo homeland, comfortably distant from the territory's population centers, offering plentiful arable land for agriculture, and already the home of Mescaleros descended from the same parent stock and speaking the same language. "I know these views are practical, practicable, and humane," he concluded; "are just to the suffering [New Mexican] people, as well as to the aggressive, perfidious, butchering Navajos."[30]

Governor Connelly agreed wholeheartedly, as did James L. Collins, Superintendent of Indian Affairs for six years and now publisher of the *Santa Fe Gazette*. Standing in lonely opposition was Collins' successor as superintendent, the long-time Apache agent Michael Steck. Bosque Redondo was indeed an admirable location for the Apaches, he conceded, but for thousands of Navajos in addition it was woefully inadequate. The arable land there, estimated at no more than six thousand acres by the territorial surveyor general, could not begin to support so many Indians and their extensive flocks and herds. Moreover, even if some relationship did bind Navajo and Apache in antiquity, the two groups had been "inveterate enemies" for a

[30] *Ibid.*, pp. 134 passim.

century or more, and it was folly to suppose that they could now share a reservation in amity. Instead, a reservation should be marked out for the Navajos on the edge of their own country, somewhere on the Little Colorado River. This had been the intention of General Canby, Steck ascertained, who also shared Steck's views about the impracticability of Bosque Redondo. Although both the Commissioner of Indian Affairs and the Secretary of the Interior were persuaded, Carleton did not wait for higher authority to resolve the issue, and by April the Interior Department had decided to acquiesce in the arrangement. The decision did not silence Steck's dissent, and for another year, over this and other issues, he and Carleton exchanged vituperation and maneuvered zealously in every corner of the bureaucracy to topple each other.[31]

Yet in the end Steck's predictions came true. Carleton's vision of the Navajos in ten years forming the "happiest and most delightfully located pueblo of Indians in New Mexico—perhaps in the United States,"[32] shattered on the hard realities forecast by the superintendent. Navajos and Mescaleros could not get along—especially after the troops at Fort Sumner began using Mescaleros to pursue bands of Navajos that slipped off on an occasional raid. The four hundred Mescaleros, their tolerance finally exhausted by the bullying of eight thousand Navajos, in November 1865 fled the reservation and hid in the familiar haunts of the Sierra Blanca, Guadalupes, and Sacramentos. The Pecos bottoms indeed failed to support so many Navajos, and floods, drouths, and clouds of grasshoppers combined to ravage the few crops that could be coaxed to germinate. Government food issues barely staved off starvation. Disease joined with Kiowas and Comanches from the Plains to prey on the hapless prisoners. Stubbornly, as the death toll rose, Carleton clung to his scheme, and not until 1868, two years after his departure, was failure officially acknowl-

[31] Steck's position in evolution and summary is set forth in his annual report for 1864 with appended correspondence in CIA, *Annual Report* (1864), pp. 183-87, 203-15. See also Connelly to Stanton, March 12, 1864, encl. to Canby to SI, April 8, 1864, W409/1864, RG 75; Collins to Dole, Dec. 6, 1863, C615/1863, RG 75; Canby to Usher, March 29, 1864, War Dept. LB, vol. 53C, pp. 201-2, RG 98; Dole to Usher, April 4, 1864, SI LR, Indian Div., RG 48. All in NARS. For the Steck-Carleton feud, see correspondence in Senate Reps., 39th Cong., 2d sess., No. 156, passim; and in Steck Papers.
[32] Senate Reps., 39th Cong., 2d sess., No. 156, p. 162.

edged and the tribe by treaty permitted to return to its home-land.[33]

Although the Bosque Redondo project ended in utter fail-ure, Carleton had after all accomplished the principal task he set for himself. Bosque Redondo ended warfare with the Nava-jos forever. The four-year exile crushed their independence, self-confidence, and morale. They came home in 1868 a beaten people, determined at any cost to avoid another such catas-trophe. Like other tribes, the Navajos had been defeated; unlike other tribes, they had also been subjugated. No provoca-tion or injustice could make them forget Bosque Redondo and fight back. Carleton attained his major goal—but at a terrible cost and a lasting consequence to a proud and accomplished people. As late as 1946, two authoritative students of the Nav-ajos could write:

Fort Sumner was a major calamity to The People; its full effects upon their imagination can hardly be conveyed to white readers. Even today it seems impossible for any Navaho of the older gener-ation to talk for more than a few minutes on any subject without speaking of Fort Sumner. Those who were not there themselves heard so many poignant tales from their parents that they speak as if they themselves had experienced all the horror of the "Long Walk," the illness, the hunger, the homesickness, the final return to their desolated land. One can no more understand Navaho atti-tudes—particularly toward white people—without knowing of Fort Sumner than he can comprehend Southern attitudes without know-ing of the Civil War.[34]

General Carleton saw himself as much more than a simple soldier with purely soldierly duties to perform. Military con-quest of the Mescaleros and Navajos fell short of the perma-nent solution he sought, so he laid out a visionary blueprint for their cultural transformation and proceeded to carry it out

[33] Voluminous correspondence bearing on Bosque Redondo is printed in Senate Reps., 39th Cong., 2d sess., No. 156, passim. Other important material is in the Steck Papers. For a synthesis see Charles Amsden, "The Navajo Exile at Bosque Redondo," New Mexico Historical Review, 8 (1933), 31-50. See also Underhill, The Navajos, chap. 11.

[34] Kluckhohn and Leighton, The Navajo, pp. 9-10. For another penetrat-ing analysis of the effect of Bosque Redondo on the tribe see Charles Amsden, Navaho Weaving: Its Technic and History (2d ed.; Albuquerque, 1940), pp. 168-69.

with supreme contempt for civil authorities more legitimately concerned than he. Not content with guarding against another Confederate invasion, in the name of wartime security he trampled individual liberties and flouted or intimidated any part of the judiciary attempting to uphold them. With an easily manipulated executive in the governor's chair, the commanding general came close to subserving Civil War New Mexico to a military dictatorship.[35] It was wholly in character, then, that Carleton conceived himself as an empire builder—an agent of Manifest Destiny obligated not only to bring safety to pioneer settlers but also to forward the great work of subduing and exploiting the wilderness.

Carleton's tenure in New Mexico coincided with exciting new mineral strikes around the headwaters of the Gila and among the mountains of central Arizona, which was detached from New Mexico in February 1863 and created a separate Territory. With optimism characteristic of fortune-seekers on every mining frontier of the American West, Carleton pronounced the vast tract of territory "from the head of the Gila northwestwardly to the Colorado River" a region "of unequalled wealth in the precious metals." In the midst of the great crisis of Civil War:

Providence has indeed blessed us. Now that we need money to pay the expenses of this terrible war, new mines of untold millions are found, and the gold lies here at our feet, to be had by the mere picking of it up! The country where it is found is no fancied Atlantis; is not seen in golden dreams; but it is a real, tangible El Dorado, that has gold that can be weighed by the steelyards—gold that does not vanish when the finder is awake.

Providence had disclosed the new riches at a propitious time: "It seems providential that the practical miners of California" —a full brigade of them—"should have come here to assist in their discovery and development." To Carleton the implications appeared obvious. In the national interest, more troops, preferably "practical miners" from California, should be sent to him—not only to sweep aside the Indians and provide security to the miners, but also to aid in developing the mines and peopling the country. Every regiment sent, he predicted, "would

---

[35] See Rogan, "Military History . . . ," chap. 11.

virtually be a military colony when the war ended, whose interests would lead the officers and soldiers to remain in the new El Dorado."[36]

To Adjutant General Lorenzo Thomas, General-in-Chief Halleck, Secretary of the Treasury Salmon Chase, Postmaster General Montgomery Blair, and others high in authority, Carleton wrote in this vein throughout 1863. His petitions aroused little response and won him no reinforcements, and his glowing prophesies turned out to be somewhat overstated. But for three years he sought by every means at his command to facilitate the opening of the mining districts and to crush the Apaches who denied them to exploitation. At the close of the Civil War, moreover, many a discharged California Volunteer did indeed make his home in New Mexico or Arizona.

The discovery of gold at Pinos Altos, near the old Spanish copper mines, brought about two thousand miners to the southern foothills of the Mogollon Mountains in the spring and summer of 1860. This was the domain of the Gila Apaches—Mimbres, Copper Mine, Warm Spring, and Mogollon—and of the giant chieftain Mangas Coloradas. Short-lived Fort McLane, twenty miles south of Pinos Altos, exerted a stabilizing influence on the area through the winter of 1860–61, but with the collapse of federal authority in southern New Mexico at the beginning of the Civil War, hostilities broke out between miners and Apaches.

Making common cause with the neighboring Chiricahuas, bitterly hostile since Lieutenant Bascom's fumbling attempt to bully Cochise had misfired earlier in the year, Mangas Coloradas led a bloody effort to expel the intruders from his homeland. He waylaid and wiped out a mail party, besieged Charles Hayden's freight train, fought a series of skirmishes with a company of "Arizona Rangers" operating under Confederate authority, and attacked and partly burned Pinos Altos itself. By mid-1862, as the California Column approached from the west, Mangas had nearly succeeded in depopulating the Pinos Altos area of miners.[37]

---

[36] Senate Reps., 39th Cong., 2d sess., No. 156, pp. 110, 113–14, 135–37, 140.
[37] Collins to Dole, June 8, 1861, C1231/1861, RG 75, NARS. R. S. Allen, "Pinos Altos, New Mexico," *New Mexico Historical Review*, 23 (1948), 302–32. William F. Scott, Paper read before Society of Arizona Pioneers, July 6,

Both Cochise and Mangas seem to have interpreted the departure of federal troops and the withdrawal of Butterfield's mail coaches as a consequence of Apache prowess, and their success against the Pinos Altos prospectors had not diluted their sense of power. As contingents of Californians began appearing out of the west, therefore, the two chieftains laid plans to dispute the passage in the tangled recesses of Apache Pass, for Cochise the scene of so many vivid memories. On July 15, 1862, several hundred Chiricahua and Gila warriors lay in ambush on the slopes of the pass when Captain Thomas L. Roberts led his infantry company into its west entrance.

Fired on from both sides, Captain Roberts had no choice but to press forward: his parched troops had to reach the water of Apache Spring or perish of thirst. The enemy commanded the spring from rock breastworks on the neighboring heights. Bursting shells from two howitzers cleared them out. Leaving part of his command to hold the position, Roberts retraced his path to the west, joined with a company of cavalry, and returned the next day. The Apaches renewed the engagement, only to be blasted from their fortifications once more by the artillery. An Apache participant later confessed that sixty-six warriors had been slain, all but three by artillery. "We would have done well enough," he added, "if you had not fired wagons at us."[38]

Carleton arrived at Apache Pass on July 27. Roberts' fight had convinced him that the security of his lines of communication with California depended importantly on the security of the vital spring in Apache Pass, favorite haunt of the Chiricahuas. On July 27, in the abandoned Butterfield mail station, his adjutant general penned an order for the erection of a fort on a hillside overlooking the spring. Named in honor of the colonel of the 5th California Infantry, Fort Bowie began its long and colorful role in the Apache wars of the Southwest.[39] For the next three years its garrison of California Volunteers

---

1894, Arizona Pioneers Historical Society, Tucson. W. S. Oury, "Cook's Canyon: A Scene of Carnage Enacted There in July, 1861," *Arizona Daily Star* (Tucson), July 27, 1879. W. W. Mills, *Forty Years at El Paso, 1858–1898*, Rex Strickland, ed. (El Paso, 1962), pp. 195–96.

[38] Cremony, *Life Among the Apaches*, p. 164. Captain Cremony, the cavalry commander, gives a detailed account of the action on pp. 157–67. For Roberts' report see *O.R.*, ser. 1, vol. 50, pt. 1, pp. 128–32.

[39] *Ibid.*, pp. 100–5.

accomplished Carleton's aim of denying the strategic pass to Cochise and his warriors.

From the Mimbres River in August 1862 Carleton sent a company to the relief of Pinos Altos, which Mangas Coloradas' warriors had reduced to a population of about thirty American, French, and German prospectors and a handful of Mexicans, all in starving and destitute straits.[40] At the moment they were not too troubled by Apaches. Mangas had caught a carbine ball in the chest at the Battle of Apache Pass, and his men had taken him to Sonora, where they forced a Mexican doctor, on penalty of death, to remove it.[41] By the close of 1862, however, the Gilas were back in familiar haunts, tightening the vise on Pinos Altos and raiding eastward to the Rio Grande and the Jornada. Enthusiastic over the supposed mineral potential of the Pinos Altos mines, Carleton set high priority on making them safe for exploitation. During a visit to Mesilla early in January 1863, he ordered General West to establish a new post, Fort West, near Pinos Altos and to take decisive measures against Mangas and his "band of murderers and robbers."[42]

With elements of the 1st California Cavalry and 5th California Infantry, West set forth at once for abandoned Fort McLane, on the Mimbres River, sending Captain E. D. Shirland with his cavalry company in advance to seek out the quarry. On January 18 Shirland rejoined West at Fort McLane. With him was Mangas Coloradas himself—"captured," according to Shirland's report; lured into camp by a white flag invitation to parley and then seized, according to a prospector, Daniel E. Conner, who was present. West had no intention of letting Mangas go. Having "voluntarily placed himself in my power," the chief could not be executed, as he deserved. But "he was told that the remainder of his days would be spent as a prisoner" and that if he tried to escape "his life would be the immediate forfeit." That night Mangas "made three efforts to escape and was shot on the third attempt." Unsaid in West's official report but observed by prospector Conner, the guards

40 *Ibid.*, pp. 105-6.
41 Cremony, *Life among the Apaches*, pp. 175-76.
42 GO 1, Hq. Dept. NM, Mesilla, Jan. 6, 1863, encl. to Carleton to Thomas, Feb. 1, 1863, N41/1863, RG 94, NARS.

thrice applied heated bayonets to the chief's bare feet and at his third vigorous protest riddled him with musket balls—probably with the tacit approval if not in response to explicit orders of General West.[43]

Within two days after the death of Mangas, Captain Shirland and Captain William McCleave had skirmished twice with portions of his band, inflicting losses of twenty killed and many wounded. From Fort West, officially established on January 24 near Pinos Altos, four California companies combed the surrounding mountains throughout February and March. On March 22 McCleave fell on a ranchería and in a hard-fought contest killed twenty-eight Gilas. By the beginning of May, West could report that "the savages are pretty well cleared out from the headwaters of the Gila River." In truth, Mangas' band had been nearly obliterated—an ambush set up by Captain James H. Whitlock in February 1864 was thought to have wiped out the last of it—and Pinos Altos, although its wealth failed to come up to Carleton's expectations, enjoyed a security interrupted by only an occasional depredation. Fort West was abandoned early in 1864 and replaced by Fort Cummings, at strategic Cooke's Spring about fifty miles to the southeast, on the road to Tucson.[44]

Although Mangas Coloradas' immediate band had been decimated, West's operations had not cleared the mountains around the head of the Gila of Apaches, and a rising young Warm Spring leader named Victorio gave promise of attaining all the stature once boasted by Mangas. Principal targets for these bands from 1863 to 1865 were the settlements around Socorro and Mesilla and the ninety-mile stretch of the Santa Fe–El Paso road that lay across the parched Jornada del Muerto in between. Favored for generations as a plundering ground by Gila and

[43] For the official version of Mangas' capture and death see West's report, Jan. 28, 1863, *O.R.* ser. 1, vol. 50, pt. 2, pp. 296–97, and Shirland to McCleave, Jan. 22, 1863, encl. to *ibid.*, N41/1863, RG 94, NARS. Conner's extended account, together with an assessment of his and other testimony, is in Daniel E. Conner, *Joseph Reddeford Walker and the Arizona Adventure*, Donald J. Berthrong and Odessa Davenport, eds. (Norman, Okla., 1956), pp. 34–42. In 1865 Superintendent of Indian Affairs Steck stated that Mangas was "murdered . . . after being invited in by the Military under promises of friendship and protection." Steck to Dole, Feb. 15, 1865, S606/1865, RG 75, NARS.

[44] *O.R.*, ser. 1, vol. 50, pt. 2, pp. 296–97; vol. 34, pt. 1, pp. 122–23. Reports of Shirland and McCleave, Jan. 22, 1863, N41/1863, RG 94, NARS. Senate Reps., 39th Cong., 2d sess., No. 156, pp. 247–48. West to McFerran, May 2, 1863, W105/1863, RG 94, NARS.

Mescalero Apaches as well as by Navajos, the middle Rio Grande suffered greater and more constant loss of life and property than any other section of New Mexico.

With more than four hundred men at Fort Craig, northern bastion of the Jornada defenses, Colonel Edwin A. Rigg strove in vain to turn back the raiders. In April 1863 Carleton planted Fort McRae on the Rio Grande opposite the midpoint of the Jornada to block a mountain pass favored by Apaches and Navajos coming from the west, and in May 1865 he established Fort Selden as the southern anchor of the Jornada defenses. Yet none of his efforts had much effect on the scale of raiding, and the Indians dramatized it by preying on the soldiers themselves. Repeatedly they infuriated Carleton by running off the stock herds at the three posts. In June 1863 they surprised Captain Pfeiffer and his family bathing in the mineral hot springs near Fort McRae, slaughtered his wife and servant, and chased the naked captain all the way back to the fort. In the same month they annihilated a mail party and its escort on the Jornada, carrying off as trophies the head and heart of the lieutenant in charge of the escort. Spurred by a wrathful commanding general, the troops labored mightily to exact vengeance and win Carleton's approval, but to no avail.[45]

The conquest of the Mescaleros and Navajos brought little relief, for war parties slipped off the Bosque Redondo Reservation to interdict the Jornada road and seize sheep by the thousand from New Mexican shepherds to the north and south. A ray of hope for neutralizing some of the Gila bands appeared in the spring of 1865, when Victorio, Rinyon, Nana, and other chiefs sent word to Mesilla that they wanted Superintendent Steck, their former agent, to come to Pinos Altos and "make a chain between them and the whites that would never be broken." Steck prepared to go, but Carleton, asserting that hostile Indians were exclusively a military responsibility, served notice that this would not be permitted. Instead, he sent his inspector general, Lieutenant Colonel Nelson H. Davis, who told the chiefs that the Gilas could have peace if they all went to Bosque Redondo. Recalling the fate of Mangas when he

---

[45] See especially operations chronology for 1863 and 1864 in Senate Reps., 39th Cong., 2d sess., No. 156, pp. 247–64. For the Pfeiffer episode see Hubbell to Rigg, June 21, 1863, encl. to Carleton to Thomas, June 29, 1863, N178/1863, RG 94, NARS. For the massacre of Lieutenant L. A. Bargie and his party see Rigg to Cutler, June 24, 1863, Dept. NM LR, RG 98, NARS.

trusted the soldiers, the Apaches promised to think over the proposition, hastily retired to their mountain hideouts, and soon were at war once more. Davis reported that they had been acting treacherously from the beginning. "Death to the Apache, and peace and prosperity to this land, is my motto," he declared. Not until fifteen years later did Victorio's death in battle foreshadow peace and prosperity for southern New Mexico.[46]

Daniel E. Conner, the gold-seeker who in January 1863 witnessed the slaying of Mangas Coloradas by General West's soldiers at old Fort McLane, belonged to a party of twenty-six prospectors whose path had briefly crossed that of the troops trying to make the Pinos Altos district safe for miners. Turning their backs on the diminishing placer deposits of California, they had banded together to seek new gold fields in unexploited corners of the Southwest. No more experienced leader of the expedition could have been found than Joseph Reddeford Walker, who in nearly forty years as an explorer and fur trapper had come to know as much about the West as any man alive. From Fort McLane the Walker party proceeded to Tucson, then turned north. Prospecting up Hassayampa Creek, a northern tributary of the Gila, the group struck gold in the mountains of central Arizona.[47]

News of the "Walker Mines" reached Santa Fe early in June 1863. In no one did it evoke more enthusiasm than General Carleton, who fairly leaped at the opportunity to aid in opening a new mining region. At once he wrote to Walker promising to found a military post at the mines, and to General Halleck he appealed for reinforcements to man it. At once, too, he provided a company to escort New Mexico Surveyor General John A. Clark to the mines to obtain full information, instructing the escort commander to search for a good site for a fort and to permit the soldiers to do some prospecting of their own. Clark returned in September 1863 with a temperate report on the potential of the Walker finds. Praising him for a restraint designed to avoid exciting "extravagant

---

[46] Senate Reps., 39th Cong., 2d sess., No. 156, pp. 220–21, 244, 304–7. Steck to Dole, March 12, 1865, enclosing petition of Mesilla citizens of Feb. 2, 1865, Steck Papers. Steck to Dole, March 20, 1865, with enclosures, S625/1865, RG 75, NARS.

[47] See Conner, *Walker and the Arizona Adventure*, chap. 4, for a firsthand account of the discovery.

expectations," Carleton could not suppress his own extravagant prediction that, given enough troops "to whip away the Apaches," he could show that the Southwest had "mines of precious metals unsurpassed in richness, number, and extent by any in the world."[48]

In October 1863 Carleton set apart all Arizona north of the Gila River as the District of Northern Arizona and ordered Major Edward B. Willis to lead two companies of the 1st California Infantry and one of the 1st California Cavalry to the mines and establish Fort Whipple. Already he had assumed that the capital of the new Territory, created by Congress the previous February, would be erected there instead of "at the insignificant village of Tucson." Governor John M. Goodwin and other newly appointed territorial officials, arriving in Santa Fe in November, confirmed the assumption. Carleton entertained them warmly and dispatched a cavalry company to escort them to Fort Whipple. By the spring of 1864, after extensive travels throughout the Territory, Governor Goodwin had selected a site for Arizona's seat of government twenty miles south of Fort Whipple. In May Major Willis moved the fort to the new location, where a roistering mining town of some five hundred people was taking shape. That summer it was named Prescott.[49]

The burgeoning settlements of the Prescott district intruded on territory inhabited by the Yavapai Indians, a Yuman group of some two thousand people consistently called Apaches or Tonto Apaches by the whites but, though culturally similar, wholly unrelated to the various divisions of the Western Apaches.[50] Resentful of the white invasion, they responded with thievery and an occasional killing but caused little serious trouble until infuriated by the aggressions of the miners. "The sentiment here," wrote Territorial Secretary Richard McCormick in March 1864, "is in favor of an utter extermi-

---

[48] Senate Reps., 39th Cong., 2d sess., No. 156, pp. 113–14, 115, 117, 118, 122, 135–36, 139–40.

[49] *Ibid.*, p. 145. GO 27, Hq. Dept. NM, Oct. 23, 1863, General Orders, AGO, vol. 922, RG 94, NARS. Rogan, "Military History . . . ," pp. 428–30. For conditions at Fort Whipple and Goodwin's travels during the winter, see the series of letters to Carleton from Inspector General Davis in *O.R.*, ser. 1, vol. 34, pt. 3, pp. 200–10; and Willis to Cutler, March 18, 1864, W123/1864, RG 98, NARS.

[50] Albert H. Schroeder, *A Study of Yavapai History* (3 vols.; Santa Fe, N.M., 1959: mimeographed report for Indian Land Claims Sec., Lands Div., U.S. Dept. of Justice).

nation of the ruthless savages who have so long prevented the settlement and development of the Territory."[51]

This sentiment was translated into practice by a band of thirty Indian fighters organized by King S. Woolsey, one of Walker's party of discoverers, and enrolled as territorial militia. Throughout 1864 Woolsey and his men, rationed by the Army and aided by Pima and Maricopa auxiliaries and occasionally by detachments of Willis' troops, rampaged over the mountains drained by the Verde and Salt Rivers, destroying crops and rancherías and slaying Indians. For the Yavapais the most memorable contact with Woolsey took place in the Pinal Mountains at a place (on the edge of modern Miami) subsequently known as "Bloody Tanks." Here on January 24, 1864, Woolsey lured thirty warriors into his camp with promises of tobacco and pinole and then fell on them and slaughtered twenty-four. Criticized after a series of fights in March that took sixty Indian lives, Woolsey responded: "It sir is next thing to impossible to prevent killing squaws in gumping a rancheria even were we disposed to save them. For my part I am frank to say that I fight on the broad platform of extermination."[52]

So, less boastfully, did Willis' troops, but they enjoyed much less success than Woolsey's partisans and were, besides, largely occupied during the winter of 1863–64 in locating and building Fort Whipple. In any event, they were too few to conduct the kind of comprehensive campaign that the scale of Yavapai hostility now seemed to require. Besides the Yavapais, nearly all the Western Apaches were hostile and had been since the withdrawal of the Regulars in 1861. Chiricahuas, Coyoteros, and Pinals interdicted the California road and carried depredations to the edge of Tucson. California Volunteers from Tucson and Fort Bowie occasionally struck back, as when the energetic Captain Thomas T. Tidball wiped out a ranchería in Aravaipa Canyon in May 1863, killing 50 Apaches, taking 10 prissoners, and seizing 60 head of stock;[53] and as when Captain Whitlock surprised a Chiricahua ranchería at the south base

[51] McCormick to Poston, March 5, 1864, OIA NM Field Papers, RG 75, NARS.

[52] Woolsey to Carleton, March 29, 1864, W244/1864, and Sept. 14, 1864, W284/1864. RG 98 NARS. Clara T. Woody, ed., "The Woolsey Expeditions of 1864," *Arizona and the West*, 4 (1962), 157–76.

[53] Senate Reps., 39th Cong., 2d sess., No. 156, p. 249.

of Mount Graham in April 1864, killed 21 Indians, captured 45 mules, and destroyed more than a ton of dried mescal and mule meat.[54] But there had been little thought of a general offensive until the opening of the Prescott mines focused Carleton's attention on Arizona and set him to planning a large-scale operation aimed at conquering all the Apaches (among whom he classed the Yavapais) of the new Territory. By the spring of 1864, with the Navajo campaign ended, he was ready to wage against them, as he had against the Navajos, "a serious war; not a little march out and back again."[55]

Carleton's plan was to blanket Arizona with numerous fast-moving light columns of soldiers, miners, and Indian allies, all aggressively seeking Apaches at the same time. He provided two hundred stand of arms to equip four fifty-man contingents of Pimas and Maricopas. He welcomed the eager participation of King Woolsey's Prescott-based partisans. He solicited the aid of Governor Goodwin in getting "every citizen of the Territory who has a rifle to take the field." "In this way, where many parties are in pursuit of Indians at the same time, the Indians, in endeavoring to escape from one, run into others." And as all this activity could be expected to drive some of the enemy into Mexico, he also urged the governors of Chihuahua and Sonora to send forth state militia and bands of armed citizens in the same sort of undertaking. "Every effort must be made," he explained to Colonel Bowie on April 20, "to have a general rising of both citizens and soldiers, on both sides of the line, against the Apaches."[56]

General orders of May 1, 1864, spelled out the Army's role in the "general rising." The main force, five hundred officers and men of the 1st and 5th California Infantry, 1st New Mexico Infantry, and 1st California Cavalry, would march west from Las Cruces under Colonel Edwin A. Rigg and establish a base of operations, Fort Goodwin, somewhere on the middle Gila. Inspector General Davis, who had pointed out that Fort Whipple was not strategically placed for such a base, would select the site. From Fort Goodwin Rigg would send detachments in every direction to search out and fight the enemy. The troops would travel lightly, relying on packmules for transportation

[54] *O.R.*, ser. 1, vol. 50, pt. 2, pp. 827–28.
[55] Senate Reps., 39th Cong., 2d sess., No. 156, p. 172.
[56] *Ibid.*, pp. 177–79.

—"to be encumbered with more is not to find Indians." At the same time, similar detachments would move north from Tucson through Canyon del Oro and down the San Pedro, from Fort Bowie south through the Chiricahua Mountains, from Fort Whipple southeast across the Salt River, from Fort Canby south along the west base of the Mogollon Mountains, from Fort Wingate south to the head of the Gila, from Forts Craig and McRae west and south to Pinos Altos, and from Fort Cummings south toward the Mexican boundary. "This covering of so much ground by detachments of determined men," hoped Carleton, "must produce a moral effect upon the Indians" and "convince them of the folly long to hold out against us."[57]

The most notable success of the campaign occurred before it got fairly underway. Escorted by Captain Tidball with eighty-six California infantrymen and a platoon of cavalry, Lieutenant Colonel Davis left Fort Bowie on May 9 to scout the Gila Valley in search of a suitable location for Fort Goodwin. Moving down the river and examining its tributaries, including the San Carlos, the troops pursued and skirmished with Apaches whenever opportunity offered. On May 29 Tidball surrounded a ranchería in a canyon of the Mescal Mountains, just below present Coolidge Dam, and killed or captured all but 7 of its 49 occupants. Arriving in Tucson on June 3, Davis and Tidball totaled the results: 51 Indians killed, 17 wounded, 16 captured, and large quantities of crops, food stores, and camp equipage destroyed.[58]

This was the kind of campaigning that Carleton believed would bring the Apaches to terms, but no other detachment was to enjoy the same measure of success. Rigg's column reached the Gila in late June and began building Fort Goodwin north of Mount Graham. Through the summer and autumn months his detachments wore themselves out struggling in furnace-like heat over the cactus-covered mountains shouldering both sides of the Gila. Several conflicts in August felled a handful of Apaches, but usually the quarry succeeded in avoiding the hunters. A few skirmishes were all the other columns could boast too. Captain Pfeiffer and the Fort Canby troops, for example, dropped five Apaches in a running fight

[57] *O.R.*, ser. 1, vol. 34, pt. 3, pp. 387–89.
[58] *Ibid.*, pt. 1, pp. 917–20; pt. 4, pp. 252–56; vol. 50, pt. 2, pp. 869–72.

near the Little Colorado, then let two come into camp with peace signs. They sacrificed themselves by opening fire, seriously wounding the captain and a soldier. By late autumn reports from the field disclosed that three months of the hardest campaigning had produced a total of nearly fifty dead Apaches—less than Davis and Tidball had counted in a single scout. By late autumn, too, many of the California companies had reached the end of their term of service, and in order to muster them out Carleton had to suspend the Apache campaign and assume the defensive.[59]

In contrast to the Mescalero and Navajo campaigns, and even that against the Kiowas and Comanches (see pp. 297–99), the offensive against the Western Apaches and Yavapais had been an unqualified failure. As a young Tucson resident wrote in mid-September to his brother in New York: "The troops in their two months campaign have killed enough of the Apaches to enrage and irritate them without breaking their spirit, and we are still in such condition that every settlement must be a small military post of itself."[60] The diminished garrisons at Bowie, Goodwin, and Whipple strove vainly throughout the winter to hold back the Apaches and Yavapais whom Carleton's campaign had managed to "enrage and irritate," but the Apache wars of Arizona had in reality just begun. They ceased to be Carleton's problem in January 1865, however, when the War Department transferred Arizona to the Department of the Pacific.

General Carleton commanded in New Mexico for another year, until mustered out of the Volunteers with a brevet of major general in the Regular Army and appointed lieutenant colonel of the 4th U.S. Cavalry. In 1873, at San Antonio, pneumonia ended his life at the age of fifty-eight. Although a thoroughly unlikable man, Carleton brought a dynamic leadership to the Department of New Mexico. He fired his troops with

[59] Senate Reps., 39th Cong., 2d sess., No. 156, pp. 262–63. *O.R.*, ser. 1, vol. 50, pt. 1, pp. 360–77; vol. 41, pt. 1, pp. 81–86, 125–30, 867–78. Carleton to Goodwin, Oct. 13, 1864, Dept. NM LB, RG 98, NARS. Rogan, "Military History," pp. 452–55.

[60] William Wrightson to G. Wrightson, Sept. 17, 1864, quoted by G. Wrightson to Charles Poston, Nov. 14, 1864, encl. to Poston to SW Stanton, Dec. 28, 1864, P1889/1864, RG 107, NARS. On Feb. 17, 1865, a band of Apaches attacked a military vidette station at old Fort Buchanan. Among the slain was William Wrightson. *O.R.*, ser. 1, vol. 50, pt. 1, pp. 401–2.

an energetic and persevering drive that New Mexicans had never before observed in their military protectors. He also brought a rare understanding of Indian warfare and a ruthlessness in applying it reminiscent of General Harney. A measure of the achievement produced by this combination may be glimpsed in statistics collected by his adjutant general. During 1863 and 1864, besides killing 34 citizens and wounding 17, Indians in the Department of New Mexico ran off 29,879 head of stock, some from the Army but most from civilians. During the same period Carleton's troops, with a loss of 4 officers and 37 enlisted men killed and 6 officers and 39 men wounded, seized 49,722 head of stock from the Indians, killed 664 Indians, wounded 227, and through capture or surrender took 8,793 prisoner.[61] Carleton had not rid New Mexico of the Indian menace, but he had badly shaken all the tribes and had vanquished the most formidable altogether.

[61] Senate Reps., 39th Cong., 2d sess., No. 156, pp. 256–57, 267.

THIRTEEN

Sibley, Sully, and the Sioux, 1862-64

THE Plains Indians had yet to experience a catastrophic impact of the westward movement such as had shaken, dispossessed, and in some instances actually destroyed tribes inhabiting the mineral regions of the Rockies, the Sierra, and certain lesser mountain ranges beyond the Great Plains. There the white man had come to stay, and he peremptorily brushed aside any natives who got in his way. On the Plains, the Indian's principal contact with the westward movement had occurred along the travel corridors by which the emigrants reached the mineral regions. The government's attempts to keep the Plains tribes clear of these corridors disturbed traditional migratory patterns, and the flow of white people through the corridors strained resources of game and forage on which the tribes depended. To these causes for resentment the violence that had flared briefly in the 1850s and sent Harney, Sumner, Van Dorn, and others storming across the Plains had added a background of armed conflict that further aggravated the Plains Indian's attitude toward the whites. But except along the eastern margins of the Great Plains, very few white men had come to stay, and in the Indian mind the white threat had yet to crystallize into a sense of impending calamity.

The expansion of the mineral frontier in the early 1860s, however, brought a stepped-up tempo of activity to the Great Plains. Mining developments in Montana, Idaho, and New Mexico attracted new emigrants over established travel routes, led to the opening of new ones, and produced a rising tide of traffic on all as freight trains shuttled back and forth between

the mountain settlements and the sources of consumer goods
to the east. For Plains Indian and white traveler, the threat
to each of the other grew steadily more explicit. In 1862 a
bloody outbreak in Minnesota set off a chain reaction that in
three years had locked Sioux, Cheyenne, Arapaho, Kiowa, and
Comanche in a war with the whites that overspread the Great
Plains from the upper Missouri to the Red River.

In little more than a decade the woodlands and prairies surrounding the upper Mississippi River were transformed from
a remote meeting ground of trader and Indian into a thriving
agricultural region. Barely six thousand inhabitants supported
creation of the Territory of Minnesota in 1849; in the following decade the population soared to nearly two hundred thousand and led to statehood in 1858. St. Paul, the capital, bustled
with more than ten thousand people in 1860. Across the river
the town of Minneapolis grew up next to Fort Snelling, which
had guarded the strategic confluence of the Mississippi and
Minnesota Rivers since 1819. Up the Minnesota to the southwest the farmers advanced. Largely German and Scandinavian
immigrants, they carpeted the fertile valley and its tributaries
with neat farms and towns.

The Santee Sioux acquiesced unhappily.[1] Weakened by several generations of warfare with the more numerous and bet-
ter-armed Chippewas to the north, these woodland Sioux by
the Treaty of 1851 sold their hunting grounds for $3 million
payable in fifty yearly installments. They retained a reservation twenty miles wide extending for 150 miles along both sides
of the upper Minnesota River. By the Treaty of 1858 they
sold the ten-mile-wide strip on the north side of the river for
$266,880.[2] The Wahpeton and Sisseton tribes settled in vil-
lages around the Upper or Yellow Medicine Agency, the
Mdewkanton and Wahpekute around the Lower or Redwood
Agency. Fort Ridgely, founded in 1853 ten miles below Redwood Agency, kept watch on the reservation and its six thousand occupants.

[1] The Santee or Eastern Sioux consisted of the Mdewkanton, Wahpeton,
Wahpekute, and Sisseton tribes. The Western or Prairie Sioux consisted of the
Yankton and Yanktonai tribes living between the Red River of the North
and the Missouri River and the seven tribes of Teton Sioux living west
of the Missouri. Swanton, *Indian Tribes of North America*, p. 282.
[2] Kappler, *Indian Affairs*, 2, 588–93, 781–89. William W. Folwell, *A History
of Minnesota* (2 vols.; St. Paul, Minn., 1956), 1, 266–304, 352–54.

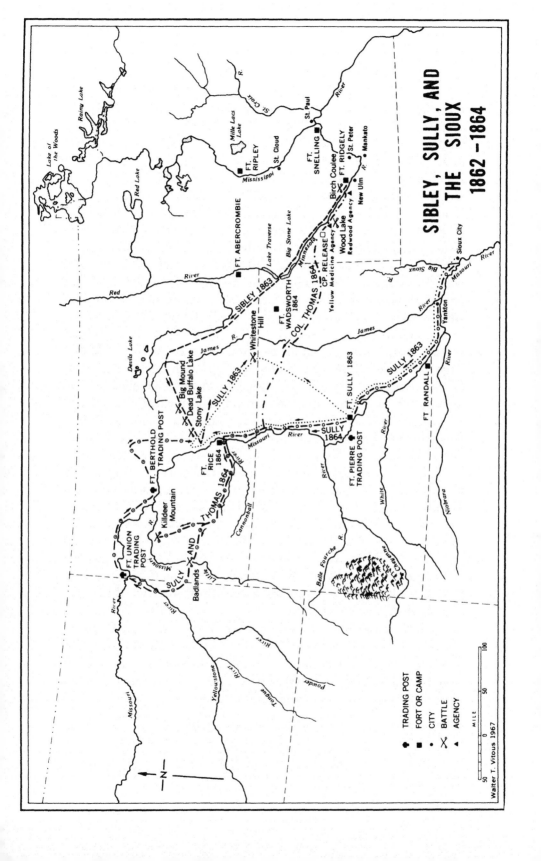

SIBLEY, SULLY, AND THE SIOUX 1862–1864

Walter T. Vitous 1967

For the Santees the 1850s were traumatic years. The engulfing tide of white settlement and the government effort to transform them into farmers and Christians produced frustration, resentment, and tribal factionalism. The yearly ⌐ash payments authorized by the treaties attracted unscrupulous traders who kept the Indians debauched and debt-ridden and who, often fraudulently, gained possession of nearly the whole sum of annuity money before it reached the intended recipients. Although the Indians brooded over these wrongs, the thought of a resort to violence never seems to have entered their minds. True, nearly fifty settlers in northern Iowa and southern Minnesota perished in the Spirit Lake Massacre of 1857, but this was the work of some renegade Wahpekutes under a violent outlaw named Inkpaduta who had left their people rather than subscribe to the Treaty of 1851. Little Crow, most powerful of the agency chiefs, even aided the troops from Fort Ridgely in the unsuccessful attempt to apprehend Inkpaduta.[3] Knowledge that the white men were fighting each other, departure of the Regulars from Fort Ridgely, mismanagement by the new agent appointed by the Lincoln administration, and the long delay in the 1862 annuity issue deepened the bitterness. But still no one suggested that the remedy lay in killing white people.[4]

Then on August 17 four Wahpeton youths hunting in the vicinity of Acton, north of Redwood Agency, murdered five settlers. There was no premeditation; one had dared another to prove his courage. But for the Sioux this act crystallized the grievances of a decade. In a stormy council that night, the aggressive Chiefs Red Middle Voice and Young Shakopee, bolstered by a riotous mob of young men shouting for blood, won the pledge of a reluctant Little Crow to lead them in a war against the whites.

At dawn on August 18 the warriors swept through Redwood Agency, killed the men, took the women and children captive, and put the buildings to the torch. In wide-ranging parties they spread over the countryside, killing, raping, pillaging, and burning. Surprised, unequipped for defense, unversed in fron-

---

[3] Folwell, *A History of Minnesota*, 2, 400–15. Russell W. Fridley, "Charles E. Flandrau, Attorney at War," *Minnesota History*, *38* (1962), 116–25.

[4] The literature of the Sioux War of 1862 is vast. I have relied heavily on C. M. Oehler, *The Great Sioux Uprising* (New York, 1959). Background is treated in chaps. 2–5 and causes summarized on pp. 235–37. See also Kenneth Carley, *The Sioux Uprising of 1862* (St. Paul, Minn., 1961).

tier life, the farmers fell by the score, dispatched with a savagery rarely equalled in the history of Indian uprisings—families burned alive in their cabins, children nailed to doors, girls raped by a dozen braves and then hacked to pieces, babies dismembered and their limbs flung in the mother's face. By evening some four hundred whites had been slain and hundreds more were flying in panic toward Fort Ridgely.[5]

Captain John Marsh's company of the 5th Minnesota Infantry, 2 officers and 76 men, held Fort Ridgely. When word of the uprising reached Marsh on the morning of the eighteenth, he took 46 men and marched for the agency. At the ferry across the river a strong force of warriors fell on the detachment and cut it to pieces; 23 men were killed, Marsh drowned in the river, and the rest made it back to the fort that night. Detachments called in from downriver augmented the garrison, and when Little Crow massed his warriors for an assault the next day, 2 lieutenants, 153 soldiers, and 25 armed civilians manned the defenses, while some 300 noncombatant refugees worked feverishly making cartridges. Ordnance Sergeant John Jones, an old Regular, posted the fort's three howitzers and instructed improvised crews in their operation.[6]

Divided counsels overtook the Indians. Little Crow, contemptuous of those who killed women and children, wished to make this a conventional war. Others preferred the less dangerous and more profitable business of slaughtering helpless settlers. As a result, about two hundred warriors declined to follow him in an attack on Fort Ridgely, instead crossing the river to ride against the town of New Ulm. On August 20, however, Little Crow mustered enough men to move on the fort. Desperate fighting raged throughout the day and again on the twenty-second, when he was able to hurl eight hundred warriors against the post. Sergeant Jones's howitzers proved crucial to the defense. Canister charges shredded every assault that reached for the outbuildings and finally so discouraged the attackers that they gave up the struggle.[7]

[5] Oehler, *The Great Sioux Uprising*, chaps. 4–6.
[6] *Ibid.*, chap. 8. *Minnesota in the Civil and Indian Wars* (2 vols.; St. Paul, Minn., 1899), 2, 166–70, 178–82. This is a compilation of official correspondence and other pertinent documents.
[7] Oehler, *The Great Sioux Uprising*, chap. 12. *Minnesota in the Civil and Indian Wars*, 2, 171–73, 182–86. Amazingly, considering the ferocity of the fighting, Fort Ridgely's defenders lost only three killed and thirteen wounded. Based on the number of graves subsequently counted in the vicinity, the Indian loss was estimated at about a hundred.

Many then rode to join their comrades at New Ulm. But Judge Charles E. Flandrau, youthful, frontier-wise lawyer, had hastened 125 men from St. Peter to the town's relief. Under Flandrau, they and about 75 of the community's own citizens met the determined attack of some 350 warriors on August 23. All day they fought in the streets and among the stores and dwellings, many of which were burned or wrecked. Stubbornly the defenders held on, at a cost finally tallied at 36 killed and 23 wounded, and at nightfall the Sioux withdrew.[8]

The defense of Fort Ridgely and New Ulm contained the outbreak and secured the settlements below. It probably also decided uncommitted chiefs not to lend Little Crow the aid on which he had counted. Some Sissetons and Wahpetons of Yellow Medicine Agency had been drawn to the hostile force, as had a few Yanktons and Yanktonais of eastern Dakota. Several hundred warriors who on September 3–6 laid siege to Fort Abercrombie, situated at the head of navigation of Red River, could only have come from these groups.[9] But their chiefs, notably the powerful Standing Buffalo of the Sissetons, cast their influence against the war.[10] No more could Little Crow assemble even the force that had assailed Fort Ridgely, much less the fifteen hundred he had hoped for. After Fort Ridgely and New Ulm, it remained for Minnesotans to avenge the death of some eight hundred citizens slain in the week's orgy of bloodletting, to liberate several hundred white and half-blood captives held by the hostiles, and to reopen the upper country to settlers.

These tasks fell to Henry Hastings Sibley, pioneer fur trader and first governor of the young state. A cultured gentleman of many talents and undoubted integrity, he laid claim to no military experience but knew the Minnesota Sioux intimately. On August 19, the day after the outbreak, Governor Alexander Ramsey commissioned Sibley a colonel in the state militia and

---

[8] Oehler, *The Great Sioux Uprising*, chap. 13. *Minnesota in the Civil and Indian Wars*, 2, 203–8. Fridley, "Charles E. Flandrau."

[9] Roy P. Johnson, "The Siege at Fort Abercrombie," *North Dakota History*, 24, (1957), 1–77.

[10] SI, *Annual Report* (1863), pp. 393–94. *Minnesota in the Civil and Indian Wars*, 2, 187–89. About four hundred warriors pressed Fort Abercrombie, held by a company of the 5th Minnesota, and at one time gained some of the outbuildings. As at Fort Ridgely, artillery fire was decisive in holding off the Indians. Two soldiers were killed and two wounded. Indian casualties probably exceeded twenty.

charged him with relieving the settlers in the Minnesota Valley.[11]

Cautiously Sibley moved up the river. At first he counted only four companies hastily assembled at Fort Snelling, but within a week his command swelled to nearly fifteen hundred men—mainly the newly organized 6th Minnesota Infantry but also including militia units and improvised volunteer groups. Savagely the press castigated the colonel for the slowness of the advance. Not until August 28 did he reach Fort Ridgely.

On August 31 Sibley ordered out a detachment of 150 men —an infantry company and a mounted ranger company plus a 20-man fatigue detail—under Captain Hiram P. Grant to reconnoiter the Redwood Agency and bury any bodies in the vicinity. After examining the charred agency and interring more than eighty victims of the first day's massacre, the command camped on the night of September 1 near the head of Birch Coulee, which emptied into the river opposite the agency. Next morning at dawn several hundred warriors under Big Eagle, Mankato, and Gray Bird fell on the camp. The first charge nearly overran the surprised detachment, killing 22 and wounding 60, but after an hour of close-range combat the attackers drew off. For the rest of the day, as the soldiers dug shallow rifle pits, the two sides exchanged fire. The sound carried dimly to Fort Ridgely, sixteen miles downstream, and Sibley started Colonel Samuel McPhail with fifty rangers and three infantry companies to the rescue. Within sight of Grant's beleagured men, however, McPhail found himself surrounded by Indians. Howitzer fire drove them off, but he withdrew to a defensible position and sent back a call for reinforcements. Not until the afternoon of September 3, thirty-one hours after the first attack on Grant, was the siege lifted by Sibley and the entire command.[12]

The Battle of Birch Coulee hardly fired Sibley with new boldness. Newspapers cried for a more aggressive commander. But the colonel could, and did, list cogent reasons for delay: raw troops; an insufficiency of rations, ammunition, clothing,

[11] A biography is Nathaniel West, *The Ancestry, Life, and Times of Hon. Henry Hastings Sibley* (St. Paul, Minn., 1889). See also Kenneth Carley, "The Sioux Campaign of 1862: Sibley's Letters to His Wife," *Minnesota History*, 38 (1962), 99–125. This Sibley was not related to Confederate Brigadier General Henry Hopkins Sibley.

[12] *Minnesota in the Civil and Indian Wars*, 2, 212–23.

blankets, forage, and transportation; less than fifty mounted men; and fear of precipitating execution of the prisoners still held by the Indians. The lack of experienced troops was partly remedied by the arrival of 275 men of the 3d Minnesota. The regiment had been captured by the Confederates at the Battle of Stone's River and the enlisted complement paroled to help defend their home state against Indians. A major was detailed from the 1st Minnesota to command them, and sergeants took over the companies. At last logistical conditions improved somewhat, and on September 19, with 1,619 officers and men of the 3d, 6th, 7th, and 9th Minnesota Infantry regiments and the mounted company of Renville Rangers, Sibley broke camp near Fort Ridgely and marched up the river.[13]

Meanwhile, the hostiles had gathered in camps located a short distance above Yellow Medicine Agency. That they would make a stand was by no means so certain as Sibley supposed. In stormy councils the factions argued over what to do. Some favored flight to the west, some death to Little Crow and prompt surrender to Sibley, some an advance against the soldiers, and some execution of the prisoners. Sibley encouraged the dispute by sending in messages calling on the Indians to give up the captives and surrender themselves. On the night of September 22, however, word reached the Indians that Sibley's army had camped near Wood Lake, just below Yellow Medicine Agency. After much debate the chiefs agreed to ambush the soldiers as they marched from their camp next morning.[14]

By daybreak of the twenty-third, perhaps seven hundred warriors lay concealed in the tall grass lining the road the column would follow. While the soldiers breakfasted, however, a small party from the 3d Minnesota took several wagons and stole out of camp on a foraging expedition aimed at a nearby pumpkin field. This unmasked the trap prematurely and brought some two hundred warriors swarming to the attack; most of the rest, posted farther up the road, never got into combat.

When firing broke out between the foragers and their assail-

[13] Ibid., pp. 199–200, 227–29, 230–32, 234–37. O.R., ser. 1, vol. 13, pp. 631, 637–38, 644, 650–52. Carley, "Sioux Campaign," pp. 102–7.
[14] Robinson, History of the Dakota, pp. 228–93. Oehler, The Great Sioux Uprising, pp. 184–93.

ants, Major Abraham K. Welch formed the 3d as skirmishers and plunged into the fray. Quickly pressed on three sides and disconcerted by a mistaken bugle call, the regiment lost its formation and got badly mauled before extricating itself. A ball shattered Major Welch's leg. The Renville Rangers finally came to the aid of the 3d and a defense line was formed. Howitzers raked the grass and broke up several attempted assaults before portions of the 6th and 7th Regiments arrived. A charge by all put the Indians to flight and won the field. The troops suffered casualties of seven killed and thirty wounded, mostly in the 3d Regiment, while thirty Indians were estimated to have been killed and many more wounded.[15]

The Battle of Wood Lake proved decisive. Defectors from Little Crow's standard swelled the camps of those who had opposed the war. During the battle, moreover, the peace chiefs seized the captives and placed them under protective custody. On September 26 Sibley's army bivouacked at the friendly villages twenty miles above Yellow Medicine Agency, and here, at "Camp Release," he received the surrender of the Indians and their captives. Altogether, on this and subsequent days, some 270 half-breeds and more than 100 whites were set free. During the month that the troops remained at Camp Release, scattered bands continued to come in or be driven in by scouting expeditions, and by the end of October Sibley had about 2,000 Sioux under guard. A "military commission" of dubious legality began taking evidence against warriors accused of murder, rape, or other crimes. By November 3 it had sentenced 303 to death by hanging. Although Minnesotans clamored for their immediate execution, President Lincoln called for the trial records and found that they justified the conviction of only 40, who were hanged at Mankato in December.

In truth, the genuine hostiles, knowing full well the fate that surrender held for them, had scattered over the Dakota plains immediately after the Battle of Wood Lake. Little Crow and a small following headed north, made a half-hearted attack on Fort Abercrombie on September 26, and took refuge for the winter on the shores of Devil's Lake, in northeastern Dakota Territory. Preoccupied with his prisoners, still hampered by a

[15] *Minnesota in the Civil and Indian Wars*, 2, pp. 249–50. *O.R.*, ser. 1, vol. 13, pp. 278–81.

shortage of supplies, and with winter rapidly coming on, Sibley abandoned his plans for pursuing the fugitives into Dakota.[16]

After Wood Lake Sibley informed Governor Ramsey that he wished to hand in his militia commission and retire to his Mendota home. The battle, however, won him a commission of brigadier general of U.S. Volunteers and General-in-Chief Halleck's dictum that he "be kept in command of that column." The emergency had also prompted the War Department to create the Department of the Northwest and place it under command of Major General John Pope, whose star had recently fallen so spectacularly at Second Manassas. Pope had set up his headquarters at St. Paul on September 16, a week before Wood Lake, and so played little part in bringing Sibley's campaign to a close. For more than two years, however, despite shattered reputation and pompous, bellicose nature, Pope ably administered the department. His two principal subordinates were Sibley and Brigadier General Alfred Sully, a hard-bitten Regular of long experience, son of artist Thomas Sully, and sometime painter himself. Sibley commanded the District of Minnesota and Sully the District of Iowa.[17]

Throughout the winter of 1862–63 reports reached General Pope that Little Crow was assembling a great army of Indians at Devil's Lake and exhorting them to join in an alliance against the whites. Refugee Santees as well as Yanktonais were said to be securing arms from British traders and preparing to descend on the Minnesota settlements in the spring.[18] Equally if not more alarming was news that the seven Teton tribes west of the Missouri had been aroused. As early as 1857, agreeing that they had submitted too meekly to General Harney's threats the year before, these proud warriors had vowed to resist further white

[16] Oehler, *The Great Sioux Uprising*, chaps. 22–24. *Minnesota in the Civil and Indian Wars*, 2, 249–92. Robinson, *History of the Dakota*, pp. 295–98. Carley, "Sioux Campaign of 1862," pp. 108–14.

[17] The department also included Wisconson, which was constituted a district. Dakota Territory at this time embraced all of present Montana and part of Wyoming, as well as the later states of North and South Dakota. Thian, *Military Geography*, p. 82. *Minnesota in the Civil and Indian Wars*, 2, 254–55, 258, 269–70. An able history of Pope's administration is Robert H. Jones, *The Civil War in the Northwest: Nebraska, Wisconsin, Iowa, Minnesota, and the Dakotas* (Norman, Okla., 1960). Of the eccentric Sully the story was told that he once made up a deficiency of horses in his quartermaster records by promoting some surplus mules to the rank of "brevet horses." D. Alexander Brown, *The Galvanized Yankees* (Urbana, Ill., 1963), p. 102.

[18] Oehler, *The Great Sioux Uprising*, chap. 25. *O.R.*, ser. 1, vol. 22, pt. 2, pp. 116–17.

encroachment.[19] The line of settlement in 1862, still at Yankton below Fort Randall, was not such an encroachment. But in the summer of this year five to six hundred gold-seekers, hastening to the new Beaverhead and Salmon mines, had trekked overland or come up the Missouri on the steamboats that supplied the long-established fur-trading posts of Forts Pierre, Berthold, Union, and Benton. Clearly they foreshadowed far more to come. The Tetons "declared to me," reported Agent Samuel Latta in August 1862, "that their treaty only gave the right of way on the river for trading; that no emigration was ever contemplated either by land or water; and they would not submit to it, as emigrants brought disease and pestilence into their country, which destroyed their people, and on the other hand, the buffalo would not return to that section of the country where they had been pursued by white men."[20]

General Pope shared the concern of Dakotans, rightly judging that the border settlements of Dakota and the Missouri River pathway to the mountains stood in greater peril than the Minnesota frontier. But the fears of Minnesotans, expressed by no less an authority than General Sibley, were not to be ignored either. Pope's plan of operations, therefore, was to have Sibley push up the Minnesota River and cross the Dakota prairies to Devil's Lake while Sully ascended the Missouri and turned northeast to cooperate. In this manner Pope hoped to awe the Tetons along the Missouri and break up any force of Santees and Yanktonais that might be massing around Devil's Lake.[21]

As a matter of fact, Little Crow's effort to rally support, whatever its dimensions, came to naught. In June 1863 he and his son slipped into Minnesota to steal horses, intending afterward to retire deep into the British possessions and remain there. Near the town of Hutchinson a settler surprised them picking berries, opened fire, and killed the chief. Remaining at Devil's Lake were Standing Buffalo's Sissetons, who regarded themselves at peace

[19] Hyde, *Red Cloud's Folk*, p. 82. See pp. 118–19, above. The Tetons were parties to the Fort Laramie treaty of 1851 and the unratified Harney treaty of 1856. Only about one-third of the Missouri River Tetons had taken the treaties seriously. Under Bear's Rib, Hunkpapa leader appointed head chief by Harney, they came to Fort Pierre each year to receive their annuities and thereby earned the contempt of tribesmen who refused to accept the presents. The assassination of Bear's Rib in June 1862 dispersed the treaty Tetons. By this act the Tetons in effect broke diplomatic relations with the government.

[20] CIA, *Annual Report* (1862), p. 196. See also SI, *Annual Report* (1863), pp. 280–85.

[21] *O.R.*, ser. 1, vol. 22, pt. 2, pp. 115–16, 123, 186, 304–5.

and whose main concern in the summer of 1863 was to shoot enough buffalo to subsist on through the winter. Somewhat to the south, however, were other Sissetons and some Yanktonais who had fallen under the influence of Inkpaduta and who did not regard themselves as peaceful. And finally, bands of Tetons— mainly Hunkpapa and Blackfeet Sioux that included three rising young warriors named Sitting Bull, Gall, and Black Moon—had crossed the Missouri from the west and were also following the buffalo. Neither Sibley nor Sully would have much difficulty finding Sioux.[22]

Sibley's brigade numbered nearly three thousand officers and men of the 6th, 7th, and 10th Minnesota Infantry, the 1st Minnesota Mounted Rangers, and the 3d Minnesota Battery. Sully led about twelve hundred horsemen of the 6th Iowa and 2d Nebraska Cavalry plus a battery of four howitzers. This column was to draw its supplies from steamboats on the Missouri. But low water prevented the vessels from getting up the river on schedule. Although Sully had enough wagon transportation to carry his supplies by land, to Pope's vast annoyance he slowed his march to keep pace with the boats. By mid-July he had advanced only to the Fort Pierre trading post, while Sibley had reached the upper James River about forty miles south of Devil's Lake and established a supply base.

Standing Buffalo's Sissetons had meanwhile left Devil's Lake and traveled southwest toward the Missouri, searching for buffalo. They had fallen in with Inkpaduta's people engaged in the same activity. Sibley's scouts picked up Standing Buffalo's trail, and, leaving a third of the brigade to guard the supply depot, the general set forth on July 20 with fourteen hundred footmen and five hundred horsemen. On the 24th the column overtook the Indians near Big Mound, northeast of present Bismarck.

Arrangements were made for a parley, for Standing Buffalo and his Sissetons had no heart for a fight. But during the tense preliminaries one of Inkpaduta's hotheads treacherously shot and killed the surgeon of the Minnesota Rangers, and the fight was on. Victims of the first fire were the friendly Sisseton chiefs on their way to the council with Sibley. The warriors, perhaps a thousand in number, fought a delaying action to cover the flight of their families. Supported by the artillery, the Minnesotans ad-

---

[22] Robinson, *History of the Dakota*, pp. 316–18. Oehler, *The Great Sioux Uprising*, pp. 229–32.

vanced in battle line, methodically driving the Sioux from one defensive position to another until they broke and ran, pursued closely by the cavalry. Nightfall ended the conflict.

On July 26 Sibley took up the march again, burned the abandoned Sioux village as he passed, and went into camp on Dead Buffalo Lake. Knots of warriors massed threateningly on all sides. Although the Sissetons had pulled out and headed for the British Possessions, Inkpaduta had united with the Hunkpapa and Blackfoot buffalo hunters. About sixteen hundred angry warriors closed in on the Minnesota brigade. Sibley turned his howitzers on them and met several thrusts at his lines with vigorous counterattacks.

On July 27 the troops followed the Indian trail twenty-one miles to Stony Lake. Next morning they had no sooner formed for the day's march than the whole force of Sioux hit the column head-on. The 10th Minnesota deployed in front and split the charging mass with concentrated fire. In two divisions the warriors rolled along the flanks and reached for the baggage train in the rear. Musketry and howitzer fire threw them back, and after several probes for a weak point they abandoned their effort and rode for the Missouri.

Sibley reached the river on the twenty-ninth and found that the Sioux had sought safety on the opposite shore. Further pursuit, he concluded, would be useless, especially with the infantry exhausted and the horses and mules verging on collapse. In the actions at Big Mound, Dead Buffalo Lake, and Stony Lake, his men had slain, by his estimate, 150 warriors at a cost of less than a dozen casualties, destroyed immense quantities of food and equipage, and driven the adversary from eastern Dakota. This, in his view, was achievement enough. After three days of fruitless effort to locate General Sully, Sibley turned his column back to Minnesota.[23]

Not until late August, nearly a month later, did Sully's brigade reach the neighborhood of Sibley's victories. By this time the Tetons had gone to the Black Hills and Inkpaduta had recrossed the Missouri to hunt buffalo on the James. With General Pope singing the praises of Sibley and sniping at Sully for his slowness, the Iowa and Nebraska troops turned southeast from the

[23] *Minnesota in the Civil and Indian Wars*, 2, 297a–323. Robinson, *History of the Dakota*, pp. 317–25. The Indians acknowledged only 24 killed in the three engagements. This figure is probably as low as Sibley's is high.

274] FRONTIERSMEN IN BLUE

Missouri to search for Inkpaduta. On September 3 a scouting battalion of four companies of the 6th Iowa Cavalry under Major Albert E. House stumbled on to Inkpaduta's whole following—probably four thousand people, a thousand warriors—camped near Whitestone Hill, northwest of present Ellendale, North Dakota.

In an instant the battalion was surrounded by an overpowering force of Sioux. Confident of a crowning triumph, Inkpaduta delayed the slaughter for the men to paint themselves and the women to prepare a great feast. But House had managed to get word to Sully, twelve miles to the west, and just as the Sioux massed for the assault the rest of the brigade stormed to the rescue. The charge drove the startled Sioux into a ravine. For an hour, as dusk settled on the battlefield, they fought savagely to break free from the trap. Before nightfall covered their escape, 300 warriors had died, 22 soldiers had been killed and 50 wounded, and 250 women and children had been seized as prisoners.[24]

Whitestone Hill restored Sully to Pope's favor. To the Sioux it was a catastrophe, for in their style of warfare such casualties were unprecedented. Although the summer's fighting moved some of the Blackfeet and Yanktonais to put out peace feelers, it made most of the Sioux more determined than ever to resist. By the spring of 1864, intelligence reports from the upper Missouri trading posts and from the British Red River settlements left little doubt that the Santee exiles would join with the larger portion of the Yanktonais and Tetons to interdict navigation on the Missouri, to dispute the overland passage of several hundred Montana-bound gold-seekers gathering at St. Paul, and to fight any soldiers who came their way.[25]

General Halleck, harried by pleas for reinforcements from Union generals in the South, hoped fervently for peace on the Indian frontier, and he urged Pope to seize on the Yanktonai and Blackfoot overtures to conclude treaties if at all possible. "If we want war in the spring," he wrote, "a few traders can get one up on the shortest notice." But Pope was already plotting the summer's strategy. Sibley would extend military occupation into

[24] O.R., ser. 1, vol. 22, pt. 1, pp. 555-68. Robinson, *History of the Dakota*, pp. 326-29.

[25] Robinson, *History of the Dakota*, p. 329. O.R., ser. 1, vol. 22, pt. 2, pp. 612, 642; vol. 34, pt. 2, pp. 69-70, 625-26, 664, 712, 743-44; pt. 3, pp. 33-34, 219-20, 356, 368-69.

Dakota by establishing permanent posts on Devil's Lake and the James River. To Fort Sully, erected in 1863 on the Missouri below the Fort Pierre trading station, General Sully would add another fort farther upstream, in the vicinity of Heart River, and still another on the Yellowstone somewhere around the mouth of the Powder. Defining a military line running roughly from Devil's Lake to the Yellowstone, the new forts would hope-fully hold the hostiles comfortably distant from the Minnesota and Dakota settlements and also provide waystations on the emigrant routes from the upper Minnesota River to the Montana mines. Besides locating two new forts, Sully was to hunt down such of the Sioux as massed and bring them to battle.[26]

Not until early July 1864 did Sully reach the upper Missouri. Again he had relied on steamboats for his supplies, and again the perverse Missouri had not risen early enough to permit the vessels to go up on schedule. But here on the bleak Dakota prairie, eight miles above the mouth of the Cannonball, he had assembled a mighty expedition to war on the Sioux. The First Brigade he himself had led up the Missouri from Sioux City. Consisting of parts of the 6th and 7th Iowa Cavalry, a two-company squadron of Dakota Cavalry, Brackett's Minnesota Cavalry Battalion, and a howitzer battery under Captain Nathaniel Pope, the department commander's nephew, the brigade num-bered about eighteen hundred horsemen. The Second Brigade had formed at Fort Ridgely and marched to the Missouri under Colonel Minor T. Thomas. (Sibley had asked Pope for permis-sion to remain in Minnesota during this season's campaign.) Composed of elements of the 8th Minnesota Infantry, the 2d Minnesota Cavalry, and the 3d Minnesota Battery, this brigade mustered about sixteen hundred soldiers. In addition, four com-panies of the 30th Wisconsin Infantry had come up by boat to build and man the first of the new posts, which was to be named Fort Rice.[27]

[26] O.R., ser. 1, vol. 22, pt. 2, p. 633; vol. 34, pp. 109-11, 152-56, 256-59, 540-41, 608-9, 622-24.

[27] Official reports and correspondence relating to the expedition are in O.R., ser. 1, vol. 41, pt. 1, pp. 131-74, 795-96; pt. 2, pp. 38-39, 80-81, 228, 591 616-17, 628, 675-79, 737, 739, 767-68; pt. 3, pp. 219, 466-67, 626-68, 698-701. Revealing accounts by participants are Abner M. English, "Dakota's First Soldiers: History of the First Dakota Cavalry, 1862-1865," South Dakota His-torical Collections, 9, (1918), 241-337; John Pattee, "Dakota Campaigns," ibid., 5 (1910), 275-350; David L. Kingsbury, "Sully's Expedition against the Sioux in 1864," Collections of the Minnesota Historical Society, 8 (1898); and Nicolas

Accompanying the Minnesota Brigade, much to Sully's disgust, was a train of 123 wagons bearing some 200 men, women, and children bound for the Montana mines. And farther back on the trail from Fort Ridgely labored still another train of gold-seekers, about the same size, led by Captain James L. Fiske. An officer of large conceit and small intellect, Fiske was one of several volunteer captains mustered in the Quartermaster Department under an act of Congress providing funds for company-size escorts to see the summer's emigration across the plains and mountains. Congress had authorized such escorts each year since 1861. Fiske had successfully piloted trains from St. Paul to the Montana mines in 1862 and again in 1863.[28] Sully's officers and men held the emigrants in contempt, not only because they got in the way but because they were viewed as draft dodgers or Confederate sympathizers.

Whether the Sioux would fight now that the soldiers had come was a question in Sully's mind. Certainly by words and deeds they had left no doubt of their hostile disposition. Actually, Hunkpapas, Blackfeet, Sans Arc, Miniconjous, some Yanktonais, and the perenially troublesome Santee fugitives from Minnesota were gathering in the vicinity of the Little Missouri Badlands. They were thoroughly frightened by the approach of so many soldiers and especially by an outrage that had put them on notice that the soldier chief meant business. Word had spread like lightning through the tribes that three young Sioux had slain an officer who strayed from Sully's column on June 28 and in turn had been killed by pursuing Dakota cavalrymen. Sully had ordered their heads chopped off and mounted on poles as warning of the retribution designed for hostile Sioux. The tribes were now seeking safety from the troops in the wild country between the Missouri and the Yellowstone, but largely at the instigation of Inkpaduta and like-minded refugees from Minnesota they agreed to fight if the soldiers found them.[29]

Reliable reports of the location and temper of the Sioux

Hilger, "General Alfred Sully's Expedition of 1864," *Contributions to the Historical Society of Montana*, 2 (1896), 314-28. A good synthesis is Rev. Louis Pfaller, O.S.B., "The Sully Expedition of 1864 Featuring the Killdeer Mountain and Badlands Battles," *North Dakota History*, 31 (1964), 1-54.

[28] Howard E. Briggs, *Frontiers of the Northwest: A History of the Upper Missouri Valley* (New York & London, 1940), pp. 56-57.

[29] Robinson, *History of the Dakota*, pp. 330-31, 334-35, 345-46. The death of Captain John Fielner, topographical officer for the expedition, and Sully's response are detailed in English, pp. 275-78.

reached Sully through wide-ranging scouts and from the great Jesuit missionary Father Pierre Jean De Smet, who paused at the site of Fort Rice on July 9 on his way downriver from the Fort Berthold trading post after an abortive peace-making effort sponsored by the Indian Bureau.[30] While awaiting additional supplies, Sully laid plans to move westward in search of the camps reported by De Smet. What to do with the emigrants in the meantime plagued him. "I can't send them back. I can't leave them here, for I can't feed them. . . . Therefore I am forced to take them with me."[31] "Gentlemen," he told them on the eve of departure, "I am damn sorry you are here, but so long as you are, I will do my best to protect you." Even though he expected "to jump an Indian camp and give them hell," he would assign four hundred soldiers to escort the emigrants and their ox-drawn wagons through to the Yellowstone, where they would be on their own.[32] On July 19, nearly three thousand strong, the procession moved up the north fork of the Cannonball.

Scouts soon picked up the trails of the Tetons Father De Smet had reported as traveling northward from the Black Hills. The column crossed the divide to Heart River on July 23. Here Sully corralled the emigrant train, left it under heavy guard, and on the 26th continued northward on the Indian trail with 2,200 officers and men. In two days' march they approached Killdeer Mountain, whose wooded slopes concealed the enemy camps. Sully estimated that six thousand mounted warriors drew up in battle line to meet him on the morning of the twenty-eighth; the Indians placed their own fighting strength at sixteen hundred.

Judging that the hilly terrain made a cavalry charge inadvisable, Sully formed his brigades dismounted in a huge square, more than a mile on each side, enclosing the artillery and horses. Thus posted, the troops advanced slowly toward the Indian villages. Clusters of warriors dashed at the front, flanks, and rear, firing volleys of arrows and rifle balls and seeking weak points. Only once, when a large force fell on the rear, did they seriously threaten the formation, and this assault was turned back by howitzers rushed to the scene. Late in the afternoon the Sioux fell back to the timbered ravines cutting the slope of Killdeer

[30] De Smet's informative reports are in CIA, *Annual Report* (1864), pp. 276–83.

[31] *O.R.*, ser. 1, vol. 41, pt. 2, p. 228.

[32] Quoted in Pfaller, p. 13.

Mountain and took up defensive positions to afford their families an opportunity to escape. Sully gave permission to Major Alfred B. Brackett to mount his battalion and charge. The assault dispersed a large group of warriors and drove them up the mountain with saber-wielding troopers in their midst, but Brackett lost two killed and eight wounded. One of the dead was the famous scout George Northrup, "the Kit Carson of the Northwest." Rather than risk further fighting in the timber, where the enemy would have the advantage, Sully brought up his two artillery batteries and until nightfall bombarded the enemy positions.

In the day's fighting Sully had lost only 5 killed and 10 wounded. He judged that 100 to 150 Sioux had been killed, although the Indians later admitted to only 31. Outnumbered and badly outgunned, they had no choice but to flee in the night, leaving their villages and immense quantities of food and other provisions to be destroyed by the soldiers next day. Whatever the casualties, they were not nearly so damaging to the Sioux as the loss of these stores. As Sully shrewdly observed, "I would rather destroy their supplies than kill fifty of their warriors."[33]

After the Battle of Killdeer Mountain the expedition turned back to the Heart River corral, picked up the emigrants, and struck westward toward the Yellowstone. It was a memorable trek across a forbidding wasteland. The Little Missouri Badlands, a desolate tangle of many-hued buttes and cones, lay across the path. "Hell with the fires burned out," Sully reputedly observed, to the benefit of future generations of writers. For three days, August 6 to 9, the caravan struggled through this fantasyland as hundreds of Sioux stabbed at the front, rear, and flanks. Howitzers and muskets kept the warriors at a distance and finally, on the last day, sent them fleeing—with a hundred dead, thought Sully. Rations dwindled perilously. Water holes grew increasingly scarce. Grain supplies vanished, and grasshoppers had stripped the land of the vegetation that might have substituted. Horses and oxen by the score fell victim to starvation and alkaline water. At last, on August 12, the terrible march ended on the shores of the Yellowstone. That evening, almost providentially it seemed to the exhausted soldiers and emigrants, two supply steamers nosed up to the river bank.

Sparsity of grass discouraged Sully from plunging once more into the Indian haunts northeast of the Yellowstone, and a falling

[33] Quoted in *ibid.*, p. 27.

river precluded laying in enough stores to support the projected fort at the mouth of the Powder. The expedition therefore forded the Yellowstone, marched down to the Missouri, and crossed to the trading post of Fort Union. All the stores intended for the Powder River post had been deposited here under guard of a company of the 30th Wisconsin. Judging the mouth of the Yellowstone a strategic point for future operations, Sully caused a military reservation to be surveyed a few miles downstream from Fort Union. (Fort Buford was built here in 1866.)

Here, too, he parted with the emigrants, who hired a guide to pilot them up the Missouri to the mines. With them went a considerable quantity of U.S. property—horses, mules, oxen, arms, and ammunition—obtained by the liberal application of whisky among the soldiers, some of whom, deciding that panning for gold was preferable to fighting Sioux, went along themselves. The general "sent a force after the Idaho gentlemen," but it returned empty-handed.

Leaving the Wisconsin company to guard his supply depot through the winter, Sully took up the march down the east bank of the Missouri on August 21. A week later he reached Fort Berthold, home of the Arikaras, Mandans, and Hidatsas (or Gros Ventres). Decimated by smallpox and warfare with other Indians, these once-powerful tribes now lived in constant terror of the Sioux. To stiffen them as a barrier of sorts against the Sioux and to facilitate communication with Fort Union, Sully assigned a company of the 6th Iowa Cavalry to garrison the trading post during the winter.

The column marched from Fort Berthold on September 1, made a wide sweep to the northeast in a fruitless search for Yanktonais said to be fleeing toward the British Possessions or Devil's Lake, and arrived at Fort Rice on September 8. Sully found that Colonel Daniel J. Dill's Wisconsin infantrymen had "done an immense amount of labor in the last two months" and predicted that "the post when finished will be one of the best posts in the West."

At Fort Rice Sully also discovered that he had not rid himself of troublesome emigrants. Captain Fiske's train had pushed off from Fort Rice about two weeks earlier and now had sent back an appeal for help. The wagons were corralled on the plains about two hundred miles to the west under siege by three thousand Sioux. Fiske wanted a relief expedition to lift the siege and escort him to the Yellowstone. But as Sully exploded in a dispatch to Pope: "They can't go forward on their trail; there is no grass and very little water. Fisk[e] was told of this before he started from here, but he, though he had never been over the country, knew better. 'It was a damned trick of the traders; they wanted him to go ninety miles out of his way, by Berthold, to get money out of his men.' " Sully dispatched Colonel Dill and 850 men to bring the train back to the Missouri. Most of the emigrants, pleased enough to be rescued from their predicament, returned to Minnesota, but Fiske was furious over Sully's refusal to escort him on to the Yellowstone.

In some ways the summer's operations had not fulfilled the program laid out by Pope. The forts on Devil's Lake and the Yellowstone had not been established, and the Sioux had not been crushed. But they had twice been defeated in combat and put to rout, and with winter approaching they gave undoubted evidence of wishing to be at peace. Of more lasting effect, the military frontier had advanced toward the James and leaped far up the Missouri. During the summer a Minnesota battalion had built Fort Wadsworth (later Fort Sisseton) about midway between Lake Traverse and the James River. Forts Sully and Rice planted the Army firmly on the Missouri as far up as the Cannonball, and the companies at the Berthold and Union trading posts clearly foreshadowed a further spread of military occupation to the mouth of the Yellowstone.

The new forts reflected the mounting importance of the Missouri River as an avenue of commerce and travel. Montana was organized as a territory in 1864, and new mineral strikes drew a swelling stream of prospectors to her rich mountain valleys. The Missouri, navigable each summer to Fort Benton trading post, would be a vital link with the outside world. The northern overland routes pioneered by Fiske and others, however, would fall increasingly into discard. Fiske would make two more trips, in 1865 and 1866, but already the tried and tested Platte road, joining northward trails in the vicinity of the Great Salt Lake, was recognized as the best if not the shortest route to the Montana and Idaho mines. Already, too, as Sully disbanded his 1864 expedition, Indian warfare had spread from the Missouri to the Platte and even to the Arkansas.

FOURTEEN

Plains Aflame, 1864

NEWS of the Minnesota uprising, reported in all its hideous details, horrified the Nation and spread consternation among westerners. In their state of anxiety, the slightest offense by an Indian portended another Minnesota massacre. Nowhere was the apprehension deeper than on the central Plains, peopled by tribes claiming ties of culture and even kinship with those fighting Sibley and Sully. Kansas and Nebraska farmers, Colorado miners, and travelers on the roads up the Platte and Arkansas did not understand that if these Indians went to war it would be for reasons much more immediate than events occurring far to the north. Ironically, the shock waves from Minnesota and Dakota had an important effect in producing such reasons, for the climate of fear and distrust that descended on the frontier in 1862 and 1863 encouraged Colorado officials to pursue the blundering—or cynical—course that provoked the Plains war of 1864–65.

In truth, the only serious hostilities on the central Plains during 1862 and 1863 centered on the emigrant and mail routes west and south of Fort Laramie. Although some Sioux, Cheyenne, and Arapaho warriors may have been involved, the chief offenders were Shoshonis and Utes. So costly did depredations become in the spring of 1862 that overland mail service was suspended and stagecoach king Ben Holladay sought a route less convenient to Indian raiders. He settled on the Bridger's Pass route, or Cherokee Trail, one hundred miles south of the emigrant road and telegraph line up the North Platte and the Sweetwater.[1]

---

[1] J. V. Frederick, *Ben Holladay, The Stagecoach King: A Chapter in the Development of Transcontinental Transportation* (Glendale, Calif., 1940), pp. 94–95, 176–79.

Brigadier General James Craig, Missouri political general assigned to command the District of Nebraska, supported the change. But no sooner had it been accomplished in July 1862 than he saw the mistake. He had less than five hundred troops, chiefly Kansans and Ohioans, to protect the overland route from the Missouri to the Green River. Now, in addition to guarding 300 miles of road from Omaha to the forks of the Platte, he had to divide his meager force west of that point between two widely separated routes, one 600 miles long, the other 650. Fort Laramie remained the headquarters for operations on the emigrant road and telegraph line, while Fort Halleck was built as a base for guarding the mail road.[2]

The pressures on Craig lessened considerably after the arrival of Colonel Connor's California brigade in the Salt Lake Valley in October 1862. Connor garrisoned Fort Bridger and by aggressive campaigning, notably the Battle of Bear River in February 1863, conquered the Shoshonis (see pp. 223–25). His operations against the Ute bands around Utah Lake, however, seem to have stirred up the affiliated bands that ranged eastward from the Wasatch to the Rockies. Raids on the mail line west of Fort Halleck began in February 1863, and by June six hundred to one thousand Utes were said to be in this area. Although the troops believed them to be refugees from Connor's offensive ("Salt Lake Utes"), they were subsequently ascertained to be Grand River and Uinta Utes. They fired on mail stations and coaches, stole 173 horses and 34 mules from the company, and for a time threatened to close the line altogether. Early in July, however, Kansas troops from Fort Halleck succeeded in bringing on a decisive clash with an estimated 250 warriors, dropped 60 in killed or wounded, and drove them from the field. This action, coinciding with Connor's successful peace negotiations in the Salt Lake Valley and with similar overtures from officials of the Colorado superintendency, marked the end of the Ute and Shoshoni threat to the Fort Halleck division of the mail line.[3]

Farther east, despite fears engendered by the Minnesota bloodbath, the Plains tribes remained relatively placid during

---

[2] O.R., ser. 1, vol. 13, pp. 362, 451, 459, 466, 468–69, 483–84, 607–8; ser. 3, vol. 2, pp. 449, 453.

[3] Ibid., ser. 1, vol. 22, pt. 1, pp. 443–44; pt. 2, pp. 234, 362–63. Frederick, Ben Holladay, p. 279. SI, Annual Report (1863), pp. 243–44, 256–57. CIA, Annual Report (1864), pp. 241–42.

1862 and 1863. Kiowas, Kiowa-Apaches, and Arapahoes, attracted by whisky peddlers to the road up the Arkansas, occasionally exacted tribute from trains bound for New Mexico and were "impudent and insulting" enough to keep military authorities on edge. Comanches now and then joined in these displays of belligerence but more often kept south of the Arkansas. The "Sioux of the Platte"—Southern Oglalas and Brules who hunted on the Republican River—kept up their ancient war on the Pawnees, and the Cheyennes and Arapahoes continued to fight their traditional enemies, the Utes. These wars within the Indian world usually had incidental effects on the white world: "When out on these expeditions against each other," noted Agent Samuel G. Colley, warriors "are not very particular from whom they steal."[4] To such sporadic criminal activity rather than to any tribal war policy may be attributed the scattered depredations recorded in 1862-63.[5]

Of all the tribes, the Cheyennes and Arapahoes probably gave least offense to the whites. Colonel Sumner had scared them badly in 1857 (see pp. 121–25), and they had not permitted even the trauma of the Pike's Peak gold rush and its aftermath of spreading settlement and mounting travel to provoke them into antagonizing the whites. Still, ominous tensions were building. Early in 1861 the Cheyenne chiefs Black Kettle and White Antelope and the Arapaho Little Raven, well known for their pacifism, had joined with a few lesser chiefs to sign the Treaty of Fort Wise. This compact bound the two tribes to relinquish all the territory assigned them by the Fort Laramie Treaty of 1851 and to settle on a reservation on the upper Arkansas, where they would be allotted land in severalty and taught how to subsist by farming.[6] The signatory chiefs did not represent all the Arkansas River bands nor any of the bands residing between the North and South Platte. These leaders endured much abuse for bargain-

---

[4] SI, *Annual Report* (1863), p. 252.

[5] For conditions on the Plains in 1862-63 see Hyde, *Spotted Tail's Folk*, pp. 83–88; Berthrong, *Southern Cheyennes*, chap. 7; Grinnell, *Fighting Cheyennes*, chap. 11; *O.R.*, ser. 1, vol. 13, pp. 381–84, 395–96, 547–49; vol. 22, pt. 2, pp. 302–3, 316–17, 339–40, 507–8. Although the central Plains are often portrayed as in the throes of war in the summer of 1863, even Colorado Governor John Evans, one of the chief makers of the war of 1864-65, wrote in October 1863: "Depredations have thus far been committed by single bands, or small parties, on their own account, without any general responsibility of the tribes to which they belong." SI, *Annual Report* (1863), p. 240.

[6] Kappler, *Indian Affairs*, 2, 807-11.

ing away Cheyenne and Arapaho territory and for consenting to so radical a change in the traditional way of life. Instead of settling on the new reservation, most of these people continued to follow the buffalo between the Platte and the Arkansas.

A major objective of Colorado Governor John Evans was to engage all the Cheyenne and Arapaho bands to the Fort Wise Treaty and to consolidate them on the Upper Arkansas Reservation, thus clearing Indian title from land already being appropriated by miners and farmers. During the summer of 1863 his emissaries visited the Cheyenne and Arapaho camps to announce a great treaty council with the governor in September. But not an Indian appeared, and from one of his half-breed intermediaries Evans learned why. The Fort Wise Treaty was a swindle, the chiefs alleged, and they had no intention of going to the reservation. On the Republican and Smoky Hill the buffalo would last for one hundred years; on the Arkansas they had vanished already. Also, a sentry at Fort Larned had killed a Cheyenne, and although restitution had been made, the episode still rankled. "The white man's hands were dripping with their blood, and now he calls on them to make a treaty."[7]

This response, together with additional reports that reached him in the late autumn, moved Evans to predict open war with the Cheyennes and Arapahoes in the spring of 1864, and his actions during the winter, including a trip to Washington, were geared to this eventuality. It has been suggested that the alarmist tales of a self-seeking "squawman," Robert North, made the governor "lose his head."[8] But it has also been charged that, his treaty efforts having collapsed, "Evans moved systematically to prove that the Plains Indians were hostile," hoping thereby to "force a situation which would enable him to clear Indians from all the settled regions of Colorado Territory."[9]

The local military commander proved an eager accomplice, one in fact who was to take the initiative away from the governor. A man of giant physique with ego and ambition to match, Colonel John M. Chivington had foresaken the Meth-

[7] Berthrong and Grinnell, cited in n. 5 above. Stan Hoig, *The Sand Creek Massacre* (Norman, Okla., 1961), chap. 2. SI, *Annual Report* (1863), pp. 239–60. The Indian was Little Heart, who on July 9 while drunk tried to ride down a sentinel.

[8] Grinnell, *Fighting Cheyennes*, pp. 134–35.

[9] Berthrong, *Southern Cheyennes*, p. 169.

odist ministry to win fame as Colorado's "Fighting Parson." At Apache Canyon and Glorieta Pass he played a decisive role in stopping the Confederate invasion of New Mexico. Promoted to colonel of the 1st Colorado Cavalry, he assumed command of the District of Colorado when the regiment came back from New Mexico late in 1862. The office provided a ready springboard for adventures in territorial politics. No ethical and few legal bars interfered with a quest for power often pursued in an aura of divine endorsement. From a former military superior—and victim—Chivington earned the characterization of "a crazy preacher who thinks he is Napoleon Bonaparte," but this does not fully convey the deep capacity for evil of the ranking army officer in Colorado.[10]

The geographical command system afforded Chivington unusual freedom from higher headquarters. From 1862 to 1864 the central Plains fell within the Department of the Missouri, whose commanders, Major Generals Samuel R. Curtis and John M. Schofield, were too busy fighting Confederates in Arkansas and Missouri to devote much thought to Indians. A reorganization of January 1864 restored the Department of Kansas, under General Curtis, an honorable man of moderate ability who knew almost nothing about Indians. Two of Curtis' districts, Chivington's Colorado and Brigadier General Robert B. Mitchell's Nebraska, were wholly concerned with Indians; but the Districts of North and South Kansas, while burdened with Indian responsibilities through Forts Riley and Larned, were still almost entirely absorbed with operations against Confederates in Indian Territory and bushwhackers in Kansas. In faroff Denver Colonel Chivington enjoyed large autonomy indeed.

The origins of the plains war that broke out in the spring of 1864 lay largely in the prevailing belief of Colorado officials that the Plains Indians intended to go to war in the spring of 1864. A few warriors may well have been guilty of

[10] This assessment is standard in the voluminous literature of the war of 1864–65. A perceptive portrayal of Chivington emerges in Michael Straight, *A Very Small Remnant* (New York, 1963), which, though fiction, is not, in the author's words, "fiction that stands in opposition to fact." Cf. also James C. Enochs, "A Clash of Ambition: The Chivington-Tappan Feud," *Montana, The Magazine of Western History*, 15 (Summer, 1965), 58–67. Two vocal dissenters should be noted: Reginald S. Craig, *The Fighting Parson* (Los Angeles, Calif., 1959), and Nolie Mumey, "John Minton Chivington, The Misunderstood Man," *Brand Book of the Denver Westerners* (Denver, Colo., 1956).

thefts, but the weight of the evidence subsequently obtained reveals that at this time all the tribes of the central Plains considered themselves at peace with the white men. In April, however, stock disappeared simultaneously from a herd camp southeast of Denver and from ranches along the South Platte. Although some of the animals turned up in Cheyenne custody, it seems probable that they were strays rounded up on the plains rather than actually stolen. But to Governor Evans and Colonel Chivington this marked the beginning of the expected war. Blame fell on the Cheyennes, and Chivington sent out detachments to find the thieves and take positive action—or as one of his officers put it, to "burn villages and kill Cheyennes wherever and whenever found." Major Jacob Downing and Lieutenants Clark Dunn and George S. Eayre fought a series of skirmishes, in each of which the Colorado cavalrymen were the aggressors, that to the Cheyennes marked the beginning of war by the white men.[11]

A few retaliatory raids fell on Kansas, principally along the road between Forts Riley and Larned, but considering the provocation the response was not very violent. General Curtis' inspector-general, journeying to Fort Larned in mid-June, did not believe that a war had yet commenced. But a general war would soon overspread the Plains, he warned, if great caution were not exercised. Military policy should be to conciliate the Indians and guard the travel routes, not to lace the countryside with Indian-killing forays as Chivington was doing. Roving columns composed of men "who do not know one tribe from another and who will kill anything in the shape of an Indian" could wreck all efforts at peace. "It will require but

[11] The origins and progress of this war are voluminously documented. Richest sources are the records of three official inquiries: one by the Joint Committee on the Conduct of the War ("Massacre of Cheyenne Indians," Senate Reps., 38th Cong., 2d sess., No. 142), one by an army commission convened in Denver in 1865 (Senate Ex. Docs. 39th Cong., 2d sess., No. 26), and one by the Senate's Doolittle Committee ("Condition of the Indian Tribes," Senate Reps., 39th Cong., 2d sess., No. 156). Additional correspondence is in O.R. ser. 1, vol. 34, pts, 1, 3, and 4; vol. 41, pts. 1–4; and in CIA, *Annual Report* (1864), pp. 216–58. Although the play of special interest made this evidence wildly contradictory, sound and careful syntheses are Hoig, *Sand Creek Massacre;* and in the Sand Creek centennial issue of *Colorado Magazine,* 41 (1964): Raymond G. Carley, "The Puzzle of Sand Creek," pp. 279–98; William E. Unrau, "A Prelude to War," pp. 299–313; and Janet Lecompte, "Sand Creek," pp. 315–35. See also Grinnell, *Fighting Cheyennes,* chaps. 12–14; Berthrong, *Southern Cheyennes,* chaps. 8–9; Hyde, *Spotted Tail's Folk,* chap. 4; and Eugene F. Ware, *The Indian War of 1864,* ed. Clyde C. Walton (New York, 1960).

few murders on the part of our troops to unite all these war-like tribes of the plains."[12]

Such murders had already occurred, and in the middle of July thoroughly aroused Cheyenne war parties struck back. They returned to their camps laden with stolen goods of such variety and splendor that no chief could restrain his young men. Kiowas, Comanches, Arapahoes, and Sioux observed this with envy and, often without the sanction of their chiefs, joined in the fun.[13] On the trails up the Platte, the Smoky Hill, and the Arkansas, marauding bands attacked stagecoaches and wagon trains, burned ranches and stage stations, seized hundreds of head of cattle, horses, and mules, and killed dozens of people. The Kansas frontier receded eastward under the pressure of raids on the Saline, Solomon, and Little Blue. Near Denver the brutal murder of the Hungate family in June sent a wave of terror over the Colorado settlements. Fed by declarations of alarm emitting from the governor's office and the public exhibition of the mutilated bodies of the Hungates, it emptied the outlying ranches and hamlets and swept most of the population into Denver.

In late July General Curtis hastened to Fort Riley, assembled a column of four hundred men, chiefly in two skeleton regiments of Kansas militia, and pushed through to Fort Larned, where he met four companies of Chivington's regiment ordered down the Arkansas from Fort Lyon (the former Fort Wise). Here he discovered that all Indians, even friendlies, had fled beyond reach. In three columns, during early August, his command scouted south, west, and north of Larned. Back at Fort Leavenworth by August 8, the general could claim no contact at all with the adversary, but there had been concrete results all the same. Traffic to Denver and Santa Fe along the Arkansas once more flowed freely, guarded by strengthened garrisons at Larned and Lyon, by the new forts of Zarah and Ellsworth (later Harker), and by fortified strong

[12] O.R., ser. 1, vol. 34, pt. 4, pp. 402–4.
[13] An incident at Fort Larned late in July set off the Kiowas. The celebrated warrior Satanta tried to enter the post. Threatened by a sentry, he fired two arrows into him and ran. The Kiowa warriors camped nearby then seized 150 head of army stock and fled the area. No official report of this has been found, although it was referred to by Agent Colley on July 26 (CIA, Annual Report [1864], p. 253) and by General Curtis on July 30 (O.R., ser. 1, vol. 41, pt. 1, p. 484). A full account from Kiowa sources is in Mooney, Calendar History of the Kiowa Indians, pp. 313–14.

points between. He had taken another important step, too, by creating the District of the Upper Arkansas to embrace all these posts and Fort Riley in a single district instead of three. The command went to Major General James G. Blunt, a prominent Kansan with little military talent and a penchant for meddling in politics. On August 9 Curtis directed Blunt to begin organizing a six-hundred-man striking force to take the offensive. The object would be to harass the hostiles during the crucial autumn months when they would cease raiding and concentrate on laying in the winter's supply of buffalo meat. No talk of peace would be permitted, Curtis enjoined, until double the amount of stolen stock had been forfeited.[14]

While Curtis searched vainly for Indians around Fort Larned, General Mitchell was finding more than he could cope with along the Platte. On August 15 he reached Fort Kearny after a trip to Fort Laramie that revealed scenes of devastation and an appalling military weakness. Like Curtis, he made some organizational changes. He divided the district into two subdistricts, assigning responsibility for the Platte road as far as Julesburg, Colorado, to Colonel Samuel W. Summers and for the three roads into which it divided beyond that point to Lieutenant Colonel William O. Collins.[15] The latter commanded the 11th Ohio Cavalry, which operated out of Forts Laramie and Halleck. Lieutenant Eugene F. Ware remembered him as "a very fine old gentleman . . . finely preserved, energetic and soldierly."[16] He had come to the Plains ignorant of Indians, but by diligent study and observation he had developed insights that made him an officer of unusual aptitude for Indian duty. Colonel Summers, an Iowa village lawyer of advanced age, commanded four companies of the 7th Iowa Cavalry at Fort Kearny and the rude stockade of Fort Cottonwood (later Fort McPherson) at Cottonwood Spring. Happily, Colonel Robert R. Livingston soon replaced the lethargic Summers, bringing with him the seasoned 1st Nebraska Cavalry.[17]

---

[14] O.R., ser. 1, vol. 41, pt. 2, pp. 368-69, 378-79, 413, 428, 445-46, 483-85, 491, 545, 610, 629-30.

[15] The Platte road divided at Julesburg into the emigrant-stage-telegraph route to Denver, the stage road to California via Fort Halleck, and the emigrant-telegraph route via Fort Laramie to Oregon and California. See pp. 281-82.

[16] Ware, The Indian War of 1864, p. 120.

[17] O.R., ser. 1, vol. 41, pt. 2, pp. 276, 429, 447, 462, 483, 722, 752, 765.

No sooner had Mitchell returned to Kearny than word came that Cheyennes had raided along the Little Blue, killing fifteen settlers and carrying others into captivity. Curtis rushed up from Fort Leavenworth and at Fort Kearny assembled a 628-man task force composed of elements of the 1st Nebraska, 7th Iowa, and 16th Kansas Cavalry, some Nebraska militia, and a company of Pawnee scouts. With Curtis, Mitchell, and Colonels Livingston and Summers, it was a rank-heavy outfit. Striking south on September 3, the column reached the Solomon on the 7th. Here Curtis turned east with half the troops, Mitchell west with the remainder. Curtis was back at Fort Leavenworth by the seventeenth, and Mitchell, after searching the upper Solomon and Republican, emerged on the Platte at Fort Cottonwood on the sixteenth. Not a single Indian had shown himself to either detachment.[18]

General Blunt's offensive enjoyed scarcely more success. With four hundred troops, he marched east from Fort Larned on September 22, intending to cross the Arkansas and push down the Cimarron Cutoff of the Santa Fe Trail into Kiowa-Comanche country. At the Cimarron Crossing, however, he learned that a command from the Department of New Mexico had already penetrated this area. At the same time word came of Indians to the north, so Blunt turned his march in that direction. On September 25 an advance party of two Colorado companies under Major Scott J. Anthony turned up a large camp of Cheyennes and Arapahoes on the upper reaches of Walnut Creek. When Blunt reached the field Anthony was fighting desperately to break free from an overwhelming force of Indians that had surrounded him. Blunt put the warriors to rout and pursued for two days until his horses gave out, then returned to Fort Riley.[19]

The operations of Curtis and Blunt, so barren of results, were cut short by the sudden raid of General Sterling Price's Confederate army into Missouri. Blunt and most of his troops hastened to the threatened area, and Curtis turned his whole attention to organizing a defense against the invasion. With Curtis distracted and a mere major left in command of the District of the Upper Arkansas, Chivington gained still

---

[18] *Ibid.*, pt. 3, pp. 36, 37, 98, 179–80, 218, 231.
[19] *Ibid.*, pt. 1, p. 818. Grinnell, *Fighting Cheyennes*, pp. 161–64, gives the Indian side of the Blunt fight.

greater mastery of military affairs on the south-central Plains.

At the same time, the ardor of the hostiles cooled as their thoughts turned to the approaching winter and the autumn buffalo hunt that necessarily preceded it. The chiefs who had counseled against the war from the start regained some of their influence. One of these was Black Kettle. Through William Bent, this perennial peace chief of the Cheyennes had learned in late July of a proclamation published by Governor Evans on June 27. It invited friendly Indians to separate themselves from the hostiles and camp near certain military installations in order to avoid conflict with the troops. Interpreting this as a peace bid, Black Kettle in early September sent emissaries to Fort Lyon with an offer to end the war and exchange prisoners. With considerable skepticism, Major Edward W. Wynkoop gambled on the chief's sincerity and marched his small command of 125 men of the 1st Colorado to the Smoky Hill for a parley. Here the Cheyenne and Arapaho chiefs surrendered four white captives and agreed to let a seven-man delegation headed by Black Kettle accompany Major Wynkoop to Denver to conclude a peace with Governor Evans.[20]

The appearance of the peace delegation in the Colorado capital badly embarrassed the governor. Much had happened since the June proclamation, to which few "friendlies" had responded. Coloradoans had suffered little bloodshed, but they had lived through a summer of stark terror, and Denver had nearly strangled as a result of raids that choked off the flow of food and merchandise from the East. The governor had also all but rescinded his June proclamation by publishing another in August calling on citizens to kill and seize the property of "all hostile Indians of the plains"—an invitation to indiscriminate slaughter and plunder. Furthermore, he had won authority to raise a one-hundred-day regiment of U.S. Volunteers, the 3d Colorado Cavalry, and Chivington had it almost ready to take the field. In short, the tentative and qualified peace policy of June had by September become a bristling war policy. To make peace now would antagonize the vociferous segment of the population that cried for revenge,

[20] The Cheyenne and Arapaho camps here were immense, and their fighting force could have annihilated Wynkoop's command with ease. After the departure of the chiefs with Wynkoop for Denver, the village moved southeast and was camped on Walnut Creek when attacked by General Blunt on September 25. See p. 289.

allow the 3d Regiment's enlistment to expire before it saw action, cast doubt in Washington on the governor's assessment of the Indian danger, leave unresolved the question of Indian title to Colorado lands, free the Indians from retribution just when they were most vulnerable and when Chivington was best prepared to exact it, and embolden the tribes to try the same thing the next season.

With the cooperation and perhaps the prodding of Chivington, who fully appreciated the importance of a successful Indian battle to his political aspirations, Evans got out of his dilemma by dumping the problem in the willing arms of the district commander. At a council held at Camp Weld near Denver on September 28, Evans informed Black Kettle and his associates that they could still take advantage of his June proclamation to separate themselves from the hostiles but that he would not make peace with them; this they must arrange with the military authorities. Disconcertingly, the chiefs agreed to all the conditions under which they might come in—including aiding the Army against their brethren—and Chivington could not well avoid giving them permission to report at Fort Lyon when they were ready "to lay down their arms and submit to military authority." Since they had already said they were ready to do this, they left the council content in the belief that peace had been made and unaware of the nuances that qualified the agreement in the minds of Evans and Chivington. The Colorado officials both made haste to publicize the fact that no peace had been concluded.[21]

Exactly what had been concluded no one could quite say, except that any Indians willing to offer themselves as prisoners of war would be received. As such, Major Wynkoop received Little Raven and Left Hand with 113 Arapaho lodges at Fort Lyon early in October and prepared also to receive Black Kettle, who was out rounding up such Cheyennes as could be persuaded to forget the fight with Blunt and become prisoners. As prisoners the Arapahoes could not hunt, and since they were destitute Wynkoop issued them rations.

Word of this heresy reached Major B. S. Henning, command-

[21] O.R., ser. 1, vol. 41, pt. 3, pp. 195–96, 242–43, 399, 462. The transcript of the council proceedings is in "Condition of the Indian Tribes," Senate Reps., 39th Cong., 2d sess., No. 156, pp. 87–90. See also Hoig, The Sand Creek Massacre, chap. 7; Berthrong, Southern Cheyennes, pp. 210–12; and Grinnell, Fighting Cheyennes, pp. 160–61.

ing the District of the Upper Arkansas at Fort Riley while Blunt
helped Curtis rout Price. (Although an officer in Chivington's
regiment, Wynkoop fell under Henning's command.) Major
Henning knew full well Curtis' attitude toward the Plains Indians. The general had scarcely concealed his annoyance at the
compromising effect on his war plans of Major Wynkoop's peace
project. "I want no peace till the Indians suffer more," he had
telegraphed Chivington on September 28, the day of the Camp
Weld talks. To Henning the friendly intercourse between soldiers and Arapahoes appeared wholly contrary to Curtis' policies.
On October 17, therefore, he issued orders replacing Wynkoop
with Major Scott J. Anthony, also an officer of Chivington's regiment and, it turned out, a man of somewhat elastic convictions.[22]

Taking command of Fort Lyon on November 5, Major Anthony inherited the understandings already reached between Wynkoop and the Indians. He made the Arapahoes surrender their
arms and certain stock said to have been stolen and persuaded
them to move down the Arkansas to the mouth of Sand Creek.
He also declined to give them provisions but expressed the hope
that orders would soon arrive authorizing him to resume issues.
When Black Kettle appeared with about seventy of his men to
report his village camped on the upper reaches of Sand Creek,
forty miles to the northeast, Anthony advised the chief to remain
there and hunt buffalo until he could get permission to feed the
Indians at Fort Lyon.[23] In all these deliberations the deposed
Wynkoop, whom the Indians trusted implicitly, assisted Anthony
and vouched for his integrity. His participation quieted the anxiety of the chiefs over the abrupt change of command and led
them to express satisfaction with the new arrangements. On November 26 Wynkoop left by stagecoach for Fort Riley to explain
his conduct to the district commander.

In Denver, meanwhile, Colonel Chivington prepared to inject

[22] O.R., ser. 1, vol. 41, pt. 3, pp. 495, 524; pt. 4, pp. 62, 433.

[23] Anthony thus made a valiant effort to reconcile the realities of Fort
Lyon with his instructions from district headquarters. His orders directed
him to investigate the rumors that "stores, goods, or supplies" had been issued to "hostile Indians" in violation of Curtis' orders. An accompanying
letter from Major Henning also emphasized that Curtis would allow no
"agreement or treaty" without his approval and pointed out that the general's
instructions were to permit no Indians "to approach any post on any excuse
whatever." Anthony had cut off issues and acted to hold the Cheyennes and
Arapahoes at a distance from Fort Lyon, but he had come to certain agree-
ments by giving the chiefs to understand that they would be accepted as
prisoners as soon as Curtis gave permission to issue rations.

himself into the ambiguous situation at Fort Lyon. A bruising
political contest that had engaged much of his attention since
summer was ended, and the 3d Colorado Cavalry—the "Bloodless
Third"—was about to close its one-hundred-day enlistment without having killed any Indians. Recruited from the dregs of the
territory's population, the "Hundred Dazers" left much ⁄to be
desired, but by the middle of November Colonel George L.
Shoup, formerly one of Chivington's subalterns, had them organized and mounted. Another unexpected stimulus suddenly
materialized in the person of General Patrick E. Connor, commander of the District of Utah. He had received orders from
Washington to aid in protecting the overland route east of his
district and had interpreted them as an invitation to organize an
offensive against the Plains Indians. Although General Halleck
quickly set him straight on this score, his appearance in Denver
on November 14 alarmed Chivington and hastened campaign
preparations.

In October Chivington had talked vaguely of aiming his offensive at some Indian camps said to be on the headwaters of the
Republican, but from the moment he began the final concentration of his striking force early in November his every movement
was directed at loosing an overwhelming surprise attack on Black
Kettle's Cheyennes. Technically, they were hostile Indians waiting for Major Anthony to win permission from General Curtis
for them to camp at Fort Lyon as prisoners. History has not condemned them for failing to appreciate this fine distinction.

Chivington's column arrived at Fort Lyon at noon on November 28. Its appearance took the garrison completely by surprise—
a source of deep satisfaction to the colonel, for success depended
on secrecy of movement. To insure that news of the advance did
not precede him, he had stationed guards at ranches along the
line of march, and he ringed Fort Lyon with pickets under orders
to shoot anyone who tried to leave.

Major Anthony warmly welcomed his colonel and, informed of
the objective, at once fell in with the plan. Some of his officers,
those who had accompanied Wynkoop on the dangerous peace
journey to the Smoky Hill in September, protested vehemently
that Black Kettle's people were regarded as prisoners of the Army
and that an attack on them would violate pledges made by both
Wynkoop and Anthony. Chivington's furious response, recalled
Lieutenant Joseph A. Cramer, was "that he believed it to be right

and honorable to use any means under God's heaven to kill Indians that would kill women and children, and 'damn any man
that was in sympathy with Indians,' and such men as Major
Wynkoop and myself had better get out of the United States
service."[24]

That night, scarcely eight hours after his arrival, Chivington
formed the command and marched out of the fort. Behind him
rode nearly seven hundred men—all of Colonel Shoup's 3d
Colorado and more than half of the 1st. Part of the 1st had come
with Chivington, and the rest, under Major Anthony, had joined
from the garrison of Fort Lyon. Four mountain howitzers composed an artillery battery. By sunup of the twenty-ninth the
column had covered forty miles and halted on the ridge overlooking Sand Creek. Below, in a wooded bend of the stream, lay
Black Kettle's village of about a hundred lodges—some five
hundred Cheyennes and a handful of Arapahoes, about two-thirds
of them women and children.[25]

Chivington deployed for an assault. Three companies crossed
the creek and raced around the village on the north, cutting off
a pony herd. Two more companies seized a herd grazing south of
the creek. Anthony's Fort Lyon battalion also crossed to the north
side, while Chivington strung the 3d Regiment and the howitzers
along the creek on the south edge of the camp. Watching these
movements with mounting apprehension, Black Kettle failed to
comprehend what was happening. Over his tepee he hoisted an
American flag and a white flag, then took station in front of his
lodge exhorting the people to be calm and assuring them that
there was no danger. White Antelope ran toward the soldiers
waving his arms and shouting pleas not to fire. Then the firing
began, and he stopped and stood silently in the creek bed, his
arms folded across his chest.

From all sides carbines exploded. White Antelope fell dead.
Indians fled wildly in all directions as bullets tore among them.
Briefly the warriors tried to form a defense line among the tepees
nearest the creek, but the howitzers on the other side quickly
broke this up. In the stream bed above the village about one
hundred Indians took refuge behind a sheltering bank and

[24] Senate Ex. Docs., 39th Cong., 2d sess., No. 26, p. 47.
[25] Chivington persisted in maintaining that the village contained at
least seven hundred fighting men and that his troops killed about six hundred, nearly all warriors. The weight of the testimony later elicited brands
these assertions as wild exaggerations. See sources cited in n. 11, above.

scooped depressions in the sand. (Chivington later contended that these were prepared entrenchments that demonstrated Black Kettle's hostile disposition.) For most of the morning these people stood off the surrounding soldiers. Interpreter John Smith later counted about seventy bodies here. "There may have been thirty warriors, old and young," he testified; "the rest were women and small children."[26]

These were the only Indians who managed to offer anything that could be described as an organized defense. The rest sought safety in frantic flight. Chivington had let it be known that he wanted no prisoners. The soldiers of the 1st for the most part shrank from carrying out his wishes; those of the 3d, outpourings of Denver's saloons, complied enthusiastically. For the rest of the day squads of troopers ranged the battlefield and surrounding hills, seeking out and slaughtering the living, scalping and mutilating the dead. It was an orgy of bloodletting that revealed the white men of Colorado fully as capable of barbarism as the red men of Minnesota.

"All manner of depredations were inflicted" on the fallen victims, recalled John Smith; "they were scalped, their brains knocked out; the men used their knives, ripped open women, clubbed little children, knocked them in the head with their guns, beat their brains out, mutilated their bodies in every sense of the word."[27] Perhaps Smith was biased. He had been in the village when the troops attacked, and that night soldiers of the 3d assassinated his half-blood son Jack.[28] But other observers fully corroborated Smith's testimony and added more.

Soldiers cut off White Antelope's ears, nose, and testicles—the latter, it was said, in order to make a tobacco pouch from the scrotum.[29] A sergeant watched Major Hal Sayre scalp an Indian,

---

[26] Senate Reps., 38th Cong., 2d sess., No. 142, p. 6.

[27] Senate Reps., 39th Cong., 2d sess., No. 156, p. 42.

[28] Before the Joint Committee on the Conduct of the War, Major Anthony, in testimony corroborated by other witnesses, said: "I went to Colonel Chivington and told him that Jack Smith was a man he might make very useful to him; . . . 'but,' said I to him, 'unless you give your men to understand that you want the man saved, he is going to be killed. . . .' Colonel Chivington replied, 'I have given my instructions; have told my men not to take any prisoners.'" (Senate Reps., 38th Cong., 2d sess., No. 142, p. 22.) That night Smith was shot and killed in his tent. Two days later, writing to his brother of the Sand Creek fight, Anthony declared: "We, of course, took no prisoners, except John Smith's son, and he was taken suddenly ill in the night, and died before morning." (Senate Reps., 39th Cong., 2d sess., No. 156, p. 92.)

[29] Ibid., p. 67. Senate Ex. Docs., 39th Cong., 2d sess., No. 26, p. 138.

and a corporal saw probably the same officer discover a wounded boy among some bodies, "take out his pistol and blow off the top of his head."[30] Lieutenant James Olney observed Lieutenant Harry Richmond approach a small party of prisoners being conducted from the battlefield by a few soldiers. Richmond "immediately killed and scalped the three women and five children while they were screaming for mercy."[31] Major Anthony watched a naked child, "just big enough to walk," toddling through the sand in the wake of some escaping adults. A soldier fired at the infant but missed. "Let me try the son of a bitch," said a second: "I can hit him." But he missed too. A third cavalryman took better aim and dropped the child.[32]

Some two hundred Indians lay dead and mutilated in and around the village when the troops marched away next morning. Probably two-thirds of these were women and children. At least nine important chiefs had been killed. John Smith identified a badly mangled body as that of Black Kettle, but this chief had in fact escaped, only to fall four years later in another dawn attack on his village. Chivington reported a loss of 9 killed and 38 wounded. "All did nobly," he added.

Chivington now headed down Sand Creek to its mouth, intending to deal similar treatment to the Arapaho village that Major Anthony had sent there from Fort Lyon three weeks earlier. But the Arapahoes had fled, and the troops returned to Fort Lyon and, ultimately, Denver. "The 'Bloody Thirdsters' made an imposing procession" as they marched into the city on December 22, reported the *Rocky Mountain News*.[33] Denver citizens acclaimed the heroes of Sand Creek, and one hundred scalps were displayed to the enthusiastic patrons of a local theater. Not displayed, in fact never produced, was the single white scalp said to have been found in the Cheyenne camp. And this scalp grew in the telling to "several scalps of white men and women . . . also various articles of clothing belonging to white persons."[34]

From Fort Lyon, once more commanded by Major Wynkoop, word soon reached higher headquarters that contested Chivington's version of the victory. During 1865 three separate investi-

---

[30] *Ibid.*, p. 143. Senate Reps., 39th Cong., 2d sess., No. 156, p. 74.
[31] *Ibid.*, p. 61.
[32] Senate Reps., 38th Cong., 2d sess., No. 142, p. 27.
[33] Quoted in Hoig, *The Sand Creek Massacre*, p. 161.
[34] *Rocky Mountain News*, Dec. 17, 1864, quoted in *ibid.*, pp. 161–62.

gative bodies, one military and two congressional, amassed testimony that overwhelmingly branded the attack as perfidious and the slaughter as wanton. But Chivington and all the "Bloody Thirdsters" had been mustered out of the service and thus beyond the reach of military justice. Only in dashing his political hopes did the castigations of the investigators injure the late "Fighting Parson."

Chivington and his followers played out their roles in a climate of fear and hatred not without roots in reality and in a context of civil and military policy that favored their course of action. Governor Evans, General Curtis, and the population of Colorado helped to create the conditions that made possible the immorality and barbarity of Sand Creek. But it was Chivington who took advantage of these conditions and on whom fell the ultimate responsibility. Of him the congressional Joint Committee on the Conduct of the War declared: "He deliberately planned and executed a foul and dastardly massacre which would have disgraced the veriest savage among those who were the victims of his cruelty."[35] It was a just indictment, one since pronounced by history.

Only four days before Sand Creek, nearly 250 miles to the south, other Plains Indians, these of less ambiguous demeanor than Black Kettle's Cheyennes, suffered a belated reprisal for their summer depredations. During July and August the Kiowas and Comanches had raided trains on the Santa Fe Trail, then in September drifted southward into the Texas Panhandle. From here, in October, war parties ravaged the Texas frontier and clashed with Confederates near old Fort Belknap. By November these tribes had sought out their winter havens.

The raids of July and August, threatening lines of supply and communication vital to U.S. forces in the Southwest, had alarmed General Carleton, commanding in New Mexico. "Our first care should be the defensive—the preservation of the trains," he informed army headquarters in late August. "When they are secure, the offensive may be begun in earnest." At once he sent strong contingents of cavalry and infantry to strategic locations on both branches of the Santa Fe Trail.[36] This was the military

---

[35] Senate Reps., 38th Cong., 2d sess., No. 142, p. v.

[36] Senate Reps., 39th Cong., 2d sess., No. 156, pp. 191–92, 193, 194, 195, 241. I have treated the subject of this section at greater length in "Kit Carson and the Adobe Walls Campaign," *The American West*, 2 (1965), 4–11, 73–75.

activity that diverted General Blunt from his intended operations south of the Arkansas and led to his engagement of September 25 with the Cheyennes and Arapahoes.

The defenses taken care of, Carleton planned his offensive. To command the striking force, he once more selected his trusted subordinate Kit Carson. During late October and early November Carson assembled about 350 horsemen of his own regiment and the 1st California Cavalry at Fort Bascom, in eastern New Mexico, and also induced seventy-five Ute warriors to go along as auxiliaries. Carleton had been led to hope that General Blunt might march south from Fort Larned and cooperate, but Price's raid in Missouri made this impossible. The expedition marched out of Fort Bascom on November 12 and headed down the Canadian River toward Texas. Rattling in the wake of the column were two 12-pounder mountain howitzers that were to prove decisive in the coming battle.[37]

Carson had known his objective since mid-October, when New Mexican *Comancheros*—traders who exchanged arms and ammunition for the plunder of Indian raids—returned from the Staked Plains with word that three thousand Comanches were wintering on the Canadian River at Red Bluff, about two hundred miles northeast of Fort Bascom. Kiowas and Kiowa-Apaches had camped there, too, laying out their village upstream a few miles from the Comanches, near the eroding adobe ruins of a trading post built twenty years earlier by William Bent. These were the people of the aged Chief Little Mountain. In the village was Satanta, the prominent warrior who had shot the sentinel at Fort Larned in July (see p. 287, n. 13).[38]

At dawn on November 25, in a surprise attack, Colonel Carson fell on Little Mountain's village of 150 lodges. After a brisk action among the tepees, the women and children got safely out of the way and the warriors retreated downstream to rouse their Comanche allies. At the "Adobe Walls," with some 350 Comanche lodges in view beyond, the troops ran into a combined Kiowa-Comanche force estimated at more than one thousand warriors. Dismounting, the cavalrymen spread out in a wide arc to defend themselves. In several hours of fighting, only the exploding shells of the two howitzers prevented the enemy horsemen from over-

[37] Senate Reps., 39th Cong., 2d sess., No. 156, pp. 197–205, 210–11, 268. *O.R.*, ser. 1, vol. 41, pt. 3, pp. 260, 295–96, 314, 429, 550, 696, 770–72.

[38] *O.R.*, ser. 1, vol. 41, pt. 3, p. 771. Nye, *Carbine and Lance*, pp. 33–35, and Mooney, *Calendar History of the Kiowa Indians*, pp. 314–17.

running the skirmish line. Late in the afternoon, Carson retraced his path back to the Kiowa village. Indians harassed the column all the way, and repeatedly, as they pressed too closely, he had to halt and turn the howitzers on them. The Kiowas had reoccupied their lodges and had to be blasted out with artillery before the soldiers could gain possession once more.

Appropriating such of the Kiowa possessions as could be carried, the cavalrymen and the Utes set torches to the rest. Buffalo robes, dried meat and berries, cooking utensils, clothing, gunpowder, 150 skin lodges—all went up in the flames of huge bonfires. The tepees also yielded abundant evidence of Kiowa raids on the Santa Fe Trail and the Texas and Kansas frontier settlements: a buggy and a spring wagon belonging to Little Mountain himself, the uniform and accouterments of a soldier killed the previous summer, and dresses, shoes, and bonnets of white women and children. In fact, as Carson later learned, five captive white women and two children were in the village when he attacked, but the Indian women concealed them in the breaks north of the river during the battle.

Back at Fort Bascom by December 10, Carson reported a slight loss of two killed and ten wounded and, probably with some exaggeration, set enemy casualties at not less than sixty. Although he claimed victory in the Battle of Adobe Walls—and in fact had badly hurt the Kiowas by destroying their village at the onset of winter—he counted himself lucky to have extricated his command at all. According to one of his officers, the Indians later stated that but for the "guns that shot twice," no white man would have left the Canadian Valley. "And I may say," he added, "that this was also the often expressed opinion of Colonel Carson."[39]

[39] George H. Pettis, "Kit Carson's Fight with the Comanche and Kiowa Indians," *Publications of the Historical Society of New Mexico*, *12* (1908), 34–35. Carson's official reports, Dec. 4 and 15, are in *O.R.*, ser. 1, vol. 41, pt. 1, pp. 939–43.

☆ FIFTEEN ☆

Plains Campaigns, 1865

Although Kit Carson's attack at Adobe Wall's impelled one Comanche chief to come to Fort Bascom under a white flag seeking peace,[1] most of the Kiowa and Comanche bands simply drifted east and north and chose new locations for their winter camps.[2] Except for the catastrophe to Little Mountain's Kiowas, the encounter seems to have produced no particular effect on these tribes, either in rousing a war spirit or in inducing a desire for peace. That question could be decided in the spring.

Not so devoid of consequence was Chivington's attack at Sand Creek. Word of the treachery and butchery perpetrated by the Colorado soldiers sped to all the winter camps of the central Plains. From their villages at the head of the Smoky Hill, where the survivors of Sand Creek had taken refuge, the enraged Cheyennes sent runners bearing war pipes to the Southern Sioux and Northern Arapahoes on the Solomon and Republican Rivers. (The Northern Arapahoes had come south to visit the Southern Arapahoes, found that they had fled south of the Arkansas after Sand Creek, and settled for the winter with the Sioux.) Nearly all the chiefs smoked the pipes; the shock and revulsion of their people left them no other choice.

Before the end of December a great village had assembled on Cherry Creek, one of the head streams of the Republican. Numbering eight to nine hundred lodges, it contained about fifteen hundred warriors and their families. Present besides the Chey-

---

[1] *O.R.*, ser. 1, vol. 48, pt. 1, pp. 611–12.
[2] In February they were reported 150 miles southwest of Fort Larned. *Ibid.*, p. 923. See below, p. 311.

ennes, now under Leg-in-the-Water and Little Robe, were Tall Bull's perennially belligerent Cheyenne Dog Soldiers, the Southern Oglalas of Bad Wound and Pawnee Killer, the Southern Brules of Little Thunder and Spotted Tail, and the Northern Arapahoes. By smoking the war pipe, the chiefs had made a formal declaration of war, committing the full band or tribe to hostility. The raids of the previous summer had been carried out largely by young warriors defying the will of their chiefs. Now the tribes could truly be described as hostile. "We have now raised the battle-axe until death," declared Leg-in-the-Water.[3]

To the Indians, this did not really mean a fight to the finish but rather a massive raid or two, followed by a return to customary pursuits. For the first month and a half of 1865, however, the battleax raised by Sand Creek fell repeatedly and ferociously along the South Platte.

The first attack hit Julesburg, Colorado, site of a stage station, store, and warehouse guarded, a mile to the west, by stockaded Fort Rankin, held by Captain Nicholas J. O'Brien's company of the 7th Iowa Cavalry. On the morning of January 7 a thousand Sioux and Cheyenne warriors concealed themselves in the sandhills south of the settlement. A decoy party lured the Iowa troopers from the fort, but excited young warriors sprang the trap prematurely. In a hard-fought retreat, O'Brien got his command back to the fort with a loss of fourteen soldiers and four civilians killed. Meanwhile, the inhabitants of Julesburg and the passengers of a westbound stagecoach that had just arrived succeeded in reaching the stockade. The rest of the day the Indians spent pillaging the store and warehouse. (Hacking open a strongbox left in the coach by an army paymaster, they were disappointed to find that it contained nothing more useful than bundles of green paper.) In the evening, their pack animals laden with a wondrous assortment of food and provisions (including such delicacies as canned oysters), the Sioux and Cheyennes made their way from the valley.[4]

After the Julesburg raid the village moved to Frenchman's

[3] Senate Ex. Docs., 39th Cong., 2d sess., No. 26, pp. 73–74. For information of the alliance and the Indian movements, see Grinnell, *Fighting Cheyennes*, chap. 15; Berthrong, *The Southern Cheyennes*, pp. 224–32; Hyde, *Red Cloud's Folk*, pp. 108–13; Hyde, *Spotted Tail's Folk*, pp. 93–98.

[4] Ware, *The Indian War of 1864*, chap. 32. Hyde, *Red Cloud's Folk*, pp. 110–11. Hyde, *Spotted Tail's Folk*, pp. 94–95. Grinnell, *Fighting Cheyennes*, pp. 182–88.

Creek. Here the chiefs held a council to decide future policy. They concluded to abandon their homeland between the Platte and the Arkansas, where their camps stood in constant danger of attack, and unite with the Northern Sioux and Cheyennes on the Powder River. On the way they would lay waste to the road up the South Platte. Black Kettle, still a champion of peace, argued against this course and, when the tribes struck their tepees for the northward journey, led some eighty families in the opposite direction to join the Southern Arapahoes south of the Arkansas.

In the weeks following the Julesburg raid, as General Mitchell and a hastily assembled force searched fruitlessly along the Republican, raiding parties spread along 150 miles of the South Platte Valley. They attacked and burned stage stations and ranches, captured trains, ran off cattle, and ripped up miles of telegraph line. On January 28 the tribes crossed the South Platte twenty-five miles west of Julesburg and established their village on the north bank. For the next six days the warriors made one final sweep of the valley, the Cheyennes west, the Sioux east, and the Arapahoes in the immediate vicinity of Julesburg. On February 2 the raiders united for a final descent on Julesburg, which they ransacked and burned while the troops and civilians watched helplessly from Fort Rankin.[5]

While the men finished off Julesburg, the women broke camp on the South Platte and resumed the northward journey. On February 4 warriors attacked the telegraph station at Mud Springs, between Lodgepole Creek and the North Platte. Nine soldiers and five civilians held the station, but on the 5th and 6th reinforcements from Forts Mitchell and Laramie under Colonel Collins augmented the defenders to more than 160. Until the evening of the seventh the Indians, numbering between five hundred and a thousand, pressed the attack, but the Ohio and Iowa cavalrymen held firm.

On February 8 Collins marched to Rush Creek and down to the North Platte. Across the frozen river the entire warrior force covered the hills, screening the movements of the village. Collins at once corralled his transportation and dug rifle pits. Shortly the Indians had him surrounded. "They dashed up very boldly, but soon fell back from our bullets, and resorted to their old game of skulking and sharpshooting." For the rest of the day and

[5] *O.R.*, ser. 1, vol. 48, pt. 1, pp. 88–92.

part of the next the two sides exchanged fire. Then the attackers drew off and rode to overtake their families.[6]

The allied tribes had left the Platte roads and settlements an appalling shambles. For more than a month no stagecoach, freight train, or telegraph message had reached Denver from the east. The telegraph line to Salt Lake was wholly destroyed for a distance of ten miles on the North Platte and that to Denver intermittently for a distance of a hundred miles on the South Platte. All twelve ranches and stage stations from Julesburg to Junction, eighty miles, had been burned, and, reported Colonel Livingston, "the charred remains of every inmate who failed to escape tell of the brutality they were subjected to." In the raids the Indians had also killed nearly fifty people, stolen fifteen hundred head of cattle, burned one hundred tons of government hay, and carried off stores beyond calculation of food, forage, and other merchandise. Truly did Colonel Livingston, surveying this wreckage, advise his superior: "Feel assured, general, that this is no trifling Indian war."[7]

General Mitchell did not have to be reminded of the fact. In March he tried desperately to get an expedition off from Fort Laramie in pursuit of the fugitives, but high water, deep snow, and cold weather retarded the movement of troops and supplies. (One regiment, the 16th Kansas Cavalry, left Fort Leavenworth in February for Fort Kearny and still had not reached its destination two months later; its disappearance, Mitchell remarked acidly, was "the most miraculous event of the war.") By late March, with his cavalry "snowed in and water-bound all along the road," the general could only conclude that "The elements are evidently partial to the Indians" and give up in disgust.[8]

The Indians meanwhile had traveled to the northeastern edge of the Black Hills. Here the Brules began to worry about the future. Game animals were scarce in this land, a condition that had impelled the Northern Sioux and Cheyennes to spread westward and seize the Crow homeland. To join their brethren on the Powder would strain the food resources there and wear thin their welcome. In order to return to their own country south of the Platte, however, they would have to make peace with the whites. Thus the Brules decided to separate themselves from the

---

[6] Collins' report, Feb. 15, 1865, *ibid.*, pp. 92–98.

[7] *O.R.*, ser. 1, vol. 48, pt. 1, pp. 40–44, 675, 735–36, 793–94.

[8] *Ibid.*, pp. 1015, 1069, 1194, 1242, 1243, 1285; pt. 2, p. 42.

alliance. Early in April sixty lodges of Brules under Little Thunder and Spotted Tail surrendered at Fort Laramie and joined the friendly camps of Northern Oglalas and Brules that for years had lived in its vicinity. The Oglalas, Cheyennes, and Arapahoes, adhering to the original plan, circled north of the Black Hills and headed west to the Powder.[9]

On November 30, 1864, the day after Sand Creek, Major General John Pope arrived at City Point, Virginia, headquarters of the Army of the Potomac. He had been summoned by telegraph from St. Paul to report in person to Lieutenant General Ulysses S. Grant, since the previous March commander-in-chief of all the armies of the Union. Grant informed Pope that he had decided to create a new geographical command, the Division of the Missouri, to bring the Departments of the Northwest, Missouri, and Kansas under a single head. Pope would be the commanding general.

Behind the decision lay Grant's growing dissatisfaction with the manpower requirements of the Indian frontier. "As a rule," he wrote to President Lincoln on December 7, "only one point is threatened at a time, and if all that territory is commanded by one man he can take troops from one point to satisfy the wants of another. With separate commanders they want to keep what they have and get all they can." Behind the decision, too, lay Grant's growing disenchantment with Generals Rosecrans and Curtis. "The importance of this change," he informed Chief-of-Staff Halleck, "is much increased because of the inefficiency of two of the commanders of the departments named, one of whom I suppose cannot well be removed." And behind the decision, finally, lay Grant's growing admiration of Pope—a measure of his recovery from the disgrace of Second Manassas. "With Pope in command we secure at least two advantages we have not heretofore had, namely, subordination and intelligence of administration."[10]

General Curtis' political connections made it unwise to attempt his removal, but he was nonetheless effectively shunted to the sidelines. The Department of Kansas was merged into the Department of the Missouri, which in turn was enlarged to include

[9] Hyde, *Spotted Tail's Folk*, pp. 97–98. Grinnell, *Fighting Cheyennes*, pp. 202–3.

[10] *O.R.*, ser. 1, vol. 41, pt. 4, pp. 709, 716, 717, 784–85.

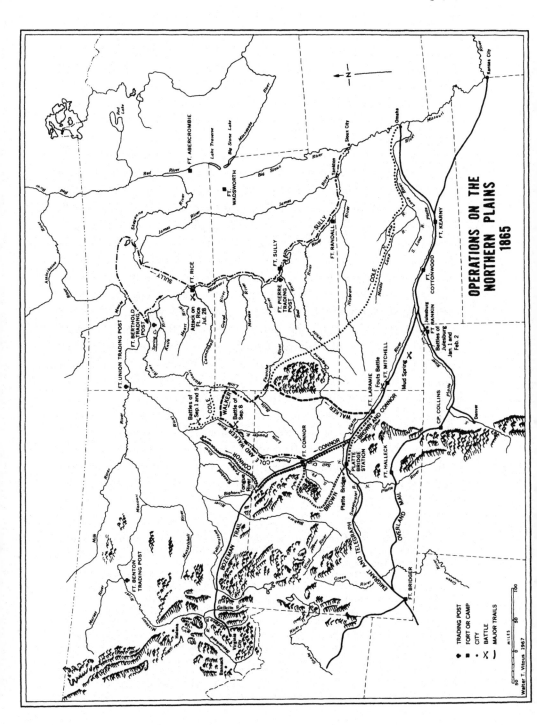

OPERATIONS ON THE
NORTHERN PLAINS
1865

TRADING POST
FORT OR CAMP
CITY
BATTLE
MAJOR TRAILS

MILES
0   50   100

Walter T. Vitous 1967

306 J FRONTIERSMEN IN BLUE

Utah and some of Dakota Territory, the latter formerly part of Pope's old Department of the Northwest. Then Curtis was assigned to command the Department of the Northwest. To replace Rosecrans as head of the expanded Department of the Missouri, Grant selected Major General Grenville M. Dodge, an able engineer and railroad builder who had commanded a corps under Sherman and was now recovering from wounds received at the Battle of Atlanta.[11]

Sibley and Sully remained the principal subordinate commanders in the Department of the Northwest, but the reorganization produced important command changes within the Department of the Missouri. Brevet Brigadier General James H. Ford, colonel of the 2d Colorado Cavalry, brought vigor and ability to the District of the Upper Arkansas following the departure of the unfortunate General Blunt, whose proclivity for detecting conspiracies against himself and the Union among nearly all his associates had kept the Kansas military scene in turmoil since 1861.[12] And along the Platte General Mitchell was finally eased out of an office in which he had consistently displayed the most abysmal ignorance of Indians. Considerable pressure built up for creating a separate Department of the Plains under General Connor, a move promoted mainly by the Overland Mail Company and, without much doubt, by the ambitious Connor himself. Pope, Halleck, and Grant saw merit in the proposal, but Secretary of War Stanton killed it. In the end, nonetheless, the Districts of Colorado, Nebraska, and Utah were consolidated into the District of the Plains and Connor placed in command, under Dodge, with responsibility for the Overland Mail Route all the way from the Little Blue to Salt Lake City.[13]

[11] Thian, *Military Geography*, pp. 67, 75, 82. For a biography of Dodge see J. R. Perkins, *Trails, Rails and War: The Life of General G. M. Dodge* (Indianapolis, Ind., 1929).

[12] See "General Blunt's Account of His Civil War Experiences," *Kansas Historical Quarterly*, I (1931–32), 211–65. In 1873 the Justice Department brought charges against Blunt for conspiracy to defraud the government but dropped them two years later. In 1879 Blunt was institutionalized in an insane asylum and died there in 1881.

[13] *O.R.*, ser. 1, vol. 41, pt. 4, p. 923; vol. 48, pt. 1, pp. 498–99, 714, 778–79, 849, 1069, 1285. The command changes took several months to effect. Dodge assumed command of the Department of the Missouri on December 9, 1864; Ford of the District of the Upper Arkansas on December 22; Pope of the Division of the Missouri on February 3, 1865; Curtis of the Department of the Northwest on February 17; and Connor of the District of the Plains on March 28.

Throughout the early months of 1865 General Pope and his subordinates laid plans for a grand offensive against the Indians of the Great Plains. With the area between the Platte and the Arkansas now all but deserted by the enemy, the plans focused on the regions south of the Arkansas and north of the Platte. South of the Arkansas were the Kiowas, Kiowa-Apaches, and Comanches, together with refugee Arapahoes and Cheyennes from north of the river. North of the Platte and extending to the upper Missouri were the Sioux, Northern Cheyennes, and Northern Arapahoes, now joined by the divisions of these tribes that had fled their homeland south of the Platte after Sand Creek.

In the tribes south of the Arkansas the Army saw a continuing threat to the established travel corridors from Missouri to Colorado and New Mexico as well as to the Kansas settlements spreading down Walnut Creek and the Little Arkansas. North of the Platte the problem was not solely to bring security to the established routes up the Missouri and the Platte, now bearing heavier travel than ever as the wealth of the Montana mines gained wide publicity in the East. Complicating this task were attempts to shorten the established routes around the Indian country by blazing new ones through its heart. Captain Fiske's expeditions west from Minnesota in 1862–64 were part of this effort. Iowa's bid for prominence came in March 1865 with the passage by Congress of legislation financing the opening of a wagon road from Sioux City up the Niobrara to Virginia City.

But topography still favored the Platte Valley as far as Fort Laramie, from which it had already become apparent that a good road could be projected to the northwest along the eastern base of the Bighorn Mountains. John M. Bozeman had pioneered this route in 1862, 1863, and again in 1864. His reception by the Sioux left little doubt of their negative attitude. But the Bozeman Trail, reducing the journey to Montana by several hundred miles, was destined to take on increasing importance whether the Indians liked it or not.[14] Thus, punishment for the destruction on

---

Between January 1, when Chivington relinquished command of the District of Colorado, and March 28, when Colorado came under Connor's command as part of the District of the Plains, Colonel Thomas Moonlight served as commanding officer.

[14] The standard history of this road, which is deficient in many respects, is Grace R. Hebard and E. A. Brininstool, *The Bozeman Trail* (2 vols.: Cleveland, Ohio, 1922). See *1*, 202 ff for the opening of the trail.

the South Platte and security for the travel routes along the edge
of the Indian country north of the Platte and west of the Missouri
formed only part of the motivation for the campaigns of 1865 in
this region; clearing the way for new roads furnished the rest.

By late March 1865, Generals Pope and Dodge had evolved a
strategy for smashing the Plains Indians. All of Pope's available
cavalry units were to be assembled in three striking columns at
Forts Larned, Laramie, and Rice. With about twelve hundred
men, General Ford would thrust at the tribes south of the
Arkansas. With another twelve hundred, General Sully would
push across Dakota north of the Black Hills and establish the
Powder River fort for which supplies had been stockpiled at Fort
Union trading post the previous autumn. And with two thousand
men, General Connor would march against the Powder River
camps and, hopefully, cooperate with Sully.[15]

To help fill in behind the cavalry as guardians of the travel
routes, Pope planned to use "Galvanized Yankees"—Confederate
enlisted men recruited during the winter at the prisoner-of-war
camp at Rock Island, Illinois, and formed into infantry regiments
under federal officers. Early in March 1865 the 2d U.S. Volunteers, Colonel Andrew P. Caraher, left Fort Leavenworth to
garrison the Arkansas route, while the 3d U.S. Volunteers,
Colonel Christopher McNally, pushed up the Platte to guard
the mail and telegraph lines. The 1st Regiment, organized the
previous summer in Virginia, was already on the upper Missouri.
Under its twenty-three-year-old colonel, Charles A. R. Dimon,
the 1st had reported to General Pope in the autumn of 1864 and
had spent the winter at the Minnesota and Dakota forts. Ultimately, six regiments of Galvanized Yankees were to be recruited
and to perform creditable if brief service in policing the Great
Plains.[16]

Pope had hoped to get his striking columns off in April or at
the latest by May. But a number of circumstances conspired to
delay and finally to alter the plans for a spring offensive. Heavy
roads and bankful streams continued to impede the movement
of troops, supplies, and fresh cavalry mounts. Transportation
and supply contracts, let in Washington by quartermaster officers

---

[15] *O.R.*, ser. 1, vol. 48, pt. 1, pp. 1212, 1295–96; pt. 2, pp. 162–63, 237–38.
[16] The story of these regiments is told in Brown, *Galvanized Yankees*.
See chap. 2 for the 2d and 3d Regiments in the 1865 campaigns, chap. 4 for
the 1st on the upper Missouri.

unfamiliar with frontier conditions, were not signed until May 1 and then were drawn to allow contractors until December 1 to meet their obligations. "This alone was almost fatal to my operations north of Fort Laramie," observed Dodge. The close of the Civil War early in May suddenly released unexpected reinforcements for the western commands. Aside from throwing additional strain on a logistical system already verging on collapse, the new troops arrived in the West without mounts. Dangerously dissatisfied and at times openly mutinous over their retention in the service, they deserted by the hundreds. Many units no sooner reached their destination than orders came to muster them out. A chaos largely beyond the control of the generals produced one delay after another and frustrated every attempt to launch the campaigns during the spring or early summer.[17]

Further complicating the projected operations was a peace offensive that had its origins in the wave of revulsion against the frontier army that had swept the Nation following Sand Creek. On the eve of adjournment Congress enacted two measures. One created a joint congressional committee to investigate "the condition of the Indian tribes and their treatment by the civil and military authorities of the United States." Headed by Senator James R. Doolittle of Wisconsin, the committee divided up the Indian country and in three contingents headed west in the spring. With Senator LaFayette S. Foster and Representative Lewis W. Ross, Doolittle himself traveled up the Arkansas to get at the truth of Sand Creek and, in the process, intervene in the military operations being mounted at Fort Larned. The other measure, fathered by Governor Newton Edmunds of Dakota Territory and sponsored by Senator Doolittle, added $20,000 to the Indian Appropriations Act to finance a treaty-making venture to the upper Missouri Sioux under the leadership of Edmunds.[18]

The projects of Doolittle and Edmunds swiftly collided with the policies of General Pope. In February 1864 Pope had written a bristling indictment of U.S. Indian policy. Published in the

---

[17] O.R., ser. 1, vol. 48, pt. 1, pp. 329-35, 335-48, 1078-79; pt. 2, pp. 36, 100-101, 162-63, 617-18, 646, 950-51.

[18] The full report of the Doolittle Committee, "Condition of the Indian Tribes," is a mine of information and has been frequently cited in this volume: Senate Reps., 39th Cong., 2d sess., No. 156. For the background of the Edmunds Commission see CIA, *Annual Report* (1865), pp. 191-93, and sources reprinted in *South Dakota Historical Collections*, 9 (1918), 409-15.

Army and Navy Gazette in April, it had received wide and favorable notice. Ever since, the general had been regarded in the Army, and especially by himself, as something of an authority on the subject. He had accordingly taken it upon himself to specify the kind of treaty that would be made with the Indians in the territory under his military jurisdiction. It was not a treaty that bribed the Indians with annuities to keep the peace. "The treaties I have directed military commanders to make are simply an explicit understanding with the Indians that so long as *they* keep the peace the United States will keep it, but as soon as they commit hostilities the military forces will attack them, march through their country, establish military posts in it, and, as a natural consequence, their game will be driven off or killed." Such a treaty would cost nothing and, he believed, prove far more effective in maintaining the peace. Far from aiding any commission bent upon concluding the usual form of treaty, he would employ his military forces to prevent it unless otherwise instructed by superior authority.[19]

Pope should have known that he could not arbitrarily substitute his own policies for those established by Congress and entrusted for execution to the Department of the Interior. And while his superiors sympathized with his point of view, they appreciated more clearly than he the bounds of their authority as drawn by law. Also, beset by a rising clamor to disband the volunteer armies and cut military expenditures, they could not help but view the peace overtures of 1865 as an attractive alternative to the costly campaigns being planned by Pope. As the summer wore on, the resolution with which the War Department supported the aggressive designs of the generals on the Plains weakened and finally collapsed.

Of ambiguous disposition were the Indians south of the Arkansas River—Kiowas, Kiowa-Apaches, and Comanches who had tangled with Kit Carson in November, together with Little Raven's Arapahoes and Black Kettle's Cheyennes who had fled

[19] For Pope's policy letter of Feb. 6, 1864, see *O.R.*, ser. 1, vol. 34, pt. 2, pp. 259-64. Similar views were developed at length in a letter to Grant on May 23 and June 14, 1865, *ibid.*, vol. 48, pt. 2, pp. 565-68, and CIA, *Annual Report* (1865), pp. 196-99. These views were fully set forth personally in a conference in Washington with Secretaries Stanton and James Harlan in June 1865. *O.R.*, ser. 1, vol. 48, pt. 2, pp. 1149-53. For orders to Sully on how to apply the policy in the field, see *ibid.*, pt. 1, pp. 718-19.

south of the Arkansas after Sand Creek. Early in March scouts spotted their camps about 150 miles southwest of Fort Larned scattered in a thirty-mile radius on the Cimarron River and Crooked Creek. Aggregating about 1,500 lodges, they were estimated to contain 3,500 fighting men.[20]

Whether or not these Indians ought to be regarded as hostile stood in dispute between military and civil authorities. Jesse H. Leavenworth, lately colonel of Colorado Volunteers and now Indian agent for the Upper Arkansas Agency, was convinced that peace could be made. In February a delegation of nearly a hundred Indians from these tribes conferred with him at Fort Riley and promised not to make war. With high hopes, Leavenworth planned to "visit them for a full and complete burying of the hatchet." Generals Dodge and Ford viewed Leavenworth as a visionary and the southern tribes as hostile. "One good thrashing will gain a peace that will last forever," wrote Ford, "while if we now make peace without punishing them severely they will be as proud, defiant, and troublesome as though they were victors and we sueing for peace." The scattered depredations of early 1865 along the Santa Fe Trail seemed to support this view, for only warriors from the Cimarron camps could have been guilty. Yet Leavenworth could point to an undeniably strong sentiment for peace among these tribes that, in his opinion, ought to be encouraged. Probably the most accurate generalization about the disposition of the Indians south of the Arkansas came from a party of Shawnee hunters who visited the Kiowas in April: "Some for peace, some for fight; not good."[21]

Agent Leavenworth sought desperately to get the southern tribes fully committed to peace and just as desperately to prevent General Ford from marching before this could be achieved. In the latter quest he enjoyed more immediate success than in the former. In March 1865, as Ford began moving his twelve hundred cavalrymen from Fort Riley to Fort Larned, Leavenworth hastened to Washington and with Senator Doolittle called on General Halleck. The Kiowas had behaved badly, Leavenworth conceded, and perhaps deserved punishment, but the Comanches and Little Raven's Arapahoes had given no offense and should not be warred upon. Halleck blandly assured his visitors that

20 *Ibid.*, vol. 48, pt. 1, p. 1204.
21 *Ibid.*, pp. 57-58, 923-24, 1011-12, 1078-79, 1231; pt. 2, p. 287. CIA, *Annual Report* (1865), pp. 388-89.

the Army did not fight friendly Indians, then telegraphed Dodge to have Ford exercise great care not to come into collision with friendly Indians, specifically Comanches and Arapahoes.[22]

The new guidelines reached Ford on April 1, just as he was ready to march and just as Leavenworth was ready to journey to the Indian camps to talk peace. "It places me in a difficult position," complained Ford. "He starts on a peaceful mission at the same time I start on a campaign against them, and as these Indians are all camped together it would be impossible for me to distinguish between the different tribes." An attack on the Indians under such circumstances would have all the appearance of another Chivington affair, and Ford therefore suspended the operation.[23]

Leavenworth failed to reach his destination, for, in Dodge's words, "The Indians stole all his stock, and very nearly got his scalp." Already the tribes had taken alarm at Ford's preparations and moved south to the Washita Valley, lately Confederate territory, where they concentrated in the vicinity of old Fort Cobb. In May Dodge and Pope appealed their case to the War Department. Assured by the new Secretary of the Interior, James Harlan, that the agent had no authority to negotiate a formal peace treaty, Secretary Stanton on April 29 flashed word for Ford to proceed.[24]

With clear authority to take the field and "pay no attention to any peace movements or propositions," Ford once more concentrated his own 2d Colorado Cavalry and part of the 7th Iowa and 11th Kansas on the Arkansas. Here he found the river too high to ford, and here, too, orders arrived to muster out all troops whose enlistments expired before October 1. While he fumed over these delays, another threat to the campaign appeared at Fort Larned on May 31 in the person of Senator Doolittle and his congressional colleagues Foster and Ross, accompanied by Major General Alexander McD. McCook, whom Pope had sent along to make sure the committee got the army side of the story.[25]

Even before reaching Fort Larned, both McCook and Doolittle had succumbed to the persuasion of Agent Leavenworth.

[22] CIA, *Annual Report* (1865), pp. 387–91. *O.R.*, ser. 1, vol. 48, pt. 1, p. 1242; pt. 2, pp. 11–12.

[23] *Ibid.*, pt. 2, pp. 59, 67, 91.

[24] *Ibid.*, pp. 141, 243–45, 687–88, 722, 796–97.

[25] *Ibid.*, pp. 385–86, 761, 868–69.

Kiowas, Comanches, Cheyennes, and Arapahoes, they conceded, were indeed hostile. If Ford had managed to cross the Arkansas, he would surely have been beaten as was Kit Carson in November. Then a war requiring 5,000 cavalry and $25 to $50 millions of expenditure would be necessary. "It is time," Senator Doolittle wrote the Secretary of the Interior, "that the authorities at Washington realized the magnitude of these wars which some general gets up on his own hook, which may cost hundreds and thousands of lives, and millions upon millions of dollars." Leavenworth had argued convincingly that peace could be had if only he were permitted to carry out his plans without Ford's interference, and General McCook, certain that Ford's column was too weak to accomplish much anyway, ordered the offensive suspended for the second time. At the same time, Doolittle won authority from President Andrew Johnson to constitute his committee as a special commission to negotiate formal treaties with the tribes south of the Arkansas.[26]

Now that there was clear authority for a peace offensive, the objects of all this bureaucratic maneuvering gave clear evidence of their attitude toward peace. From Fort Zarah to Fort Lyon and from Fort Dodge, newly established near the Cimarron Crossing, to Fort Union, raiding parties struck at freight trains and express riders almost daily during June and collided a half-dozen times with army patrols. On the eighth a group of Kiowas dressed in army uniforms boldly ran off the post herd at Fort Dodge. Kiowas and Comanches attacked trains on the Cimarron Cutoff of the Santa Fe Trail and skirmished with California cavalrymen sent from New Mexico by General Carleton to police the road and establish a post, Camp Nichols.[27]

Furious, Dodge instructed Ford to ready three striking columns at bases on the Arkansas, then sought permission to send them southward to converge on the Indian haunts and, hopefully, draw the raiders away from the Santa Fe Trail to defend their homes. Writing directly to Secretary Harlan on July 13, he inquired whether Leavenworth's mission was to be construed as barring retaliation for the raids that had fallen on the Arkansas. Fortuitously Harlan had just concluded an exchange of correspondence with General Pope concerning the friction that

---

[26] *Ibid.*, pp. 707–08, 868–69. CIA, *Annual Report* (1865), pp. 391–94.

[27] *O.R.*, ser. 1, vol. 48, pt. 1, pp. 308–16, 320–21; pt. 2, pp. 796–97, 922, 941, 949–50.

had long aggravated relations between army officers and Indian agents, and on July 11 the Secretary had issued instructions to the Indian Bureau designed to clarify the authority of its agents. A copy reached Dodge shortly after he had addressed Harlan. Agents, the directive said, would subordinate themselves to military authority in dealings with hostile Indians, and army officers would hopefully conduct themselves similarly in dealings with peaceful Indians. This was all Dodge needed, for the June raids left little room for debate over whether the tribes south of the Arkansas were friendly or hostile. On July 19, attaching a copy of Harlan's directive, Dodge issued orders for the campaign to commence.[28]

Ford had been mustered out of the service, and his successor, Brigadier General John B. Sanborn, moved circumspectly. He called on Leavenworth, now at the mouth of the Little Arkansas, for evidence of a "moral certainty" that his mission would end in an honorable peace. This of course the agent could not produce, but he could point out that no hostilities had been committed for more than a month, and he could set forth a record of progress sufficient to give Sanborn further pause. Leavenworth had indeed made contact with the hostile leaders, who had heard that the "big chiefs" from Washington wanted to talk with them. Arrangements had now been concluded for him to meet personally with representatives of the tribes and make plans for bringing them together with the commissioners for a treaty council as they returned from Denver. If Sanborn marched, Leavenworth warned, he would violate assurances conveyed to the Indians on authority of General McCook, and "an angel from heaven could not convince them but what another Chivington massacre was intended."[29]

Word of Leavenworth's arrangements had already reached General Pope in St. Louis. Perhaps recognizing the inevitability of some form of accord and hoping to influence its content, he wired Sanborn on August 4 to call off the invasion and proceed himself to the mouth of the Little Arkansas for the appointed conference. Arriving there on the fifteenth, Sanborn found nearly all the important leaders of the southern Plains tribes engaged in amiable dialogue with Agent Leavenworth. Among them were

[28] *Ibid.*, pt. 1, pp. 329-35, 359; pt. 2, pp. 796-97, 1075-76, 1115-17. For the exchange between Pope and Harlan, see CIA, *Annual Report* (1865), pp. 196-203.

[29] *O.R.*, ser. 1, vol. 48, pt. 2, pp. 1009, 1115-16, 1162-63, 1164.

Little Mountain, Lone Wolf, and Heap-of-Bears of the Kiowas; Poor Bear of the Kiowa-Apaches; Ten Bears, Drinking Eagle, Horse Back, Iron Mountain, and even old Buffalo Hump of the Comanches; Little Raven, Big Mouth, and Storm of the Arapahoes; and, appearing a day later, Black Kettle and Little Robe of the Cheyennes. With the legendary old frontiersman Jesse Chisholm looking on as official witness, twenty-eight chiefs joined with Leavenworth and Sanborn to sign a truce suspending hostilities and appointing October 4 as the date for meeting with the Doolittle Commission to conclude a formal and lasting peace.[30]

Of more pressing concern than the southern tribes to Pope and Dodge in the spring of 1865 were those north of the Platte and west of the Missouri. Around Fort Laramie, after the surrender of Little Thunder's people in April, were nearly two hundred lodges of Brules and Oglalas, about half recent hostiles and the other half the traditionally friendly "Laramie Loafers."[31] All the rest of the Teton Sioux and their allies were either avowedly hostile or of uncertain temper.

Scattered along the headwaters of the Powder and Tongue Rivers lived Oglalas, Miniconjous, and Sans Arcs, together with the Northern Cheyennes. Numbering more than a thousand lodges, they had remained generally at peace since the Harney expedition of 1855–56. But in March 1865 the fugitives from south of the Platte, now reduced to six hundred lodges of Oglalas, Southern Cheyennes, and Northern Arapahoes, arrived in their midst with stories of Sand Creek and the lucrative forays that had followed on the South Platte. The counsels of Man-Afraid-of-His-Horse and other moderates were drowned in a clamor for war against the whites on the Platte.[32]

To the northeast, occupying the country between the upper Missouri and the lower Powder, were other Tetons— Hunkpapas, Blackfeet, Two Kettle, the rest of the Miniconjous and Sans Arcs —also representing more than one thousand lodges. Together with the Yanktonais and Santees from east of the Missouri, with close to one thousand lodges of their own, these Tetons had fought General Sully in 1864, then returned to the Missouri at the onset of winter to raise their tepees in winter camps west of

[30] Ibid., pt. 1, pp. 361–63; pt. 2, 1171–72. CIA, Annual Report (1865), pp. 394–97. Berthrong, Southern Cheyennes, pp. 239–40.
[31] Hyde, Spotted Tail's Folk, pp. 102–03.
[32] Hyde, Red Cloud's Folk, pp. 114–18.

the river between Forts Berthold and Rice. Conflicting assessments of their attitude reached the officers at the two forts. The Santees were known to be, as they had been since 1862, "malignantly hostile." The Tetons and Yanktonais were divided, some favoring accommodation with the whites, others promoting resistance. British traders visited the villages several times during the winter, selling arms and ammunition and inciting the tribes to fight again in the summer.

In the spring the Yanktonais and Santees went east of the Missouri to hunt, while the Tetons moved to the upper Heart River. Here emissaries from the Powder River groups came among them with accounts of Sand Creek and proposals to join in hostilities. Peace and war factions quarreled endlessly over whether to accept the pipes and clean out Fort Rice or move to the Missouri and make peace with the soldiers.[33]

Actions of military authorities at Forts Rice and Laramie did little to tip the balance in favor of peace. Youthful Colonel Dimon, protégé of the controversial Massachusetts political general Benjamin F. Butler, commanded Fort Rice. His unacclimated "Galvanized Yankees" of the 1st U.S. Volunteers had passed a harrowing winter—11 per cent of the command dead of scurvy and diarrhea, 206 on sick report in April, and communication with the outside world uncertain because of weather and roving parties of Indians that attacked the mail carriers. Under weak leadership, the garrison might well have disintegrated; but Dimon's strict discipline, reinforced by an unshakable confidence in his own military capacity, held it intact. A certitude of equal strength that governed his approach to Indian relations proved less fortunate.

On March 30 twenty Indians were seen passing down the river on the east side. Dimon sent a squad in pursuit. The Indians scattered, but two took refuge in a camp of friendly Yanktonais near the fort, and old Chief Two Bears turned them over to his friend the colonel. They were Santees, who said they had come over from the James to hear the news. On April 12 about two hundred warriors, chiefly Yanktonais and Santees but thought to include some Platte River Cheyennes as well, swept down on the herd guard within sight of the fort, killed two

[33] O.R., ser. 1, vol. 48, pt. 1, pp. 439-40, 700-01, 1106-07; pt. 2, pp. 208-9, 434-35. Fairly reliable estimates of all the above groups were made by Governor Edmunds in 1865: CIA, Annual Report (1865), pp. 189, 194. The customary multiple was six people to a lodge.

soldiers, and ran off some sixty head of stock. That evening Colonel Dimon had his two Santee prisoners shot. The reprisal did not discourage another and more determined attack on the herders two weeks later, but it did mark the beginning of a constantly deepening distrust of Fort Rice in the minds of the Sioux that was to complicate General Sully's summer operations on the upper Missouri.[34]

A similar incident occurred at Fort Laramie, where the wise and experienced Colonel Collins had been succeeded by the excitable Colonel Thomas Moonlight. Throughout the spring the friendly Sioux camps east of the fort had grown steadily as groups of Indians who wished no part of the trouble brewing in the Powder River country came in to seek forgiveness. Prevented from hunting by threats from the hostiles, these Indians had become dependent on the Army for food. Regarding them as prisoners of war, General Dodge had ordered them fed condemned military rations for which, in return, they were to serve as scouts and camp police. Trader Charles Elliston commanded the paramilitary unit that had been organized in response to the order.[35]

In mid-May some of Elliston's police apprehended the Oglalas Two Face and Black Foot, on their way with a small following to join the friendly camps near Fort Laramie. To demonstrate his pacifism, Two Face had purchased a white woman, Mrs. Lucinda Eubanks, from Cheyennes who had seized her on the Little Blue the previous August. "She was almost naked," reported Colonel Moonlight, "and told some horrible tales of the barbarity and cruelty of the Indians"—not only of her Cheyenne captors but of Two Face and Black Foot as well. According to Moonlight, both Indians boasted of killing white men, "so I concluded to tie them up by the neck with a trace chain, suspended from a beam of wood, and leave them there without any foothold."[36]

The hanging of Two Face and Black Foot had no effect on the Powder River Indians. They were already fully committed to war. But it could not fail to create doubts among the friendlies about the wisdom of placing themselves so completely within

[34] *O.R.*, ser. 1, vol. 48, pt. 1, pp. 208–9, 434–35. Brown, *The Galvanized Yankees*, pp. 89–90.

[35] *O.R.*, ser. 1, vol. 48, pt. 1, p. 1104. Hyde, *Spotted Tail's Folk*, p. 101; and Hyde, *Red Cloud's Folk*, p. 119.

[36] *O.R.*, ser. 1, vol. 48, pt. 1, pp. 276–77. Hyde, *Red Cloud's Folk*, pp. 119–20, and *Spotted Tail's Folk*, pp. 101–2. Brown, *The Galvanized Yankees*, pp. 33–34.

the power of the soldiers. Doubt soon gave way to certainty. Secretary of War Stanton had decided that Indian prisoners of war should be confined at a convenient military post and made to put in crops for their own support until the Indian Bureau assumed responsibility for them. The Laramie Sioux were to be transferred to Fort Kearny, in the heart of enemy Pawnee territory.

On June 11, under escort of Elliston's uniformed Indian police company and 135 cavalrymen of the 7th Iowa commanded by Captain William D. Fouts, a procession of 1,500 to 2,000 Sioux got underway. Three days later, breaking camp for the approach to Scotts Bluff and Fort Mitchell, the Indians tarried as the troops marched out. Captain Fouts, returning to hurry them up, found the camp rocking with a quarrel between peace and war factions. Someone shot and killed Fouts, and the whole force of Indians, police included, stampeded for the Platte. Lieutenant John Wilcox brought the Iowans back at a gallop, but the warriors, screening the flight of their families crossing the river, advanced on his front and flanks so aggressively that he hastily pulled back to the shelter of his wagons. Wilcox reported a loss of four killed and four wounded besides Captain Fouts and averred that not less than twenty to thirty Sioux had been slain.

That afternoon word of the affair reached Colonel Moonlight at Fort Laramie by telegraph from Fort Mitchell. Scraping together a mixed force of 234 California, Ohio, and Kansas cavalry, he crossed the Platte and struck out in pursuit with such haste that, in three days, 103 men had turned back with broken horses. On the morning of the seventeenth, 120 miles northeast of Laramie, some 200 Sioux surprised the command at breakfast and stampeded every horse, leaving the unfortunate colonel to burn the saddles and lead his weary men back to Fort Laramie on foot.

Connor promptly relieved Moonlight from command and Dodge ordered him mustered out of the service, but the colonel's blunder was only a postscript to the larger blunder of Dodge and his superiors in attempting to move the friendlies to Fort Kearny. Many joined their kinsmen on Powder River, although the Loafers soon returned to their familiar haunts around Fort Laramie.[37]

---

[37] *O.R.*, ser. 1, vol. 48, pt. 1, pp. 322–28, 1303. Hyde, *Spotted Tail's Folk*, pp. 103–6, and *Red Cloud's Folk*, pp. 120–22. Moonlight had served an enlist-

The Fouts and Moonlight affairs only confirmed the Powder River tribes in the wisdom of a declaration of war already formally agreed on. Raids on the mail and telegraph lines had begun in April and steadily built up through July. War parties skirmished with detachments from Laramie and Halleck, repeatedly cut the telegraph line west of Laramie, and so interdicted the Bridger's Pass road that the Overland Mail Company abandoned its stations, leaving Colonel Carroll H. Potter, whose 6th U.S. Volunteers reached the upper Platte in June, to keep the mail running by using his own men and stock.[38]

Yet these raids did not represent the formal offensive planned by the Powder River groups. The Indians were nearly all together in one big village and, during May and June, more concerned with killing enough buffalo to subsist such a large gathering than with giving effect to their declaration of war. By late July, however, the chiefs decided that the time had come for the massive war expedition they had been plotting since May. The objective selected was Platte Bridge Station, 130 miles west of Fort Laramie, where a company of the 11th Kansas Cavalry guarded the Oregon-California Trail crossing of the North Platte.[39]

Major Martin Anderson commanded the troops sheltered in the stockade at Platte Bridge. On July 26 he had 96 regularly assigned officers and men—70 of his own 11th Kansas and a scattering from the 11th Ohio and 3d Volunteers—together with another 23 lying over en route to other stations. Among the transients was Lieutenant Caspar W. Collins, the youthful and much-liked son of the colonel of the 11th Ohio. The troops knew that hostiles were in the vicinity, for small parties had been observed on the two preceding days and a brief skirmish had taken place two miles east of the fort on the twenty-fifth. Thus, on the morning of the twenty-sixth Major Anderson considered it expedient to send a detachment to bolster the twenty-five-man escort of a train of five empty wagons approaching from the

ment in the Regular Army, 1853-58. Later a prominent Kansas politician, he was appointed by President Cleveland governor of Wyoming Territory and, in 1893, Minister to Bolivia. *Kansas Historical Quarterly, I* (1931-32), 211 n. 2.

[38] Brown, *The Galvanized Yankees,* pp. 143-46. *O.R.,* ser. 1, vol. 48, pt. 1, pp. 164, 198-99, 294-96, 305-6; pt. 2, pp. 690, 1045, 1060-61.

[39] Hyde, *Red Cloud's Folk,* pp. 117-18. For the Platte Bridge Fight, see *ibid.,* pp. 122-26, and the careful, book-length reconstruction by J. W. Vaughn, *The Battle of Platte Bridge* (Norman, Okla., 1963). See also Agnes Wright Spring, *Caspar Collins* (New York, 1927).

west. None of the Kansas officers, momentarily expecting release from the service, cared to face the danger, so Anderson ordered Lieutenant Collins to undertake the mission with about twenty of the Kansas cavalrymen.

Although the lieutenant expected the assignment to end in death—he rode forth attired in a dress uniform recently purchased at Laramie—neither he nor anyone else at the fort suspected that between one and three thousand Sioux, Cheyenne, and Arapaho warriors had been concealed in the hills north of the Platte for several days and now lay in ambush watching the little detachment leave the stockade. The cavalrymen had crossed the bridge and followed the road for half a mile when the Indians sprang the trap. A body of horsemen dashed for the bridge to seal off the escape route while the rest converged on the troops from all sides. Wheeling into two ranks, the soldiers discharged their carbines in a volley, then drew their pistols. "Retreat to the bridge," shouted Collins. In a strung-out column of twos, they dashed madly back on the trail. Warriors mingled with them, wielding spears and tomahawks to avoid firing into their own men. "The Indians suffered dreadfully," thought Sergeant Isaac Pennock, "as our pistols were pushed right against their bodies and fired doing great execution." Collins, a wound in his hip, paused to aid a fallen soldier. An arrow buried itself in his forehead and milling warriors engulfed him. At the bridge detachments from the stockade, aided by a howitzer, fought desperately to keep open the escape path. All but Collins and four men made it to safety, though eight bore serious wounds and none emerged unscathed.

Approaching from the west with the wagon train, Sergeant Amos Custard heard the explosion of howitzer shells and sent four men ahead to investigate. They ran into hordes of warriors, now riding to cut off the train. Veering to the river and splashing across, three made it safely to the stockade. Custard and the rest of the escort corralled the wagons and, with careful fire, discouraged the Indians from a mounted assault. But for four hours a circle of warriors inched forward on their stomachs behind piles of dirt and slowly drew closer around the doomed soldiers. Finally they leaped to their feet and in overpowering numbers swarmed into the corral, killed and mutilated the defenders, and set fire to the wagons.

The allied tribes had successfully concluded their offensive—at

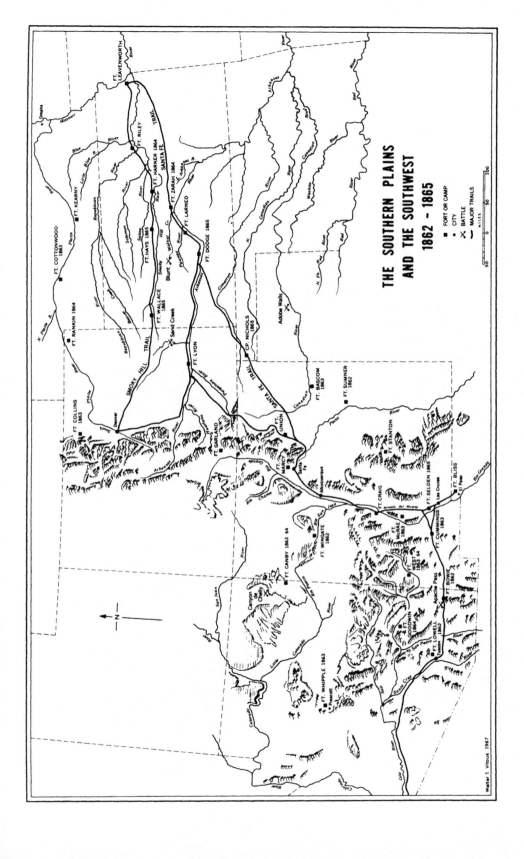

THE SOUTHERN PLAINS
AND THE SOUTHWEST
1862 – 1865

■ FORT OR CAMP
● CITY
✕ BATTLE
〰 MAJOR TRAILS

MILES

Walter T. Vitous 1967

a loss at Platte Bridge of about 60 killed and 130 wounded. The
war was over. It was time to break up the huge village and
scatter to hunt buffalo. They remained unaware that, for General
Connor, the war had hardly begun.

From March through July, while the Indians raided along the
Platte between Julesburg and Platte Bridge, Connor labored to
mount his offensive. Muddy roads, dilatory contractors, mutinous
troops, lack of horses and forage, and changing signals from
higher headquarters caused one delay after another. The Indians
forced the assignment of heavy escorts to the freight trains, which
"uses up troops beyond conception," complained Dodge. Ignoring
the appeals for speed, contractors loitered along the road, waiting
for the ripening prairie grass to strengthen the animals and thus
conserve forage. "I wish [the Indians] had Contractor Buckley
under their scalping knives," grumbled Connor as he finally
mobilized government trains to hasten the supplies.

The promised reinforcements, designed to give him twelve
thousand men altogether, were not so easily hastened. Most did
not reach Fort Leavenworth until June, horses to mount them
until July. In order to get the campaign underway at all, Connor
had to strip 2,500 men from the Platte defenses. And when the
reinforcements did reach the upper Platte in August to take the
place of the troops in the field, they numbered less than four
thousand "mutinuous, dissatisfied, and inefficient" Volunteers
who wanted their discharge and were almost at once marched
back to the States to get it.[40]

To add to the confusion, developments in Minnesota and
Dakota had led to a modification of the program originally projected for Connor and Sully. In the spring a party of sixteen
Santees, thought to be from Devil's Lake, had slipped through
the Minnesota defenses and raided as far south as Mankato. Both
Sibley and Curtis shared the alarm of Minnesotans and joined in
urging Pope to have Sully send an expedition against "the hive of
hostile Sioux" at Devil's Lake. Pope regarded eighteen companies
of cavalry and four of infantry as ample protection for Minnesota
and was furious over the "want of vigilance" and "inefficiency
(to call it no worse)" that permitted the raiders to penetrate the
settlements. He deprecated the tendency of his subordinates to
join in the "stampedes" that occurred in Minnesota every spring

40 *O.R.*, ser. 1, vol. 48, pt. 1, pp. 329-48; pt. 2, pp. 646, 950-51, 1132.

and autumn, and he judged an expedition against Devil's Lake, even if a "hive of hostile Sioux" were actually there, as useless until the British withdrew their refusal to allow pursuit across the international boundary. Nevertheless, when word reached Pope from the upper Missouri that many of the Teton Sioux had signified an intention to come to Fort Rice for peace talks with Sully, he gave in to the pressures. In late May he authorized Sully to drop his plans to thrust west from the Missouri and instead, after parleying with the Tetons at Fort Rice, to march on Devil's Lake.[41]

No sooner had the plans been changed than intelligence from the upper Missouri made it clear that not all the Sioux had decided to talk peace with General Sully. On June 2 Colonel Dimon got into another fight with Indians at Fort Rice and scattered them with howitzer fire. Reports also reached Pope of large numbers of Tetons, Cheyennes, and Arapahoes assembled at Bear Butte, on the northeastern edge of the Black Hills, spoiling for a fight. Sully expressed concern over leaving such a force in his rear while he went to Devil's Lake. More important to Pope, Representative Asahel W. Hubbard, the Iowa congressman who sponsored the legislation authorizing a wagon road to Montana from Sioux City, expressed concern. Under James A. Sawyers, the road-building expedition was about to push up the Niobrara toward the Black Hills, and the Indians thought to be at Bear Butte were a disquieting shadow on the horizon. Accordingly, now that Sully had been diverted, Pope had to find other units to put in this area. Besides furnishing an escort to Sawyers' road-builders, he gave Sully's former mission to Dodge and Connor. "You must deal with these Indians in the Black Hills and establish the post at Powder River," he informed Dodge on June 3.[42]

General Connor's Powder River Expedition moved in three

---

[41] *Ibid.*, pt. 2, pp. 391, 413–14, 486, 492–94, 501, 515, 532, 556, 557–58, 575, 579. Sibley's dire prediction of "a desolating war involving frontier settlements of Minnesota, Iowa, and Wisconsin in one common ruin" so disgusted Pope that he gave vent to a disenchantment with Sibley that had been building for more than a year. Such communications, he wrote Grant on June 2, "exhibit a panic which I hardly know how to deal with, except by asking you to send me an officer to command in Minnesota who is not subject to such uneasiness." *Ibid.*, p. 731.

[42] *Ibid.*, pt. 1, pp. 304–5; pt. 2, pp. 617–18, 756. For Sawyers' report, see House Ex. Docs., 39th Cong., 1st sess., No. 58. This report and related documents, together with source material bearing on Connor's operations, are printed in LeRoy R. and Ann W. Hafen, *Powder River Campaigns and Sawyers Expedition of 1865* (Glendale, Calif., 1961).

columns, all to join about September 1 at a rather vaguely appointed rendezvous on Rosebud Creek, a tributary of the Yellowstone lying between the Tongue and Bighorn Rivers.[43] The "Right Column," organized in June at Omaha by Colonel Nelson Cole, consisted of the 2d Missouri Light Artillery, equipped as cavalry, eight companies of the 12th Missouri Cavalry, a section of three-inch rifled guns, and a train of 140 wagons. Numbering fourteen hundred men, it set forth on July 1 to march up the Loup Fork of the Platte and strike at the Indians reported at Bear Butte, then march around the north edge of the Black Hills to the rendezvous point.

Lieutenant Colonel Samuel Walker led the "Center Column," composed of some six hundred men of his own 16th Kansas Cavalry, a small detachment of the 15th Kansas, two mountain howitzers, and a train of thirteen wagons. Walker was to march from Fort Laramie northeast to the Black Hills, north along their western base to the headwaters of the Little Missouri, then northwest to meet Connor on the Rosebud. Shouting that their enlistment would expire before they could return, the men of the 16th Kansas refused to march. But after Connor lined up his loyal companies of the 2d California and a couple of howitzers, the Kansans perceived that he was not to be trifled with and finally got off from Laramie on August 5, more than a month after Cole's departure from Omaha.

The "Left Column," Connor accompanying, marched from Fort Laramie on July 30. Numbering 90 each of the 7th Iowa and 11th Ohio Cavalry, 116 of the 2d California Cavalry, 95 Pawnee scouts under Captain Frank North, and 84 Omaha Indian scouts, it was accompanied by 200 of the 6th Michigan Cavalry under Colonel James H. Kidd who were to build and garrison the new fort on Powder River. Supplies traveled in 184 wagons. Venerable Jim Bridger went along as guide. With most of the command, Connor struck directly up the Bozeman Trail, while Captain Albert Brown and a smaller column made a wide sweep

[43] This was all imperfectly known country in 1865. Connor's map showed the Panther Mountains running northwesterly from the Tongue to the Bighorn, and in his orders to column commanders he fixed the "general rendezvous" on the Rosebud in relation to the north base of these mountains. Although the Panther Mountains may be roughly equated with the modern Wolf Mountains, which separate the Rosebud and Little Bighorn watersheds, the inaccuracy of the expedition maps was to cause great confusion.

to the west, by way of Platte Bridge, planning to meet Connor on the head of the Powder.[44]

Although much smaller than at first planned, the Powder River Expedition was still one of the most comprehensive yet to take the field against the Plains Indians. Only the Sibley-Sully operations of 1863 and 1864 paralleled it in strength and scope of undertaking. But as all three column commanders were to discover, it was one thing to assemble such an expedition, another to maintain it in the hostile country between the Black Hills and the Bighorn Mountains, and quite another yet to inflict any serious punishment on angry Indians who did know how to maintain themselves in such country.

Connor's column reached the upper Powder, just below its forks, on August 11. Three days later, near the Bozeman Trail crossing of the river, the Michiganders began felling timber for the stockade of Fort Connor. Patrols radiating from the fort during the week that Connor tarried here turned up plentiful evidence of Indians and clashed three times with parties moving north from the Platte Bridge fight. One of the encounters was a triumph for Frank North's Pawnees. After a pursuit of twelve miles, they overwhelmed a group of twenty-seven Cheyennes and came back to camp with twenty-seven scalps, which set off two nights of uninhibited celebration and dancing that sorely tried the general's patience.

Leaving Colonel Kidd and his Michigan cavalry to complete Fort Connor, the general on August 22 marched to the northwest on a route roughly paralleling, at times intersecting, the Bozeman Trail. Captain Brown with his Californians and the Omaha scouts, having found no Indians west of the Bighorn Mountains, caught up with Connor shortly after he left the Powder. Reaching the Tongue, the column turned downstream, toward the appointed junction with Cole and Walker. On August 28, however, Pawnee scouts brought word of an Indian village forty miles upstream, near the head of the Tongue. Leaving part of the command with the train, Connor led 125 cavalrymen and 90 of the Indian scouts in a swift night march back up the river.

---

[44] *O.R.*, ser. 1, vol. 48, pt. 1, pp. 366–67; pt. 2, pp. 1048–49, 1129–31. Significant documents covering all three columns are reprinted in Hafen and Hafen, *Powder River Campaigns and Sawyers Expedition*, on which the following account is mainly based. See also Rogers, *Soldiers of the Overland*, chaps. 18–24.

Early on the twenty-ninth Black Bear's Arapahoes were just dismantling their lodges, two to three hundred in number, when Connor's men stormed into the village. The warriors made a brief stand while their families scattered, then fled up a creek valley to the south. Connor followed at a gallop for ten miles, only to be driven back at a gallop when the Arapahoes saw that only fourteen men had kept up with him. While the Pawnees rounded up the horse herd and the troops destroyed the village, the Arapahoes launched an aggressive counterattack that continued until dark as the command conducted a defensive withdrawal down the Tongue. Only the howitzers, holding the Indians at a distance, saved the outnumbered soldiers from serious loss. Connor reported enemy casualties at about 35 killed and his own at 7 wounded.[45]

During the first week of September, as equinoctial storms dumped rain and snow on the valleys draining north to the Yellowstone, Connor's soaked and mud-spattered horsemen slogged down the Tongue, then back up the Tongue. Apprehension mounted as scouting parties crossed to the Rosebud and Powder in search of Cole and Walker, whose supplies would now be nearly exhausted. But it was Sawyers' road-builders who first made contact with the Powder River Expedition.

Actually, the road-builders built no road but sought only to pioneer—and publicize—a route linking Sioux City with the Bozeman Trail and hence with Montana. Sawyers had 53 men and 15 wagons, permitted 5 emigrant and 35 private freight wagons to accompany him, and secured from General Pope an escort of 143 men in 2 companies of the 5th U.S. Volunteers and a detachment of Dakota cavalry, with 25 wagons of their own. Leaving the mouth of the Niobrara on June 13, the expedition advanced without particular incident until the second week in August, when it got tangled up in the badlands around Pumpkin Buttes, between the Belle Fourche and Powder Rivers. Here the train was set upon by several hundred warriors—Cheyennes under Dull Knife and Oglala Sioux under Red Cloud—and har-

[45] Five of the seven, including Connor's aide-de-camp, were in his headquarters group, which places him clearly in the thick of the fight. One of the wounded had an arrow enter his open mouth and lodge in the root of his tongue, which had to be cut out in order to remove the arrow. Accounts of the battle, which took place near present Ranchester, Wyoming, are in Hafen and Hafen, *Powder River Campaigns*, pp. 46-48 (Connor's report), 129-36 (diary of Captain Henry E. Palmer), and 365-70. See also, for the Indian side, Grinnell, *Fighting Cheyennes*, pp. 209-11.

assed for nearly four days. Sawyers and the escort commander, Captain George Williford, quarreled bitterly over whether to continue to Montana or head for the safety of Fort Laramie, but the discovery of Fort Connor taking shape on the Powder resolved the issue.[46]

Colonel Kidd, after communicating by express with Connor, detained Williford's infantry at Fort Connor and furnished Sawyers with a cavalry escort up the Bozeman Trail. On August 31, on the upper Tongue, Indians waylaid and killed a Michigan officer scouting in advance and next day forced the train to corral. Sawyers sent three couriers down the Tongue to seek aid from Connor, and for two weeks, through the early September storms, the expedition kept its position as several hundred Indians, now menacing, now professing friendship, camped nearby. They were principally Black Bear's Arapahoes, with whom Connor had fought on August 29, and their fluctuating demeanor doubtless reflected a conflict between desire for revenge and hope that, through Sawyers, they might retrieve their ponies from the Pawnee scouts. Finally, despairing of help and quarreling among themselves, the Sawyers party turned back on the trail to Fort Connor. That very evening, however, Captain Brown arrived from Connor's command with a company of California cavalry and some Omaha scouts. The couriers had reached their destination on the lower Tongue on September 4, but storms and bankful streams had so slowed the relief column that it took nine days to travel fifty miles. A resolute leader, Captain Brown took charge, restored harmony, and piloted the would-be road-builders as far as the Bighorn, where they were beyond danger from hostile Indians.[47]

Not until September 11 did Connor gain any hint of the whereabouts of Cole and Walker. On that day North and his Pawnees returned from a scout to report the discovery in the Powder River Valley of hundreds of dead cavalry horses and the charred remains of their saddles and other trappings. They rep-

[46] George Bent, St. Louis-educated son of William Bent, was with these Indians, having ridden with them ever since Sand Creek. Through him Sawyers tried to buy passage through the Indian country with a wagon load of provisions. The Indians acceded, but more, coming up later and not sharing in the goods, continued the attack. Bent told Sawyers that the only condition on which the Indians would make peace was the hanging of Colonel Chivington.

[47] Principal sources for the Sawyers Expedition are Sawyers' report, in journal form, and Albert M. Holman's detailed account, both printed in Hafen and Hafen, *Powder River Campaigns*, pp. 219-346.

resented the last and most grievous of a series of misfortunes that had dogged the trail of Cole and Walker from the beginning.

Cole's heavy column, burdened by a long wagon train, had passed the month of July in a slow march up the Loup Fork and through the White River Badlands to Bear Butte, reported haunt of the Indians whose threat to the Sawyers Expedition Cole was to neutralize. Finding no Indians here, Cole continued up the Belle Fourche River and on August 18 fell in with Colonel Walker and his regiment, two weeks out of Fort Laramie. For the balance of the campaign, although Walker did not come under Cole's command, the two columns followed substantially the same route and kept close enough to each other to permit frequent communication.[48]

Crossing from the Belle Fourche to the Little Missouri, the two columns descended this valley on heavy and increasingly fresh Indian trails. Cole later stated that he wanted to follow them but felt bound by his orders to head for the rendezvous on the Rosebud. It was well that he did. Both columns were in bad shape. Days of marching over a country nearly destitute of grass and water had seriously weakened the horses. Scurvy swept Cole's units. Rations were running alarmingly low. On August 28, after an agonizing march over grassless badlands, the two commands reached the Powder fifty miles above its mouth.

A scouting party sent to the west returned on September 1 to report no sign of Connor on either the Tongue or the Rosebud and that the valleys of these streams, even if they could be reached, offered no grass. Placing the command on half-rations, Cole at once decided "to move toward rations"—up the Powder toward Fort Laramie. Before he could give the order, however, four to five hundred warriors attacked his herd a mile from camp. They were Hunkpapa Sioux from the villages he had followed down the Little Missouri. Oriented toward Sully's zone of operations on the Missouri, until now they had taken no part in the war being waged by their kinsmen against the soldiers on the Platte. Nearly all Cole's force rushed to meet the threat and drove off the attackers, losing six killed in the process.

Now Cole changed his plans and headed down the Powder

---

[48] For the movements of Cole and Walker see *ibid.*, pp. 69–91 (Cole's report), 92–100 (Walker's report). Reports of subordinates are in *O.R.*, ser. 1, vol. 48, pt. 1, pp. 383–88. For the Indian movements see Hyde, *Red Cloud's Folk*, pp. 130–33, and Grinnell, *The Fighting Cheyennes*, pp. 212–15.

toward smoke columns that he judged to represent either more Indians or Connor attempting to communicate with him. A broiling day's march followed by a stormy, frigid night was enough to turn him back—with 225 horses and mules dead of "excessive heat, exhaustion, starvation, and extreme cold." On September 4 the march up the Powder began, Walker forging ahead with his more mobile command, Cole tarrying at a patch of grass to graze his animals. Much property had been abandoned because of the lack of mules to haul it, and a detachment sent back to finish the work of destruction had a final encounter with seventy-five Hunkpapas, who rode down the Powder when pressed.

But upstream, near the mouth of the Little Powder, lay the big village of Sioux, Cheyennes, and Arapahoes that had mounted the attack on Platte Bridge, and on the morning of the fifth more than a thousand warriors from this camp issued from the hills west of both Cole and Walker. "All the hilltops, divides, and margins of the nearest bluffs were literally covered with Indians," recalled Cole. For three hours parties from both sides launched small-unit attack and counterattack as Cole's artillery kept the warriors from attempting a general assault. A cavalry detachment that crossed the river got cut off and nearly wiped out before relieved. Parties of warriors tried to stampede the led horses of the dismounted skirmishers, but each attempt was thwarted by rapid fire from the new Spencer repeating carbines that some of the troops carried. Fifteen miles up the valley, the Indians who had surrounded Walker did not attack. Leaving a battalion to guard his packs, he took the rest of the regiment back to Cole's aid but arrived after the warriors had broken off the fight.

After this encounter the Cheyennes went off to the Black Hills to hunt buffalo, but the Sioux remained near the mouth of the Little Powder, where on September 8 Walker and Cole nearly blundered into their village. The warriors came out to slow the advance of the soldiers while the women took down the tepees. Walker, three miles in advance, rode into this resistance. Cole corralled his train and hastened the 12th Missouri and the rifled cannon into the fight. After some confused skirmishing, the troops headed for a river crossing while the warriors gathered in surrounding timber to dispute the passage. Cole's cannon caught them in enfilade and they scattered from the field.

That night a norther hit the military camp. The temperature plummeted, and gales pounded men and animals with rain, sleet, and then snow. Weakened horses dropped by the score. "God forbid I shall ever have to pass such another night," wrote Walker. Moving to a more sheltered location next morning, the men surrounded the stock with great log fires and spent the day gathering cottonwood boughs for forage, but when the storm finally blew itself out on September 10 Cole counted 414 dead animals and Walker at least 100.

"Vulture like," as Cole moved on up the Powder, the Sioux "hovered around my starving and exhausted command." Artillery held them off when they grew too aggressive. Starvation was not so easily held off. Now on less than quarter-rations and these rapidly vanishing, the troops verged on catastrophe. As horses dropped dead, Walker observed, "if they happened to be in good flesh 20 men would pounce on them and in less time than I can tell it his bones would be stripped and devoured raw."

The last reserves of endurance were summoned on September 13 when some of Connor's Pawnees found the command, and the men learned that Fort Connor lay less than eighty miles up the Powder. By the twentieth Cole and Walker had brought their thoroughly used-up troops into camp near the fort. Here Connor arrived with his column on September 24, to unite the three divisions of the Powder River Expedition.

Connor had planned to assemble another striking force from Cole's and Walker's commands at Fort Connor and take the field again, but two days before reaching the fort he had been met by a courier bearing orders, dated August 22, breaking the vast District of the Plains into four separate districts and assigning him to his old command, the District of Utah. As he was now operating in the new District of Nebraska, Brigadier General Frank Wheaton commanding from Fort Laramie, there was nothing to do but disband the Powder River Expedition and head for Salt Lake City.[49]

The orders were part of a general reorganization of the postwar Army, but they also reflected a growing disenchantment in St. Louis and Washington with Connor. Pope had taken alarm when Connor, disgusted with dilatory quartermaster and commissary contracting officers, began making contracts himself. And Connor's orders to Cole and Walker to kill every male Indian over twelve years of age had filled Pope with nightmarish

---

[49] *O.R.*, ser. 1, vol. 48, pt. 2, p. 1201. Palmer diary in Hafen and Hafen, *Powder River Campaigns*, pp. 148–49.

visions of another Chivington massacre. "These instructions are atrocious," he wired Dodge on August 11. "If any such orders as General Connor's are carried out, it will be disgraceful to the Government, and will cost him his commission, if not worse. Have it rectified without delay."[50]

Coincident with the reorganization came orders for retrenchment that sprang from a mounting alarm over the expense of conducting offensives against the Indians. By the end of July the skyrocketing cost of the expeditions operating in Dodge's department had assumed the proportions of a scandal in Washington. "I cannot too strongly impress upon you the necessity of reducing both troops and supplies in your command," Pope scolded Dodge on July 31. "You don't understand the pressure from Washington on this subject." Quartermaster General Montgomery Meigs went to Fort Leavenworth himself to investigate. Reporting costs of nearly $10 million for rations and forage and another $10 million for other supplies, he concluded ominously, "It remains to wait for results commensurate with the expense." The Secretary of the Treasury declared that he could not meet such large and unexpected obligations, and Secretary of War Stanton appealed to General Grant for some assurance to relieve the President's anxiety over the situation.[51]

Dodge stood by Connor, whose expenses attracted the most attention, and asserted his "desire that the Government may understand that it has either got to abandon the country west entirely to the Indians or meet the war issue presented." But his protests could not overcome the swelling clamor for retrenchment. In August the decision was reached to muster out the Volunteers, reduce the troop commitment on the plains, and confine military activity to defense of the travel routes.[52]

Incensed over the interruption of his campaign and stung by the personal repudiation implied by the orders that reached him on September 22, Connor at once left for Salt Lake City. He traveled by way of Denver, where the populace soothed his injured ego with a rousing reception and feast at the Planters' Hotel. Dodge also defended Connor. Recommending him for promotion to major general, he pointed out that his operations had drawn

---

[50] *O.R.*, ser. 1, vol. 48, pt. 1, pp. 356–57. Conner received Pope's orders on August 20 near Fort Connor and replied that they would be "implicitly obeyed."
[51] *Ibid.*, pt. 1, p. 350; pt. 2, pp. 1154–55, 1156–59, 1167, 1178.
[52] *Ibid.*, pt. 1, p. 351; pt. 2, pp. 1203–11.

the Indians off the Platte road and punished one tribe "in a manner seldom before equaled and never excelled."[53]

But Dodge's accolade and the festivities in Denver, while helping to restore Connor's reputation, could not obscure the failure of the Powder River Expedition. Even the Battle of Tongue River, the only serious damage inflicted on the Indians, ended with Connor's withdrawal from the field under fire. Cole and Walker had presided over a near disaster—losing nearly a thousand horses and mules and immense quantities of quartermaster and ordnance supplies besides 13 killed, 5 wounded, and 2 missing in combat. And although Cole estimated that the troops had killed or wounded 200 to 500 Indians, Walker conceded that "I cannot say as we killed one." Neither Cole nor Walker, inexperienced in Indian fighting and plains campaigning, had managed their assignments very well, but neither had Connor, who was experienced, given them very clear assignments. Connor had attempted a complex and intricately timed operation in a region too vast and imperfectly mapped to permit success. Far from defeating the hostiles, he had been decisively defeated himself—not by the Indians but by weather and terrain.

Yet there was one important effect of the Powder River Expedition. Focusing public attention on the Bozeman Trail, gaining new knowledge of the country through which it ran, and planting a fort at its crossing of the Powder, the campaigners of 1865 insured that the road would attract mounting emigrant travel in 1866. And with the emigrants would come fresh demands on the Army to finish the job begun by Connor.

The same frustrations that plagued Connor also delayed the departure of General Sully from Sioux City. He had planned to get off by May 10, but wet roads across Iowa and high water in the Missouri slowed the buildup of supplies. As late as May 26, lamenting that "three boatloads found the bottom of the Missouri," he reported his command hardpressed simply to maintain itself at Sioux City. Not until June 7 did the column—840 Iowa, Minnesota, and Dakota cavalrymen—leave Sioux City, trailing a long supply train manned by 200 teamsters.[54]

The first task—now that his objective had been changed from

[53] *Ibid.*, pt. 1, pp. 335–48. Hafen and Hafen, *Powder River Campaigns*, pp. 150, 371–76.
[54] *O.R.*, ser. 1, vol. 48, pt. 2, pp. 162, 617–18.

the Black Hills to Devil's Lake—was to talk with the Teton Sioux. The report that three thousand lodges were en route to Fort Rice to make peace had been responsible for Pope's decision to yield to the imprecations of Curtis and Sibley and send Sully to Devil's Lake. Yet Pope's intentions toward these Sioux were somewhat unclear. On the one hand, he had informed Governor Edmunds that they were openly hostile, clearly a military responsibility, and therefore not Indians with whom the governor could be allowed to treat even though armed with the authority of an act of Congress. On the other hand, Pope instructed Sully, "If you can make a treaty with the Indians at Fort Rice such as I have suggested, it will be well to do so and I trust you will not leave anything undone to effect this." The key to this seeming contradiction lay in the qualification, "such as I have suggested." Edmunds could be expected to negotiate the usual kind of treaty, bribing the Indians with presents and annuities to keep the peace and thus in effect rewarding them for past hostilities and encouraging them in future ones. Sully, following Pope's design, would conclude a treaty that was no more than a "mere understanding": if the Indians kept the peace, so would the Army; if they broke it, they would be pursued and killed by the Army.[55]

This neat solution, of course, ignored the fact that the Army's record of pursuing and killing Indians had not been so impressive as to make this a frightening prospect. It ignored, too, the Army's inability to make good the implicit guarantee of protection to the Indians from aggressive whites. Most significant, it ignored the will of Congress as registered in the act empowering Edmunds to treat with the Sioux. But Pope's dogmatic stand, forcing Edmunds to postpone his undertaking until the obstinate general in St. Louis could be circumvented, did buy time for Sully to try the Pope formula first.

Foreshadowing the fate of the Pope formula, near old Fort Pierre late in June Sully learned that one thousand lodges of Sioux had come to hear what he had to say but had tired of the wait and gone east of the river to hunt. That he missed the chance to talk with them was not serious, for these were Indians with whom he had made peace in 1864. That they had chosen to intercept him here, however, was a disquieting indication of the distrust in which the Sioux increasingly held Fort Rice. There had been too many unpleasant incidents there—full-dress

[55] *Ibid.*, pt. 2, pp. 357–58, 492–94, 557–58, 961–62.

skirmishes on April 12 and 26 and June 2, the execution by Colonel Dimon of the two Santee captives on April 12, and, as Sully later learned, a disconcerting tendency of the Volunteers to shoot first and inquire later whether the target happened to be friendly or hostile.[56]

This abiding fear of Fort Rice prevented Sully from even testing the Pope formula. Reaching the east bank of the Missouri opposite the fort on July 13, he found, instead of the anticipated three thousand Sioux lodges, only two hundred, augmented during the week he remained there to three hundred. The chiefs, mainly Hunkpapa, Blackfoot, and Yanktonai, reported bitter dissension rocking the "hostile" camp, now on Knife River about fifty miles southwest of Fort Berthold. They also said that many more groups wanted to come in for the talks but were "deathly afraid" of Fort Rice. Sully observed the depth of the fear on the very day of his arrival. As the boat bearing him from the expedition camp on the east bank docked at the fort, the proper Colonel Dimon fired an artillery salute in honor of the commanding general of the district. At the same moment, 130 lodges of very suspicious Blackfeet and Hunkpapas were approaching the fort. Certain that the soldiers were perpetrating a massacre, they stampeded homeward. Several nights later, when a steamboat crossed from Rice with a load of rations, a rumor swept the Indians that Sully intended to bring his soldiers back on it and kill them all. Another stampede occurred. Dimon succeeded in restoring order, but not before many warriors had fled beyond recall. As the chiefs averred that any other meeting place would draw sufficient Sioux for a meaningful council, Sully told them to spread the word that he would meet them at Fort Berthold, then set forth on July 21 for Devil's Lake.[57]

Much of the Sioux antipathy toward Fort Rice Sully blamed on Colonel Dimon. Impressed by his "energy and pluck," he also had come to view him as "too young—too rash—for his position." "He is making a good deal of trouble for me," he had already advised Pope, "and eventually for you, in his overzealous desire to do his duty." He was too much like his mentor, Ben Butler, thought Sully, for the delicate business of dealing with Indians, and what he saw at Fort Rice confirmed his decision to clear the

---

[56] *Ibid.*, pt. 2, p. 1013. CIA, *Annual Report* (1865), p. 209.

[57] Sully's reports to Pope, July 14, 15, 17, and 20, *O.R.*, ser. 1, vol. 48, pt. 2, pp. 1080, 1084–85, 1090–91, 1109–10.

way for an "older and cooler head." Dispatching Dimon to Washington on an "important mission," Sully assigned Fort Rice to Lieutenant Colonel John Pattee of the 7th Iowa Cavalry, a moccasin-shod frontiersman who promptly dropped the parade-ground formality of his predecessor.[58]

As Pope and Sully had expected, the three-week march to Devil's Lake and back to the Missouri proved thoroughly un-rewarding. The expedition found no Indians and very little In-dian sign. Parties of Red River half-breeds met along the way confirmed that the hostile Santees who had not joined the Tetons and Yanktonais had scattered into the British possessions. After scouting Devil's Lake for a suitable site for the long-heralded military post (it would be established as Fort Totten in 1867, several years after the need had passed), the column turned back to the Missouri, arriving opposite Fort Berthold on August 8.[59]

Much had happened since the preliminary talks at Fort Rice three weeks earlier. Runners had taken Sully's message to the camps on the Knife: he would meet all who wanted peace at Fort Berthold and then make war on the rest. According to the gen-eral's intelligence, the arrival of the runners on the Knife had set off a great controversy, in which peace currents ran strong. But a rising Hunkpapa chief named Sitting Bull, "who wishes to lead the war party," circulated among the bands "cutting himself with a knife, and crying out that he was just from Fort Rice; that all those that had come in and given themselves up I had killed, and calling on the nation to avenge the murder." Or-ganizing an expedition of five hundred warriors, Sitting Bull led them against hated Fort Rice.[60]

When the Sioux appeared in the hills around Fort Rice on July 28, Lieutenant Colonel Pattee turned out the garrison—four companies of the 1st Volunteers, two of the 4th, and one of the 6th Iowa, to form a long skirmish line curling around the north, west, and south flanks of the post. The warriors raced up and down the line at close range, loosing clouds of arrows as the de-fenders responded with musketry. Howitzers soon turned the contest into a long-range exchange of fire that lasted for three hours. Throughout, Pattee kept his outnumbered men in a firmly defensive stance that enabled his superior firepower to prevail.

---

[58] *Ibid.*, pt. 2, pp. 851–52. Brown, *The Galvanized Yankees*, pp. 93, 103.

[59] Sully's reports of July 31 and August 8, *O.R.*, ser. 1, vol. 48, pt. 2, pp. 1136–38, 1172–74.

[60] Sully's report of August 8, *ibid.*, pt. 2, pp. 1172–74.

What the impulsive Colonel Dimon might have done may be conjectured.[61]

The peace proponents in the Knife River villages were never very confident that Sully did not meditate treachery. "They are convinced that it is only a trap I have set to capture and slay them," he lamented. Now they lost their enthusiasm for the Fort Berthold meeting altogether. Sitting Bull's war expedition to Fort Rice would be sure to make Sully angry, and it seemed foolhardy to place themselves in his power. Many, perhaps all, the camps withdrew to the Little Missouri, and in early September some of their warriors rode over to the lower Powder to contribute to the discomfiture of Colonels Cole and Walker.

"I am in considerable of a quandry what to do," complained Sully on August 8, before learning that the Sioux had left the Knife. If he crossed the Missouri and failed to win a clear victory, the Indians would interpret his subsequent withdrawal as defeat and the war faction would gain strength. If he marched down the Missouri without even trying, "matters will be nearly as bad." When he heard that the Sioux camps had dissolved in a general movement to the west, he chose the latter course.[62]

By the close of summer nothing was more certain than that the military solution had not produced the "results commensurate with the expense"—nearly $20 million exclusive of pay, it turned out—that Quartermaster General Meigs skeptically awaited. At enormous cost Connor's 2,500 men had scoured the Powder River country in three columns, Sully's 800 had made a profitless march up the Missouri and back, and Ford and then Sanborn with more than 1,000 had frittered away the summer on the Arkansas trying to get a clear mandate to attack the loose concentration of southern Plains tribes. In addition, to make certain that the country between the Platte and the Arkansas remained free of Indians, Dodge had sent a 350-man column up the Republican and another of 250 up the Smoky Hill. During the entire summer these 6,000 offensive troops probably killed no more than 100 Indians—less than the defensive troops had accounted for in protecting the travel routes and settlements. Perhaps unintentionally, General Sully repudiated the basic concept

[61]Brown, *The Galvanized Yankees*, pp. 104–7, based on accounts in *Frontier Scout*, a newspaper published by the 1st Volunteers at Fort Rice. Pattee, "Dakota Campaigns," pp. 339–41. *O.R.*, ser. 1, vol. 48, pt. 2, pp. 1181–82.

[62] Reports of August 8 and 13, *O.R.*, ser. 1, vol. 48, pt. 2, pp. 1172–74, 1181–82.

of the 1865 operations by concluding that a scalp bounty "would be cheaper and more effective than sending large bodies of troops, who can never be successful in hunting small bodies of Indians in their broken, mountainous country."[63]

The absence of any apparent result to show for all the costly military activity, coupled with the economy-motivated directives to assume the defensive on the Plains, left Pope with the unenviable prospect of losing all influence on the course of Indian affairs in his division unless he swallowed his pride and cooperated in the Indian Bureau's peace effort. This dawning reality probably underlay his abrupt decision in August to have General Sanborn join with Agent Leavenworth in arranging the truce with the tribes south of the Arkansas. At the same time the Indian Bureau, doubtless reflecting the moderation of the able Interior Secretary Harlan, softened its uncompromising stance toward the Army. It must have been apparent, too, that military participation in the peace effort would tend to commit the Army to the Bureau's rather than Pope's view of the proper peace solution. Thus the peace commissions that went forth in the autumn of 1865 to negotiate with the tribes of the northern and southern Plains were composed of high-ranking army officers as well as civilian functionaries.

On the southern Plains Agent Leavenworth's long quest for peace, which with some powerful aid from Senator Doolittle had thrice confounded Dodge's aggressive plans for war, culminated in the Little Arkansas treaties. Generals Sanborn and Harney, the latter back in familiar frontier haunts after an unhappy Civil War interlude, joined with Leavenworth, Kit Carson, William Bent, James Steele of the Indian Office, and Superintendent of Indian Affairs Thomas Murphy to compose the commission that met with the chiefs of the southern Plains tribes on the Little Arkansas between October 12 and 24, 1865. The result was a series of treaties establishing peace between the United States and the Cheyenne, Arapaho, Kiowa, Kiowa-Apache, and Comanche tribes. In return for the annual annuities that so distressed

---

[63] CIA, *Annual Report* (1865), p. 211. For the overview, see Dodge's summary report, Nov. 1, 1865, *O.R.*, ser. 1, vol. 48, pt. 1, pp. 335–66; and Dodge, *The Battle of Atlanta and other Campaigns* (Council Bluffs, Ia., 1911), in which he devotes two chapters to his frequently erroneous version of the 1864–65 campaigns. For the detailed breakdown of the cost see House Ex. Docs., 39th Cong., 2d sess., No. 5. Expenditures of the Quartermaster Department in supporting operations against Indians in 1865 were $19,263,856, of the Subsistence Department $359,788, and of the Pay Department $1,132,512.

General Pope, the Indians promised to stop depredations on the travel routes and withdraw to specified tracts of territory south of Kansas and east of New Mexico. The Cheyenne and Arapaho treaty also contained more liberal annuity provisions than the others and expressly repudiated "the gross and wanton outrages perpetrated" by U.S. troops at Sand Creek.[64]

Generals Curtis and Sibley joined with Governor Edmunds, Superintendent of Indian Affairs Edward B. Taylor, and two other civilians to compose the commission that Edmunds had been laboring to assemble, over Pope's obstructionism, since spring. In October, at Fort Sully, they met with chiefs of the Teton and Yanktonai Sioux and concluded a series of treaties restoring peace, binding the signatories to withdraw from the emigrant routes, and providing for annual annuity payments. Altogether there were nine treaties, one each with the Miniconjou, Lower Brule, Two Kettle, Blackfeet, Sans Arc, Hunkpapa, Oglala, and Upper and Lower Yanktonai Sioux.[65]

Actually, only one chief of any importance—old Lone Horn of the Miniconjous—had participated in the Fort Sully councils. The rest were peace leaders who in no sense expressed the temper of the tribes out on the Little Missouri and Powder Rivers. Whether the commissioners overrated the representative character of the chiefs in ignorance or with deliberate intent to deceive, they did concede that the chiefs who were not present would have to be contacted when the season again permitted travel. This, they naively assumed, would involve no more than inviting the nonsignatories to come in the next spring and place their marks on the paper. As it turned out, they could not have been more wrong.[66]

The treaties of October 1865, approved by the Senate in the spring of 1866, assuaged a national conscience troubled by memories of Sand Creek and momentarily seemed to authenticate the

<hr/>

[64] Council proceedings are in CIA, *Annual Report* (1865), pp. 515-36. The treaties are printed in Kappler, *Indian Affairs*, 2, 887-95. See Berthrong, *Southern Cheyennes*, pp. 241-44, for an account of the council. See also "Diary of Samuel A. Kingman at the Indian Treaty of 1865," *Kansas Historical Quarterly, 1* (1931-32), 442-50.

[65] CIA, *Annual Report* (1865), pp. 183-96; (1866), pp. 168-76. Correspondence from various official sources relating to the origins and activities of the Edmunds Commission is printed in *South Dakota Historical Collections, 9* (1918), 409-65. For the treaties see Kappler, *Indian Affairs*, 2, 883-87, 896-908.

[66] Hyde, *Red Cloud's Folk*, pp. 135-39.

uncomplicated view of Indian relations enjoyed by the theorists of the Indian Office and their like-minded supporters in the widening circle of Eastern humanitarians concerned with the Indian problem. But as they—and the Indians—were to discover within the year, it was easier to sign treaties than to live up to them.

The treaties of Fort Sully and Little Arkansas ended, however briefly, the second stage in the progress of hostilities with the Plains tribes. The first, more in the nature of a preliminary skirmish, subsided after the conflicts at Blue Water, Solomon's Fork, and Rush Spring. The second had begun with the massacre of whites by Minnesota Sioux and the massacre of Cheyennes by Colorado soldiers. This stage of the Plains wars featured some of the most elaborate campaigns and powerful expeditions ever projected against Indians as well as some of the most tenacious combat yet to erupt on the military-Indian frontier.

The massive scale on which the armies of blue and gray contended farther east perhaps conditioned the military thought of Plains commanders, who were closer in spirit and distance to the theaters of formal war than their brother officers in the Southwest and on the Pacific. Generals such as Pope, Dodge, and Connor went after the Indians with regiments and brigades instead of companies and battalions, and in such conflicts as Whitestone Hill, Killdeer Mountain, Tongue River, and Adobe Walls they saw evidence that heavy columns could indeed bring Indians into open and decisive battle. That there had been open battles at all, however, was in truth due less to the efficacy of heavy columns than to the extraordinary carelessness of a people just learning the conditions of serious warfare with a better armed and organized aggressor. And that the battles were anything but decisive eluded the generals until the War Department's decision to abandon offensive operations provided a convenient rationalization for the increasingly apparent reality.

The Plains operations of 1863-65 held certain lessons of importance for the future. The experiences of Cole and Walker on the Powder and of Sully in the Badlands dramatized the perils of inadequate logistics, and yet the enormous logistical effort necessary to support heavy columns in a country uncovered by a network of forts ran the risk of paralyzing the tactical effort. The experiences of Sully on the Missouri and Ford and Sanborn on

the Arkansas testified to an increasingly irreconcilable diver-
gence between military and civil policies that foreshadowed a
time when the Army could be less cavalier about defining all
Indians in a zone of operations as hostile and correspondingly
less certain about the identity of friend and foe. And Sully's
burst of disgust over the outcome of his 1865 campaign—better
a scalp bounty than large bodies of soldiers—suggested that the
Plains Indians were beginning to learn that the best defense
against a heavy column was to avoid it altogether.

The lure of the large-scale offensive never wholly dimmed.
But the peacetime army, struggling with swelling responsibilities and shrinking resources, never again summoned the
strength to test it on anything like the comprehensive scale of
1863–65.

SIXTEEN

Legacy and Prospect, 1866

THE POSTWAR demand for peace and retrenchment dashed the plans of western commanders to throw the vast military resources freed by the accord between Grant and Lee at Appomattox Court House against the Indians of the West. The Southern Rebellion had been crushed at enormous cost in blood and treasure. Now it was time to divert the national energies generated by the war to a quest for individual and national prosperity. The quest would produce commercial and industrial revolution, exploration of horizons of technology revealed by the war, unprecedented exploitation of natural resources, and rapid destruction of the western frontiers. For the West, the postwar mood brought not only the expected military cutback but also a rising clamor for nonmilitary solutions to the Indian problem. If men of good will could sit down and talk with the Indian in a spirit of justice and generosity, ran the thesis, he could be removed from the paths of expansion without resort to bloodshed and expensive armies.

But where to remove him? In less than two decades Americans had scattered themselves over half a continent. Already, with the postwar westward surge yet to begin, there remained no blocks of territory large enough for the Indian to pursue his traditional mode of life and still stay out of the white man's way. Already, as General Sherman observed during his western tour of 1866, the Indian found himself "hemmed in" by white settlements, and already "the poor devil naturally wriggles against his doom."[1] Unless national expansion was to be arrested, the Indian

[1] House Ex. Docs., 39th Cong., 2d sess., No. 23, p. 10.

would have to make do with less territory. This meant that he must yield his old way of life for another requiring less territory. And since people rarely make such a fundamental change voluntarily, even at the behest of men of good will motivated by a spirit of justice and generosity, the white man and the Indian hardly stood on the threshold of peace in 1865.

Like its predecessor of the 1850s, the postwar Regular. Army would be a peacetime army only in name—and strength. With even more truth than earlier could the Regulars complain, as one expressed it, that "while Indian campaigns may not constitute a state of war within the meaning of the Revised Statutes of the United States, they do present the most active peace establishments recorded in the history of the country."[2] Because the Indian was now cornered, because the pace of the westward movement of which they were a part had accelerated, the Regulars of 1865–90 belonged to an even more active peace establishment than those of earlier years. Before the Indians stopped wriggling against his doom, they conducted twenty-four operations officially recorded as wars, campaigns, or expeditions, engaged in nearly a thousand armed conflicts,[3] played a large role in shaping federal Indian policy, and contributed importantly to the painful and tragic beginnings of the Indian's acculturation. But what they were and what they did in these years owed much to the frontiersmen in blue, Regular and Volunteer alike, who confronted the Indian between 1848 and 1865.

Among the legacies the frontier army of 1848–65 bequeathed its successor was an accumulation of wisdom produced by seventeen years of experience with the western environment and its aboriginal inhabitants. Coming from eastern woodlands after the Mexican War, the soldiers had to learn for themselves how to survive and operate in this new kind of land, where vast distances, climatic extremes, and scarcity of life-sustaining resources confounded the newcomer and aided his enemy. They had to learn, too, the customs and traits that differentiated the western Indian tribes, particularly strengths and weaknesses of military import, and how to turn them to military advantage. Never formally codified, this was a lore in part susceptible to articulation, in part an instinct implanted by long experience. Never did the Army consciously study and master it, but enough

[2] Price, *Across the Continent with the Fifth Cavalry*, p. 39.
[3] See Heitman, 2, 299, 426–48.

officers and men made the effort for veteran to pass on to recruit an expanding body of knowledge that, despite a large content of misinformation, was of high value in postwar relations between soldier and Indian.

A more important and more tangible legacy was a group of regional defense systems whose main outlines governed command relationships and distribution of troops until the passing of the frontier. Divisions, departments, and districts underwent continuous geographical redefinition, but the western command organization of 1890 still bore a recognizable identity with that placed in effect by the War Department in 1853. In each of the geographical commands, while making extensions and readjustments, successive commanders did not fundamentally alter the basic framework of forts erected in the 1850s and 1860s.

On the Great Plains, where Sioux, Cheyenne, and Arapaho were to make their last stand in the next fifteen years, the great transcontinental thoroughfares continued to provide the skeleton for the distribution of troops. The Oregon and Santa Fe Trail defenses laid out by Colonels Loring and Sumner in 1849 and 1850–51, and the Smoky Hill stations founded by Volunteers in 1864–65, took on new importance as railroads crept westward from the Missouri along trails rutted by the wagons of emigrants and freighters. On the northern Plains, where traffic on the Missouri River and Bozeman Trail pathways to the mountains had so recently inflamed the Sioux, postwar commanders had only to build on beginnings made by Generals Sully and Connor.

In Texas, plagued by Kiowa and Comanche raiders until 1875 and by hostile Mescalero Apaches until 1881, the defensive concept authored by General Persifor Smith in 1851–52 and refined by General Twiggs in 1857–61 remained intact. A line of forts sweeping from Red River to the Rio Grande shielded the settlements, another guarded the Rio Grande boundary with Mexico, and still another thrust westward along the wagon road—soon to become a railroad—to El Paso.

In the Southwest, tormented for another twenty years by Apache hostilities, army stations formed a pattern on the map vaguely resembling a great tree, with the Rio Grande the trunk and with limbs reaching east and west to cover lines of travel and pockets of settlement. Colonel Sumner sketched the pattern in 1851–52, and Generals Garland and Carleton introduced more limbs to cover new roads and settlements. Their postwar successors did the same, principally in Arizona, but none reshaped the basic pattern.

So thoroughly had the tribes of the Great Basin and the Pacific Coast been eliminated as a military problem that only the barest rudiments of the defense systems laid out by Generals Smith and Hitchcock survived in the postwar years. The Indians of the Snake River watershed, however, had some fight left in them, and here the Regulars operated from a network of forts for the most part founded by Oregon and Washington Volunteers between 1862 and 1865.

That the basic patterns of defense endured did not testify to a strategic insight among early commanders denied their successors. Only in General Smith's Texas, in fact, was there a conscious effort to design a comprehensive system responsive to the conditions and needs of a region, and the success of that effort hardly bespoke the value of strategic planning. Elsewhere, the systems evolved piecemeal as specific conditions and needs called forth specific responses. That later commanders saw no reason to make more than minor adjustments, however, suggests, if not the soundness of the early decisions, at least an adequacy that discouraged sweeping revision.

The expansion of the regional defense systems in the postwar period indicated that the fundamental issue of military strategy on the Indian frontier had been resolved in the earlier period. No longer was there much debate over the merits of roving columns as a substitute for fixed posts. Rarely did military leaders seriously advocate the concentration of the frontier army at a few large and easily supplied stations from which, each summer, strong mounted columns would sweep through the Indian country and show the flag. Officers would continue to echo Captain Marcy's complaint that "the system of small garrisons has a tendency to disorganize the troops in proportion as they are scattered, and renders them correspondingly inefficient."[4] Inefficiency, though, was the price of congressional economy in military appropriations rather than of unsound strategy. When first propounded by General Stephen Watts Kearny in 1845, the roving summer column seemed the ideal strategy to reconcile large responsibility with small resources. The spread of settlement and the demand of settlers for visual assurance of protection had made the concept politically if not militarily unrealistic even by

[4] Marcy, *Thirty Years of Army Life*, p. 48.

the time it was most seriously debated in the middle fifties and certainly so by the middle sixties. If manpower limitations prevented the attainment of Tom Fitzpatrick's ideal of many powerfully garrisoned forts, then the Army would take comfort in the assurance of Colonels Mansfield and Sumner that a military presence close to the Indian homeland, however insignificant, would have a beneficial effect (see p. 55).

That the fixed-post system prevailed over roving summer columns did not signify that a purely defensive strategy had prevailed. The forts served as bases for offensive as well as defensive operations. The columns of Harney, Sumner, Van Dorn, Bonneville, and Wright in the 1850s, and of Sibley, Sully, and Connor in the early 1860s, differed from the roving summer variety envisaged by General Kearny only in their character as specific rather than general task forces. They were formed to accomplish a specified mission and then disbanded rather than sent each season to make a show and if necessary an application of force. By 1865 the practice of responding to Indian aggressions with an offensive directed at the tribe harboring the aggressors had become well established, and the regional systems of forts continued to provide the framework for wedding offensive with defensive strategy.

By 1865, also, two important and related precedents had been set in the conduct of offensive operations that would be further developed by postwar commanders, notably General Philip H. Sheridan. One was the winter campaign. In latitudes of heavy snow and subzero temperature, winter made the Indian highly vulnerable. It was a time of the year when he remained stationary for long periods, when he was least alert to danger, when he had to conserve food supplies and the waning strength of his stock, when the consequences of defeat were most devastating, and when, therefore, he was ill prepared psychologically as well as materially to offer firm resistance. Winter confronted a striking force with staggering logistical obstacles, and not least of the challenges was one of sheer survival, but if the problems could be mastered the dividends could be high. Just how high Colonels Connor and Carson demonstrated to the Shoshonis and Navajos in 1863–64 (see pp. 223–24, 242–44).

The other precedent was the growing practice of "total war." This meant warring on a whole enemy population, combatant and noncombatant alike. Rarely, with the notable exception of

Sand Creek, were women and children deliberately killed, although this happened regularly enough through avoidable or unavoidable accident. More often this warfare took the form of destruction of food, shelter, clothing, stock, and all other possessions that could be seized, leaving the hapless victims destitute in a less than bountiful land to starve, find succor with kinsmen, or come in and surrender. Demoralizing in its effect, total war undermined the will to resist and strengthened the faction, present in every tribe or band, that favored peace at any price. Harney, Van Dorn, Wright, and Bonneville all won a measure of success in this way, but again it remained for Kit Carson, coupling total war with the winter campaign, to dramatize the full possibilities. Sherman and Sheridan, who applied the technique in Georgia and Virginia during the Civil War, would give it further significance in the postwar years.

A network of physical facilities produced by seventeen years of labor and a body of knowledge and precedent developed by seventeen years of experience were not the only legacies inherited by the new Regular Army. If these were assets, then there were liabilities, too. Seventeen years of experience had also developed certain dilemmas inherent in the nature of the Army's role on the Indian frontier, and these were to grow still more vexing as the conflict between Indian and white escalated in the decade after 1865.

For one, the increasing reliance on total war raised a distressing moral dilemma. On the one hand, total war could produce quick and decisive results, and its proponents argued that in the long view this was more humane than slow strangulation by broken treaties, encircling settlements, and inconclusive military action. On the other hand, officers and gentlemen of chivalrous heritage could not quite convince themselves of the justice of warfare that took the lives of women and children or cast them without food or shelter on a hostile landscape.

And this formed part of a larger moral dilemma deriving from their mission on the Indian frontier. To be sure, a minority of the frontier army joined with a vocal segment of the western population in viewing the Indian as a savage beast, deserving the sympathy of civilized man no more than the wolves that scavenged on the prairies. But most officers and men, especially those who came to know and understand the Indian, saw him as degraded and inferior but still a human being upon whom a great wrong was being inflicted. Frontier settlers demanded peremptory military action against the Indian, even to the point of extermination. Peremptory action outraged an eastern population made keenly sensitive to humanitarian issues by the crusade against slavery. And the soldiers, wrestling with their own consciences, buffeted by extremes of opinion, had to fight an enemy with whom they sympathized in wars provoked by their own countrymen.

Complicating the moral dilemma was another, destined also to find no solution and to be exacerbated by postwar developments. This dilemma, which further imprisoned the frontier army by forces beyond its control, sprang from the division of federal authority over Indian affairs between military and civil arms of the government, and it focused on both personalities and policies. Army officers regarded Indian agents as corrupt and incompetent and Indian policy as tragic in its effect on Indians and whites alike. Over neither agents nor policy did the Army exert any influence, yet for the pernicious consequences of both it had to pay a high price in blood, blame, and frustration. The outspoken General Pope expressed the military view of the dilemma: "Whenever Indian hostilities or massacres occur on the frontier the military are held responsible for them, and by none are they so held more promptly and violently than by the officials of the Indian Department who have made treaties with the very Indians concerned which could not fail to lead to an outbreak."[5]

Indian Bureau officials, of course, held similar opinions about military personalities and policies, and both sides could cite plenty of specific examples to lend credibility to their contentions. By 1865, after sixteen years of civil involvement in Indian affairs, the confusions and consequences of divided authority had so infuriated military leaders that they openly championed transfer of the Indian Bureau back to the War Department and fundamental revision of the whole edifice of treaties, annuities, agents, and reservations that the civilian officials and associated vested interests had erected. That the Indian problem was not one for military techniques alone had been amply demonstrated by 1865. Thus the key issue was whether military or civil officials could best apply the nonmilitary techniques. The battle between the proponents of military and civil rule would rock Washington for a decade after 1865.

Still another dilemma, one that faced the Indian Bureau as

[5] Pope to Grant, June 11, 1865, *O.R.*, ser. 1, vol. 48, pt. 2, p. 881.

well as the Army, lay in the powerful influence on policies and courses of action of the vested interests. In a sense the whole western population, so dependent economically on federal expenditures, was a vested interest. "All the people west of the Missouri river look to the army as their legitimate field of profit and support," observed General Sherman in 1866.[6] But the pressures originated mainly with the traders, contractors, freighters, manufacturers, and financiers whose profits derived from federal expenditures for feeding or fighting Indians. The location of forts and the size of their garrisons often owed as much to commercial aspirations masquerading under exaggerations of Indian danger as to legitimate strategic requirements. And often minor Indian disturbances set off a sequence in which, as General Pope described it, "troops are immediately demanded, and then begins an Indian war, which the greed of contractors and speculators interested in its continuance, playing upon the natural apprehensions of the people and influencing the press, makes it very difficult to conduct successfully or bring to an end."[7] How to shape military policies and actions to needs as assessed by the Army instead of as portrayed by commercial interests was a problem that military leaders never mastered.

A chronic dilemma sprang from a promise seemingly implied by the Army's principal mission in the West—to protect the settlements and travel routes from Indians. The western population tended to construe this as a guarantee of absolute protection and to blame the Army for every murder or robbery perpetrated by Indians. "Each spot of every road," complained General Sherman, "and each little settlement along our five thousand miles of frontier, wants its regiment of cavalry or infantry to protect it against the combined power of all the Indians, because of the bare possibility of their being attacked by the combined force of all these Indians."[8] Westerners ought to help protect themselves, Sherman thought. "Denver needs no protection," he declared in 1866. "She could raise in an hour's notice one thousand men; and instead of protection, she can and should protect the neighboring settlements that tend to give her support and business."[9] But as

---

[6] Sherman to Rawlins, Sept. 30, 1866, House Ex. Docs., 39th Cong., 2d sess., No. 23, p. 13.

[7] Pope to Stanton, Feb. 6, 1864, O.R., ser. 1, vol. 34, pt. 2, p. 261.

[8] SW, Annual Report (1867), p. 8.

[9] Sherman to Rawlins, Sept. 12, 1866, House Ex. Docs., 39th Cong., 2d sess. No. 23, p. 13.

in the past, so in the future the people would demand an absolute security that an army tenfold that of 1866 could not begin to provide.

A final dilemma, and in many ways the most troublesome of all, centered on the imperative to conduct war on a peacetime budget. Rarely since 1848 had there been a time when the Army was not engaged in open war with Indians somewhere in the West, and never had there been a time when troops were not contending with guerrilla-style raiders in some part of nearly every geographical command. Yet, except for the four years of Civil War, a Nation at peace with itself and the world declined to recognize frontier conditions that, while not quite adding up to a state of war, still demanded much more than the static military establishment of peace. The dilemma would grow even more acute after the Civil War, when frontier conditions brought about the final test between Indian and white and when a prolonged period of national peace and prosperity induced a national mood smothering to all manifestations of militarism.

Weak though it was, the Army in the future as in the past would play an influential role in the westward movement and in the process of destroying the freedom and way of life of the western Indians. No more in the future than in the past, however, would the role lend itself to precise definition or the influence to precise measurement. Certainly, exploration, mapping, internal improvements, and indirect subsidization of the economy contributed enormously to the opening of the West. Certainly, such tribes as Navajo and Spokane earlier, Nez Perce, Kiowa and Comanche, Sioux and Cheyenne later, could view the Army as the primary instrument of their final conquest. Yet in every war or pacification in which the Army engaged, there were other and often more determining forces at work. As in the seventeen years after the Mexican War, so in the twenty-five years after the Civil War, the Army alone did not conquer the Indians and make the West safe for settlement. Rather it was but one of many groups, some organized, some not, joined in a largely uncontrolled and uncontrollable movement that, in the course of subjugating a wilderness empire, also subjugated one people to another.

☆ BIBLIOGRAPHY ☆

MANUSCRIPTS

This work has been approached on the assumption that printed original sources and monographic literature were together adequate to support a history such as I envisioned. Certain portions of the text, however, rest in large part on manuscript sources that I had already investigated for other purposes. These documents are principally in the Michael Steck Papers at the University of New Mexico in Albuquerque and in the National Archives and Record Service, Washington, D.C., in Record Groups 75 (Bureau of Indian Affairs), 94 (Adjutant General's Office), 98 (U.S. Army Commands), and 107 (Secretary of War).

GOVERNMENT DOCUMENTS

U.S. Army. *Army Regulations*, 1857.

U.S. Commissioner of Indian Affairs. *Annual Reports*, 1848–66.
   Also in U.S. Serials as follows:

1848:	House Ex. Doc. No. 1,	30th Cong., 2d sess.,	Vol. 1 (Serial	537).
1849:	House Ex. Doc. No. 5,	31st Cong., 1st sess.,	Vol. 3 (Serial	569).
1850:	House Ex. Doc. No. 1,	31st Cong., 2d sess.,	Vol. 1 (Serial	595).
1851:	House Ex. Doc. No. 2,	32d Cong., 1st sess.,	Vol. 2 (Serial	633).
1852:	House Ex. Doc. No. 1,	32d Cong., 2d sess.,	Vol. 1 (Serial	673).
1853:	House Ex. Doc. No. 1,	33d Cong., 1st sess.,	Vol. 1 (Serial	710).
1854:	Senate Ex. Doc. No. 1,	33d Cong., 2d sess.,	Vol. 1 (Serial	746).
1855:	Senate Ex. Doc. No. 1,	34th Cong., 1st sess.,	Vol. 1 (Serial	810).
1856:	Senate Ex. Doc. No. 5,	34th Cong., 3d sess.,	Vol. 2 (Serial	875).
1857:	Senate Ex. Doc. No. 11,	35th Cong., 1st sess.,	Vol. 2 (Serial	919).
1858:	Senate Ex. Doc. No. 1,	35th Cong., 1st sess.,	Vol. 1 (Serial	974).
1859:	Senate Ex. Doc. No. 2,	36th Cong., 1st sess.,	Vol. 1 (Serial 1023).
1860:	Senate Ex. Doc. No. 1,	36th Cong., 2d sess.,	Vol. 1 (Serial 1078).
1861:	Senate Ex. Doc. No. 1,	37th Cong., 2d sess.,	Vol. 1 (Serial 1117).
1862:	House Ex. Doc. No. 1,	37th Cong., 3d sess.,	Vol. 1 (Serial 1156).
1863:	House Ex. Doc. No. 1,	38th Cong., 1st sess.,	Vol. 3 (Serial 1182).
1864:	House Ex. Doc. No. 1,	38th Cong., 2d sess.,	Vol. 5 (Serial 1220).
1865:	House Ex. Doc. No. 1,	39th Cong., 1st sess.,	Vol. 2 (Serial 1248).
1866:	House Ex. Doc. No. 1,	39th Cong., 2d sess.,	Vol. 2 (Serial 1284).

U.S. Congress. *Congressional Globe:*
   30th Cong., 2d sess. (1848–49).
   31st Cong., 1st sess. (1849–50).
   31st Cong., 2d sess. (1850–51).
   32d Cong., 1st sess. (1851–52).

33d Cong., 2d sess. (1854–55).
35th Cong., 1st sess. (1857–58).

U.S. Congress. House of Representatives.
House Ex. Doc. No. 69, 30th Cong., 1st sess., Vol. 8, 1848, Serial 521. "Treaty with Mexico."
House Ex. Doc. No. 59, 33d Cong., 1st sess., Vol. 8, 1853, Serial 721. "Army Register, 1853."
House Ex. Doc. No. 93, 34th Cong., 1st sess., Vol. 11, 1856, Serial 858. "Indian Hostilities in Oregon and Washington."
House Ex. Doc. No. 118, 34th Cong., 1st sess., Vol. 12, 1856, Serial 859. "Indian Hostilities in Oregon and Washington Territories."
House Ex. Doc. No. 130, 34th Cong., 1st sess., Vol. 12, 1856, Serial 859. "Council with Sioux Indians at Fort Pierre."
House Ex. Doc. No. 24, 34th Cong., 3d sess., Vol. 3, 1856, Serial 879. "Army Register, 1856."
House Ex. Doc. No. 39, 35th Cong., 1st sess., Vol. 9, 1858, Serial 955. "Indian Affairs in the Territories of Oregon and Washington, Report of Special Agent J. Ross Browne."
House Ex. Doc. No. 45, 35th Cong., 1st sess., Vol. 9, 1858, Serial 955. "Expenses of the Indian Wars in Washington and Oregon Territories."
House Ex. Doc. No. 114, 35th Cong., 2d sess., Vol. 12, 1859, Serial 1014. "Topographical Memoir of the Department of the Pacific," by Capt. T. J. Cram.
House Ex. Doc. No. 24, 36th Cong., 2d sess., Vol. 6, 1860, Serial 1097. "Indian Disturbances in New Mexico."
House Ex. Doc. No. 58, 39th Cong., 1st sess., Vol. 8, 1866, Serial 1256. "Wagon Road from Niobrara to Virginia City."
House Ex. Doc. No. 5, 39th Cong., 2d sess., Vol. 5, 1866, Serial 1287. "Suppression of Indian Hostilities."
House Ex. Doc. No. 20, 39th Cong., 2d sess., Vol. 6, 1866, Serial 1288. "Military Posts."
House Ex. Doc. No. 23, 39th Cong., 2d sess., Vol. 6, 1866, Serial 1288. "Protection across the Continent."
House Ex. Doc. No. 45, 39th Cong., 2d sess., Vol. 7, 1866, Serial 1289. "Inspection by Generals Rusling and Hazen."
House Ex. Doc. No. 111, 39th Cong., 2d sess., Vol. 11, 1866, Serial 1293. "General Ingalls' Inspection Report."

U.S. Congress. Senate.
Senate Ex. Doc. No. 1, 29th Cong., 1st sess., 1846. "Report of a Summer Campaign to the Rocky Mountains . . . in 1845."
Senate Ex. Doc. No. 7, 30th Cong., 1st sess., Vol. 3, 1848, Serial 505. "Notes of a Military Reconnaissance from Fort Leavenworth . . . to San Diego," by Lt. William H. Emory.
Senate Ex. Doc. No. 22, 33d Cong., 2d sess., Vol. 6, 1855, Serial 751. "Report of Secretary of War on Indian Hostilities."
Senate Ex. Doc. No. 26, 34th Cong., 1st sess., Vol. 10, 1856, Serial 819. "Indian Disturbances in California."
Senate Ex. Doc. No. 66, 34th Cong., 1st sess., Vol. 13, 1856, Serial 822. "Indian Disturbances in the Territories of Washington and Oregon."

Senate Ex. Doc. No. 96, 34th Cong., 1st sess., Vol. 18, 1856, Serial 827.
"Statistical Report on the Sickness and Mortality in the Army of the
United States [1839–55]," by Richard H. Coolidge.
Senate Ex. Doc. No. 34, 34th Cong., 3d sess., Vol. 7, 1857, Serial 880.
"Pay and Emouluments of Lt. Gen. Scott."
Senate Ex. Doc. No. 58, 34th Cong., 3d sess., Vol. 8, 1857, Serial 881.
"Battle of Bluewater."
Senate Ex. Doc. No. 62, 34th Cong., 3d sess., Vol. 8, 1857, Serial 881.
"Purchase of Camels for Military Purposes."
Senate Ex. Doc. No. 32, 35th Cong., 2d sess., Vol. 10, 1859, Serial 984.
"Topographical Memoir of Colonel Wright's Campaign," by Lt.
John Mullan.
Senate Rep. No. 142, 38th Cong., 2d sess., Vol. 4, 1865, Serial 1214.
"Massacre of Cheyenne Indians."
Senate Ex. Doc. No. 26, 39th Cong., 2d sess., Vol. 2, 1867, Serial 1277.
"Sand Creek Massacre."
Senate Rep. No. 156, 39th Cong., 2d sess., 1867, Serial 1279. "Condition
of the Indian Tribes."

U.S. Secretary of War. *Annual Reports*, 1848–61:
1848: House Ex. Doc. No. 1, 30th Cong., 2d sess.,   Vol. 1 (Serial   537).
1849: House Ex. Doc. No. 5, 31st Cong., 1st sess.,   Vol. 3 (Serial   565).
1850: House Ex. Doc. No. 1, 31st Cong., 2d sess.,   Vol. 1 (Serial   595).
1851: Senate Ex. Doc. No. 1, 32d Cong., 1st sess.,   Vol. 1 (Serial   611).
1852: Senate Ex. Doc. No. 1, 32d Cong., 2d sess.,   Vol. 2 (Serial   659).
1853: Senate Ex. Doc. No. 1, 33d Cong., 1st sess.,   Vol. 2 (Serial   691).
1854: Senate Ex. Doc. No. 1, 33d Cong., 2d sess.,   Vol. 2 (Serial   747).
1855: Senate Ex. Doc. No. 1, 34th Cong., 1st sess.,   Vol. 2 (Serial   811).
1856: Senate Ex. Doc. No. 5, 34th Cong., 3d sess.,   Vol. 3 (Serial   876).
1857: Senate Ex. Doc. No. 11, 35th Cong., 1st sess., Vol. 3 (Serial   920).
1858: Senate Ex. Doc. No. 1, 35th Cong., 2d sess.,   Vol. 3 (Serial   976).
1859: Senate Ex. Doc. No. 2, 36th Cong., 1st sess., Vols. 2–3 (Serial 1024).
1860: Senate Ex. Doc. No. 1, 36th Cong., 2d sess.,   Vol. 2 (Serial 1079).
1861: Senate Ex. Doc. No. 1, 37th Cong., 2d sess.,   Vol. 2 (Serial 1118).

U.S. Statutes at Large. Vols. 9, 10, 11, 12.

U.S. War Department (Also printed in U.S. Serials):
*The War of the Rebellion: A Compilation of the Official Records of the
Union and Confederate Armies.*
Series 1: Vols. 1, 3, 4, 8, 9, 13, 15, 22 (2 parts), 26 (2 parts), 34 (4 parts),
41 (4 parts), 48 (2 parts), 50 (2 parts), 51, 52, 53.
Series 3: Vols. 1–5.

ARTICLES

Allen, R. S. "Pinos Altos, New Mexico." *New Mexico Historical Review*,
23 (1948), 302–32.
Amsden, Charles. "The Navaho Exile at Bosque Redondo." *New Mexico
Historical Review*, 8 (1933), 31–50.
Anderson, Harry H. "Harney v. Twiss; Nebraska Territory, 1856."
Westerners Brand Book (Chicago), 20 (1963), 1–3, 7–8.

———. "The Controversial Sioux Amendment to the Fort Laramie Treaty of 1851." *Nebraska History*, *37* (1956), 201–20.

Anderson, T. M. "Vancouver Barracks—Past and Present." *Journal of the Military Service Institution of the United States*, *35* (1904), 267–79.

Barrett, Lenora. "Transportation, Supplies, and Quarters for the West Texas Frontier under the Federal Military System, 1848–1861." West Texas Historical Association *Year Book*, *5* (1929), 87–99.

Bischoff, W. N., S.J. "Yakima Campaign of 1856." *Mid-America*, *31* (1949), 162–208.

———. "Yakima Indian War, 1855–1856: A Problem in Research." *Pacific Northwest Quarterly*, *41* (1950), 162–69.

Bliss, Zenas R. "Extracts from the Unpublished Memoirs of Maj. Gen. Z. R. Bliss." *Journal of the Military Service Institution of the United States*, *38* (1906), 120–34, 303–13, 517–29.

Blunt, James G. "General Blunt's Account of His Civil War Experiences." *Kansas Historical Quarterly*, *1* (1931–32), 211–65.

Burns, Robert Ignatius, S.J., ed. "Pere Joset's Account of the Indian War of 1858." *Pacific Northwest Quarterly*, *38* (1947), 285–314.

Carley, Kenneth. "The Sioux Campaign of 1862: Sibley's Letters to His Wife." *Minnesota History*, *38* (1962), 99–125.

Carley, Raymond G. "The Puzzle of Sand Creek." *Colorado Magazine*, *41* (1964), 279–98.

Clark, Robert C. "Military History of Oregon, 1849–1859." *Oregon Historical Quarterly*, *36* (1935), 14–59.

Crimmins, Martin L., ed. "Freeman's Report on the Eighth Military Department [1853]." *Southwestern Historical Quarterly*, *51* (1947–48), 57–58, 167–74, 252–58, 350–57; *52* (1948–49), 100–8, 227–33, 349–53, 444–47; *53* (1949–50), 71–77, 202–8, 308–19, 443–73; *54* (1950–51), 204–18.

———. "Col. J. K. F. Mansfield's Report of the Inspection of the Department of Texas in 1856." *Southwestern Historical Quarterly*, *42* (1938–39), 122–48, 215–57, 351–57.

———. "The First Line of Army Posts Established in West Texas in 1849." West Texas Historical Association *Year Book*, *19* (1943), 121–27.

"Dick" [Capt. William Dickinson]. "Reminiscences of Fort Defiance, 1860." *Journal of the Military Service Institution of the United States*, *4* (1883), 90–92.

Dorris, J. T. "Federal Aid to the Oregon Trail before 1850." *Oregon Historical Quarterly*, *30* (1929), 305–25.

Drum, Richard C. "Reminiscences of the Indian Fight at Ash Hollow." *Collections of the Nebraska State Historical Society*, *16* (1911), 143–51.

Ellison, William H. "The Federal Indian Policy in California, 1849–1860." *Mississippi Valley Historical Review*, *9* (1922), 37–67.

Emerson, Arthur W. "The Battle of Pyramid Lake." Potomac Westerners, *Great Western Indian Fights*. New York, 1960.

English, Abner M. "Dakota's First Soldiers: History of the First Dakota Cavalry, 1862–1865." *South Dakota Historical Collections*, *9* (1918), 241–337.

Enochs, James C. "A Clash of Ambition: The Chivington-Tappan Feud."

Montana, the Magazine of Western History, 15 (Summer, 1965), 58–67.

Espinosa, J. Manuel. "Memoir of a Kentuckian in New Mexico, 1848–1884." *New Mexico Historical Review, 13* (1937).

Fridley, Russell W. "Charles E. Flandrau, Attorney at War." *Minnesota History, 38* (1962), 116–25.

Haller, Theodore N. "Life and Public Services of Colonel Granville O. Haller." *Washington Historian, 1* (1899–1900), 102–4.

Harmon, George D. "The United States Indian Policy in Texas, 1846–1860." *Mississippi Valley Historical Review, 17* (1930), 377–403.

Heyman, Max, Jr. "On the Navaho Trail: The Campaign of 1860." *New Mexico Historical Review, 26* (1951), 44–63.

Hilger, Nicolas. "General Alfred Sully's Expedition of 1864." *Contributions to the Historical Society of Montana, 2* (1896), 314–28.

Holden, W. C. "Frontier Defense [in Texas], 1846–1860." West Texas Historical Association *Year Book, 6* (1930), 36–65.

Hoopes, Alban W. "Thomas S. Twiss, Indian Agent on the Upper Platte, 1855–1861." *Mississippi Valley Historical Review, 20* (1933), 353–64.

Hughes, W. J. "Rip Ford's Indian Fight on the Canadian." *Panhandle-Plains Historical Review, 30* (1957), 1–26.

Johnson, Roy P. "The Siege at Fort Abercrombie." *North Dakota History, 24* (1957), 1–77.

Kingman, Samuel A. "Diary of Samuel A. Kingman at the Indian Treaty in 1865." *Kansas Historical Quarterly, 1* (1931–32), 442–50.

Kingsbury, David L. "Sully's Expedition against the Sioux in 1864." *Collections of the Minnesota Historical Society, 8* (1898).

Lammons, Frank B. "Operation Camel: An Experiment in Animal Transportation in Texas, 1857–1860." *Southwestern Historical Quarterly, 61* (1957), 40–48.

Lecompte, Janet. "Sand Creek." *Colorado Magazine, 41* (1964), 315–35.

Lindgren, Raymond E. "A Diary of Kit Carson's Navaho Campaign of 1863–64." *New Mexico Historical Review, 31* (1946), 226–46.

McCann, Lloyd E. "The Grattan Massacre." *Nebraska History, 37* (1956), 1–26.

Mantor, Lyle E. "Fort Kearny and the Westward Movement." *Nebraska History Magazine, 29* (1948), 175–207.

Merriam, C. Hart. "The Indian Population of California." *American Anthropologist,* n.s. 7 (1905), 594–606.

Meyer, M. C. "Letters of a Santa Fe Army Clerk." *New Mexico Historical Review, 40* (1965), 141–64.

Miller, Nyle H., ed. "Surveying the Southern Boundary Line of Kansas: From the Journal of Col. Joseph E. Johnston." *Kansas Historical Quarterly, 1* (1931), 104–39.

Morgan, M. R. "Memories of the Fifties." *Journal of the Military Service Institution of the United States, 37* (1905), 147–67.

Mumey, Nolie. "John Minton Chivington, The Misunderstood Man." *Brand Book of the Denver Westerners* (Denver, 1956).

Neighbours, Kenneth F. "Chapters from the History of the Texas Indian Reservations." West Texas Historical Association *Year Book, 33* (1957), 3–16.

———. "Robert S. Neighbors and the Founding of the Texas Indian Reservations." West Texas Historical Association *Year Book, 31* (1955), 65–74.

———. "The Marcy-Neighbors Exploration of the Headwaters of the Brazos and Wichita Rivers in 1854." *Panhandle-Plains Historical Review*, 27 (1954), 26–46.

———. "The Assassination of Robert S. Neighbors." West Texas Historical Association *Year Book*, 34 (1958), 38–49.

———. "Indian Exodus out of Texas in 1859." West Texas Historical Association *Year Book*, 36 (1960), 80–97.

Oneal, Ben G. "The Beginnings of Fort Belknap." *Southwestern Historical Quarterly*, 61 (1957–58), 508–21.

Oury, William S. "Cook's Canyon: A Scene of Carnage Enacted There in July, 1861." *Arizona Daily Star* (Tucson), July 27, 1879.

Pattee, John. "Dakota Campaigns." *South Dakota Historical Collections*, 5 (1910), 275–350.

Peck, Robert M. "Recollections of Early Times in Kansas Territory from the Standpoint of a Regular Cavalryman." *Transactions of the Kansas State Historical Society*, 8 (1904), 484–507.

Pettis, George H. "Kit Carson's Fight with the Comanche and Kiowa Indians." *Publications of the Historical Society of New Mexico*, 12 (1908).

Pfaller, Louis, O.S.B. "The Sully Expedition of 1864 Featuring the Killdeer Mountain and Badlands Battles." *North Dakota History*, 31 (1964), 1–54.

Reeve, Frank D. "The Government and the Navaho, 1846–1858." *New Mexico Historical Review*, 14 (1939), 82–114.

———, ed. "Puritan and Apache: A Diary." *New Mexico Historical Review*, 23 (1948), 269–301; 24 (1949), 12–53.

Rippy, J. Fred. "The Indians of the Southwest in the Diplomacy of the United States and Mexico, 1848–1853." *Hispanic-American Historical Review*, 2 (1919), 363–96.

Robbins, Harvey. "Journal of the Rogue River War, 1855." *Oregon Historical Quarterly*, 34 (1933), 345–58.

Roland, Charles P., and Richard C. Robbins, eds. "The Diary of Eliza (Mrs. Albert Sidney) Johnston [1855]." *Southwestern Historical Quarterly*, 60 (1956–57), 463–500.

Sacks, Benjamin H., ed. "New Evidence on the Bascom Affair." *Arizona and the West*, 4 (1962), 261–78.

———. "The Origins of Fort Buchanan, Myth and Fact." *Arizona and the West*, 7 (1965), 207–26.

Santee, J. F. "Pio-Pio-Mox-Mox." *Oregon Historical Quarterly*, 34 (1933), 164–76.

Smith, Marian W. "The War Complex of the Plains Indians." *Proceedings of the American Philosophical Society*, 78 (1938), 425–64.

Smith, Ralph A. "The Comanche Invasion of Mexico in the Fall of 1845." *Southwestern Historical Quarterly*, 38 (1934–35), 157–76.

———. "The Comanche Bridge between Oklahoma and Mexico, 1834–1844." *Chronicles of Oklahoma*, 39 (1961), 54–69.

Strobridge, Truman R., and Bernard C. Nalty. "And Down Came the Indians: The Defense of Seattle, 1856." *Pacific Northwest Quarterly*, 55 (1964), 105–10.

Taylor, Morris F. "Action at Fort Massachusetts: The Indian Campaign of 1855." *Colorado Magazine*, 42 (1965), 292–310.

Thoburn, Joseph P. "Indian Fight in Ford County in 1859." *Kansas Historical Collections*, 12 (1911–12), 312–29.

Todd, John B. S. "The Harney Expedition against the Sioux: The Journal of Capt. John B. S. Todd," Ray H. Mattison, ed. *Nebraska History, 43* (1962), 110–11.

Unrau, William E. "A Prelude to War." *Colorado Magazine, 41* (1964), 299–313.

———. "The Story of Fort Larned." *Kansas Historical Quarterly, 23* (1957), 257–80.

Utley, Robert M. "The Bascom Affair: A Reconstruction." *Arizona and the West, 3* (1961), 59–68.

———. "Kit Carson and the Adobe Walls Campaign." *The American West, 2* (1965), 4–11, 73–75.

———. "Fort Union and the Santa Fe Trail." *New Mexico Historical Review, 36* (1961), 36–48.

———, ed. "Captain John Pope's Plan of 1853 for the Frontier Defense of New Mexico." *Arizona and the West, 5* (1963), 149–63.

Watkins, Albert. "History of Fort Kearny." *Collections of the Nebraska State Historical Society, 16* (1911), 227–67.

Woody, Clara T., ed. "The Woolsey Expeditions of 1864." *Arizona and the West, 4* (1962), 157–76.

Wyman, Walker D. "The Military Phase of Santa Fe Freighting, 1846–1865." *Kansas Historical Quarterly, 1* (1932), 415–28.

BOOKS

Abel, Annie H., ed. *The Correspondence of James S. Calhoun.* Washington, D.C., 1915.

Amsden, Charles. *Navaho Weaving: Its Technic and History.* 2d ed. Albuquerque, N.M., 1940.

Ashburn, P. M. *A History of the Medical Department of the United States Army.* Boston, Mass., 1929.

Bailey, Lynn R. *The Long Walk: A History of the Navajo Wars, 1846–68.* Los Angeles, Calif., 1964.

Bancroft, Hubert H. *History of Arizona and New Mexico.* San Francisco, Calif., 1889.

Bandel, Eugene. *Frontier Life in the Army, 1854–1861.* Ralph P. Bieber, ed. Glendale, Calif., 1932.

Bender, A. B. *The March of Empire: Frontier Defense in the Southwest, 1848–1860.* Lawrence, Kans., 1952.

Bernardo, C. S. and E. H. Bacon. *American Military Policy: Its Development since 1775.* Harrisburg, Pa., 1955.

Berthrong, Donald J. *The Southern Cheyennes.* Norman, Okla., 1963.

Birkheimer, William E. *Historical Sketch of the Organization, Administration, Materièl, and Tactics of the Artillery, United States Army.* Washington, D.C., 1881.

Bledsoe, A. J. *The Indian Wars of the Northwest.* San Francisco, Calif., 1885.

Brackett, Albert G. *History of the U.S. Cavalry.* New York, 1865.

Brooks, Clinton R., and Frank D. Reeve, eds. *Forts and Forays: James A. Bennett, A Dragoon in New Mexico, 1850–1856.* Albuquerque, N.M., 1948.

Briggs, Harold E. *Frontiers of the Northwest: A History of the Upper Missouri Valley.* New York and London, 1940.

Brown, D. Alexander. *The Galvanized Yankees.* Urbana, Ill. 1963.

Burns, Robert Ignatius, S.J. *The Jesuits in the Indian Wars of the North-west.* New Haven, Conn., and London, 1966.

Carley, Kenneth. *The Sioux Uprising of 1862.* St. Paul, Minn., 1961.

Chamberlain, Samuel E. *My Confession.* New York, 1956.

Conner, Daniel E. *Joseph Reddeford Walker and the Arizona Adventure.* Donald J. Berthrong and Odessa Davenport, eds. Norman, Okla., 1956.

Craig, Reginald S. *The Fighting Parson.* Los Angeles, Calif., 1959.

Cremony, John C. *Life among the Apaches.* San Francisco, Calif., 1868.

Crook, George. *General George Crook, His Autobiography.* Martin F. Schmitt, ed. Norman, Okla., 1946.

Curtis, E. S. *The North American Indian.* 20 vols. Norwood, Mass., 1907–30.

Davis, William W. H. *El Gringo, or New Mexico and Her People.* New York, 1856; Santa Fe, N.M., 1938.

Dillon, Richard H. *J. Ross Browne, Confidential Agent in Old California.* Norman, Okla., 1965.

Dodge, Grenville M. *The Battle of Atlanta and Other Campaigns.* Council Bluffs, Ia., 1911.

DuBois, John Van Deusen. *Campaigns in the West, 1856–1861.* George P. Hammond, ed. Tucson, Ariz., 1949.

Dunbar, Roland, ed. *Jefferson Davis, Constitutionalist: His Letters, Papers, and Speeches.* 10 vols. Jackson, Miss., 1923.

Dunn, J. P. *Massacres of the Mountains: A History of the Indian Wars of the Far West, 1815–1875.* New York, 1886.

Elliott, Charles W. *Winfield Scott, the Soldier and the Man.* New York, 1937.

Emmett, Chris. *Fort Union and the Winning of the Southwest.* Norman, Okla., 1965.

Ewers, John C. *Teton Dakota History and Ethnology.* Berkeley, Calif., 1938.

Folwell, William W. *A History of Minnesota.* 2 vols. St. Paul, Minn., 1956.

Ford, John S. *Rip Ford's Texas.* Stephen B. Oates, ed. Austin, Tex., 1963.

Forman, Sidney. *West Point: A History of the United States Military Academy.* New York, 1950.

Frazer, Robert W. *Forts of the West.* Norman, Okla., 1965.

——, ed. *Mansfield on the Condition of Western Forts, 1853–1854.* Norman, Okla., 1963.

Frederick, J. V. *Ben Holladay, The Stagecoach King: A Chapter in the Development of Transcontinental Transportation.* Glendale, Calif., 1940.

Fuller, Charles E. *The Breech-Loader in the Service.* New York, 1933.

Fry, James B. *The History and Legal Effect of Brevets in the Armies of Great Britain and the United States.* New York, 1877.

Ganoe, William A. *The History of the United States Army.* New York, 1924.

Garrard, Lewis H. *Wah-To-Yah and the Taos Trail.* 2d ed. Glendale, Calif., 1938.

Glassley, Ray H. *Pacific Northwest Indian Wars.* Portland, Ore., 1953.

Gluckman, Arcardi. *United States Muskets, Rifles and Carbines.* Buffalo, N.Y., 1948.

——. *United States Martial Pistols and Revolvers.* Buffalo, N.Y., 1944.

Goetzmann, William H. *Army Exploration in the American West, 1803–1863*. New Haven, Conn., and London, 1959.

Grinnell, George B. *The Cheyenne Indians*. 2 vols. New Haven, Conn., 1923.

———. *The Fighting Cheyennes*. 2d. Norman, Okla., 1956.

Guie, H. Dean. *Bugles in the Valley: Garnett's Fort Simcoe*. Yakima, Wash., 1956.

Hafen, LeRoy R., and Ann W. Hafen., eds. *Powder River Campaigns and Sawyers Expedition of 1865*. Glendale, Calif., 1961.

———, eds. *Relations with the Indians of the Plains, 1857–1861*. Glendale, Calif., 1959.

Hafen, LeRoy R. and W. J. Ghent. *Broken Hand: The Life Story of Thomas Fitzpatrick, Chief of the Mountain Men*. Denver, Colo., 1931.

Hafen, LeRoy R., and Francis M. Young. *Fort Laramie and the Pageant of the West*. Glendale, Calif., 1938.

Hall, Martin H. *Sibley's New Mexico Campaign*. Austin, Tex., 1960.

Hamersly, Thomas H. S., comp. *Complete Regular Army Register of the United States*. Washington, D.C., 1881.

Hamlin, Percy G., ed. *The Making of a Soldier: Letters of General R. S. Ewell*. Richmond, Va., 1935.

Harmon, George D. *Sixty Years of Indian Affairs, 1789–1850*. Chapel Hill, N.C., 1941.

Hebard, Grace R., and E. A. Brinnistool. *The Bozeman Trail*. 2 vols. Cleveland, Ohio, 1922.

Heitman, Francis B., comp. *Historical Register and Dictionary of the U.S. Army*. 2 vols. Washington, D.C., 1903.

Heyman, Max, Jr. *Prudent Soldier: A Biography of Major General E. R. S. Canby, 1817–1873*. Glendale, Calif., 1959.

Hicks, James E. *Notes on United States Ordnance*. Mount Vernon, N.Y., 1946.

Hitchcock, Ethan Allen. *Fifty Years in Camp and Field: The Diary of Major General Ethan Allen Hitchcock*. W. A. Croffut, ed. New York, 1909.

Hodge, Frederick Webb, ed. *Handbook of American Indians North of Mexico*. 2 vols. Washington, D.C., 1912.

Hoig, Stan. *The Sand Creek Massacre*. Norman, Okla., 1963.

Hollon, W. Eugene. *Beyond the Cross Timbers: The Travels of Randolph B. Marcy, 1812–1887*. Norman, Okla., 1955.

Hoopes, Alban W. *Indian Affairs and their Administration, with Special Reference to the Far West, 1849–1860*. Philadelphia, Pa., 1932.

Hunt, Aurora. *Major General James Henry Carleton, 1814–1873; Western Frontier Dragoon*. Glendale, Calif., 1958.

———. *The Army of the Pacific: Its Operations in California, Texas, Arizona, New Mexico, Utah, Nevada, Oregon, Washington, Plains Region, Mexico, Etc., 1860–1866*. Glendale, Calif., 1961.

Hyde, George E. *Spotted Tail's Folk: A History of the Brulé Sioux*. Norman, Okla., 1961.

———. *Red Cloud's Folk: A History of the Oglala Sioux Indians*. 2d ed. Norman, Okla., 1957.

Ingersoll, L. D. *A History of the War Department of the United States*. Washington, D.C., 1879.

Johnson, Richard W. *Memoir of Maj. Gen. George H. Thomas.* Philadelphia, Pa., 1881.

Jones, Robert H. *The Civil War in the Northwest: Nebraska, Wisconsin, Iowa, Minnesota and the Dakotas.* Norman, Okla., 1960.

Josephy, Alvin M., Jr. *The Nez Perce Indians and the Opening of the Northwest.* New Haven, Conn., and London, 1965.

Kappler, Charles J., comp. *Indian Affairs: Laws and Treaties.* 2 vols. Washington, D.C., 1904.

Keyes, Erasmus D. *Fifty Years Observation of Men and Events.* New York, 1884.

Kip, Lawrence. *Army Life on the Pacific: A Journal of the Expedition against the Northern Indians . . . in the Summer of 1858.* New York, 1859.

Kluckhohn, Clyde, and Dorothea Leighton. *The Navaho.* Cambridge, Mass., 1946.

Kroeber, A. L. *Handbook of the Indians of California.* Bureau of American Ethnology Bull. 78. Washington, D.C., 1925.

Lane, Lydia Spencer. *I Married a Soldier, or Old Days in the Army.* Philadelphia, Pa., 1910.

Lavender, David. *Bent's Fort.* New York, 1954.

Lesley, Lewis B., ed. *Uncle Sam's Camels: The Journal of May Humphreys Stacy Supplemented by the Report of Edward F. Beale, 1857–1858.* Cambridge, Mass., 1929.

Lowe, Percival. *Five Years a Dragoon.* Kansas City Mo., 1906. 2d ed., Don Russell, ed. Norman, Okla., 1965.

Lockwood, Frank C. *The Apache Indians.* New York, 1936.

Luomala, Katharine. *Navaho Life of Yesterday and Today.* Berkeley, Calif., 1938.

McFarling, Lloyd, ed. *Exploring the Northern Plains, 1804–1876.* Caldwell, Ida., 1955.

McKnitt, Frank, ed. *Navaho Expedition: Journal of a Military Reconnaissance from Santa Fe, New Mexico, to the Navaho Country Made in 1849 by Lieutenant James H. Simpson.* Norman, Okla., 1964.

Mack, Effie Mona. *Nevada: A History of the State from the Earliest Times through the Civil War.* Glendale, Calif., 1936.

Madsen, Brigham D. *The Bannock of Idaho.* Caldwell, Ida., 1958.

Majors, Alexander. *Seventy Years on the Old Frontier.* Denver, Colo., 1893.

Malin, James C. *Indian Policy and Westward Expansion.* Bull. of the University of Kansas, Vol. 22, No. 17. Lawrence, 1921.

Marcy, Randolph B. *Thirty Years of Army Life on the Border.* New York, 1866.

Maury, Dabney H. *Recollections of a Virginian in the Mexican, Indian and Civil Wars.* New York, 1894.

Mattes, Merrill J. *Fort Laramie and the Forty-Niners.* Estes Park, Colo., 1949.

Mayhall, Mildred P., *The Kiowas.* Norman, Okla., 1962.

Meneely, A. Howard. *The War Department, 1861.* New York, 1928.

Meyers, Augustus. *Ten Years in the Ranks of the U.S. Army.* New York, 1914.

Millis, Walter. *Arms and Men: A Study of American Military History.* Mentor ed. New York, 1956.

Mills, W. W. *Forty Years at El Paso, 1858–1898*. Rex Strickland, ed. El Paso, Tex., 1962.

[Minnesota, State of.] *Minnesota in the Civil and Indian Wars*. 2 vols. St. Paul, Minn., 1899.

Mishkin, Bernard. *Rank and Warfare among the Plains Indians*. Monographs of the American Ethnological Society, *3*, New York, 1940.

Mooney, James. *Calendar History of the Kiowa Indians*. 17th Annual Report of the Bureau of American Ethnology. Washington, D.C., 1898.

Mordecai, Alfred. *Artillery for the Land Service of the United States*. Washington, D.C., 1848.

Nye, Wilbur S. *Carbine and Lance: The Story of Old Fort Sill*. Norman, Okla., 1943.

———. *Bad Medicine and Good: Tales of the Kiowas*. Norman, Okla., 1962.

Oehler, C. M. *The Great Sioux Uprising*. New York, 1959.

Ogden, H. A. *The Army of the United States: Illustrated by Forty-Four Fac-simile Plates from Water Color Drawings by H. A. Ogden*. Washington, 1890. 2d ed., Thos. Yoseloff. New York, 1959.

Parks, Joseph H. *General Edmund Kirby Smith*. Baton Rouge, La., 1954.

Perkins, J. R. *Trails, Rails, and War: The Life of General G. M. Dodge*. Indianapolis, Ind., 1929.

Peterson, Harold L. *Notes on the Ordnance of the American Civil War*. Washington, D.C., 1959.

Price, George F. *Across the Continent with the Fifth Cavalry*. New York, 1883. 2d ed., New York, 1959.

Pride, W. F. *The History of Fort Riley*. Fort Riley, Kans., 1926.

Prucha, Francis Paul, S.J. *Guide to the Military Posts of the United States*. Madison, Wis., 1964.

Richardson, James D., comp. *Messages and Papers of the Presidents*. 20 vols. New York, 1897.

Richardson, Rupert N. *The Frontier of Northwest Texas, 1846 to 1876*. Glendale, Calif., 1963.

———. *The Comanche Barrier to South Plains Settlement*. Glendale, Calif., 1933.

Risch, Erna. *Quartermaster Support of the Army: A History of the Corps, 1775–1939*. Washington, D.C., 1962.

Rister, C. C. *Border Captives: The Traffic in Prisoners by Southern Plains Indians, 1835–1875*. Norman, Okla., 1940.

Robinson, Doane. *A History of the Dakota or Sioux Indians*. 2d ed. Minneapolis, Minn., 1956.

Rockwell, Wilson. *The Utes, A Forgotten People*. Denver, Colo., 1956.

Rodenbough, Theo. F. *From Everglade to Canon with the Second Dragoons*. New York, 1875.

Rodenbough, Theo. F., and William L. Haskin, eds. *The Army of the United States*. New York, 1896.

Rogan, Francis E. "Military History of New Mexico Territory during the Civil War." Ph.D. dissertation, University of Utah, 1961.

Rogers, Fred B. *Soldiers of the Overland: Being Some Account of the Services of Gen. Patrick Edward Connor and His Volunteers of the Old West*. San Francisco, Calif., 1938.

Roland, Charles P. *Albert Sidney Johnston, Soldier of Three Republics*. Austin, Tex., 1964.

Sabin, Edwin L. *Kit Carson Days: Adventures in the Path of Empire.* 2 vols. New York, 1935.

Schroeder, Albert H. *A Study of Yavapai History.* 3 vols. Santa Fe, N.M. 1959. Mimeographed report of U.S. Dept. of Justice.

———. *A Study of the Apache Indians.* 5 vols. Santa Fe, N.M., 1960. Mimeographed report for U.S. Dept. of Justice.

Settle, Raymond W., ed. *The March of the Mounted Riflemen from Fort Leavenworth to Fort Vancouver, May to October 1849.* Glendale, Calif., 1940.

Settle, Raymond W., and Mary L. *Empire on Wheels.* Palo Alto, Calif., 1940.

Sheridan, Philip H. *Personal Memoirs of P. H. Sheridan.* 2 vols. New York, 1888.

Sherman, William T. *Memoirs of William T. Sherman.* Civil War Centennial ed. Bloomington, Ind., 1957.

Spier, Leslie. *Tribal Distribution in Washington.* Menasha, Wis., 1936.

Spring, Agnes Wright. *Caspar Collins.* New York, 1927.

Stanley, David S. *Personal Memoirs of Maj. Gen. D. S. Stanley, U.S.A.* Cambridge, Mass., 1917.

Stern, Theodore. *The Klamath Tribe: A People and their Reservation.* Seattle, Wash., 1965.

[Stevens, Isaac I.] *Message of the Governor of Washington Territory.* Olympia, Wash., 1857.

Stevens, Hazard. *Life of General Isaac I. Stevens.* 2 vols. New York, 1901.

Strode, Hudson. *Jefferson Davis, American Patriot, 1808–1861.* New York, 1955.

Swanton, John R. *The Indian Tribes of North America.* Bureau of American Ethnology Bull. 145. Washington, D.C., 1952.

Thian, Raphael P., comp. *Notes Illustrating the Military Geography of the United States.* Washington, D.C., 1881.

———. *Legislative History of the General Staff of the Army of the United States.* Washington, D.C., 1901.

Trenholm, Virginia C., and Maurine Carley. *The Shoshonis: Sentinels of the Rockies.* Norman, Okla., 1964.

Twitchell, Ralph E. *Historical Sketch of Governor William Carr Lane.* Santa Fe, N.M., 1917.

———. *The Military Occupation of New Mexico, 1846–1851.* Denver, Colo., 1909.

Underhill, Ruth. *The Navajos.* Norman, Okla., 1956.

Upton, Emory. *The Military Policy of the United States.* Washington, D.C., 1917.

Vaughn, J. W. *The Battle of Platte Bridge.* Norman, Okla., 1963.

Vestal, Stanley. *Sitting Bull, Champion of the Sioux.* 2d ed. Norman, Okla., 1957.

Viele, Mrs. Egbert L. *Following the Drum: A Glimpse of Frontier Life.* New York, 1858.

Wallace, Ernest, and E. Adamson Hoebel. *The Comanches, Lords of the South Plains.* Norman, Okla., 1952.

Ware, Eugene F. *The Indian War of 1864.* Clyde F. Walton, ed. New York, 1960.

Webb, Walter Prescott. *The Texas Rangers: A Century of Frontier Defense.* Boston, Mass., 1935.

White, Leonard D. *The Jacksonians: A Study in Administrative History, 1829–1861.* New York, 1963.

Weigley, Russell. *Towards an American Army: Military Thought from Washington to Marshall.* New York, 1963.

West, Nathaniel. *The Ancestry, Life, and Times of the Hon. Henry Hastings Sibley.* St. Paul, Minn., 1889.

Whitford, William C. *Colorado Volunteers in the Civil War: The New Mexico Campaign of 1862.* Denver, Colo., 1906.

Wilbarger, J. W. *Indian Depredations in Texas.* 2d ed. Austin, Tex., 1935.

Winfrey, Dorman H., ed. *Texas Indian Papers, 1846–1859.* Austin, Tex., 1960.

Wissler, Clark. *North American Indians of the Plains.* 2d ed. New York, 1938.

Woodward, Arthur. *Journal of Lt. Thomas W. Sweeny, 1849–1853.* Los Angeles, Calif., 1955.

———. *Feud on the Colorado.* Los Angeles, Calif., 1955.

Young, Otis E. *The West of Philip St. George Cooke, 1809–1895.* Glendale, Calif., 1955.

Index